Please return to Marian

"To name the goddesses and heroines is a powerful act of invocation, of bringing them into our consciousness and thereby into the world. I am grateful to Pat Monaghan for returning our suppressed legacy to us."

—Deena Metzger
What Dinah Thought

"Pat Monaghan knows an amazing amount about the history and traditions of the goddess and her peoples. The next best thing to spending an afternoon with her is reading her book about goddesses and heroines. The book is a compilation of information about goddesses' myths, traditions, and facts from cultures both well-known and obscure.

The Book of Goddesses & Heroines is a great source of information arranged in an easy-to-access alphabetical form with many cross-references. It is a great reference for serious work, or a wonderful resource when you're looking for a name for your new cat."

—Jade River
Of a Like Mind

"Some of the entries in this book that are seven lines long represent facts on goddesses taken from seven different sources. Many of these sources were rare, academic works. I wanted to bring these obscure fragments into one complete and shining whole."

—Patricia Monaghan

This is exactly what The Book of Goddesses & Heroines *is—a complete, shining whole of goddess myths from around the globe. Each goddess is viewed from her people's perspective rather than the usual Western tradition. Discover the goddess in Australia, India, the Americas, Japan, throughout the world—and experience her as she truly is.*

CALDRON CRAFTS
915 MONTPELIER ST.
BALTO., MD 21218

About the Author

For nearly 15 years, Patricia Monaghan has been researching goddesses of the world for her women's spirituality lectures, slide presentations, and this volume. She has viewed the dance rituals of Korean women shamans as well as experienced the winter solstice sunrise from within Newgrange's megalithic mound. Although a native of New York, she was raised in Alaska. She has a master's degree in English literature from the University of Minnesota as well as a Master of Fine Arts from the University of Alaska. She now lives in Beverly on Chicago's South Side and teaches writing at St. Xavier College and at South Shore Bank, a minority-owned enterprise devoted to community redevelopment. She also writes poetry and contributes book reviews to *Booklist*, the magazine of the American Library Association. Currently, she is the Director of Continuing Education at St. Xavier College and is adapting goddess myths for children.

About the Cover

The statue on the cover is one of the treasures of the Field Museum of Natural History in Chicago—itself one of the world's treasures for its collection of world art. Found in the Philippines, the four-pound gold figure is unusual for that area in representing a Hindu goddess or Devi, perhaps Gauri the Golden. The goddesses of the Field Museum, pictured in this book, reach beyond images familiar in Western culture; like the text they illustrate, they embody some of the diverse energies depicted through history in feminine form.

To Write to the Author

We cannot guarantee that every letter written to the author can be answered, but all will be forwarded. Both the author and the publisher appreciate hearing from readers, learning of your enjoyment and benefit from this book. Llewellyn also publishes a bi-monthly news magazine with news and reviews of practical esoteric studies and articles helpful to the student, and some readers' questions and comments to the author may be answered through this magazine's columns if permission to do so is included in the original letter. The author sometimes participates in seminars and workshops, and dates and places are announced in *The Llewellyn New Times*. To write to the author, or to ask a question, write to:

Pat Monaghan
c/o *The Llewellyn New Times*
P.O. Box 64383-573, St. Paul, MN 55164-0383, U.S.A.
Please enclose a self-addressed, stamped envelope for reply, or $1.00 to cover costs.

THE BOOK OF
Goddesses
& Heroines

(revised and enlarged edition)

Patricia Monaghan

Photos from the Field Museum of Natural History, Chicago

1990
Llewellyn Publications
St. Paul, Minnesota 55164 0383, U.S.A.

FIRST LLEWELLYN EDITION

First published by E.P. Dutton Publishing Co., Inc. 1981
Copyright © 1981 by Patricia Monaghan

Cover photo: Devi, Field Museum of Natural History (Neg# 109935ᶜ), Chicago

Interior photos from the Field Museum of Natural History, Chicago

Book design by Terry Buske

Library of Congress Cataloging-in-Publications Data

Monaghan, Patricia.
  The book of goddesses and heroines / by Patricia Monaghan.
    p. cm.
  Reprint. Originally published: 1st ed. New York : Dutton, c1981.
  Includes bibliographical references (p.).
  ISBN 0-87542-573-9
  1. Goddesses. 2. Mythology. I. Title. II. Series.
[BL473.5.M66   1990]
291.2'114—dc20   89-77418
                                                        CIP

90 91 92 93   10 9 8 7 6 5 4 3 2 1

Llewellyn Publications
A Division of Llewellyn Worldwide, Ltd.
P.O. Box 64383, St. Paul, MN 55164-0383

to the Circle

Other Books by Patricia Monaghan

Unlacing: Ten Irish-American Women Poets. Editor.
Hunger and Dreams: The Alaskan Women's Anthology. Editor.

Forthcoming Books

Oh Mother Sun! A New View of the Cosmic Feminine
The Worship of Sex
Home Deaths (poetry)

•Acknowledgments•

In the ten years since this book was first published, the community of women reclaiming the goddess, and that of friends who support such work, has grown so magnificently that any acknowledgment can only be partial. So I thank each of you who, through reading and research, through poetry and artwork, through ritual and performance, and through personal devotion, has let the many-featured, many-named goddess into today's world. And I thank in advance you who, over the next decades, will continue the work.

Anyone working in feminist spirituality must acknowledge, as I do here, the writings of Marija Gimbutas, Merlin Stone and Mary Daly. In addition, the works and words of Charlene Spretnak, Z Budapest, Jade River and Lynn Levy are invaluable. Production of this second edition was helped immeasurably by Diane Stein, who put me in touch with Llewellyn Publications, and the entire Llewellyn staff. The indexes would not have been possible without the indexing crew: Jean McKenzie, Margaret Arnd-Caddigan, Paula Schiller, Deborah Neidermeier, Sherry Mack, Jeanne D'Amico, Pamela Meyer, and especially M.P. McKenzie. A special thanks to Nina Cummings of the Field Museum for assistance in gathering illustrations.

For personal and scholarly sustenance over the last decade, thanks to Antiga, Barbara Bruno, Janet Baird, Jim Duran, Susan Gitlin-Emmer, Helen Farias, Renny Golden, Karen Johnson, Natalie Kusz, Joe Meeker, Mary Jo Neitz, Ray Olson, Judith Roche, Allen Schwartz, Laverne Sandler, Terri Vierick, B.J. Webb, Barbara Wallant; my women's circles in Alaska and in Chicago; the Re-Formed Congregation of the Goddess in Wisconsin; and my family, especially Roland Wulbert.

·Contents·

Introduction
xiii

Families of Goddesses and Heroines
xvii

Glossary
1

Calendar of Goddess Feasts
371

Index of Associations
373

Index of Alternative Names and Minor Goddesses
393

Bibliography
413

"Whatever is unnamed, undepicted in images, whatever is omitted from biography, censored in collections of letters, whatever is mis-named as something else, made difficult-to-come-by, whatever is buried in the memory by the collapse of meaning under an inade-quate or lying language—this will become, not merely unspoken, but unspeakable."

—ADRIENNE RICH

"In naming all of these, we are practicing an age-old rite. Such lists . . . are a form of ritual worship. The abundance of manifes-tations is a characteristic of the archetype, and the plethora of names by which the powers are invoked among all people is an expression of their numinous ineffability."

—ERICH NEUMANN

"We need the goddess because she breaks stereotypes of the fem-inine and thus frees women from the limitations of that stereotype. Woman can be strong *and* beautiful, feminine *and* wise teachers, mothers *and* participants in cultures. If the goddess provided that much it would have been enough. But it seems that she brings much more . . . The goddess completes the image of the god and brings wholeness."

—RITA M. GROSS

•Introduction•

In the spring of 1980, on entering the antiquities wing of a major museum, I spied a Cretan goddess whose image I had seen in at least a dozen mythology books. I rushed to her, one of the most famous images of female divinity, only to find the statuette unnamed and labeled merely "votive figure."

Later, in another large museum, I toured the Chinese section, seeking sculptures of a favorite goddess, the merciful Kuan-Yin. And indeed, there she was: a lovely girl, almost life-size, her sweet expression framed by long curls, her robes full and elaborate. Her label read "deity of mercy."

Why not "goddesses"? And why not named? This custom is not limited to museum labelers. The conspiracy (to use a stronger term) of misnaming goddesses, hiding their sex, or dismissing them as subsidiary deities runs throughout literature as well.

Mythographers use three tactics to restrict information about goddesses. First, they simply ignore them. Reading many "comprehensive" mythological dictionaries, one would think that divinities all over the world have been primarily male. Some works ignore even major goddesses like Anat and Cerridwen, while including relatively minor gods of the same people like Baal and Lugh.

Second, mythographers fail to give a goddess's name. The story of the Eskimo sun-goddess is told in virtually every book on Eskimo religion, but no name is recorded for her. Several days of research uncovered her name, Akycha or Seqinek, as a footnote in Boas's journals. I was unable, however, to locate the names of many African goddesses who were called merely "earth mother," as though they lacked proper names of their own.

One form of this nominal subterfuge is to call a goddess or heroine "Potiphar's wife" or "the Daughters of Zelophehad" as though relationship to a god or patriarch sufficiently defines her. These labels not only hide the goddess's name but often deceive the reader about the actual relationship. Omphale, for instance, is listed in many texts as "a wife of Heracles," when in legend she was an Amazonian queen who purchased the hero as a sexual slave; Daphne is described as a "beloved of Apollo" rather than a victim of attempted rape; and Parvati is seen as the "consort" of Shiva, rather than the force that animates him.

Third, most writers organize their works to emphasize the gods rather than the goddesses. At the start, the stories of the gods are told individually, then those of the goddesses are lumped together in a single chapter. This is followed by another section devoted to the exploits of male heroes, heroines being named only in footnotes. If this order is sometimes changed, the proportion of information remains constant. For many goddesses listed in *The Book of Goddesses and Heroines*, there was no complete recitation of their legends in any available source. Instead, the stories had to be pieced together from multiple sources: a detail here, a quotation there.

Even when they do remember to write about goddesses, mythographers show their biases through their choice of language. All goddesses, most writers tell us, are symbols of the earth—even Tanith, the sky-goddess of the Carthaginians, and Tara, the Tibetan star-goddess. Goddesses may be either virgins or mothers or whores, despite evidence that virgin goddesses may take lovers (Anat), mother-goddesses may have no children (Kunti), and harlot-goddesses may be magicians (Arianrhod). Goddesses who convey a spirituality alien to modern Western thought are derided (as in the case of European nature deities described as fairies or spirits) or shunned (like Durga, the fierce Indian death-goddess, described as ugly and horrible).

Finally, stories are always told from the viewpoint of the god, even when the major character is clearly a goddess. Thus in the story of Inanna, her lover Dumuzi is the focal point.

In retelling these stories, I found that the study of conventional mythological writings—necessary to gather information—limited my ability to tell the stories freshly. I found myself automatically relying on conventional vocabulary, which often conflicted with the spiritual meaning of these stories. Read over and over, the words impressed themselves on my mind until it seemed I had no language of my own.

I solved the problem by telling each story as though the goddess were my own goddess, a divinity I truly revered. I made her the focus of her own story, told it from her point of view. For instance, I accepted the dancing lady of death, Kali, on her own terms, and she became something other than merely grotesque or terrifying; she became a vehicle for spiritual understanding, as she is to the millions who revere her.

Many of these stories, therefore, depart drastically from the conventional ways in which they have been told. Here there are tales of rape and murder where other versions tell of love and death. The goddesses evolve and grow, rather than being eternally fixed presences. And similar god-desses are not grouped together as "forms of" each other, any more than the Holy Ghost is a "form of" the Divine Son.

Although over a thousand goddesses and heroines are listed in the text, an exhaustive or even definitive survey would be impossible here or any-where. Maybe it's just as well, for I encourage others to seek out goddesses. I see this book as the first of many devoted to the long-needed work of renam-ing the goddess and thereby restoring a lost world.

·Families of Goddesses & Heroines·

African, Carthaginian, Egyptian, North African and Phoenician

Abuk
Ahemait
'Aisha Qandisha
Akusaa
Ala
Al-Lat
Al-Uzza
Ama
Ament
Ankt
Anuket
Asase Yaa
Astronoe
At-Em
Athtar
Au Set
Avaris
Ba'Alat
Bakkah
Bast
Bau
Belqis
Beruth
Candace
Dea Caelestis
Dhat-Badan
Dido
Elat
Ermutu
Genea
Hathor
Hekt

Het
Isis
Isong
Kalisha
Kla
Lat
Lemkechen
Maat
Mafdet
Maruwa
Mawu
Mehit
Mehurt
Menat
Meri
Mertseger
Meskhoni
Mut
Mylitta
Nahab
Naila
Nambi
Nana Buluku
Neb-Ti
Neith
Nekhebet
Nephthys
Nsomeka
Nut
Oba
Ochumare
Oddudua

Ogdoad
Olosa
Oshun
Oya
Qadesh
Qebhsnuf
Renenet
Renpet
Ri
Sabulana
Sambatu
Saosis
Sati
Sekhmet
Sela
Selkhet
Shait
Shamshu
Sheshat
Sige
Ta-Dehnet
Tanetu
Tanith
Tauret
Tefnut
Uadgit
Umm Attar
Uzza
Wazit
Yemaya
Ymoja

FAMILIES OF GODDESSES AND HEROINES

Ainu, Japanese, and Korean

Amaterasu
Aryong-Jong
Aze
Basho
Benten
Byul-Soon
Chup-Kamui
Dae-Soon
Fuji
Hae-Sun
Hiedo-no-Ame
Himiko
Ikutamayorihime
Inaba
Inari
Ishikore-Dome
Iwa-Naga-Hime
Izanami
Izushio-Tome
Jingo
Kaguya-Hima

Kamui Fuchi
Kaya-Nu-Hima
Kishimogin
Kongsim
Kono-Hana-Sakuya-Hime
Kuzu-no-Ha
Mama
Mulhalmoni
Naru-Kami
Ningyo
Nish-Kan-Ru Mat
No-Il Ja-Dae
Ootonobe-no-Kami
O-Ryu
Oto-Hime
Pali Kongju
Rafu-Sen
Samsin Halmoni
Sayo-Hime
Seyadatarahime
Shino-To-Be

Shita-Teru-Hime
Sinjang Halmoni
Suhijini-no-Kimi
Sungmo
Tamayorihime
Tatsuta-Hime
Toyota-Mahime
Toyo-Uke
Tsuru
Turesh
Uke-Mochi
Uso-Dori
Uzume
Wakahirume
Yamato-Hime-no-Miko
Yama-Uba
Yaya-Zakura
Yondung Halmoni
Yuki-Onne

Anatolian, Armenian, Hattian, Hittite, Hurrian, and Persian

Aka
Anahita
Ararat
Armaiti
Cybele
Halmasuit
Hannahanna
Hebat
Hulla
Inaras

Istustaya
Jaki
Jeh
Kait
Kamrusepas
Kupapa
Lilwani
Muzulla
Myrrha
Nasa

Saris
Semiramis
Shauskha
Sipylene
Tarkhu
Tasimmet
Tharatha
Wurusemu
Zintuki

Australian, Maori and Pacific Islands

Agusan Devi
Aponibolinayen
Atanea
Bara
Bila

Biliku
Bugan
Darago
Djanggawul Sisters
Doh Tenagan

Eingana
Gnatoo
Gnowee
Goga
Hainuwele

Haumea
Hikuleo
Hina
Hit
Indara
Iro Duget
Julunggul
Junkgowa
Kalwadi
Kapo
Koevasi
Kunapipi
La'i-la'i
Laka
Le-Hev-Hev
Ligoapup
Ligoband

Liomarar
Lorop
Luminu-Ut
Madalait
Mahui-Iki
Makore-Wawahiwa
Matariki
Mayi-Mayi
Miru
Nevinbimbaau
Numma Moiyuk
Nyapilnu
Pani
Papa
Pare
Parewhenua-Mea
Pele

Rabie
Rona
Satine
Tapa
Taranga
Tuli
Wahini-Hai
Walo
Walutahanga
Waramurungundji
Wari-Ma-Te-Takere
Wawalag Sisters
Whaitiri
Wuriupranili
Yak

Baltic, Germanic, Icelandic, and Scandinavian

Ahrenkonigin
Alfhild
Amberella
Angerboda
Angeyja
Aspelenie
Asynjr
Atla
Audhumbla
Austrine
Bestla
Dil
Breksta
Brynhild
Buschfrauen
Dag
Dekla
Dis
Dugnai
Edda
Eir
Embla
Fangge
Fengi and Mengi
Frau Holle
Freya
Frigg

Fulla
Fylgja
Gefjon
Gerd
Gna
Gollveig
Gondul
Gonlod
Groa
Hariasa
Harimela
Hedrun
Heith
Hel
Hertha
Hervor
Hild
Hlin
Hlodyn
Hnossa
Hrede
Huldra
Hyrrokin
Iarnvithja
Idunn
Imd
Ingebord

Ivithja
Jord
Juras Mate
Jurate
Kornjunfer
Kveldrida
La Reine Pedaque
Laima
Laumes
Lofn
Ma-Emma
Maria
Mari-Ama
Matergabiae
Modgud
Mora
Myrkrida
Nana
Nerthus
Nixies
Norns
Nott
Oddibjord
Perchta
Perkuna Tete
Ran
Rind

Rugiu Boba
Saga
Saule
Saules Meita
Sibilja
Sif
Sigurdrifta
Silige Fraulein
Sjofn
Sjojungru
Sjora
Skadi

Skogsnufvar
Skuld
Snotra
Sunna
Swan Maidens
Sweigsdunka
Syn
Tamfana
Thordis
Thorgerd
Vakyrine
Valkyries

Var
Voluspa
Vor
Waldmichen
Wanne Thekla
Weisse Frauen
Wilden Wip
Zemyna
Zisa
Zytniamatka

Caribbean, Central American, Macumban, Mesoamerican, and South American

Aida-Wedo
Akewa
Alaghom Naom Tzentel
Anuanaitu
Atabei
Auchimalgen
Bachue
Cavillaca
Ceiuci
Chalchiúhtlicue
Chantico
Chicomecóatl
Cihuacóatl
Cihuateteo
Cipactli
Coatlícue
Coatrischie
Cocomama
Coyolxauhqui
Dabaiba
Evaki

Ezili-Freda-Dahomey
Guabancex
Guatauva
Huitaca
Huixtocíhuatl
India Rosa
Itiba Tahuvava
Ituana
Itzpapálotl
Ix Chebel Yax
Ix Chel
Ixtab
Iztaccihuatl
Korobona
Kualchink
Mama Allpa
Mama Cocha
Mama Ocllo
Mama Quilla
Maman Brigitte
Mamapacha

Marinette
Masaya
Mayáhuel
Metzli
Mictecacíhuatl
Mu Olokukurtilisop
Obatallah
Omecíhuatl
Oshun
Oya
Quetzapetlatl
Sibilaneuman
Sicasica
Teczistecatl
Tlazoltéotl
Toci
Tonan
Xochiquetzal
Yemanja
Yohuatlicetl
Zaramama

Celtic: British, Continental, Irish, Scottish, and Welsh

Achall
Achtan
Achtland
Aeracura
Aeron
Aeval

Aibheaog
Aife
Aige
Ailinn
Ain
Aine

Airmed
Almha
Andraste
Anne
Anu
Ardwina

Argante
Arianrhod
Arnamentia
Artio
Badb
Ban Naomha
Banba
Ban-Chuideachaidh Moire
Banshee
Basilea
Bean Nighe
Bebhionn
Becuma
Belisima
Benvarry
Berecyntia
Biddy
Biddy Mannion
Black Annis
Blathnat
Blodewedd
Bo Find
Boann
Branwen
Bri
Brigantia
Brigid
Bronach
Buan
Caer
Cailleach
Caireen
Cally Berry
Campestres
Canola
Caolainn
Carlin
Carman
Carravogue
Cartimandua
Cathubodia
Ceasg
Ceibhfhionn
Cerridwen
Cessair
Cethlion
Cetnenn

Chlaus Haistic
Clidna
Corchen
Corra
Coventina
Cred
Creiddylad
Crobdh Dearg
Dahut
Dames Vertes
Damona
Danu
Dea Nutrix
Deae Matres
Dechtere
Deirdre
Devorgilla
Dia Griene
Dil
Domnu
Don
Druantia
Dubh Lacha
Eadon
Ebhlinne
Echtghe
Edain
Ele
Emor
Eostre
Epona
Eri of the Golden Hair
Eriu
Ess Euchen
Estiu
Etain
Ethne
Fachea
Fand
Feithline
Fideal
Finchoem
Findabar
Finncaev
Fiongalla
Fionnuala
Fithir

Flidais
Gentle Annie
Gillagriene
Glas
Godiva
Grainne
Grainne ni Malley
Grian
Guinevere
Gwyar
Gwyllion
Habetrot
Habondia
Henwen
Inghean Bhuidhe
Korrigan
Latiaran
Latis
Lavercam
Leanan Sidhe
Liban
Logia
Luaths Lurgann
Mabb
Macha
Maeve
Magog
Mal
Mala Liath
Marcia Proba
Melusine
Minerva Medica
Momu
Moncha
Morgan Le Fay
Morgay
Moriath
Morrigan
Moruadh
Muime Chriosda
Muireartach
Munanna
Nar
Natosuelta
Nehalennia
Nemain
Nemetona

Nessa
Niamh
Nicnevin
Nimue
Oanuava
Odras
Olwen
Oona
Ratis
Rhiannon

Rosmerta
Saba
Sabrina
Scathach
Scota
Sequana
Sheila na Gig
Silkie
Sin
Sinann

Sirona
Sulis
Suliviae
Taillte
Triduana
Turrean
Uairebhuidhe
Varia
Veleda
Viviane

Chinese, Manchurian, and Mongolian

Aigiarm
Altan-Telgey
Chang-O
Chih Nu
Chuang-Mu
Etugen
Feng Pho-Pho
Fu-Pao
Ho Hsien-Ku
Hsi-Ling Shih
Hsi Wang Mu
Hsian Fu-Jen

Hu-Tu
Kuan-Yin
Lan Ts'ai-Ho
Lo Shen
Ma Tsu-Po
Ma-Ku
Meng-Po Niang-Niang
Nu Kua
Pa
Pao-Yueh
Pi-Hsia Yuan-Chin
Sao-Ts'ing Niang

Shiju-Gara
Sien-Tsang
Tai Yuan
Teleglen Edzen
Tien-Hou
Tien-Mu
Tou-Mou
Tsan-Mu
Tsi-Ku
Vatiaz

Cretan, Greek, pre-Hellenic, and Hellenistic

Acantha
Adamanthea
Aedon
Aega
Aella
Agave
Agdos
Aithuia
Alcippe
Alecto
Alectrona
Althaea
Amalthea
Amazons
Amphitrite
Amymone
Anadyomene

Ananke
Anaxarete
Andromeda
Anesidora
Anieros
Anthiea
Antianara
Antigone
Antiope
Aphrodite
Arachne
Arete
Ariadne
Artemis
Artemisia
Asteria
Atalanta

Até
Athana Lindia
Athene
The Augralids
Aura
Basile
Basilinna
Baubo
Bia
Biblys
Bontene
Brimo
Britomartis
Caenis
Caligo
Callisto
Calypso

Campe
Carya
Cassandra
Cassiopeia
Castalia
Cer
Cerberus
Ceto
Charila
Charybdis
Chelone
Chera
Chimera
Chloë
Chrysothenius
Circe
Cleone
Clymene
Clytemnestra
Clytie
Cotys
Crocale
Cydippe
Cynosura
Cyone
Cyrene
Da
Dactyls
Damia
Danae
The Danaids
Daphne
Dejanira
Demeter
Despoina
Dione
Doris
Dryads
Dryope
Echenais
Echidna
Echo
Eileithyia
Eireisone
Electra
Eos
Erigone

Erinyes
Eumenides
Europa
Eurydice
Eurynome
Gaea
Galatea
Ganymeda
Gorgons
Graces
Graeae
Halcyone
Harmonia
Harpies
Hebe
Hecate
Hegemone
Helen
Heliades
Helle
Hera
Hero
Hesperides
Hestia
Hiera
Hippia
Hippo
Hippodamia
Hippolyta
Horae
Horephoros
Hydra
Hypermnestra
Ia
Iambe
Iaso
Ida
Idothea
Ino
Io
Iphigenia
Iphis
Irene
Iris
Ismene
Jocasta
Kakia

Karpophoros
Kore
Lada
Lamia
Lampetia
Latona
Leda
Lemna
Leto
Leucippe
Limnades
Litae
Lotis
Lygodesma
Lysippe
Lyssa
Macaria
Macris
Maenads
Maia
Malophoros
Manto
Marpesia
Marpessa
Medea
Medusa
Megaera
Meilichia
Melanippe
Meliae
Melissa
Menalippe
Mentha
Meroe
Merope
Meta
Metanira
Meter
Metis
Mnasa
Mnemosyne
Moirae
Mormo
Muses
Myrine
Naiads
Nausicaa

Nemesis
Nephele
Nereids
Nike
Niobe
Nympheuomene
Nyx
Oceanids
Omphale
Oreads
Oreithyia
Orthia
Otiona
Otrere
Pallas
Pamphile
Pandia
Pandora
Panope
Pantariste
Paphos
Pasiphae
Penelope
Penthesilea
Perasia
Pero
Perse

Persephone
Phaedra
Pheraia
Pherenice
Philemon
Philomena
Phoebad
Phryne
Phyllis
Pitho
Plataia
Pleiades
Poine
Polycaste
Polydamna
Praxidike
Procris
Protagenia
Psyche
Pyrrha
Pythia
Python
Rhea
Rhode
Rumor
Salmacis
Scylla

Selene
Semele
Sibyl
Sirens
Smilax
Spako
Sparta
Spes
Sphinx
Styx
Syrinx
Teleia
Telesilla
Telphassa
Telphusa
Tethys
Thalassa
Thalestris
Thea
Themis
Thesmophoros
Thetis
Thyone
Tomyris
Urania

Etruscan, Italic, and Roman

Abeona
Abundita
Acca Larentia
Adeona
Aetna
Alemona
Amata
Angerona
Angitia
Anima Mundi
Anna Perenna
Antevorta
Aricia
Arria
Aurora
Aventina

Befana
Bellona
Bona Dea
Caca
Camenae
Camilla
Candelifera
Cardea
Carmenta
Carna
Ceres
Claudia Quinta
Concordia
Copia
Cuba
Cunina

Damatre
Damatres
Dea Dia
Devera
Diana
Disciplina
Diuturna
Edusa
Egeria
Fama
Felicitas
Feronia
Fides
Flora
Fons
Fornax

Fortuna
Fraud
Fulgora
Furrina
Galiana
Ggigantia
Giane
Hybla
Intercidona
Juno
Lalal
Lara
Lasa
Laverna
Libera
Liberalitas
Libertas
Libitina
Lignaco-Dex
Lucina
Luna
Luperca
Magna Mater
Maia
Mania
Marcia
Matuta
Meditrina
Mellonia

Menrva
Mens
Minerva
Moneta
Naenia
Necessitas
Nona
Nortia
Ocrisia
Ops
Ossipago
Pales
Pallor
Panacea
Parca
Partula
Pavor
Pietas
Pomona
Postvorta
Potina
Proserpine
Providentia
Puta
Rhea Silvia
Rumina
Salus
Seia
Sentia

Sipna
Spes
Strenua
Tanaquil
Telete
Tellus Mater
Tempestates
Thalna
Titania
Tuchulcha
Turan
Tursa
Uni
Unxia
Vacuna
Vagitanus
Valetudo
Vanths
Vegoia
Venus
Veritas
Verplace
Vesta
Vesuna Erinia
Virginia
Volumna
Voluptas
Zirna

Finno-Ugric: Cheremis, Finnish, Hungarian, Mordvin, and Saami

Avfruvva
Azer-Ava
Barbmo-Akka
Beiwe
Beiwe-Neida
Bonto
Cacce-Jienne
Cuvto-Ava
Haltia
Idem-Huva
Ilma
Juks-Akka
Kalma
Keca Aba

Laugo-Edne
Loddis-Edne
Louhi
Luonnotar
Luot-Hozjit
Madder-Akka
Mardeq Avalon
Mere-Ama
Metsannetsyt
Metsarhatija
Mielikki
Nakineitsi
Ovda
Paivatar

Paive
Pohjan-Akka
Port-Kuva
Poshjo-Akka
Radien-Akka
Radien-Kiedde
Rana Neida
Rauni
Risem-Edne
Sar-Akka
Sundi-Mumi
Suonetar
Tava-Ajk
Tundr Ilona

Tuonetar	Veden Emo	Xatel-Ekwa
Tuulikki	Vellamo	Xoli-Kaltes
Uks-Akka	Viran-Akka	Yabme-Akka
Ved-Ava	Vitsa-Kuva	Zlota-Baba

Indian, South Asian, and Tibetan

Abhramu	Jyestha	Ranu Bai
Aditi	Kadru	Rati
Alakhani	Kali	Rohini
Amba	Kandiu	Rudrani
Ammavaru	Karaikkal-Asmmaiyar	Saibya
Anna Purna	Katau Kumei	Sakkala-Khatun
Armaiti	Khala Kumari	Samjuna
Banka-Mundi	Khon-Ma	Samundra
Bardaichila	Kottavi	Saning Sri
Bentakumari	Kunti	Sarasvati
Bhavani	Kurukulla	Sarna Burhi
Bisal-Mariamna	Kusumamodini	Sarvari
Bomong	Lakshmi	Sasti
Budhi Pallien	Lalita	Sati
Candi	Lla-Mo	Savitri
Challallamma	Lohasur Devi	Shakti
Chinnintamma	Mahakala	Sila
Churalin	Maitreya	Sita
Dakini	Manasa	Sitala
Davata	Marahi Devi	Srinmo
Devayani	Marici	Suki
Devi	Maya	Sunkalamma
Dharti Mata	Minachiamman	Sura
Diti	Mindhal	Surabhi
Draupadi	Muk Jauk	Surasa
Durga	Mutyalamma	Tara
Ekash-Taka	Naina Devi	Tari Pennu
Ekhe-Urani	Nirriti	Toh Sri Lam
Emboq Sri	Parooa	Trung-Trac
Ganga	Parvati	Tsun Kyankse
Gauri	Pidari	Tulsi
Gauri-Sankar	Po Ino Nogar	Ukepenopfu
Ghar-Jenti	Pok Klai	Urvasi
Hada Bai	Prakriti	Ushas
Hathay	Prithivi	Vajravaraki
Holika	Radha	Vinata
Huligamma	Rakshasi	Yamuna
Ila	Rambha	Yaparamma
Janguli	Ranaghanti	Yasodha

Mesopotamian: Akkadian, Aramaic, Babylonian, Chaldean, Elamite, Sumerian, Syrian, and Ugaritic

A
Absusu
Abtagigi
Adamu
Aja
Allatu
Amashilamma
Anat
Anatu
Anunit
Aruru
Ashnan
Atargatis
Bau
Belit-Ilani
Belit-Seri
Damkina
Dea Syria
Derceto
Egime
Eriskegal
Erua
Eshara
Gamlat
Gamsu
Gatamdug
Gestinanna
Gula
Gumshea

Hanata
Inanna
Irkalla
Irnini
Ishtar
Kadi
Kathirat
Ki
Kilili
Lahar
Lamamu
Lamasthu
Mami
Mamitu
Minu Anni
Myrrha
Nagar-Saga
Nammu
Nana
Nanshe
Ninazu
Nindum
Ningal
Ninhurra
Ninhursag
Ninkasl
Ninkharak
Ninkigal
Ninlil

Ninmah
Ninsar
Nin-Si-Anna
Ninsikilla
Ninti
Nintur
Nisaba
Orore
Sadarnuna
Sala
Sarbanda
Sasura
Seimia
Shapash
Sharrat Shame
Shatagat
Sherua
Shulamite
Siduri
Siris
Tauthe
Tiamat
Ulsiga
Uttu
Vashti
Zanaru
Zarpandit
Zib

North American

Aghyu Gugu
Ailsie
Ai-Willi-Ay-O
Akycha
Amayicoyondi
Apasinasee
Ataensic
Atse Estsan
Awitelin Tsita
Butterfly Maiden
Changing Woman

Chuginadak
Djigonasee
Dzalarhons
Estsanatlehi
Gendenwitha
Genetaska
Glispa
Gyhldeptis
Hanwi
Hastseoltoi
Hatai Wugti

Hekoolas
Hulluk Miyumko
H'Uraru
Irdlirvirisissong
Kadlu
Kanene Ski Amai Yehi
Loo-Wit
Mahakh
Mem Loimis
Nahkeeta
Nokomis

Noogumee
Norwan
Nuliayoq
Ohoyo Osh Chishba
Omamama
Onatah
Oniata
Pahto
Panes
Ptesan-Wi
Pukimna

Qamaits
Qocha Mana
Rhpisunt
Rukko
Sedna
Selu
Shiwanokia
Sneneik
Snutqutxals
Spear-Finger
Tacoma

Tahc-i
Tlitcaplitana
Unelanuhi
Uti Hiata
Utset and Nowutset
Wah-Kah-Nee
White Buffalo Woman
Yebaad
Yolkai Estsan

Semitic: Cabalistic, Canaanite, Christian, Hebrew, and Jewish

Abigail
Adah
Adath
Agasaya
Agrat Bat Mahalat
Ama
Ardat Lili
Asherah
Astarte
Athaliah
Beruryah
Bilhah
Bina
Broxa
Chaabou
Cherubim
Daughters of
    Zelophehad
Deborah

Dinah
Esther
Eve
Ganzir
Hagar
Hannah
Hawwah
Hokkma
Husbishag
Iahu Anat
Igirit
Ishara
Istehar
Jezebel
Jocebed
Judith
Leah
Leviathan
Lilith

Mahalat
Mary
The Matronit
Mehitabel
Miriam
Naamah
Ptrotka
Rachel
Rebecca
Sarah
Sheilah
Shekinah
Sheol
Tamar
Torah
Zipporah
Zuleika

Slavic: Balkan, Polish, Russian, Scythian, Siberian, and Thracian

Ajysyt
Apia-Fellus
Arganthone
Artimpaasa
Baba Yaga
Bendis
Bugady Musun
Colleda
Doda

Dolya
Dziwozony
Erce
Ja-Neba
Jezenky
Kasum-Naj-Ekva
Kikimora
Kostrubonko
Kou-Njami

Kupalo
Marzana
Mati
Mokosh
Mother Friday
Mou-Njami
Navky
Ognyene Maria
Poldunica

Poza-Mama
Rusalky
Selci Syt Emysyt
Siva
Sreca
Sroya
Sudice

Tabiti
Tu-Njami
Umaj
Ursula
Veshtitze
Vesna
Vila

Vodni Panny
Vut-Imi
Wlasca
Zima
Zonget
Zywie

THE BOOK OF

Goddesses
& Heroines

A, Aa, also **Sirdu, Sirrida**   A Chaldean moon-goddess whose emblem is a disk with eight rays, a number that—like the octagon—is associated with the goddess of light in many cultures.

A, Aja, Aya   The "bride," a Babylonian dawn-goddess whose consort was the sun-god. Like other dawn-goddesses—*Eos,** *Aurora*—she was associated with the eastern mountains, which boost the sun into the sky. Independent at first, A later merged with *Ishtar.*

Abeona   Roman goddess ruling a child's first departure from home.

Abhramu   The "cloud-knitter" was the original female elephant who—like her offspring for many generations—was a supernatural winged being who could change her shape at will, like the clouds that resemble her children. But according to Indian legend, Abhramu's tribe lost its wings and its magic by mischance.

One day a large flock of elephants was flying slowly through the sky, changing into various shapes. Tiring, they spied a huge tree and began to alight on it. Alas, the combined weight of the elephant flock broke the tree's branches.

And alas for the winged elephants, for an ascetic was sitting in yogic posture beneath the tree teaching his pupils. He was unharmed, but the falling branches and elephant bodies crushed all his students. The sage, furious at having his school destroyed, cursed the elephants and their wings dropped off. Abhramu's progeny have been earthbound ever since, trapped in the enormous cloud shapes they were wearing during the unfortunate encounter with the sage.

---

* A figure mentioned in an entry different from its own is *italicized* the first time it appears in that entry. There are two types of cross-references in the text. **See** is a direct reference and is mainly used for figures of different cultures sharing a similar story or when a figure is an aspect or form of another. **See also** is a more generalized reference.

Abigail   This woman of Hebrew legend is similar in many respects to the ancient goddesses of the eastern Mediterranean, especially in being both the sister and the spouse of a king, David of Israel. Married first to the "churlish and evil" non-Hebrew Nabal, a shepherd who grazed his flocks under David's protection along Judea's border, Abigail intervened with the Israelite king after her husband insulted him and David threatened to send 400 soldiers to punish Nabal. The shepherd, hearing how his wife had saved him, promptly died of fright, leaving Abigail available for remarriage to David, who, in other texts, is described as her brother by the same mother.

Absusu   A title of *Ishtar* the promiscuous, perhaps originally an independent Sumerian deity.

Abtagigi   A Sumerian title that means "she who sends messages (of desire)" and refers to *Ishtar* as the patron of sacramental promiscuity.

Abuk   The first woman, the Dinka people of the African Sudan say, was created very tiny but fully formed, then put like a bean in a big pot, where she swelled up overnight. The creator-god stingily gave Abuk and her mate Garang only one grain of corn to eat each day. The human race would have starved had Abuk not simply taken what people needed and ground it into meal. As patron goddess of women and gardens, Abuk has for her emblem a little snake.

Abundita   The name of this Roman farm goddess means "agricultural abundance."

Acantha   According to the Greeks, the resident spirit of the acanthus flower was once a nymph loved by the sun-god. At her death, she was transformed into a sun-loving plant.

Acca Larentia   "Lady Mother," a full-fledged goddess to the Etruscans, passed into Roman mythology as a semidivine prostitute who was benefactress of the plebeian class. She gained her great wealth, it was said, by worshiping an entire night in the temple of Heracles. As she departed, she met a rich man with whom she lived for some time. He died, leaving her a fortune; when she died, she willed the remaining vast wealth to the Roman people, who celebrated her gift each year on December 23 in the raucous festival called, after her, the Larentalia. In other legends, Acca Larentia is named as the foster mother of Rome's founders, Romulus and Remus, and even as the she-wolf who suckled them.

Achall In Irish legend, she was a loving sister who died of sorrow when her brother was killed in battle. Her love was memorialized by the Hill of Achall near Tara at the island's mystic center.

Achtan The daughter of an evil Irish Druid smith, Achtan slept with the land's high king the night before his final battle; she conceived a child and called him Cormac mac Art after the father. The baby was accidentally separated from Achtan and was suckled by a wolf. The child grew up wild and healthy and was ultimately returned to Achtan by the hunter Luinge Fer Tri.

    The reunited mother and son set out to climb the wild Irish mountains, protected by animals as they traveled. Eventually they reached the seat of Irish sovereignty, the Hill of Tara. There Cormac took his father's place as king, while his mother settled down with the hunter Luinge.

Achtland In ancient Celtic legend, this mortal queen could not be satisfied with human men and took a giant as her spouse. Her greatest pleasure came from combing his yards of long hair.

Adah Her name means "ornament," and Hebrew legend named her as one of the great matriarchs of the neighboring, non-Hebrew Edomites. In biblical legend, this was symbolized by calling her a wife of Esau, the son of Isaac who refused to worship Jehovah.

Adamanthea Long before Zeus became the preeminent Greek god, his life was in danger. His father, Cronos, intended to swallow the infant, as he had swallowed the earlier-born gods and goddesses. To spare her offspring, the earth mother *Rhea* hid the infant in Crete, in the care of the nymph (or princess) Adamanthea. The mighty Titan Cronos had dominion over the earth, the heavens, and the sea; he could see anything that existed in his realm. But the infant's new nurse was clever. Adamanthea hung a cradle from a tree and there—suspended between earth, sea, and sky—Zeus was invisible to his destructive father. In other versions of the story, the nurse of Zeus is *Ida*, Adrastea, Neda, Helice, *Aega* or *Cynosura*.

Adamu In Chaldea, this was the name of the female principle of matter. It means "red"; she represented the blood of the womb and of menstruation. See **Mens**.

Adath This Canaanite word, the counterpart of *Adonis* ("lord"), means "lady" and was applied to both goddesses and distinguished mortal women.

Adeona   Roman goddess ruling a child's return home after school.

Aditi   Some have tried to call her Mother Earth, but this Indian goddess properly is called Mother Space, a feminine embodiment of whatever transcends measurement: infinity, the cosmos, the continuing creation, divinity itself. Although unquestionably feminine, she was also "father and son," the Vedic scriptures tell us.

The preexistent first goddess was said to have no mother and no birth, to have existed from all time. She was, however, the genetrix of other divinities: some say of the powerful Vishnu, others of Indra, others, Mithra. Almost all sources agree that in her aspect of sky-goddess she produced the multiple divinities who bear her name, the Adityas.

Although Aditi was more often invoked or prayed to than described in myth, there are tales that explain how the goddess produced children. Some say she bore 12 Adityas, one for each month, and that Aditi thus marked limits on previously boundless time. It was also said that she had seven normal sons, then birthed a huge egg that rose into the sky to become the sun. Yet another version of the story says she had only one son, but one so splendid that his mere presence hurt Aditi's eyes; she divided the single son into 12, setting them to rule the order of nature. See also **Diti**.

Aedon   The queen of ancient Thebes plotted to murder the eldest son of her rival *Niobe* but accidentally killed her own child. Stricken by remorse and grief, Aedon attempted suicide and was transformed into a nightingale, which still haunts the night with its sad cry.

Aega   She was the sun's daughter and, like her sisters *Circe* and *Pasiphae,* a hypnotically beautiful woman, so beautiful that when the earthborn Titans attacked the gods of Olympus, the earth mother Gaea placed Aega in a cave to hide her shimmering loveliness. It is probable that behind these Greek legends lies a pre-Hellenic mythology in which the three sisters were a threefold goddess, possibly the ruler of the sun, for Pasiphae means "she who shines for all," and another famous sun-goddess, the Japanese *Amaterasu,* was also hidden in a cave.

Aella   The Greeks set sail for the shores of the Black Sea, intending to make war on the *Amazons* and to despoil their queen of her famous golden belt. But the women resisted. Aella flew first at the invaders like a "whirlwind" (the meaning of her name). But this heroic defender of Queen *Hippolyta*, this valiant wielder of the double-ax, was cut down by the Greek hero Heracles.

Aeracura   Celtic earth mother of the Rhine Valley.

Aeron   Welsh goddess of slaughter and war.

Aetna   The Roman mountain-goddess after whom the Italian volcano Mount Etna is named. In many cultures, fire is female; in most, mountains are considered to be so; thus people living near volcanoes often perceive the fiery mountains as particularly powerful goddesses. See also **Pele, Fuji, Chuginadak.**

Aeval   A fairy queen of Munster, the southwestern quarter of Ireland, Aeval heard a debate on whether the men in her district were satisfying the women's sexual needs. It took all night to give evidence at Aeval's "midnight court," but when the queen had heard both sides, she judged the men wrong and sentenced them to overcome their prudishness and accede to the women's wishes.

Agasaya   "Shrieker," a Semitic war-goddess who merged into *Ishtar* in her identity as fearless warrior of the sky.

Agave   The daughter of *Harmonia*, Agave had a son, King Pentheus of Thebes. Her sister *Semele* had a son, too—the god Dionysus, inventor of viniculture and leader of secret rites. Agave and another sister, Autonoe, quickly recognized the divinity of their nephew and joined the new religion as Bacchantes or *Maenads*.

Only women were allowed to participate in—even to witness—the all-night festivals of the new religion; thus the Maenads sought the privacy of forested mountains for their rituals of dancing and drinking, during which they felt themselves to be part of the divinity of life. Prudish King Pentheus, however, saw no good in such religious intoxication and deplored the attendance by his aunt and, worse yet, his mother.

Despite warnings, King Pentheus decided to spy on them. Climbing a tall pine tree near the ritual site, he thought to go unnoticed while he penetrated the women's privacy. But the Maenads spotted him, and not even a mother could ask forgiveness for such sacrilege. They dragged Pentheus from the tree and tore him to shreds as if he were a wild animal. Then the women bore his bloody remains back to Thebes—his mother bearing the head aloft—as a warning to anyone considering a similar infringement of the women's ceremonials.

Agdos   A name for the great rock of Asia Minor (*Cybele* in disguise) that Zeus tried to rape; her name survived in that of her hermaphrodite offspring Agdistis.

Aghyu Gugu "Beautiful woman" or perhaps "excellent woman," a name used of the Cherokee sun-goddess *Unelanuhi.*

Agrat Bat Mahalat, also Igirit In Jewish legend, she is the commander of 180,000 demons and roams the world on Wednesdays and Friday evenings in a chariot, hunting down anything that moves. On other days, the Talmud tells us, the "spirit of uncleanness" is contained by the power of the rabbis. But as Jewish couples were traditionally expected to have intercourse on Friday evenings, it is likely that Agrat represents unbridled sexuality, which the rabbis attempt to "bind" but which they admit will never be banished completely until the end of time. For a similar but more fully developed figure of Jewish tradition, see **Lilith.**

Agusan Devi A Hindu goddess found in the Philippines.

Ahemait The Egyptian underworld-goddess ("devourer"), part hippopotamus, part lion, part crocodile, who eats the souls of the unworthy dead. See also **Maat.**

Ahrenkonigin Austrian "queen of corn ears," a harvest-goddess.

Aibheaog Ancient fire-goddess of County Donegal in Ireland, she was worshiped at a *tobar* (well) whose alternative name—*Tobar Bride*—includes that of the pan-Celtic Great Goddess. The well's waters were held to be an effective remedy against toothache, so long as the petitioner left a little white stone beside the well as a substitute for the sore tooth. See **Brigid.**

Aida-Wedo The rainbow snake *loa* (spirit) in Haiti, she is the companion of the most popular god, Damballah-Wedo, also a serpent. She appears in voodoo ritual, slithering across the ground and, it is said, wearing a jeweled headdress that—like the treasure at the end of the rainbow—is elusive but enriches anyone who can grasp it.

Aife, Aoife A legendary Celtic queen, whose name is pronounced "ee-fa," she lived in Scotland near her rival, the amazonian queen *Scathach,* with whom she was constantly at war. They were well-matched foes; Scathach had magical powers, whereas Aife was invulnerable to them and to everything but fast horses and pretty horsewomen. Eventually, Aife was defeated by the Irish hero Cuchulain and accepted as part of the truce his demands that she bear his son; she did; he returned to Ireland and, years later, killed his son without recognizing him.

  Another—or possibly the same—Aife was the consort of the sea-

See Agusan Devi, p. 8; Devi, p. 95; Gauri, p. 131. Field Museum of Natural History (Neg # 109923), Chicago.

god Mananaan. She stole the secret alphabet of knowledge from the gods to give to humanity and was transformed into a crane in punishment. However, in a bag made from her own skin, Aife delivered the magic letters to the people.

Aige A woman of Irish legend, she was turned by elfin spite into a fawn. In this form, Aige wandered across the island until she died by plunging into a bay, which today bears her name.

Aigiarm Marco Polo said of this Mongolian princess, "She could meet no man able to conquer her." Whenever one came to woo her, Aigiarm wagered her virginity against the suitor's horses and challenged him to wrestle her to the ground. There is no record of her marrying, but it is recorded that Aigiarm won 10,000 horses.

Ailinn The heroine of one of Ireland's great romantic legends was born a princess of Leinster, the southeastern part of the island. She was passionately attached to Baile, a prince of northern Ireland, and they agreed to meet for a night of love midway between their realms.

But an evil sprite met Baile at the trysting-place and told him that Ailinn was dead; the shock killed the prince instantly. Then the wicked sprite traveled to Ailinn, this time telling the truth. Hearing that her lover was dead, the princess died of grief.

Their people, recognizing the depth of their affection, buried Ailinn and Baile in adjoining graves, from which grew two magical trees: an apple from Ailinn's grave, a yew from Baile's. As they grew, the trees twined themselves around each other. Centuries later, the famous pair was cut down by poets and made into wands on which all the tragic love songs of the Irish were cut in runes and carried to the Hill of Tara.

Ailsie A Cherokee heroine, she was a tall woman beloved by the crane and the hummingbird. Her father wished for her to marry the powerful crane, but she preferred the swift-flying hummingbird. She set her suitors a challenge: the one who could fly fastest would win her.

She trusted in the hummingbird's speed, but after five circuits around the racecourse the hummingbird had tired, and the crane won handily. Furious at the loss, Ailsie vowed never to marry rather than wed an ugly bird like the crane. But her father, happy at the race's outcome, pledged to kill her unless she married. Ailsie asked for a reprieve of seven days alone. During that time she wept so much that she turned into a deep pool in the Etowah River.

Ain   The sister of Iaine and probably her double, she was the mythical reason for women's high status in ancient Ireland. When the two sisters married their two brothers, the men invented war so that each could claim as large a share of the island as possible. As a result of the conflict, the rights of women, single or married, were spelled out carefully in the famous "Brehon Laws," which among other things guaranteed that no child be called illegitimate except those engendered by satirists who changed sides with each dispute. The laws of ancient Ireland were singularly comprehensive in assuring women's property rights and freedom, but later occupation by the Normans meant the end of the Brehon system.

Aine   One of the great goddesses of ancient Ireland survives in modern times as the queen of the fairies of south Munster, the southwest corner of the island, and is said to haunt Knockainy Hill there. Originally Aine was apparently a sun-goddess who assumed the form of Lair Derg ("red mare"), the horse that none could outrun. Her special feast was Midsummer Night, when farmers carried torches of straw in procession around Knockainy and waved them over the cattle and the fields for protection and fruitfulness.

   Two stories are told of Aine. In one, she was the daughter of an early Irish god and was infatuated with the semidivine hero Finn. She had taken a *geasa* (sacred vow) that she would never sleep with a man with gray hair, but Finn was young with no silver streaking his bushy hair. One of Aine's sisters, Miluchrach, was also interested in Finn; she enchanted a lake and tempted Finn to take a dip. When the hero emerged from the magic waters, his body was still youthful and strong, but his hair was stained gray. True to her *geasa*, Aine thereafter scorned the hero.

   In another story, Gerald, the human Earl of Desmond, captured Aine while she was combing her hair on the banks of her sacred lake. Aine bore the first Earl Fitzgerald to the man, but made Gerald promise never to express surprise at the powers his son might develop. All went well for many years until one day when Gerald saw his son jump into and out of a bottle. He could not contain an exclamation of shock and the boy disappeared, flying away in the shape of a wild goose. Disappointed in her human mate, Aine disappeared into Knockainy, where she is said still to live in a splendid castle. See **Grian.**

Airmed   She was a goddess of the Tuatha de Danaan, the most ancient deities of Ireland; like all of them, she had great magical powers. She was the particular goddess of witchcraft and herb lore, for she knew the uses of every plant, knowledge gained at the death of her beloved brother Miach. She buried him with great mourning, and

11

innumerable plants sprang from his grave. These were all the world's herbs, which instructed her in their use as she tended Miach's grave.

'Aisha Qandisha People along the coast of Northern Morocco sometimes saw this *jinniya* (female spirit), recognized by her beautiful face, pendulous breasts and goat legs. She was wanton and free, seducing young men, despite having a *jinn*-consort named Hammu Qaiyu.

Her name strongly suggests a connection to the Qadesha, the sexually free temple women of Canaan who served *Astarte*. She, like 'Aisha, was a water-goddess; a possible translation of her name may be "loving to be watered," apparently with semen. Another connection hides in the name of Astarte's consort Haman, seemingly the original of Hammu. The route of transmission was likely through Carthage, where Astarte had a temple. Carthage had colonies in Morocco; the bedouins of the Beni Ahsen, living on the site of the ancient Carthaginian colonies, were most prone to visitations by 'Aisha. See **Astarte.**

Aithuia "Diver bird" was the Greek goddess *Athene* in the shape of a seabird, or a separate goddess later assimilated into the powerful Athenian goddess.

Ai-Willi-Ay-O See **Sedna**; this name is used for her on the West Coast of Hudson Bay.

Ajysyt, Aisyt Among the Yakuts of Russia, this birth-goddess had two functions: to help laboring women bear safely, and to breathe a soul into the child once born. She was also the divinity of domestic animals, especially cattle. Perhaps her rulership of birth made this a natural evolution of her duties, for the safe birthing of cattle was necessary in economically marginal societies.

The ceremonies glorifying Ajysyt after birth were held secret by the Yakut women; a man's presence would have been sacrilege. Parts of a sacrificed animal (usually the inner organs) were served to the goddess on a special dinner table in the birth chamber. As the birth proceeded, the midwife offered butter to the goddess by placing it on the heart, praying, "We thank you, Ajysyt, for what you have given and ask for it even in future." For three days the birthing woman had to remain sequestered; her friends visited and ate butter with her. After three days, the midwife took the straw on which the new mother had lain and tied it into the top of a tall tree; after this, the goddess left the house until the next birth.

Aka, Akka, Ekki The mother-goddess in ancient Turkey; her name remains in some dialects as the common noun for "mother."

Akewa The sun-goddess of the Toba of Argentina was said to be the sister of all earthly women. Once they, like her, were shining residents of the heavens, while hairy male savages inhabited the earth. Curious about their downstairs neighbors, the women one day climbed down a vine rope to explore the earth. But one of the brutish men bit the heavenly ladder in two and stranded the angelic women on this planet forever, leaving only Akewa to remind them of what they had been.

Akusaa Egyptian goddess of sunset.

Akycha, Seqinek, Malina The people of Greenland, Canada and Alaska say that the sun and the moon, before they lived above us, were residents of the earth. The sun was the young woman Akycha, the moon was her brother, and they lived in a small village where the people gathered each night to dance in the dance hut.

Akycha lived alone. One night, while everyone else was dancing, she was surprised by a man breaking into her home. He raped her, and in the dark, Akycha could not recognize her assailant. After that she never knew when the man would come, but he frequently repeated the crime.

One night, Akycha determined to discover the identity of the man. She rubbed her fingers across her oil lamp, covering them with soot; after the attacker had finished with her, Akycha rubbed his face with her smeary fingers. He left, but she trailed him to the dance hut. There, to her horror, Akycha saw her own brother with a smeared face. She grabbed a knife and cut off her left breast, flinging it to him with the words, "Since you desire me so much, eat this."

Then Akycha grabbed a burning brand of wood and ran from the village. Her brother followed her, his desire enflamed by the sight of her blood. He too grabbed a lighting branch, but he tripped and dampened its flame in the snow. On and on they ran until they were transported to the sky, where they continue their endless pursuit.

Ala, Ale, Ane The most popular divinity of the Ibo tribe in Nigeria is the earth mother Ala, creator of the living and queen of the dead, provider of communal loyalty and lawgiver of society; her worship survives today. She is the guardian of morality, the one on whom oaths are sworn and in whose name courts of law are held. The village shrine of Ala is the central one in any Ibo village; it is at her sacred tree shrine that the people offer sacrifices at planting, at first fruits, and at the harvest.

Alaghom Naom Tzentel "Mother of mind" was the ancient Mayan goddess of thought and intellect.

Alakhani Under the bamboo groves in a mushroom-shaped plant called *alakhani-bah* ("cell of Alakhani") lived this puckish imp known to the Indian Assamese. Anyone who passed was suddenly possessed by her, though never harmed. A form of vegetation spirit, she was essentially benign, though mischievous.

Alcippe According to the Greeks, the rape of this daughter of Aglauros occasioned the first murder trial. The young goddess was criminally assaulted by a son of Poseidon whereupon her father Ares killed the offender. Called to trial by the gods to account for his actions, Ares presented the brutal facts and was swiftly acquitted. See **The Augralids.**

Alecto, Alektro One of the three Furies or *Erinyes*; sometimes a Greek goddess of war and death.

Alectrona An early Greek goddess, she was the daughter of the sun. No beast of burden could enter her sanctuary in Rhodes. Anyone bringing an ass, horse, or mule to her shrine had to undergo ritual purification.

Alemona Roman goddess who guards the fetus.

Alfhild A maiden goddess of Scandinavia who dressed as a warrior to avoid being taken in marriage by King Alf. Only when they had fought to the death, and he had proven himself as strong as she, did she agree to mate with him.

Al-Lat, Alilat, Allita, Elat, Elath, Hallat, Lat In Arabic, *Allah* means "god." Similarly, *Al-Lat* means simply "goddess," the supreme reality in female form. Al-Lat is a mythic figure of antiquity, one of the trinity of desert-goddesses that included *Al-Uzza* and *Menat*. Like the Greek *Demeter*, Al-Lat represented the earth and its fruits; it naturally follows that she ruled human generation.

    Al-Lat was worshiped at At Ta'if near Mecca in the form of a great uncut block of white granite, which her worshipers addressed as "My Lady" or Rusa ("good fortune"). Women were required to appear before her naked and circle the sacred rock; if these conditions were met, the goddess would grant all requests. Solid as the earth she represented, Al-Lat was considered unshakable and immovable. Thus her people swore their most solemn oaths by her, with the following words: "by the salt, by the fire, and by Al-Lat who is the greatest of all."

*See Ala, p. 13. Field Museum of Natural History (Neg# 96453),
Chicago.*

Allatu, Alukah Akkadian and Canaanite names, respectively, for *Eriskegal*, the queen of the underworld.

Almha, Almu Pronounced "alva," she was a goddess of the Tuatha de Danaan after whom a southern Irish hill is named. Nothing remains of her myth.

Altan-Telgey The Mongolian earth-goddess bore this name, which means "golden surface."

Althaea This Greek woman had two sons: one was a hero in campaigns against tribal enemies, the other a priest of the secret rites. When the hero Meleager killed his brother, the priest, Althaea cried out to the underworld to take the murderer away.

Al-Uzza, Uzza Before declaring himself a prophet of male divinity, Mohammed worshiped this desert-goddess of the morning star, whose name means "the mighty" or "the strongest." He turned on her, however, destroying her sanctuary of acacia trees south of Mecca, where Al-Uzza's worshipers had gathered for generations to reverence the sacred stone representing her. Belief in her power long survived the destruction of her holy place, not dying out until almost 1,000 years had passed. With *Al-Lat* and *Menat*, this goddess composed the great religious trinity of the ancient Arabians.

Ama, Am, Umm "Muse" and "mother" in Semitic and Aryan tongues. In Egypt, there was a goddess of this name whose consort was the sun-god; in Dravidian India, *Amba* is "Mother Earth." For the most developed eastern Mediterranean form of this figure, see **Mami**.

Amalthea Whatever the name of Zeus's Cretan nurse (see **Adamanthea**), she fed the infant god on the milk of this magical nanny goat. When he grew up, Zeus broke off one of Amalthea's horns and gave it to his nurse; it then turned into the magical "cornucopia." Just as the magic goat could produce milk rich and copious enough for a god, so part of her could provide sufficient nourishment for the children of earth. After thus providing for humankind, the one-horned nanny disappeared into heaven, where she was transformed into the constellation of Capricorn.

Amashilamma Sumerian cow-goddess.

Amata The name of Vestal virgins after election; see **Vesta**.

16

Amaterasu, Amaterasu-Omi-Kami   Of all the religions currently practiced by significant numbers of people, the only one whose chief divinity is female is Japanese Shinto, based on the worship of the sun-goddess Amaterasu ("great shining heaven"). In her simple shrines—notable for their architectural purity and unpretentiousness and for the central mirror that represents the goddess—Amaterasu is honored as the ruler of all deities, as the guardian of Japan's people, and as the symbol of Japanese cultural unity. Her emblem, the rising sun, still flies on Japan's flag. Even the inroads of patriarchal Buddhism have not destroyed the worship of the bejeweled ancestor of all humanity.

There is one central myth of Amaterasu. She quarreled with the storm-god Susano-o and brought winter to the world. Two reasons are given for her annoyance with him: one, because of his murder of Amaterasu's sister, the food-giving goddess *Uke-Mochi*; the other, because of his deliberately provocative acts against Amaterasu herself.

The latter version has it that Amaterasu did not trust her brother Susano-o because of his excesses and his constant shouting. One day he came to heaven to see her, claiming that he meant no harm. She was wary, but he promised that he would undergo a ritual test to prove his goodwill. He said he would give birth, and that if his intentions were peaceful, the children would all be boys.

Amaterasu grabbed Susano-o's sword and broke it with her teeth, spitting out three pieces which, striking the ground, became goddesses. Susano-o asked Amaterasu for some of her jewels: she gave him five; he cracked them open and made them into gods. But then Susano-o grew wild with excitement at his creative feat and tore through the world destroying everything in his path: he even piled feces under Amaterasu's throne. As though that was not enough, he stole into her quarters and threw a flayed horse's corpse through the roof of her weaving room, so startling one of Amaterasu's companions that she pricked herself and died.

This was too much for the sun-goddess. She left this mad world and shut herself up in a comfortable cave. Without the sun, the entire world was blanketed with unending blackness. The eight million gods and goddesses, desperate for their queen's light, gathered to call out pleas that she return. But in her cave the goddess stayed.

Uzume, shaman and the goddess of merriment, finally took matters into her hands. She turned over a washtub, climbed on top, and began dancing and singing and screaming bawdy remarks. Soon the dance became a striptease. When she had shed all her clothes, Uzume began dancing so wildly and obscenely that the eight million gods and goddesses started to shout with delight.

Inside her cave, Amaterasu heard the noise. As it grew to a commotion, she called to ask what was going on. Someone paused to answer that they had found a better goddess than the sun. Provoked—and curious—Amaterasu opened the door of her cave just a crack.

The gods and goddesses had, with great foresight, installed a mirror directly outside of the cave. Amaterasu, who had never seen her own beauty before, was dazzled. While she stood there, dazed with delight, the other divinities grabbed the door and pulled it open. Thus the sun returned to warm the winter-weary earth. Mounted again on her heavenly throne, Amaterasu punished Susano-o by having his fingernails and toenails pulled out and by throwing him out of her heaven. See also **Uke-Mochi.**

Amayicoyondi   Sky mother among the Pericu of California.

Amazons   A land populated entirely by these women—the Greeks believed in it, believed it existed on their very borders, a country on the River Thermodon. Once or twice a year. on the borders of their country. the Amazons had intercourse with men from surrounding tribes, keeping their daughters and returning the sons to the tribe of origin. (Some contend that they killed the boys.)

Two queens, one for defense and one for domestic affairs, shared sovereign rule. Under their military queen the Amazons were a mighty army of mounted warriors bearing ivy-shaped shields and double-bladed battle-axes. At home, the Amazons lived peacefully, supplying all their economic needs and producing artistic treasures coveted far outside their borders. For some 400 years (1000-600 B.C.), they held sway over the part of Asia Minor along the shores of the Black Sea. Or so the Greeks believed for hundreds of years after the legendary warriors last engaged them in battle. Later Greeks attempted to dismiss the earlier tales as untrue. The historicity of Amazonia still provokes scholarly skirmishes. Did the Amazons exist? There are many theories, some dating all the way back to the days of classical Greece.

Some attempts to disprove the nation's existence are simply ludicrous, like the suggestion that, because Greek men wore beards, they thought anyone without a beard was a woman; a beardless army would have been perceived as composed of women. Other theorists speculate that, because some northern tribeswomen fought alongside their men, their existence was extrapolated into an entire northern kingdom of women warriors. Finally, there are those who contend that the Amazons were a mere projection of the (male) Greek mind and never existed outside of psychopathology.

But if they never existed, they could never have invaded Athens as

Plutarch (among others) assures us they did. Of course, one could argue that the Greeks believed that monsters like the *Sphinx* and *Gorgons* also fought with historical kings. While the issue of historicity remains far from settled, the stories of the Amazons continue to inspire the generations.

There is a persistent rumor that the word *Amazon* means "breastless," although no convincing etymology has been established. Allegedly Amazons tore off their right breasts, the better to draw the bow and throw the javelin. This is a smear campaign, for there is not a single bit of evidence in Greek art that they considered their neighbors to be self-mutilated women. On the contrary, Amazons are invariably shown with one breast bare, and quite visibly intact.

Once, so their legend says, the strong man Heracles murdered his three children. For this crime, he was sentenced to perform 12 virtually impossible tasks. One of these was to travel to Amazonia and to bring back the women's most famous treasure, their golden belt of queenship. With a large force of men, Heracles debarked at the land of women. Bands of Amazons guarded him and his comrades as they approached the queen's residence.

But Queen *Hippolyta* liked the looks of the hefty Heracles and offered him the belt in peace, and her bed with it. Unfortunately, rumor flew among the gathered Amazons that their queen Hippolyta was under attack, and they counterattacked instantly, driving the Greeks right back to their boats. Many warriors fell on both sides before the battle could be halted. It ended poorly for the Amazons. The valiant women were no match for the superhuman strength of Heracles. They were forced to surrender their leaders *Melanippe* and *Antiope* and beautiful Hippolyta herself lay dead. Antiope was carried back to Athens as a spoil of war and given to King Theseus; this was too much of an outrage for the Amazons, who mounted an attack on Greece.

The queenless warriors fought their way the length of the Greek territories, finally entering Athens and penetrating right to the sacred hill, the Acropolis. There the battle reached an awful pitch, with Antiope dying still a captive and many other Amazons losing their lives in the heroic but futile effort. They retreated north to Amazonia, so many of the wounded dying en route that the trail home was lined with their shield-shaped gravestones. For more Amazon stories, see **Antianara, Antiope, Dejanira, Hiera, Hippolyta, Lysippe, Marpesia, Myrine, Omphale, Orthia, Otrere, Penthesilea, Thalestris,** and **Tomyris.**

Amba, Amber Possibly pre-Aryan, this Indian mother-goddess was assimilated to other divinities, among them *Durga, Parvati,* and Uma. Her very name means "mother," and near Jaipur into modern times the mother-goddess was honored under this name with dawn sacrifices of black goats. Her name is similar to the old Semitic and Aryan word for "mother"—*ama*.

Amberella In Baltic folklore, Amberella was a golden-haired woman with eyes the color of the sea in which she liked to swim. One day, grasping at a piece of floating amber, she was pulled to the bottom of the water by the Prince of the Seas, who had fallen in love with her.

Distraught, her parents walked daily by the ocean, looking for their child and calling her name. A goldfish came to the surface and offered them amber in exchange for the girl, but the mother refused. The goldfish, taking pity on the woman, vowed to find her daughter.

She descended into the ocean until she found the prince's bejeweled castle where green amber lined the hallways and foaming amber wreathed the clear amber columns. In a hall of the palace on a sun-bright throne, Amberella sat. The goldfish spoke her sad message, and while it softened the girl's heart, it made the prince furious. As he stormed, so did the sea. Mounting his raging white horses, he bore her back to the shore.

Her parents stood amazed at the vision of their daughter glowing like a goddess. She began to throw large chunks of amber to them as farewell gifts. Then, as suddenly as they had come, Amberella and her lover vanished. The people of the Baltic say when the sea rages it is Amberella coming home, and as proof they show the shores full of amber that are left when the storm subsides.

Ambika "Little Mother," a euphemistic name for the Indian death-goddess *Kali*.

Ament The "westerner," Ament was an Egyptian goddess who lived in a tree on the edge of the desert. She watched the gates to the afterworld and welcomed the newly deceased with bread and water. Those who took her offerings became "friends of the dead" and could never return to the land of the living. Originally from Libya, this goddess appears in hieroglyphs wearing an ostrich feather on her head; not only was this a common ornament among Libyans but it was the ideogram for her name. In time, the "West," which at first meant Libya to the Egyptians, began to mean the land of death as well.

Ammavaru, Ankamma North of Madras in India it is said that this ancient goddess existed before the beginning of time. Over eons she laid three eggs in the cosmic milk-sea, one at a time. The first egg spoiled. The second filled up with air, but the third hatched into the trinity of

Brahma, Vishnu and Shiva. The egg's lower half became the earth, its upper half the sky. Ammavaru may well have been a very ancient, pre-Vedic creator-goddess.

Amphitrite   A great Greek sea-goddess with a non-Greek name who Homer said was the female manifestation of the ocean itself. She may have been the pre-Hellenic sea-goddess of the Aegean, whom the invading Greeks "married" to their image of oceanic strength, the god Poseidon, demoting her to *Nereid* or sea sprite. However, Amphitrite retained her individuality and her ownership of the caves under the sea, where she stored her precious jewels and from which she emerged to tend her cattle, the fish and mammals of the deep. See also **Sedna.**

Amymone   One of the *Danaids*, she was an early earth-goddess after whom a fountain was named.

Anadyomene   "She who rises from the waves," the sea-born Greek goddess of sexuality, *Aphrodite.*

Anahita, in Greek, **Anaitis**   "Immaculate one," also called Ardvi Sura Anahita ("humid, strong, immaculate one"). One of the ruling divinities of the Persian Empire, Anahita embodied the physical and metaphoric qualities of water, the fertilizing force that flowed from her supernatural fountain in the stars. By extension she ruled semen—which flows forth and fertilizes—and thus human generation as well as all other forms of earthly propagation.

   She seems to have originated in Babylonia, whence she traveled to Egypt to appear as an armed and mounted goddess. Her worship spread east as well; she became the most popular Persian deity, worshiped, it is said, even by the great god Ahura Mazda himself. Nevertheless, Zoroaster did his best to ignore Anahita, although later writings reveal that the sage was specifically commanded by the male god to honor her.

   In this tall and powerful maiden, her people saw the image of both the mother and the warrior; she was, in essence, a protective mother to her people, generously nurturing them while fiercely defending them from enemies. In statuary, Anahita was the "golden mother," arrayed in golden kerchief, square gold earrings, and a jeweled diadem, wrapped in a gold-embroidered cloak adorned with 30 otter skins. She was also described as driving through our world in a chariot drawn by four white horses that signify wind, rain, clouds, and hail.

   "Great Lady Anahita, glory and life-giver of our nation, mother of sobriety and benefactor of mankind," the Armenians called out to their beloved goddess. They honored her with offerings of green branches and white heifers brought to her sanctuaries. They may have offered themselves as well; the traveler Strabo said that sacramental promiscuity was part of the honor due this ruler of reproduction who "purifies the seed of males and the womb and milk of females." Healer, mother, and protector of her people, she was worshiped throughout the Persian Empire for many centuries. To the west she was said to be identical to *Anat*; the Greeks contended she was *Aphrodite*, when they did not claim she was *Athene*.

Ananke, Anagke   Plato called her the mother of the *Moirae* or Fates, but she seems less an actual goddess than the Greek personification of the abstraction *necessity*, or that force of destiny perceived in most cultures as female.

Anat, Anata, Anath, Anit, Anta   The Great Goddess of the Ugaritic pantheon had four separate aspects: warrior, mother, virgin, and wanton. "Mother of nations," she remained "Virgin" in spite of being "Mistress of all gods"; she never lost her hymen despite her blatant promiscuity. Creator of her people, she could also be a bloodthirsty killer who went berserk and destroyed every living thing within reach.

The energy she personified was immense—no less than sexuality itself in all its ecstatic and terrifying aspects. The goddess of desire, Anat was the favored sex partner of her brother Baal, for whose embraces she prepared herself with a bath of dew and a shower of ambergris. Their appetite for each other was prodigious: in one case Anat, overcome by lust, sought Baal while he was hunting, whereupon they copulated 77 times in the wilderness. For this occasion, she took the form of a cow, and the progeny she bore afterward were oxen and buffalo.

Her rage for blood was equally noteworthy. Once, when her brother had waged a victorious battle, Anat ordered a huge celebratory feast prepared on the heavenly mountain, to which she invited the defeated. Retiring, Anat painted herself with rouge and henna. Then she entered the hall and closed the doors. She slew everyone in sight, wading maniacally in knee-deep blood and strapping dismembered bodies to her waist. In this, Anat embodied the fearful indifference of sexuality, which endlessly reproduces mortality: sex producing life which ends in death.

Powerful as she was, Anat was later fused with *Asherah*, a less noticeably contradictory goddess. But her worship had already traveled from Canaan to Egypt, and there she was honored as the warrior Anath even by the Jews. See **Anahita, Astarte, Freya.**

Anatu, Antu, Antum   Ruler of the earth and queen of the sky, a Great Goddess of Mesopotamia who was merged with *Ishtar*. Originally, however, it appears she was not only a separate figure but Ishtar's mother.

Anaxarete   Iphis, a commoner, loved this stonyhearted Greek princess. But she ridiculed him and his affection until, in a fit of depression, he hanged himself at her door. She laughed even then, and for this, *Aphrodite*, the goddess of sexuality who commanded all to mate, turned Anaxarete to stone.

Andraste   The "invincible one" was invoked by Celtic Britons before they entered battle. The warrior-goddess was the particular favorite of the famous queen Boudicca of the Iceni, who offered Andraste sacrifice in a sacred grove before launching an anti-Roman campaign. Boudicca was almost successful, but overpowered at last by the Roman legions, she committed suicide rather than submit to slavery and probable rape.

Andromeda, Andromena   The Greeks said that Joppa's queen *Cassiopeia* bragged once too often of her beauty; in punishment, Poseidon—proud of the beauty of his own daughters, the *Nereids*—sent a monster to ravage her land. Cassiopeia's daughter Andromeda was then exposed on a barren rock as an offering to the monster, who threatened but did not devour her. Eventually the Greek hero Perseus saw the endangered maiden and rescued her, and they lived together afterward. At her death Andromeda was placed by *Athene* among the stars as the constellation that bears her name.

Her original story may be older, and different, from this familiar version, however. Her name may be interpreted as "ruler of men" as well as "human sacrifice." Some consider her to be a personification of the moon, constantly under siege by the demon of darkness. Rather than being a victimized maiden, then, Andromeda may have originally been a pre-Hellenic moon-goddess whose legend was incorporated into that of a Greek hero.

Anesidora   "She who sends up gifts" of food plants, a title of *Demeter* or *Pandora*.

Angerboda   The "one who warns of (bodes) danger" was given a cameo role in the Scandinavian eddas, where she was called a giant and the mate of the trickster-god Loki. Her attributes were not described, but she was given credit—or blame—for bringing into the world three strange offspring. One of these was Jörmungander, a snake who grew so large that he surrounded the earth (commonly called the Midgard

Serpent or world snake). The second was the Fenris Wolf, an impressively vicious beast that will bring about the end of this world when let loose at Ragnarok, the end of this time cycle. Third, there was Angerboda's daughter *Hel*, the death queen. It seems that Angerboda was a form of the goddess of mortality, for her children circled the world of men (Jörmungander) so that they could not escape their fate (Hel) or the inevitable end (Fenris) of the entire creation.

Angerona   The Roman goddess of the winter solstice was shown with a bandaged mouth and with a finger to her lips enjoining silence. At her feast on December 21—called the Divalia or Angeronalia—the sun passed its weakest moment in the year and the sunlight began to increase. At the very moment of the solstice, however, before the balance tipped toward light, the goddess's image reminded her worshipers of the need to remember the fragility of the natural balance; for this reason she was sometimes called a death-goddess.

Angeyja   Scandinavian water-goddess and daughter of *Ran*.

Angitia   An early Italian goddess of the Oscan tribe, she ruled the powers of healing and witchcraft and was known as a great expert in verbal and herbal charms. Angitia was honored in Italy's Marsian district, still famous today for its witches. See **Medea.**

Anieros   During Roman times, in the northeastern provinces of Phrygia and the island of Samothrace, this name was given to a *Demeter*-like earth-goddess who had a *Persephone*-like daughter named Axiocersa. They were doubles of each other: the young earth of springtime and the mature earth of autumn; the young woman of promise and the fulfilled matron. Their religion was the ancient one of Asia Minor, based on the divinity of the female body, which was seen as a microcosm of the forces of life, growth, death, and rebirth.

Anima Mundi   To the Gnostic philosophers of the Roman Empire, the "soul of the world" was female, a concept that corresponds to our "Mother Nature."

Ankt, Anouke   A spear-carrying war-goddess of the Egyptians who was depicted wearing a curved and feathered crown.

Anna Perenna   The origin and original legend of this Roman goddess is a subject of conjecture, for she seems to be so ancient that even in early historical times her beginnings were unclear. One legend tells us that she was the sister of *Dido* of Carthage. Fleeing to Rome after Dido's death, she was received by Aeneas, Dido's unfaithful lover, by then married. The new wife grew jealous of the mistress's sister, and Anna Perenna ran away, changing herself into a river.

Another story has it that Anna was an old woman of the town of Bovillae; when the plebeian revolutionaries were besieged on Mons Sacer, she found a secret way to convey food to them, enabling them to endure the siege. For this, Anna Perenna was deified after her death.

Current scholarship suggests that she was originally an Etruscan goddess who ruled human and vegetative reproduction. Each year at her March 15 festival, rowdiness, merrymaking, and promiscuity were expected of all pious Romans. The spring date of the festival and its nature indicate that Anna Perenna was the goddess of the fruitful earth, who would be pleased by the reproductive activities of human beings and respond by bringing forth an abundance of edibles for them. See **Anna Purna.**

Anna Purna, Anapurna   "Food-giver" was the name of this ancient Indian goddess whom some scholars identify with Rome's *Anna Perenna*. A common household deity, often depicted enthroned and feeding a child from a full ladle, Anna Purna was especially significant to the city of Benares, where harvest festivals honored her. The Hindus, finding it necessary to systematize their complex pantheon, called her a form of *Durga* or of *Devi*, but she retained her rulership over food production and distribution.

Anne   King Arthur's twin sister, of whom little else is known.

Antevorta   Roman goddess of prophecy.

Antheia   "Flowering one" or simply "the flower," a name for *Hera* in Argos that honored the first of her three forms—the goddess as a flower-like adolescent.

Antianara   This Amazon queen, when asked why her male slaves were all crippled, replied, "The lame best perform the acts of love." This comment, recorded by the Byzantine scholar Eustathius, runs counter to the common image of *Amazons* as disinterested in, or repelled by, heterosexual relations.

Antigone   The loyal daughter of Oedipus of Thebes, she followed her blind-ed father into exile at Colonus; some say that she dug his grave. Then she returned to Thebes and found two of her brothers had been killed in a revolt against their uncle Creon, ruler of the city. Creon forbade anyone to bury the rebels, but Antigone knew that unless her brother Polynices's body were returned to the earth's womb, he could never be reborn. She risked death to spread dust over the corpse so that the earth mother would recognize Polynices's desire for reincarnation. Caught, Antigone was buried alive; some stories say, however, that her lover-cousin Haemon secretly carried her away. See also **Ismene.**

Antiope   One of the most beautiful women of her age, this *Amazon* queen was kidnapped by Heracles (some say Theseus) from her homeland north of Greece, brought to Athens, and presented to King Theseus. Some sources say he made her his legal wife, others claim he merely kept her as a captive concubine. She bore him a son, naming the child Hippolytus after her sister *Hippolyta*. But Theseus eventually tired of Antiope, as he had previously tired of the helpful *Ariadne*, and moved on to his next affair with *Phaedra*. (In some versions of the tale, the Amazon queen who lived with Theseus is Hippolyta herself.) Antiope died in the Amazon attack on Athens, either as a traitor fighting beside Theseus against her own kin or as a captive of the Greeks and a casualty of the war.

Anu, Ana, Cat Ana   One of the ancestor-goddesses of Ireland, some say she is the same goddess as *Aine*. Others say she is identical to *Danu*. In any case, she was known as a force of prosperity and abundance; two breast-shaped mountains in western Ireland are called, in her name, "the paps of Anu."

Anuanaitu   In the days just after creation, said the Carib peoples of South America, men were usually ugly and women were magnificently beautiful. But there was one handsome man, Maconaura, who lived with his mother in the peaceful jungle of primordial time, when there was no evil and no fear.

One day Maconaura found that someone had been raiding his fishnet—the world's first crime. To make matters worse, the thief had ripped the nets. Maconaura set a woodpecker to guard the nets and soon heard the bird's cry. Running back to the pond, the young man saw a water monster and swiftly shot it. Then he discovered on the shore a young girl, not yet pubescent, whom he took home and whom his mother raised.

When she grew, Anuanaitu was Maconaura's first choice for a wife. She demurred at first, for she could not marry without her parents' consent and she refused to reveal their identity. Eventually, she gave way to her affection and desire and married Maconaura. The pair decided it would still be best to travel to the woman's village and seek the blessing of her parents. Anuanaitu's mother quickly agreed to the match, but her father subjected Maconaura to near-impossible tests of skill and courage. The young man performed well and remained with Anuanaitu as her husband.

One day Maconaura decided to visit his own family; on his return to Anuanaitu's village, her father shot him dead with an arrow. War broke out between the two families, with Anuanaitu's kin being destroyed in the magical battles. She remained alive and became entranced with the spirits of the dead. Traveling in rattlesnake form to her husband's village, she determined to take her revenge. The human woman who had raised her appealed to her gentler instincts, and for a moment Anuanaitu hesitated. But then she struck her poisonous blow, revealing that the water monster slain by Maconaura had been her own brother, for she was from a race of such creatures.

Her heart had been moved, although duty had silenced love. Anuanaitu ran through the world—which turned dark and fearsome as she crossed it—until she reached the ocean. There she threw herself into the water and drowned in a place where today a dangerous whirlpool sucks; there she was reunited with her lover, and there she reigns as the Soul of the Ocean.

Anuket, in Greek, **Anukis**   At Aswan, and particularly on the sacred island of Seheil, this water-goddess was adored. Her name means the "embracer" and may refer to the embrace of the Nile waters by the river's banks. In hieroglyphs she wore a feather headdress; eventually she was merged with *Nephthys*.

Anunit, Anunitu   Originally goddess of the city of Akkad (Agade) in northern Babylonia, she was later called *Ishtar* of Akkad and finally was submerged in the powerful figure of Ishtar. While independent, Anunit ruled either the moon or the evening star and, like other light-goddesses, was symbolized by a disk with eight rays. "Mistress of battle, bearer of bow and quiver," she was called, but she proved kindly disposed toward humankind and interceded for them with the moon-god Sin, her father or brother. See **Ishtar.**

Apasinasee   Once, the Inuit of Hudson Bay say, there was a haughty young woman who refused all the men in her village; she did not wish to marry but stayed instead in her parents' home. One day, her father angrily suggested that, considering her behavior, the family dog was the proper mate for her.

The next day the dog disappeared, and a beautiful young man

27

dressed in dog-skin clothing arrived at the hut, ate sitting next to the girl, and then slept with her. They stayed together until the young woman gave birth to a litter of puppies. Her children were so noisy that Apasinasee's father put the whole lot, with the dog and his wife, into a boat and carried them across the river to live.

Apasinasee's father continued to provide for them, however; he sent meat to the family every day, tying it around the dog's neck. Eventually tiring of this, he tied rocks around the dog's neck instead, so it drowned. Apasinasee instructed her children to eat her father, and they did.

Then Apasinasee was utterly without support. So she mournfully sent her children away to forage for themselves. One group traveled far inland, where they became giants; another, living on the coast, became walrus-eating dwarfs. A few she put into a magical ship, and they disappeared entirely. And a very few stayed beside their mother—and they became the Inuit.

Aphrodite   One of the most familiar of Greek goddesses, Aphrodite was not originally Greek at all. She was the ancient mother-goddess of the eastern Mediterranean who established herself first on the islands off Greece before entering the country itself. There, her journey with the sea traders who brought her across the waters was expressed in a symbolic tale.

In the ancient days, it was said, the old heaven-god Uranus was castrated by his children, the Titans; his penis fell into the ocean and ejaculated a final divine squirt. The sea reddened where it fell, and then the foam gathered itself into a figure: the long-haired Aphrodite riding on a mussel shell. (Whence the epithet Anadyomene, "she who rises from the waves.") She shook the seawater from her locks and watched drops fall, instantly turning to pearls, at her feet. She floated to the islands off Greece, for which she is sometimes named Cytherea or Cypris. She landed at Cyprus and was greeted by the lovely *Horae,* who provided attire worthy of her beauty and who became her constant companions.

The story of her birth is an obvious description of the journey of this Near Eastern goddess to her new home in Greece. It is also allegorical: the sky impregnates the great sea womb with dynamic life, a story that the Greeks reiterated in the alternate version of Aphrodite's birth by the sea sprite *Dione* and the sky-god Zeus.

Once she arrived, the Greeks provided Aphrodite with a husband: Hephaestus, the crippled god of smithcraft. Aphrodite could not be contained in a single relationship, though, and spread her favors liberally among divine and mortal males. She bore children by half a dozen mates, none her husband. In many of these unions, the allegory is glaringly obvious, as when Aphrodite (sexuality) mates with Dionysus (wine) to produce Priapus (permanent erection).

The most famous—or notorious—of Aphrodite's affairs were those with Ares and with the beautiful young Adonis. She carried on scandalously and publicly with the god of war; their union was a fascinating symbol of the relationship of female carnality and male competitiveness. All heaven knew of their assignations, the Greeks said, before someone finally tattled to the husband. Furious at Aphrodite's unfaithfulness (although in her homeland such behavior would have been expected), the cuckolded Hephaestus fashioned a mesh of gold in which he caught the lovers. Ares and Aphrodite were the laughingstock of heaven then, naked and damp, their limbs entangled in each other's and in the golden web that held them.

As for Adonis, it was said that Aphrodite fell in love with his youthful beauty and hid him in a chest that she gave to *Persephone* for safekeeping. The queen of the underworld, however, peeked inside to see what treasure she was guarding and, smitten, refused to give Adonis back to Aphrodite. Zeus was called in to arbitrate, and he ruled that Adonis could live one-third of each year by himself, one-third with Persephone, and the remaining one-third with Aphrodite. Each year thereafter Adonis was killed while hunting a wild boar, and his spilled blood turned the Lebanese river named for him red.

The energy that Aphrodite represented, however humanly true, was almost incompatible with Greek culture. The Great Goddess of impersonal, indiscriminate lust meshed poorly with the emerging Greek intellectualism. Thus the tale of the goddess's love for the ever-dying god ceased to be central to her legend and became that of just another casual attraction to a pretty face. The rather smutty little tale is a far cry from those masterpieces of theological understanding, the stories of *Ishtar, Inanna,* and *Cybele,* with their symbolic description of the hopeless love of the earth herself for the life she continually produces and inevitably consumes.

In their attempt to assimilate the alien goddess, the Greeks converted Aphrodite into a personification of physical beauty. But she remained so problematical that Plato distinguished her by two titles: Urania, who ruled spiritualized (platonic, if you will) love; and Aphrodite Pandemos, the Aphrodite of the commoners, who retained her original character in debased form. In this form she was called Porne, the "titillator." It was this latter Aphrodite who was worshiped at Corinth, where the Near Eastern practice of sacramental promiscuity deteriorated into a costly prostitution about which the Greeks warned travelers, "The voyage to Corinth is not for everyone." However degraded the practice became in a patriarchal context, the "hospitable women" (Pindar) who engaged in it were highly valued, serving as priestesses in public festivals, and of such rank and importance that at state occasions as many hetaerae as possible were required to attend. See **Anahita, Galatea, Venus.**

Apia-Fellus Scythian earth-goddess.

Aponibolinayen In the islands now called the Philippines, it was said that this divine sky woman supported the heavens by a vine wrapped around her waist. Possibly she was a moon-goddess, for she was said to live during the day in the sun's home; Aponibolinayen produced children by him, giving birth from her little finger.

Arachne The daughter of a dyer, this proud young mortal was an exquisite weaver who challenged the goddess *Athene* to a weaving contest—a presumptuous act, as Athene was the very spirit of the craft itself. In an attempt to embarrass the goddess into making a mistake, Arachne wove a gorgeous tapestry revealing the whole Greek pantheon in indelicate poses. Athene shredded the woman's cloth in anger, and Arachne hanged herself in shame. Her spirit scurried away from the loom in the body of the first spider, and spiders (arachnids) still bear Arachne's name today.

Ararat The ancient Anatolian world-creator goddess was embodied in this famous mountain in modern Armenia.

Ardat Lili, Ardat Lilitu In Semitic lore, this storm demon caused nocturnal emissions, mounting sleeping men and capturing their ejaculations to form her demon children. See **Lilith.**

Ardwinna, Arduinna The Continental Celtic goddess of the wildwood, she demanded a "fine" of money for every animal killed in her wood; in addition, her people were expected to bring her sacrificial animals on feast days. Her favorite haunt was the forest of Ardennes, which Ardwinna was said to oversee mounted on a wild boar.

Arete The Greek goddess of justice, teacher of the hero Heracles, was a personified abstraction with no real legendary background.

Argante Legendary healer-queen of Avalon, the ancient British sacred island.

Arganthone   Thracian mistress of animals and hunting-goddess.

Ariadne, Aridella   The myth and character of this Cretan goddess come to us in confused form. Political changes in ancient Greece were mirrored in religious shifts, and Ariadne's worshipers—the losing side in one such shift—found their native religion suppressed. In her original Minoan form, Ariadne ("very holy") was apparently a goddess worshiped exclusively by women, a goddess of the underworld and of germination, a vegetation-goddess much like the Greek *Persephone*. When the Greeks arrived, they "converted" Ariadne's worshipers and demoted the former goddess to the heroine of the following tale.

The daughter of Queen *Pasiphae* and King Minos of Crete, Ariadne gave the Athenian hero Theseus the spool of thread for his escape from the Minoan labyrinth. Together they fled, but Theseus abandoned Ariadne on the island of Naxos (or Dia). There she was discovered by the newly mature god of wine, *Semele's* son, Dionysus, and they joined forces. She became the leader of the Dionysian women, the *Maenads,* and bore many children to the god before dying in childbed. (Another version has it that *Artemis* killed her; as that goddess ruled childbirth, the tale remains essentially the same.) Then Ariadne was raised to heaven and given the new name of Aridella.

Arianrhod, Arianhod   The goddess of the "silver wheel" was a Welsh sorceress who, surrounded by women attendants, lived on the isolated coastal island of Caer Arianrhod. Beautiful and pale of complexion, Arianrhod was the most powerful of the mythic children of the mother-goddess *Don.*

It was said that she lived a wanton life, mating with mermen on the beach near her castle and casting her magic inside its walls. She tried to pretend virginity, but a trial by the magician Math revealed that she had conceived two children whom she had not carried to term: in leaping over a wizard's staff, Arianrhod magically gave birth to the twins Dylan-son-of-Wave and the fetus of Llew Llaw Gyffes. Dylan slithered away and disappeared, but Arianrhod's brother, the poet Gwydion, recognized the fetus as his own child, born of his unexpressed love for his sister.

Gwydion took the fetus and hid it in a magical chest until it was ready to breathe. Arianrhod, furious at this invasion of her privacy, denied the child a name or the right to bear arms—two prerogatives of a Welsh mother—but Gwydion tricked Arianrhod into granting them. Eventually the goddess overreached herself, creating more magic than she could contain; her island split apart, and she and her maidservants drowned.

Some scholars read the legend as the record of a change from mother right to father rule, claiming that the heavenly Arianrhod was a matriarchal moon-goddess whose particular place in heaven was in the constellation called Corona Borealis. The argument has much in its favor, particularly the archetypal relation of Arianrhod to her sister moon-goddesses on the Continent, who like *Artemis* lived in orgiastic maidenhood surrounded entirely by women. Other scholars, unconvinced that the Celts were matriarchal at any time, see Arianrhod as an epic heroine. See also **Dahut.**

Aricia   The name of the most famous shrine of *Diana* was also the name of a minor Roman goddess who ruled the prophetic visions sometimes experienced in wild places far from human habitation.

Armaiti   An aspect of the androgynous divinity of Zoroastrianism, Armaiti ("devotion") is the righteous goddess who also ruled reproduction and fructification. Of the seven aspects of Ahura Mazda, three were feminine: Armaiti and the sister divinities Haurvatat ("integrity") and Ameretat ("immortality"), who ruled the physical as well as the spiritual manifestations of these qualities.

Arnamentia   The ancient British goddess of spring waters.

Arria   A heroic Roman matron, she was the wife of Caecina Paetus, who was ordered by the emperor to end his life in A.D. 42. He shrank from obeying the command, so his wife stabbed herself first, then handed the dagger to her husband with the words, "It does not hurt."

Artemis   As we see her in Western art, Artemis is the virgin moon-goddess roaming the forest with her band of nymphs, bearing the bow and quiver, avoiding men and killing any male who looks on her. But this familiar form was only one of the identities assumed by this complex Greek goddess, for she was also the many-breasted Artemis of Ephesus, a semihuman symbol of fecundity, and the warlike Artemis said to have been the special goddess of the *Amazons*. It is problematical whether she was originally an all-encompassing goddess later divided into separate identities, or if Artemis became so complex by assuming the attributes of lesser goddesses as her worshipers took control of Greece. But, like *Isis* or *Ishtar*, Artemis came to represent the variable energies of the feminine. She was therefore contradictory: she was the virgin who promoted promiscuity; she was the huntress who protected animals; she was a tree, a bear, the moon. Artemis was the image of a woman moving through her life and assuming different roles at different

Greek vessel; see Artemis, p. 32. Field Museum of Natural History (Neg# A99594), Chicago.

times; she was a veritable encyclopedia of feminine possibility.

In one form she was the Nymph and ruler of all nymphs, an elemental force whose domain was the greenwood. There an order exists so unlike human order that it seems to us formless and free, but this freedom is that of complete obedience to instinct, which animals still possess while humans do not. Artemis in this form was the "Lady of the beasts," the force of instinct who assured their individual deaths and the survival of the species. As mistress of the animals, she was the invisible game warden of the Greeks, killing with sharp arrows anyone who hunted pregnant beasts or their young. Again as instinct, she ruled reproduction, both sex and birth. She ruled the childbed; even in late legend, when her dominance was undercut by male gods, Artemis was still said to have been the elder twin of the sun (not originally her brother) and the midwife at Apollo's birth. It was to Artemis, the force of creation, that Greek mothers called when the pangs of birth began, and they found comfort in their belief that she nursed them through labor just as she did any of her other animals.

As the Nymph of the greenwood, then, she is not really different from her other most famous form: Mother Artemis, whose vast rich temple at Amazonian Ephesus was one of the wonders of the ancient world. There her massive statue stood, rising from a legless base into a huge torso ringed with breasts, then up to a head surmounted by the turret crown of her city. This Artemis was merely a different visualization of the same energy represented by the woodland Nymph: the instinct to live, to produce and reproduce constantly, to devour, and to die. There is power in the image of Ephesia—as Artemis in this form was sometimes called—a power that could be seen as terrifying, so vast and inhuman is it.

The most beloved goddess of Greece, Artemis was honored in rituals that were wildly popular although as varied as the forms of the goddess herself. At Ephesus, in her well-endowed temple, Artemis was served by chaste priestesses called *Melissae*, or "bees," and by eunuch priests. In Sparta she was Korythalia, worshiped in orgiastic dancing. The Amazons honored the war mother Astateia, the mother as protector of her children, in a circle dance amid the clashing of shields and swords and the stomping of battle-clad feet. But apparently the most popular festivals of Artemis were those celebrated on nights of the full moon, when worshipers would gather in the goddess's wood and give themselves over to her power in revels and anonymous matings. The beloved goddess of Greece was the personification of natural law, so different from the laws of society, so much more ancient, so everlasting. See **Britomartis, Despoina, Diana, Eileithyia, Hegemone,** and **Leto.**

Artemisia   A famous naval strategist of Caria in Asia Minor, she fought her way to fame in the wars between Persia and the Greek city-states.

Artimpaasa   Scythian love-goddess who ruled the moon.

Artio, Dea Artio   All across Celtic Gaul and Britain, this Great Goddess of wildlife was worshiped. She appeared to her people in the form of a bear, as did *Artemis*, a Greek goddess with a similar name.

Aruru   Aruru in some texts, she's the goddess who at other times is called *Zarpandit, Mami,* or *Ninhursag.*

Aryong-Jong   Korea's "Lady of Dragon Palace," the first queen of the land, was a goddess who controlled rainfall. In times of drought, shamans poured water through a sieve on the parched soil and Aryong-Jong opened the clouds.

Asase Yaa, Aberewa, Asase Efua   "Old Woman Earth" is a rough translation of the name of this great divinity of the Ashanti people of western Africa. She gave birth to humanity and today still reclaims her children at death. Each person who has worked a field and who, on dying, returns to Asase Yaa becomes a co-power of fertility. At planting, therefore, the Ashanti farmer prays to his ancestors and to Asase Yaa, who lent the rights of cultivation to the living.

Thursday is the sacred day of the earth-goddess; farmers then allow her a day of rest from their plows and other sharp tools. When Christianity came to western Africa with its Sunday festival, the issue of which day was the more truly sacred posed a great problem to those seeking converts. Another difficulty was that this supreme divinity does not live in houses or temples but in every plowed field; the Ashanti do not have to retreat to special places to acknowledge her power and presence. Although Christianity has nominally won the battle, vestiges of the worship of the "Old Woman" remain, and some Ashanti still pray, "Earth, when I am about to die, I lean on you. Earth, while I am alive, I depend on you."

Asherah   From a root meaning "straight," this Canaanite goddess derived a name that implied not only the moral rectitude she demanded of her followers but also the upright posts or living trees in which they perceived her essence. In her temples, Asherah's image was nonhuman, merely an unshaped piece of wood called an *asherah.* But in private devotions she was represented by a simple woman-shaped clay figurine with, instead of legs, a base for insertion in the soft earthen floor of the home. She also appeared as a naked, curly-haired goddess riding a sacred lion and holding lilies and serpents in upraised hands.

"Wet-nurse of the gods" and "she who gives birth" to 70 of them, Asherah was one of the Ugaritic mother-goddesses. Not only did she physically nurture the gods—and human rulers too—she offered spiritual sustenance through her oracular wizards. She was the force of life, experienced as benevolent and enduring, found in flocks of cattle and groves of trees, evoked in childbirth and at planting time.

"Lady Asherah of the Sea" (her full name) was also called *Elat* ("Goddess") and Athirat. Her character is vague and unclear, coming down as it does to us predominantly through the writings of her sworn enemies, the patriarchal Hebrews who often, perhaps deliberately, confused her with *Astarte* (Ashtoreth) and who officially abhorred her worship. But this official view often did not coincide with popular opinion. In the Old Testament we can read the catalogue of a centuries-long campaign against the joyfully orgiastic rites of this benevolent goddess. Asherah would apparently be rooted out of the people's hearts, only to reemerge, giving rise to another wave of reforms. Queen Maacah, mother of Asa and *Jezebel*, publicly worshiped her; Hebrew zealots, however, later took the life of Jezebel on the charge of "harlotry" during festivals of the goddess. But so popular did the worship of Asherah remain that there is substantial evidence that she was worshiped, with all attendant public pleasures, within the Jerusalem temple itself.

Ashnan   The Sumerian goddess of grain and her friend *Lahar* were charged with the provision of food and drink for the gods. Alas, they got drunk and failed in their duties, with the result that humankind was created to take up the slack.

Askefruer   "Ash women," Danish woodland spirits.

Aspelenie   This Lithuanian goddess ruled the corner of the house behind the stove. She could sometimes be spotted in her animal form as the *zaltys*, the little ringed snake that was not only harmless but useful as a rodenticide. Sometimes Aspelenie was so friendly with the family that her snake was an actual house pet.

Astarte (Ashtoreth), Athtarath   It is often difficult to distinguish the like-named goddesses of the ancient Near East, partially because the persecuting Hebrews blurred the distinctions between them and partly because over the ages tribes identified their native goddesses with those of conquering or neighboring peoples. Such is the case with

Nigerian figure; see Asase Yaa, p. 35. Field Museum of Natural History (Neg # 98087), Chicago.

Astarte, often confused or merged with *Anat, Asherah,* even *Atargatis.* Whether she was originally an independent deity whose identity grew indistinct, or whether her name was at first a title of Asherah or another goddess, may never be known. But Astarte was probably the goddess named, in other languages, *Ishtar.*

Astarte ("womb" or "she of the womb") was the goddess who appears in the Old Testament as Ashtoreth, a non-name formed by mis-reading the goddess's name Athtarath with different vowels so that the word becomes "shameful thing." What seems to have been shameful to the patriarchal Hebrews was the untrammeled sexuality of the god-dess, one of those who "conceived but did not bear" offspring for her partners. In this, her identity as the Canaanite version of Ishtar becomes clear, for in the ancient eastern Mediterranean the spirit of sexuality was the goddess who ruled the planet Venus. As morning star Astarte was, like Anat, a war-goddess robed in flames and armed with a sword and two quivers full of death-dealing arrows, flying into battle like a swallow. But as the evening star, a goddess of desire, Astarte descend-ed to the underworld to reclaim a lost lover, thereby causing all human and animal copulation to cease until she returned.

Her colors were red and white; in her honor the acacia tree pro-duced flowers in these colors, so she called it her emblem. She also loved the cypresses of her country and the stallions that she rode, the first fruits of the harvest, the firstborn of the womb, and all bloodless sacrifices. In some pictures, Astarte stands small-breasted and naked on the back of a lioness, with a lotus and a mirror in one hand and two snakes in the other. At other times, to show her fierce and hungry nature, she was shown with the head of a lioness. See also **Isis** for more of Astarte's myth.

Asteria Assaulted by the Greek god Zeus, this nymph changed herself into a quail to avoid rape. Stories like this one may allegorically record the invasion of the patriarchal Greeks and their religious persecution of the pre-Hellenic goddess worshipers native to the peninsula. In this case, the story of Asteria would contain the name and symbol of one of the many local goddesses lost in the pre-Hellenic mists.

Astronoe Phoenician mother-goddess of whom the same story was told as that which describes *Cybele.*

Asynjr Generic term for female Scandinavian giants.

Atabei The Primary Being of the pre-Hispanic people of the Antilles bore five names other than Atabei: Attabeira, Momona, Guacarapita, Iella and Guimazoa. She was served by a messenger, Guatauva, and by the hurricane-goddess *Coatrischie*. Little is known of her rites, although she was recognized as a form of the earth-goddess by the Antillean people, whose culture was such that invading Spaniards called the women "amazons" and said that they lived alone and engaged in war. In some areas, the women even spoke a different language from the men of the same group.

Ataensic   Once, said the Iroquois and their neighbors, there was no land, just a vast blue lake upon which water birds floated with otters, turtles, and other sea-dwelling creatures. High above in a heavenly land was the celestial society into which Ataensic was born.

Her father died before her birth—the first death in the universe. He was placed on a burial scaffold to which the girl used to go to converse with his spirit. He instructed her, when she was grown, to travel a long distance through heaven to Earth-Holding Chief, her intended mate.

Through tempests and danger she traveled; the chief tested her with torture, but she endured and returned to her own village, pregnant by him. Her daughter, Gusts-of-Wind, was born, but her people threw Ataensic down to the earth-lake. (Or was it an accident?—the myths differ.) She fell and fell through the blue air, her daughter returning to Ataensic's womb.

Below, a loon looking into the water saw a figure rising from the depths. He mentioned this curiosity to the bittern. The puzzled birds slowly realized that Ataensic was falling, not rising from the lake. They had never known that their lake had a bottom, which thus had formed a mirror. The knowledge came just in time, for to save the falling woman, the birds and animals had to build land from the lake mud. Otter and turtle tried, and muskrat, and finally Ketq Skwayne ("Grandmother Toad") dove deep and returned exhausted, spitting up some of the magical earth just before she died.

The earth landed on the turtle's back and instantly began to grow. By the time Ataensic reached the water—her fall broken by the water birds' wings—there was enough land for her to rest on as Gusts-of-Wind was reborn. (Some stories say that she fell onto what is now a mountain near Oswego River Falls in New York.)

Gusts-of-Wind became pregnant and died giving birth to twins; from her body Ataensic fashioned the sun and the moon, and that is the way the earth and its luminaries came into being.

Atalanta   The "impassable one," a pre-Hellenic divinity of mountainous Arcadia, was probably originally the death-goddess whom no one can outrun. The conquering Greeks told her legend this way: Atalanta's father, disappointed at the birth of a daughter, took the infant to Parthenia ("virgin hill") and left her there to die. But she survived by being suckled and raised by a mother bear. She grew wild and strong in the wilderness, grew into a centaur-killing heroine, the match of any man in Greece, a woman of vigorous beauty who took her lovers from the men at whose side she fought.

Her father eventually decided to claim fatherhood of the famous warrior, and with it he claimed such paternal rights as the choice of Atalanta's husband. But the heroine refused to marry any man whom she could outrun and demanded the right to kill any who lost to her. So compelling was her beauty that many risked, and lost, their lives racing for her hand. One competitor, given golden apples by *Aphrodite*, flung them down before the fleet woman who, stopping to scoop them out of the dust, lost the advantage. Won by guile, Atalanta nevertheless wed happily. But she and her lover, engrossed in their passion, neglected to make proper marital sacrifices and were punished by being transformed into the lions who drew *Cybele*'s chariot. See **Aigiarm.**

Atanea   The dawn-goddess of the Marquesas Islands, daughter of the high divinity Atea. (Some scholars claim that Atea, cited in most sources as a male deity, was in fact originally female, an overarching sky mother.) Atanea created the sea accidentally when she miscarried and filled the hollows of the earth with amniotic fluid.

Atargatis, Dea Syria (the Syrian goddess), **Derceto, Derketo**   No one is certain of the original name of this Syrian or Aramaic goddess. The names we now use are Greek transliterations, similar to *Isis* for *Au Set.* But philologists suggest that her original name ("divine Ata") was related to *Ishtar* and *Astarte.*

The spirit of fertilizing moisture, Atargatis descended from heaven in the form of an egg, from which the mermaid-goddess emerged. Beautiful and wise, she roused the jealousy of a rival who cursed her with consuming love for a beautiful youth. She became pregnant by the boy and bore the goddess *Semiramis,* then assured the boy's eternal fidelity by causing him to disappear. After placing her daughter in the wilderness with doves to attend and feed her, Atargatis threw herself into a lake and became a fish, the omnipotent "fish mother." In honor of her and of her daughter the Syrians refused to eat fish or doves.

Although this was the basic form of her legend, Atargatis appeared in other guises as well: as a vegetation-goddess who protected the cities that her produce enriched; as a sky-goddess in a cloudlike veil with eagles around her head; as a dolphin-crowned sea-goddess. Her sanctuaries, such as the one at Delos, were centered on quiet fish-filled ponds, and doves roosted in the sacred trees around them.

During the Roman era, Atargatis was worshiped in ecstatic dances by eunuch priests who devoted their lives to dervishlike whirlings and self-inflicted pain. Her worship was ancient by that time, for in the pre-Christian centuries her believers had come under Hebrew attack when Judas Maccabaeus lured them into her temple with assurances of safety and then ruthlessly slaughtered them. Atargatis is a figure comparable to Ishtar and *Cybele*. See **Tarkhu.**

Ate   Like the Roman goddess Discordia, she was to the Greeks the embodiment of folly, moral blindness, infatuation and mischief. Her famous toy, the Apple of Discord, was the cause of several notorious conflicts, including the Trojan War.

At-Em   The Egyptian mother-goddess who represented all-devouring time, the force that found expression in *Kali*.

Athaliah   The daughter of Queen *Jezebel*, she was, with her mother, one of the pair of women who bore the singular distinction of ruling the early Hebrews. Athaliah was a zealous worshiper of the ancient life-and-death goddess *Asherah* and, like her mother, was martyred for her faith.

Athana Lindia   This goddess of the city of Lindos was one of the early Mediterranean symbols of the united power of fruitful fields and a peaceful community. Like the Roman *Ceres*, she embodied the reproductive energies of the harvest, as well as the prosperity and culture that a stable food supply could sustain. In statuary, Athana Lindia's torso and limbs were represented simply by an uncut plank, from which rose a sculpted head crowned with the walls of her city, while across her unshaped breast were strung necklace garlands.

Athene, Athena   She was not always accepted as patron of the famous city that bears her name. Greek legend says that the sea-god Poseidon disputed with the goddess for rulership of the city. It came to a vote of the people of the town in question.

The citizens, men and women alike, gathered to cast their ballots. Naturally, the men voted for the god, the women for the goddess. As it happened, there was one more voter on the women's side, and so Athene won the day. (An alternative version has it that the Olympian deities judged the contest. They ruled that because Athene had planted the first olive tree, whereas all Poseidon could offer was the changeful

41

sea, the goddess would be a better city ruler than the god.)

The men of Athens bitterly agreed to accept the goddess as their patron. But being poor losers, they levied three heavy requirements on the women: that they should forgo being called citizens, that they should no longer vote, and that their children should be called by their fathers' rather than their mothers' names.

They then prepared a new identity for the city's goddess. They claimed that she was a virginal goddess without sexuality, a motherless goddess who sprang full-grown from the head of Zeus, a goddess "all for the father" (as Aeschylus had her say), who voted on the side of the new patriarchal order against the earlier system of mother right. But hidden in the legend of the Athenian vote are clues to Athene's original identity. If children did not bear their mothers' names, if women were not full citizens, if women did not vote, why bother to legislate against it?

It is now well established that Athene—her name is so ancient that it has never been translated—was originally a Minoan or Mycenaean household-goddess whose temple stood on the Athenian Acropolis. This original Athene was the essence of the family bond, symbolized by the home and its hearth. She ruled the implements of domestic crafts: the spindle, the pot, and the loom. By extrapolation, she was the guardian of the ruler's home, the goddess of the palace; by further extrapolation, she was the symbol of the community itself, the larger social unit based on countless homes.

A maiden goddess, apparently called *Pallas*, arrived with the Greeks; she was a warrior, a kind of *Valkyrie*, a protector of the tribe. This figure was bonded to that of the indigenous tribal symbol to form Pallas Athene, and her legend was recreated to suit the new social order. But Athene's ritual recalled her origins. Each year at midsummer her splendid image was taken from her temple on the Acropolis and borne ceremoniously down to the sea. There Athene was carefully washed and, renewed in strength and purity, was decked in a newly made robe woven by the city's best craftswomen. It was the same ritual that honored *Hera* and showed Athene as a woman's deity—the mistress of household industry and family unity. See **Anahita.**

Athtar This Arabian name for *Ishtar* seems to betray an attempt to turn the goddess into a god.

Atla Scandinavian water-goddess and daughter of *Ran.*

Atse Estsan The first woman of Navaho religion was born in the darkness of the First World and gradually rose to the surface of our Fifth World. To do so, she passed with the first man and the trickster-god Coyote through the Second World, where a man assaulted her. Coyote called together the other dwellers in the Second World, and all determined to climb farther, to the Third World.

There, in a lake-filled mountain territory, Atse Estsan and the others met a water monster named Tieholtsodi, whose children Coyote stole. The monster, unable to find his offspring but suspecting that they were in the mountains, began to raise the level of his lake. The people piled all the world's four mountains atop each other, so that they almost reached the sky. Still the waters rose until they reached the feet of the animals and people who, climbing up a water weed that punctured the sky, gained the Fourth World.

There a great argument arose between men and women. The women claimed social precedence because they were the fire makers, the childbearers, and the planters. The men contended that because they hunted and danced, they were the more important sex. The alienated sexes went their separate ways. But within four years, weary of their isolation, they agreed to reunite.

During this time the water monster's lake had been slowly seeping into their land. Finally, Tieholtsodi's waters turned the soil to mud, and the lake again rose about them. A long reed was again lifted to pierce the sky, and everyone climbed through to the Fifth World. And what did they find but the bottom of a lake! The Locust volunteered to find a way out, and passing through the ordeals set for him by the many-colored swans who lived on the lake, he brought forth the people. Behind them was the monster Tieholtsodi, in hot pursuit of his children.

Until then the people did not know that in Coyote's pack were the water monster's children. Discovering his theft, the people forced Coyote to toss back the monster babies, and the underworld waters retreated. Then Atse Estsan and her people built the earth as we know it, with its changing seasons, its moving luminaries, and the death of its inhabitants.

But the humans from the Third World grew haughty and selfish in the Fifth World. Atse Estsan began to create monsters to plague them: the giant Yeitso, the man-eating antelope Delgeth, and others. After a time, the goddess felt her people had been punished enough and she brought them a reward: the goddess *Estsanatlehi*, the Navaho savior, the wife of the sun. Leaving her on the Fifth World to combat the dangers facing her people, Atse Estsan retreated to the eastern sky where she still lives.

Au Set "Exceeding queen," the goddess whose name the Greeks translated as *Isis*.

Auchimalgen   This moon-goddess was the only kindly divinity of the Araucanians of Chile, who believed that she protected them from her subject-spirits. Auchimalgen was also a seer, foretelling great events by changing the color of her face.

Audhumbla, Audhumla   Before this creation, the Scandinavians said, there was a land of frost in the north, a land of constant fire in the south, and between them a gulf of elemental chaos. The interaction of heat and cold, expansion and contraction, eventually formed two creatures: Audhumbla, the cow rich in milk, and an evil man named Ymir, who sweated forth offspring from his armpits and feet while nursing at the teats of the divine cow. Audhumbla herself needed nothing but the salty ice of chaos, which she converted into four great rivers of milk on which Ymir fed.

Eons passed as the great cow browsed the ice fields for her food. One day, under her thirsty tongue, a hard spot appeared in the ice. It was the head of a man born of the ice just as Audhumbla had been. She licked the ice, freeing first one part, then another, of the man who after three days was free. This was Bur, grandfather of the great god Odin, and with his icy birth the world we know began.

The Augralids   Long before *Athene* came to rule the city that bore her name, there were other native goddesses in Attica. Pre-Hellenic residents worshiped a trinity of goddesses, the Augralids: Agraulos, the mother or oldest sister, and the "dewy sisters," Herse and Pandrosos. Apparently they were goddesses of the earth and its produce, signifying the social organization of the people who lived on the land. As the centuries brought social and political change to the area, the religion also changed until the ancient goddesses were bonded to the new city ruler by a complex myth.

The Augralids, it was then said, were entrusted by the goddess Athene with a box that they were told to guard but not to open. The goddesses performed their task as instructed—for a while. Eventually curiosity overtook them, and they peeked into the box, discovering the terrible snake son of Athene Erichthonius ("earthborn one"). (This, clearly, happened while Athene was still a fertile earth mother, before her transformation into a motherless virgin.) The myth then loses its way in theological complexities, for all of the following are said to have happened: Agraulos and Herse threw themselves in terror off the Acropolis; Agraulos was turned into a stone; and Agraulos was appointed Athene's first priestess. However distorted their legend became, the remnants of the Augralids' worship lasted into the days of Athens' glory.

Aura   In the intoxication of the Dionysian rituals, this *Maenad* devoured her newborn child. There are several similar tales told of the impassioned followers of the Greek god of women, and several interpretations offered. Some see infanticide as a symptom of negative female forces, usually controlled but unleashed in the Dionysian religion; others, as a clue to the tremendous oppression, which was apt to explode into violence, under which Greek women lived; still others, as a spiritual convulsion in which women, perhaps sacrilegiously, impersonated the Great Goddess of death and rebirth.

Aurora   The Roman dawn-goddess of whom the same tales are told as of the Greek *Eos*.

Austrine, Ausrine   "Lady of the morning star," the daughter of the Baltic goddess *Saule* who was raped by the moon-man Menesis.

Avaris   Egyptian form of *Anat*.

Aventina   The many-breasted *Diana* worshiped on Rome's Aventine Hill.

Avfruvva, Friis Avfruvva   This mermaid-goddess of the Finnish Saami performed a very important task for them: at appropriate times, she gathered schools of fish and herded them into the mouths of rivers, then led them upstream to their spawning ground.

Awitelin Tsita   A "fourfold vessel," the earth seemed to be a mother to the Zuni, as to most people in the world. She was thought to lie in constant intercourse with her lover the sky, until she filled her four wombs with his seed. Then she withdrew to carry and birth her children—the human race.

But men and women, confused by the new world around them, needed more than life from their mother. So she gave them directions to find their way around her surface; mountains, so that the land's divisions would be clear; clouds filled with rain, so that the earth's surface might bloom. Challenged by her generosity, the sky father waved beneficial lights over the earth dwellers. Thereafter the Zuni lived in a happy world, well provided for by their immortal parents. See also **Hatai Wugti**.

Aze   Japanese pine-tree spirit.

Azer-Ava   The Mordvins were a Finno-Ugric people who settled in eastern Russia with their pantheon of nature divinities of whom Azer-Ava, the

45

rain-bringing sky-goddess, was one of the most important. Her name, meaning "mistress," appeared in many other goddesses' names, suggesting that her people saw her as one goddess in a number of different guises.

The Mordvins invoked a goddess for each place they occupied and had a name as well for each natural phenomenon. Around the settled areas there were Jurt-Azer-Ava, the goddess of the home and its outbuildings, and Ban-Ava, the ruler of the outhouse. Farther afield we find Norov-Ava, the corn mistress, and Nar-Azer-Ava, the meadow spirit. On an even larger scale were Mor-Ava, the sea mother; Varma-Ava, the wind woman; and Tol-Ava, the spirit of fire.

A few of the goddess's most important forms were Mastor-Ava, the earth mother herself; the women's goddess, Niski-Ava; and the very ancient Otsuved-Azer-Ava. Mastor-Ava was the goddess in her most honorable form, the ruler of the earth and all its dwellers; sacrifices were offered to her by the entire community at agricultural holidays. Niski-Ava, now generally confounded with the Virgin *Mary*, was a form of the goddess worshiped by women in the privacy of their homes. Otsuved-Azer-Ava (or simply *Ved-Ava*) was the spirit of moisture who made the earth ready to bear fruit; she resided in a different form in each different body of water, just as Niski-Ava took a different form for each woman's body she occupied.

One of the most delightful forms that Azer-Ava took was Vir-Ava or Vir-Azer-Ava, the forest mother. She assumed a different shape for each forest, often looking very much like a tree. A friendly goddess, she welcomed berry pickers and mushroom hunters, directing them to the best foraging areas if gifts were left for her. Hunters, too, prayed to her for luck in the hunt and protection against accidental injury and death. The energy of the forest hostess stretched out to the fields nearby; if the right kind of attention was paid her, she would increase the crop yield for her worshipers. It was rumored that communal festivals, at certain trees which enjoyed gifts of money and food, had good results.

Ba'Alat, Baaltis, Belili, Beltis Her name means "Lady" or "Our Lady" and is equivalent to that of the god Baal ("Lord"). The chief deity of the Phoenicians, she was shown as a heavily-built naked woman whose hands supported her mature breasts, a sign of her generosity toward the children of earth. When dressed, she was a stylish matron in a shoulder-strapped, tight robe and an elaborate Egyptian hairstyle. To the Sumerians, she was the "wise old lady" of the trees; to others she was identical to *Cybele* or *Ishtar*.

Baba Yaga, Baba The "old woman" of autumn was called Baba by the Slavic inhabitants of eastern Europe, who believed she lived in the last sheaf of harvested grain; the woman who bound that sheaf would bear a child that year. Baba passed into Russian folk legend as the awesome, usually awful, Baba Yaga, a witchlike woman rowing through the air in a mortar, using a pestle for her oar, sweeping the traces of her flight from the air with a broom. A prototype of today's fairy-tale witch, she was said to live deep in the forest and to scare passersby to death. She devoured her victims, which is why her picket fence was topped with skulls. Behind this fierce legend looms the figure of the ancient birth-and-death goddess, the one whose autumnal death in the cornfield led to a new birth the next spring.

Bachue The great ancestral goddess of the Chibcha, who lived in what is now Colombia, was Bachue or Turachoque. At first she lived beneath the waters of a huge lake from which she walked one day, hand in hand with her young son. Raising him to manhood beside the lake, Bachue then had intercourse with her son to produce the human race. Teaching her offspring civilized manners and religious rites suitable to her divinity, Bachue finally satisfied herself that her human children could live without her. Transforming herself and her son-husband into dragons, Bachue returned with him to their original home.

Badb   One of the forms of the *Morrigan,* the great Irish war-goddess, Badb (pron. "beeve") usually took the form of a hooded crow, although she sometimes haunted battlefields disguised as a wolf, a bear, or a heifer. When she took human form, it was as a gigantic woman who straddled a river with one foot on each bank, washing the clothing and armor of the men she had doomed to die in battle. When she lowered her hands to the water, it ran red as blood; when she raised them, the water disappeared entirely, leaving a fordable crossing. See **Bean Nighe.**

Baduhenna   "War-maddened," a Scandinavian war-goddess.

Bakkah   Among the Arabian people, a goddess like *Aphrodite.*

Ban Naomha, Banna Naomha   Kil-na-Greina in Ireland's County Cork was the ancient well of the sun, a place of prophecy and wisdom. In it Ban Naomha swam, a magical trout invisible to all save the second-sighted. You could force the fish-goddess to show herself—thus permitting you to ask any question and be answered—by taking three drinks from the well three times, crawling around the well three times between drinks, and laying a stone the size of a dove's egg on the altar with each circle. At the end of the ritual, and ready with your question, stare into the well to catch your glimpse of the wisdom trout.

Banba   "Land unplowed for a year" is the meaning of this Irish earth-goddess's name; with *Eriu* and Folta she formed the triad of ancient rulers of the island. A talented sorceress, she met the invading troops of the Milesians at the Slieve Mish Mountains in Kerry, the farthest southwest county in modern Ireland; there she unsuccessfully tried to prevent their occupation of the country. A similar Continental Celtic goddess was named *Cathubodia.*

Ban-Chuideachaidh Moire   The "aid-woman" or midwife of the Virgin Mary, a title given to Bridget once the goddess had been Christianized as a saint.

Bandia   Old Irish generic name for "goddesses."

Banka-Mundi   Among the Khond in India, she was a hunting-goddess; merely uttering her name made one fearless against jungle beasts.

Banshee   Her gray cloak covering a green dress, with streaming hair and eyes, the Banshee or spirit woman is still said to appear to the rural Irish to foretell the coming death of a family member. Sometimes she chooses not to be seen, instead conveying her message of bereavement in an unearthly keening outside the cottage window. When more than one Banshee is heard or seen, a great person faces death.

Bara The sun daughter of Arnhem Land aboriginals; see **Walo.**

Barbmo-Akka, Loddis-Edne These goddesses of the western Saami controlled the migratory paths of birds and their nesting instincts, respectively.

Bardaichila This Assamese storm-goddess created gales when she traveled from her airy homeland to earth for the Indian festival of Bohag Bihu; thus it was traditional to speak of the two storms, one just before, one immediately after, the event.

Basho Goddess of the basho plant in Japan

Basile This ancient Greek title meaning "queen" was applied to both goddesses and mortal women.

Basilea Ancient queen of Celts who civilized her people.

Basilinna The chief woman of Athens bore this title. As the embodiment of the generative female force, the Basilinna was required to mate ritually with the gods in public festivals.

Bast, Bastet, Pasht She originated in the Nile delta, but by 930 B.C., the power of Bast was acknowledged by all Egyptians. At first she was a lion-goddess of sunset, symbolizing the fertilizing force of the sun's rays. Later her image grew tamer: she became a cat carrying the sun, or a cat-headed woman who bore on her breastplate the lion of her former self.

> Bast ruled pleasure and dancing, music and joy. At Bubastis ("house of Bast"), the center of her worship, great celebrations were held. Boatloads of worshipers—hundreds of thousands of them, Herodotus said—were greeted by pleasant flute melodies as they debarked for a worship service combined with a vast trade fair. Bast's followers believed that in return for this reverent celebration Bast bestowed both mental and physical health.

Bau, Baau, Bahu, Bohu She emerged into history as a sky-goddess ("eldest of heaven"), bearing a name that means "space." In very ancient times, Bau was the mother-goddess of Babylonia and Phoenicia, a life-giving figure who appeared in each morning's light. But she merged with *Gatamdug*, then with *Gula*, and the separate identities of these goddesses became lost, with only Gula surviving the process.

Baubo   Her name means "belly," and Baubo was the Greek goddess of belly laughter, the kind that indecent gestures and suggestive jokes provoke. Baubo was sculpted as a headless and limbless body, with her genitals forming a bearded mouth and her breasts staring like eyes. She was the sister or double of *Iambe*, the goddess of indecent speech, and a similar story is told of both: the weeping *Demeter*, searching the earth for her lost *Persephone*, reached the coastal town of Eleusis and there, convulsed with sorrow, sat down by a deep well. Baubo came to draw water and, touched by the goddess's sorrow, tried to console her. But Demeter refused her sympathy. So Baubo lifted her skirts and exposed her vulva. Demeter's sorrow was broken by a smile; the sterile earth stirred; soon Persephone returned. (Almost the same tale is told in Japan of *Uzume*.) That such a minor character should have such power over the Great Goddess seems unlikely to some, who contend that Baubo is really a form of *Hecate*, the night-riding goddess of mystery and power who also plays a significant part in Demeter's legend.

Bean Nighe   A woman who dies in childbirth, say the Irish and the Highland Scots, better not leave laundry unfinished; otherwise, she will be forced to remain on earth as a ghost, washing linens until the natural time of her death. These Washers at the Ford are a form of the *Banshee*, foretelling imminent death when they appear to human eyes. The Bean Nighe is described as a small woman dressed in green, with red webbed feet, one nostril, and one tooth. Her breasts are very long and, if you can grab and suck one of them, you will be granted any wish. Like other water spirits, the Bean Nighe are prophets; if you meet one, you can ask her three questions, which she will answer. However, she will ask you three questions in return, and if you lie in answering her, things will go badly for you thereafter.

Bebhionn, Be Bind   As huge as she was beautiful, this supernatural woman was from Maiden's Land, the Isle of Women, far off the Irish west coast. Some legends say she was originally an underworld-goddess and a patron of pleasure, that she traveled surrounded by magical birds, and that she knew all the powers of healing. Another legend says that she came from her magical island to live with the king of the Isle of Man. But he soon proved brutal and she, rather than endure his beatings, headed home. The king pursued and killed Bebhionn. See **Rhiannon.**

See Bast, p. 49. Field Museum of Natural History (Neg# 108334), Chicago.

Bechoil Early Irish ancestor-goddess like *Danu*.

Becuma In Irish legend, this goddess of the magic boat was one of the earliest divinities of the island, one of the Tuatha de Danaan, the people of the goddess *Danu*. She lived in the heart of the country on the magic Hill of Tara, where by sleeping with her a king could gain sovereignty over the countryside. The Tuatha de Danaan ostracized the beautiful goddess for this behavior, but they could not change the tide of history, for the kings remained and the Tuatha were banished from their green homeland.

Befana A figure of Italian folk legend, she is the "lady of twelfth night" in Rome, where custom still calls for an image of an old woman made of rags to be hung outside the home on January 5, probably to witness the passing of winter's darkness.

Beiwe The Saami count this sun-goddess third in order of supernatural precedence. This wonderful being, who traveled with her daughter *Beiwe-Neida* through the sky in an enclosure of reindeer antlers, brought back greenness in the Arctic spring; she made new plants grow so that reindeer could prosper and reproduce. At each solstice her worshipers sacrificed white female animals, the meat of which was threaded on a stick, then bent into rings and tied with bright ribbons. When she was invoked, a special prayer was always said for the insane; Saami scholar Rafael Karsten suggests that madness was thought to be caused by Beiwe's winter absence.

On the day when light first appeared in the Arctic, the Saami smeared their doors with butter so Beiwe could eat the rich food with her hot beams and begin her yearly recovery. On summer solstice, "sun rings"—twists of leafy branches—were hung about and butter "sun porridge" was sacramentally eaten. Prayers were offered that the sun virgin would "pour her merciful rays over the reindeer, and everything else."

Beiwe-Neida The daughter of the sun among the Saami. See **Beiwe**.

Belisama Celtic goddess of the Mersey River; see **Sequana**.

Belit-Ilani, Belit-Ile A Babylonian title meaning "mistress of the gods," Belit-Ilani was the name of the evening star of desire. Some consider it a title of *Astarte*, some of *Ninlil*, some of Nintud. In any case, Belit-Ilani is inscribed on portraits of the goddess as a woman who bears on her left arm a babe that she suckles and who blesses the child with her right hand.

Belit-Seri, Beli-Sheri, Nin-Edin   In Babylonian theology, she was the scribe of the afterlife who kept records of all human activities. The lady of the underworld wilderness, she squatted in front of the queen of the dead to call out judgments on the lives of the newly dead.

Bellona   Often described as a mere feminine shadow of the god Mars, Bellona was actually much more, for her domain included the entire arena of conflict, diplomatic as well as military. Even her name shows her importance, for the Latin word for war, *bellum*, derives from her name.

In the temple of this serpent-haired goddess who bore a bloody lash, the Romans began and ended their military campaigns. Before Bellona's temple, her priest began a war by raising a ceremonial spear and hurling it into a section of ground that symbolized enemy territory. When the war was finished, it was in Bellona's temple that the Senate determined the best reward for the victorious generals. And during wars as well as in peacetime, the Senate used Bellona's temple to receive the ambassadors of countries in conflict with Rome.

When Roman divinities began to be identified with those of the countries Rome conquered, Bellona found herself assimilating the Cappadocian goddess Mah, a late form of the Sumerian *Mami*. Both symbolized territorial sovereignty and both represented the armed conflict necessary to defend claims to rulership. The Roman goddess was called Mah-Bellona in the later days of the Roman Empire. See **Vacuna.**

Belqis   In Muslim tradition, the name of the Queen of Sheba. See **Candace.**

Bendis   Important Cappadocian earth-goddess similar to *Gaea.*

Bentakumari   As an Assamese water-goddess, she was owed the first fish caught in her area of India each season.

Benten, Benzaiten   Among the seven Japanese divinities of good luck, only one was a goddess: Benten, who brought inspiration and talent, wealth and romance to those who honored her. Benten was also queen of the sea, a dragon woman who swam in state through her domain with a retinue of white snakes. In her dragon body she protected her devotees from earthquakes by mating with the monstrous snakes who thrashed under the Japanese islands. But she could also wear the form of a lovely human woman, and in this form she was usually portrayed, mounted on a dragon who was both her steed and her paramour.

Benvarry   Friendly Manx mermaid.

Berecyntia   Old Celtic earth-goddess.

Beruryah   A Jewish heroine of the 2nd century A.D., she was a judge known for her wise sayings, her wisdom, and her kindness.

Beruth, Berit, Beroth   Her name still lives in her city—Beirut—recalling the days when she was high goddess of the Phoenicians, their image of the earth who mothered the human race. It is not known whether her name means "earth," "mother," or "covenant" (an instructive set of possibilities, nevertheless).

Bestla   The first woman-shaped female of Scandinavian mythology (the earlier creation-goddess was a cow), Bestla received scant notice in the written eddas, except for the mention of her name and status as the Norse *Eve* and mother of the great god Odin.

Bhavani   One of the common names of the Mother Goddess of India, Bhavani means "bestower of existence" and is thought to have been the goddess's name in Dravidian languages spoken by non-Aryan people of the subcontinent. But unlike *Durga, Parvati* or *Kali*, the goddess of this name developed no distinguishing legends or attributes, save that she was evoked by women in labor, who burned perfume to honor her.

Bia   A warrior maiden of Greek mythology, her name means "force." It was Bia who bound the Titan Prometheus to a rocky crag when he was condemned to perpetual torment for stealing heavenly fire for humanity.

Biblys, Biblis, Biblos, Biblus   One of a pair of Greek twins, she fell in love with her brother. But he refused her love and Biblys, tormented and ashamed, was transformed into a constantly weeping fountain.

Biddy   A shortened version of the name *Bridget*, used in Ireland on February 1 when a girl impersonating the goddess-turned-saint (or a group carrying her effigy), went begging from house to house. In Kerry, on the far southwest coast, she sang, "Something for poor Biddy! Her clothes are torn. Her shoes are worn. Something for poor Biddy!" When the group was only young men, who often dressed in women's attire, they were called "Biddy boys." Giving food and money to the Biddy callers was thought to bring a good harvest in the following season.

Biddy Mannion   A midwife of Inishshark, a tiny island off the Irish coast, she was stolen from earthly life by the king and queen of the fairies. They, it seems, had a sickly child, and Biddy's reputation for healing had spread to fairyland. Biddy did indeed bring the child back to life. Returning to her home, Biddy found a fairy double in her place; not even her family had suspected the switch.

Bil   Once she was a human girl, but Bil did not stay long on earth. One morning, she was sent to fetch water with her brother Hjuki. The moon-man, still in the sky, saw them, descended to earth, and stole them to be his servants. Thus did Norse mythology record the story, which some scholars say is the same one told in the familiar children's chant "Jack and Jill."

Bila   Among the Australian aboriginals of the Flinders Range, the cannibalistic sun-goddess provided light for the world by cooking her victims, dragged into camp by her dogs, over a huge open fire. When the lizard-man Kudnu wounded her with his boomerang, she blew up into a ball of fire and disappeared, plunging the world into darkness. When he realized what he had done, Kudnu was frightened and sent his boomerang off into the north to try to recover the sun—but to no avail. Then to the west, and the south—but still no light came forth. The lizard-man threw his boomerang to the east, and it carried the sun-goddess high above the horizon, then down again in the west, as she does to this day. Because the lizard-man saved the world from extinction, the Flinders Range aboriginals never killed a goanna or a gecko.

Bilhah   One of the great matriarchs of Jewish tradition, she was the mother of the tribes of Dan and Naphtali. She was the "handmaiden" of *Rachel* and her double, sharing her house and her husband. Little is told of her in Hebrew legend; her character presumably was merged with Rachel's.

Biliku   The chief divinity of the Andamanese Islands, Biliku was a complex goddess, both kindly and fearsome. The creator of the earth, sometimes embodied in a spider's form, she was the first to own fire. But the kingfisher stole this magic substance from her and, furious at the sacrilege, Biliku abandoned the earth forever.

Bina   Minor Cabalistic demigoddess. See **The Matronit.**

Bisal-Mariamna   This Shakti of sunlight in Mysore, India is symbolized by a brass pot full of water called the Kunna-Kannadi or "eye-mirror." Into this pot are put pepper leaves and coconut flowers; a small metal mirror leans against it. One of seven sister goddesses, Bisal-Mariamna is worshiped in an unroofed shrine into which sunlight pours.

Black Annis   A blue-faced cannibal with long white teeth who snatched people from their firesides to eat, this British form of the *Cailleach* was said to live in a cave in Argyll. There she crouched among the branches of an old pollard oak, the last remnant of her huge forest, which grew out of a cleft in the rock at the mouth of her cave—an opening she dug out with her fingernails.

In Leicester, according to Lewis Spence, Black Annis lived in a round cave in the Dane Hills. Children who dared play there "were warned that Black Agnes, or Annis, lay in wait to snatch them away to her cave, where she would scratch them to death." Annually, it was an early spring custom to drag a dead cat in front of a pack of hounds near Black Annis's bower—originally a ceremonial cat hunt, resulting in the ceremonial killing of the hag of winter.

It is axiomatic that conquered deities survive as devils and monsters, and Black Annis is an example. Although it is probable her origins are pre-Celtic, she may have melded with *Danu* as *Cat Ana* (see **Anu**). See also **Gentle Annie.**

Blathnat   "Little flower" was the daughter of Midir, the high king of the Irish fairies. She traveled across the island with three cows hitched to her magic caldron, demanding that heroes serve her with feats of superhuman strength. She was apparently a late survival of an early goddess of sex and death, another version living on in Wales as the deceitful queen *Blodewedd.*

Blodewedd   *Arianrhod,* the unwilling mother of the Welsh hero Llew Llaw Gyffes, laid a curse on him never to have a human wife. So two magicians made this creature from nine kinds of wildflowers, among them meadowsweet, oak, broom, primrose, and cockle. The magicians piled blossom upon blossom to create the goddess "Flowerface."

The most beautiful of goddesses, Blodewedd was also the most treacherous. She lived with Llew Llaw for a time. One day, though, she saw a band of hunters pass outside her window and, falling in love with one of them, plotted the death of her husband. Llew Llaw had a magical safeguard. He could be killed only under curious circumstances: in a bath by the side of a river, under a thatched roof over a caldron, while standing with one foot on a deer. Blodewedd set up those circumstances, daring Llew Llaw to stand in his only dangerous position. He took the dare and her hidden lover killed the king.

Blodewedd eventually was found out, captured by the magicians who created her, and turned into an owl. This strange legend, which parallels the Irish story of *Blathmat* and the Semitic Delilah, seems to record an ancient legend of the goddess, the clues to which are now lost. Some, like Robert Graves, see Blodewedd as a type of the May Queen, wedded ritually to the king who would eventually be sacrificed to her (see **Guinevere**). But it is also possible that the flower-goddess of betrayal was the goddess of life and death, a form of the earth-goddess who, like *Ishtar* or *Cybele*, both loved and devoured the living.

Bo Find Before Ireland became the renowned green isle, when it was still barren and unpopulated, this magical white cow appeared from the western sea, together with the red cow Bo Ruadh and the black cow Bo Dhu. Each headed in a different direction: the black cow to the south, the red cow to the north, and Bo Find to the center of the country. (She may have been a form of *Boann*, central Ireland's white cow-goddess of fertility, called Bouvinda in early Ireland.)

Bo Find stopped twice along her journey to drink: at Lough-na-Bo, the cow's lake, and Tober-Bo-Finn, the well of the white cow. When she reached the island's center, she gave birth to magical twin calves, one male and one female; from them descended all the cattle the Irish owned for centuries. Then Bo Find, having provided for the island's people, disappeared into the west again, to sink down entranced in a dark cave where she still rests.

Some legends say that Bo Find originally had a human woman's form, but that she could not regain it unless she slept for centuries on the summits of Erin's three highest mountains, even were that magical duty fulfilled, only an Irish high king would be able to wake her. The ancient divinity of fertility thus survives in Irish folklore, enchanted beneath the earth, awaiting the signal to return.

Boann Among the Celtic people, rivers were the residences—indeed, the tangible forms—of powerful goddesses of inspiration and fertility. Such was the case in Celtic Ireland, where the goddess of the mighty River Boyne was Boann ("she of the white cows").

It was said that Boann was a curious woman who heard of the magical Well of Segais at the source of the Boyne. There nine magical hazel trees grew and bore nuts of knowledge. The nuts dropped into the well, where they were eaten by a little salmon—the wisest creature in the world.

Even goddesses were forbidden to approach the grove, but Boann, undeterred, traveled to the Well of Segais. Furious and defensive of its treasure, the well rose from its depths and poured out in a mighty flood, drowning the approaching Boann. But it could never return to its original place deep in the earth, and henceforth had to carry its waters, which brought spiritual and mental food to humans, down across the Irish hills. See **Bo Find, Coventina.**

Bodua Continental Celtic war-goddess like *Badb.*

Bomong In addition to the Hindu and Buddhist pantheons of India, there are thousands of smaller goddess groups belonging to ancient tribal people. One of these is the Minyong, whose cosmic goddesses were two sisters, Bong and Bomong. Daughters of the earth and sky, they glowed from the moment they were born. Brighter and brighter they grew under the care of their treasured nurse, but when she suddenly died, they died too.

In the prolonged darkness that followed, the earth's creatures grew afraid. Thinking that the nurse had somehow stolen the light, they dug up her body. But it had rotted away—except for the eyes, which held mirror images of Bong and Bomong. The people, thinking they had the goddesses back, took the eyes to a stream and washed them for five days and five nights. Then a carpenter carefully cut the images from the reflecting eyes, and the two girls jumped back to life.

The people did all they could to keep the goddesses with them. But Bomong, dressing herself in her finest jewelry, ran away into the sky. Her intense brilliance made the earth crack and bubble. Bong followed her, shining brightly, but not unbearably.

People were fainting from the heat, so they sent a frog hunter to kill Bong. He shot her twice, and she fell dead. Her body lay for a long time until a rat dragged it to Bomong who, seeing her sister dead, covered herself with a huge rock in sorrow.

In the darkness that followed, all living beings grew frightened. A rat, a bird and a cock went to find Bomong, who said that she would never return until her sister was revived. In animating the goddess, a carpenter made her smaller so that she could become a moon. Bomong, joyous at her sister's rebirth, rose into the sky in all her splendor, and all the beasts and birds sang out in welcome.

Bona Dea The "good goddess" was originally a descriptive term—some say a mistranslation of *Damia*—but Bona Dea later became the most popular name by which the goddess Fauna or Fatua was known in Rome. She was worshiped only by women, and only in utter secrecy at rites in early December that no man could attend. Conducted by the

Vestal priestesses, these events were held at the home of a high-ranking Roman matron and may have been rather bawdy affairs; it is known that the room was decorated with vine branches and that wine flowed freely in honor of Bona Dea, goddess of abundance and of prophecy.

In 62 B.C., when the women's festival was in progress at the home of Caesar himself, a certain Publius Clodius disguised himself in women's clothing and invaded the rites; discovered, he was duly prosecuted. The crime caused considerable political upheaval. Unfortunately for curious moderns, the invader kept secret the rites he had illegally witnessed, as did Bona Dea's rightful worshipers.

Bontene   "The Mother" at Thyiateria, a Greek colony.

Bonto   Mordvin creator-goddess.

Branwen, Bronwen   The "White-Bosomed One" was the Welsh love-goddess, sometimes called "the Venus of the northern sea." In the *Mabinogion*, the Welsh epic, Branwen was said to have been married by her brothers to an Irish chieftain, who, once he got Branwen back to his land, mistreated her terribly. From the miserable kitchen where she was enslaved, the goddess sent a trained crow—possibly her spirit or familiar, for sometimes her name is translated "white crow"—across the waters to alert her brothers to her predicament. They launched a massive campaign to get her back, paying dearly in lives to reclaim Branwen.

Breksta   In Lithuania, three goddesses ruled the passing hours; *Ausrine*, the dawn; Zleja, high day; and Breksta, the darkness. They may all be forms of the great sun mother *Saule*.

Bri   Beautiful fairy queen of Ireland.

Brigantia   In Celtic Ireland, *Brigid* was one of the greatest of goddesses, and the Celtic Britons worshiped the same goddess with the title Brigantia. Ancestral goddess of the tribe that bore her name, the Brigantes, she was especially worshiped in Yorkshire; her presence is memorialized in the names of the rivers Briant in Anglesey and Brent in Middlesex. It is possible that she was never envisioned in human form, worshiped instead as the power of the rushing rivers and thrusting hills of her countryside.

Brigid, Brigit, Bridgit   Probably the clearest example of the survival of an early goddess into Christian times is Brigid, the great triple goddess of the Celtic Irish who appeared as *Brigantia* in England, Bride in Scotland,

59

and Brigandu in Celtic France. So entrenched was the devotion of the Irish to their goddess that the Christians "converted" her along with her people, calling her Bridget, the human daughter of a Druid, and claiming she was baptized by the great patriarch St. Patrick himself. Bridget took religious vows, the story went on, and was canonized after her death by her adoptive church, which then allowed the saint a curious list of attributes, coincidentally identical to those of the earlier goddess.

The Christian Bridget, for instance, was said to have had the power to appoint the bishops of her area, a strange role for an abbess, made stranger by her requirement that her bishops also be practicing goldsmiths. The ancient Brigid, however, was in one of her three forms the goddess of smithcraft. Brigid also ruled poetry and inspiration, carrying for this purpose a famous caldron; her third identity was as a goddess of healing and medicine. Not surprisingly, the Christian Bridget was invoked both as a muse and as a healer, continuing the traditions of the goddess.

The three Brigids—probably never construed as separate goddesses but as aspects of one divinity—were unified in the symbol of fire, for Brigid was "bright arrow," or simply the "bright one," as her name tells us. Almost into modern times, the ancient worship of the fire-goddess Brigid continued at her sacred shrine in Kildare, where 19 virgins tended the undying fire and where, on the 20th day of each cycle, the fire was miraculously tended by Brigid herself. There, into the 18th century, the ancient song was sung to her: "Brigid, excellent woman, sudden flame, may the bright fiery sun take us to the lasting kingdom." But for more than 10 centuries, the Bridget invoked was a saint rather than a goddess; her attendants, nuns rather than priestesses.

The Irish said that the goddess Brigid brought to humanity a number of useful things, including whistling, which she invented one night when she wanted to call her friends. And when her beloved son was killed, Brigid invented keening, the mournful song of the bereaved Irishwoman; this story draws her close to the great mother-goddesses of the eastern Mediterranean, and like them, Brigid was identified with the earth herself and with the soil's fertility.

Ritual, that most conservative of forces, preserved Brigid's name and symbols for more than 1,000 years after she ceased to be acknowledged as a goddess. But little is left of the legends told of one of the greatest of all Celtic goddesses, a deity so high that her brass shoe was the most sacred object that could be imagined, a divinity so intensely related to the feminine force that no man was allowed to pass beyond the hedge surrounding her sanctuary.

Brimo   A famous name used for *Demeter* in the Eleusinian mysteries; also applied to *Rhea, Hecate,* and *Persephone.*

Britomartis   Early Crete boasted an elaborate and wealthy culture based on the worship of the female principle of nature, embodied in such goddesses as *Rhea* and *Ariadne.* But when the patriarchal Greeks overran the island, the theology of the early settlers was passed through the distorting prism of the invaders' sensibility. Cretan goddesses were demoted to heroines, and their legends were grafted onto those of Greek heroes. The complex symbolism and imagery that expressed Minoan and Mycenaean theological insights were, in the main, reinterpreted or misunderstood.

In some cases, a goddess's picture and name are still known, but scanty legendary material survives to explain her original symbolic and psychological significance. Such a figure is Britomartis ("sweet girl"), whom some scholars suspect was the greatest goddess of Minoan Crete. We know little of her except how she was traditionally depicted: a young, lithe, and strong hunter, often carrying arrows.

This image was given as a spoil of war to the invading goddess *Artemis,* and it remained for 2,000 years the traditional depiction of that Greek deity. But Britomartis also had as her companions a suckling babe and a snake, two powerful symbols of the generative force that were never identified with the moon-goddess to whom the Cretan divinity was assimilated.

What little we know of Britomartis's myth is sketchy but suggestive. Minos of Crete, it was said, intended to rape the virginal goddess. He chased her for nine months through the forested island, but she finally eluded capture by flinging herself off a high cliff into the ocean. There she was miraculously saved, caught in the fishnets that she herself had invented as a gift to humanity.

After this, the goddess was called Dictynna ("netted one"), some sources say; others claim the great Cretan goddess was Britomartis in the eastern end of the island, Dictynna in the west. But the story that joins them, with its pursuit that lasted the length of a human pregnancy and its rebirth from the sea, suggests that this goddess, in Crete's labyrinthine theology, symbolized the integrity of the feminine soul and the promise of salvation or rebirth.

Bronach, Caileach Cinn Boirne   This goddess is a form of the *Cailleach* known in the west of Ireland, especially in the rocky northern Burren near the famous Cliffs of Moher. One of the highest of these cliffs is Hag's Head, or Ceann Cailighe. Bronach's title, Caileach Cinn Boirne, means "the hag of Black Head," another of the Moher Cliffs. See also **Mal.**

Broxa In Jewish folklore, a name for the night-stalker *Lilith* as a nightjar, a bird believed to suck the milk of goats while the family sleeps.

Brynhild, Brynhilda She was a shield-maiden, a woman warrior, when she first encountered the hero Sigurd Fafnirsbane, who desperately desired her. But this Norse heroine, aware that the *Norns* opposed their love, refused to sleep with Sigurd. His constant pleas, however, finally wore down her resolve, and the result of their union was a daughter named Aslaung.

Sigurd would not stay with Brynhild, however; he wandered south of the Rhine where he met with the powerful sorceress Grimhild. Knowing how great a hero he would become, Grimhild wanted him as spouse for her daughter Gudrun. Sigurd protested that he was promised to Brynhild, but the sorceress drugged him so that he forgot his promise. Soon Grimhild had her way: Sigurd and Gudrun were wed.

Grimhild next decided that she wanted Brynhild for her son Gunnar, whom she sent off to gain the warrior maiden. Impossible: she was lying in a trance surrounded by a ring of fire. (In some versions, she was on a glass mountain; others confound her with the *Valkyrie* named *Sigurdrifta*.) Gunnar could not get his horse to cross the barrier; he tried mounting Sigurd's magic horse but still could not cross through the flames. So Sigurd magically exchanged identities with his brother-in-law and passed safely through the fire. There he slept for three nights—albeit without having intercourse—with Brynhild, marrying her while still in Gunnar's body.

Sigurd then resumed his usual appearance, but the interlude had restored his memory and he was thereafter miserable with Gudrun. Gudrun, for her part, hastened the end of this unhappy story by teasing Brynhild with the information that she'd actually married Sigurd in Gunnar's body; Brynhild's heart was embittered toward her former lover because of the trick. When, urged on by Gudrun, Gunnar killed Sigurd, Brynhild laughed with hysterical joy. Then, remembering the fated link between them and the depth of her love for Sigurd, she committed suicide quietly by piercing her chest with a dagger. The lovers were burned on the same pyre. See **Sigurdrifta.**

Buan This Irish heroine had the psychic power of understanding her husband, Mes Gegra, after his death. When his severed head was brought home to her, she asked it questions about how he was killed, translating the faint reddening and whitening of the flesh to gain her answer. Understanding that he had died by treachery, she cried herself to death. The magical hazel tree Coll Buana grew from her grave as testimony to the steadfastness of her love.

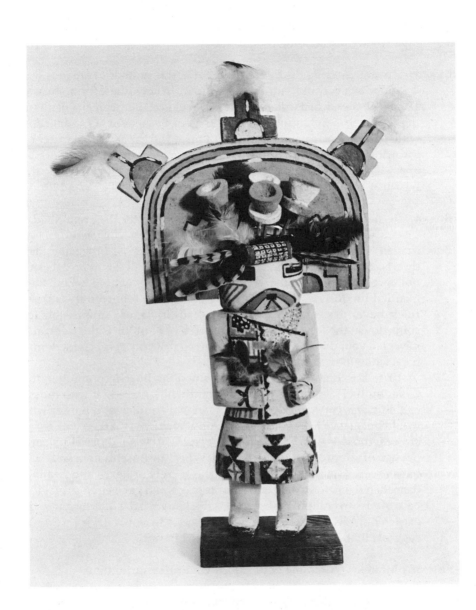

See Butterfly Maiden, p. 64. Field Museum of Natural History (Neg# 93887), Chicago.

Budhi Pallien   An Assamese forest-goddess, she appears in the shape of a tiger roving through the Indian jungle.

Bugady Musun   Among the Evenki of Siberia, this mother of animals was imagined as a very old, very strong woman. In her animal form, she was a huge female elk or a wild reindeer. She ruled all life, from the plants of the taiga to the food supplies of her villagers. Because of her connection with food, it was proper to offer bits of meat and especially fat to her by throwing them into the fire with the prayer, "Eat to satiety, do not be angry with us, protect us." She was sometimes worshiped outside the hearth at sacred rocks which looked like petrified elk or reindeer.

Bugan   In the Philippines, the mother of humanity after the great flood.

Buschfrauen   The "bush women" of central Europe were a little taller than dwarfs, golden-haired and shaggy-skinned, with pendant breasts and hollow backs. They lived in companies in old hollow trees, where they guarded the forests and the kindly people who followed their three rules: never use caraway in baking bread (it makes it impossible for spirits to eat the food), never peel off tree bark (it hurts the tree), and never tell your dreams. They also preferred that you never count dumplings while they're still cooking.

   The Buschfrauen had a queen named the Buschgrossmutter, the Grandmother of the Bushes, an ancient white-haired elf with mossy feet. She was constantly pursued by an evil spirit, a wild hunter who would only leave her alone if she sat on a fallen tree marked with three crosses; those walking through the forest who wished her aid blazed the sign of safety on trees they passed. When the Buschfrauen and their queen were pleased, they revealed the secrets of herbs and healing, danced in the fields to make the plants grow, and gave endless magical balls of yarn to knitters. Although it is not known if the Buschfrauen still exist in Europe, the fact that they were said to live only in virgin forests suggests that, if not extinct, they are hard to find.

Butterfly Maiden   A *kachina* of the Hopi who rules springtime.

Byul-Soon   Korean star-goddess. See **Hae-Sun.**

Caca Ancient Roman goddess later replaced by *Vesta*.

Cacce-Jienne "Water mother" of Russian Saami.

Caenis A woman of Thessaly in ancient Greece, Caenis was brutally raped by the sea-god Poseidon. Furious and humiliated, she appealed to the gods of Olympus for revenge: transform her, she begged, into an invulnerable man so that she might maim and murder the sex that had injured her. Her wish having been granted, she became a great hero named Caeneus, unstoppable on the battlefield, fierce and destructive. When she died a heroic death, she resumed her female body and original name, and enjoyed a hero's welcome in the afterlife.

Caer "Yew berry" was an Irish swan maiden who lived on the lake of Dragon's Mouths, swimming about decked out in a golden necklace hung with 130 chains set with golden balls. There the god of poetry, Aengus, loved her. Caer lured him into the lake where Aengus, too, became a swan. In that form the pair flew off to Brugh na Boinne—the megalithic ritual site north of Tara—singing so sweetly that everyone on the island slept for three days and three nights.

Cailleach Her name, pronounced correctly, sounds like someone clearing her throat, but "coy-luck" is a near approximation. One of the world's Great Goddesses, she went by many names: Cailleach Bheur or *Carlin* in Scotland; *Cally Berry* in northern Ireland; Cailleach ny Groamch on the Isle of Man; *Black Annis* in Britain; the Hag of Beare in Ireland. She was vastly ancient; the Irish Triads say: "The three great ages: the age of the yew tree, the age of the eagle, the age of the Hag of Beare." She could endlessly renew her youth. All the men she loved—and they were countless—died of old age as she went on, returning to the prime of life, finding another pretty young one with whom to share youth.

  She had an eye in the middle of a blue-black face, an eye of preternatural keenness. She had red teeth and matted hair "white as an apron covered with hoarfrost." Over it she wore a kerchief and over her gray clothing, a faded plaid shawl. She owned a farm and hired workers for six months with the stipulation that none would be paid who could not outwork her. Looking at the hunched old thing, many a man fell for the trick and paid with his life, dying of overwork while trying to keep the pace she set. So strong was she that she carried boulders in her apron; the ones she dropped became mountain ranges.

She controlled the seasons and the weather; she was the cosmic goddess of earth and sky, moon and sun. Because she does not appear in the written myths of Ireland and Scotland, but only in ancient tales and place-names, it is presumed that she was the goddess of the pre-Celtic settlers of the islands off Europe. She was so powerful and beloved that even when newcomers imported divinities like *Brigid* the Cailleach was remembered.

Caireen   Heroic mother of Irish legend.

Caligo   This was the name the Greeks applied to the "vaporous" condition, perceived as feminine, that preceded even primordial chaos.

Callisto, Calliste, Kalliste   In the mountains of provincial Arcadia, this pre-Hellenic goddess personified the force of instinct: in human form, as a lithe young athlete and hunter, racing barefoot through the woods she owned; in animal form, as the powerful and protective mother bear. But the invading Greek tribes had their own image for this energy, and they called her *Artemis*. A forced merger of the two similar goddesses resulted in the legend that Callisto was a mere nymph, treasured by Artemis but accidentally killed by her. The saddened Greek goddess took on the "Nymph's" name and all her symbols, calling herself Artemis Calliste ("Artemis the fairest").

Cally Berry   This was the northern Irish name for the "old gloomy woman," also called the water hag, Cailleach Bheur in Scotland and Caileach Bhera in southern Ireland. She was a spirit of the lakes and protected them from being drained; she also controlled the weather, appearing as a crane with sticks in her beak to forecast storms in Scotland. In Ireland, she was a builder of mountains, wearing an apron full of stones until the ties broke and the rocks fell in gigantic heaps.

Some scholars think that the Highland Cailleach Bheur ("hag of winter") was the same goddess who is called *Black Annis* in other places; British researcher Katherine Briggs sees her as a primitive *Artemis*-type figure who guarded the animals from predators and hunters. She may have had an alternative form as the goddess of spring, for a young maiden appears in a number of stories related to this supernatural crone. See **Cailleach.**

Calypso One of the daughters of the ocean, this *Oceanid* lived on the island of Ogygia. The wandering Greek king Odysseus was shipwrecked there; Calypso was attracted to him and offered Odysseus immortality if he would stay and sleep with her. Odysseus took advantage of Calypso's offer to stay as long as he desired her. Then, after seven years, Odysseus abandoned the disconsolate Calypso on her wave-ringed isle, which some identify with the goddess—the island Gozo off Malta.

Camenae, Casmenae In ancient Italy, these goddesses dwelt in freshwater springs and rivers, their most notable haunt being the sacred spring at the Porta Capena, just outside Rome. Their name means "foretellers," for, like many other feminine water spirits, they were prophetic forces. As Roman divinities were assimilated to those of Greece, the Camenae were seen as a local variation of the *Muses.* Their festival, the Fontinalia, was celebrated on October 13 by the tossing of good-luck wreaths into wells.

Camilla A legendary Volscian queen of ancient Italy, Camilla led their armies against Aeneas and his invading Trojans. On foot and with breasts bare, she fought at the head of the army, but was killed by a spear of the Trojan leader. Some scholars see in her the remnant of a very early territorial goddess with a name meaning "fiery one."

Campe This huge female dragon was set to guard the monster children of the Greek earth mother, *Gaea,* in their prison beneath her surface, deep in her stony womb.

Campestres Latin name for Celtic field-goddesses.

Candace In some traditions, this was the name of the Queen of Sheba who visited Solomon of the Hebrews. For at least 800 years, Candace was the name or title of the hereditary queens of the desert empire of Nubia. During the early Roman Empire, Strabo recorded that the reigning Candace was "a masculine sort of woman, blind in one eye." She may have been the same Candace who led an army of 10,000 rebels against the Roman occupation of Egypt.

Candelifera Roman goddess who assists at births.

Candi, Chandi   In ancient India, the moon was a male divinity named Chandra. The fierce goddess *Durga*, however, had a similar name: Candi ("furious"). Over the centuries, the nominal similarity gave rise to the idea that the moon was a goddess. Because this clearly contradicted earlier legend, yet another arose: that the moon was a god one month, a goddess the next.

Canola   The inventor of the Irish harp was this goddess, one of the most ancient of Eire's deities. She had a disagreement one day with a lover, legends say, and Canola left his bed to wander the night. Hearing beautiful music, she stopped and sat down; soon she fell asleep in the open air. Wakening to daylight, Canola discovered the music had been made by the wind, blowing through the rotted sinews clinging to the skeleton of a whale. Inspired by the sight and remembering its magical sound, she built the first harp.

Caolainn   A form of the *Cailleach*, she was the ruler of a healing well in County Roscommon of Ireland. A man, it was said, happened to admire this maiden's beautiful eyes, whereupon she gouged them out, throwing them at him. She then groped her way to a sacred spot, where she pulled rushes from the ground. Where the plants were uprooted, water gushed forth; when Caolainn wiped her bloody sockets with the rushes, her eyes grew back. The same story is told of three nearby wells, all devoted to *Brigid*. See also **Carlin, Cally Berry.**

Cardea   Roman religion included many minor goddesses who personified the spiritual value of certain acts, certain times of life, or certain household objects. Cardea was one of these, signifying the hinges of the front door, and therefore the comings and goings essential to family life.

Carlin   "Old woman" was the name of this Scottish spirit of the eve of Hallowmas—the Celtic festival we call Halloween—the night on which the year turned to winter, and the ghosts of the dead roamed the world of the living. Into modern times, her effigy—a figure built from the last sheaf of harvested corn—was exhibited to protect farming families from unearthly visitations.

Carman   A powerfully destructive witch of Irish legend, she was goddess of malevolent magic and could destroy anything by chanting her spells. She had three destructive sons, with appropriately violent names: Dub ("darkness"), Dother ("evil"), and Dian ("violence"). Not magicians like their mother, they wreaked havoc with their bare hands.

   Carman spitefully came to Ireland, legends say, to lay waste its fields and to blight its corn. But the Tuatha de Danaan, the deities ruled by the goddess *Danu,* fought against Carman with their most powerful weapons. First, they sent a poet to stop Carman; he failed. Second, a satirist, but he too failed. Third, the sorceress Bechuille, who was able to undo Carman's curses. The sons of the goddess were destroyed and Carman put in chains, where she died of grief. Thereafter, an annual festival was held at her death place to ensure the continued growth of food plants; this suggests that Carman was perceived as a goddess of sterility who needed to be magically propitiated.

Carmenta, Carmentes (pl.), Carmentis Originally there seems to have been one Carmenta, a Roman goddess of prophecy and midwifery. She was worshiped in magical ceremonies each January 11 and 15, celebrated by the "flamines" who were her priests. Later there were said to be many Carmentes; they appeared to assist a woman in labor and to tell the future of the newborn.

Carna Every June 1, the Romans celebrated Carna's assistance by offering her a soup of beans and bacon, thanking her for helping them maintain good health. Sometimes simply explained as a goddess of food assimilation, Carna was more than that—she was, in fact, the carnal reality of human existence, a personification of the physical processes of survival.

Carravogue, Garbhog, Cailleoch, Ghcarcagain In eastern Ireland in County Meath, a myth was told until early this century of a woman by this name who, because she ate berries on the way to church, became a monstrous snake. St. Patrick was called upon to throw holy water at her, and she dissolved into lakes from which she will someday rise again. The story, says Maire MacNeill, can be interpreted in several ways—perhaps it epitomizes Christianity's disdain for the island's original faith and its attempt to destroy it; or perhaps St. Patrick merely stands in for an earlier hero who, at the goddess's urging, banishes the Hag of Winter to bring spring to the earth.

Cartimandua A legendary British warrior queen who waged war against the Roman Empire, she was the leader of the Brigantes, descendants of the goddess *Brigantia.*

Carya, Caryatis Like *Callisto,* this goddess lost her independent identity as the religion of the great *Artemis* swept over the Greek provinces. In southern Laconia, of which Sparta was the capital in classical times, the pre-Hellenic settlers perceived the force of nature in trees, where their goddesses (*Helen* being one) were embodied. But the invading Greeks assimilated these tree divinities into their own Artemis, spirit of the wildwood. The memory of the era's social upheaval was preserved in the legend that Carya ("walnut") died and was transformed into a walnut tree. Artemis then carried the news north that the Laconian "woman" was dead. For this simple task, she was awarded the title of Caryatis ("she of the walnut tree") in a transparent tale of the destruction of an indigenous goddess's cult.

Cassandra, Alexandra   The most beautiful of the 12 daughters of Queen Hecuba of Troy, Cassandra was a priestess of the sun who caught the eye of her god. The lust-stricken Apollo promised the maiden that he would grant any wish if she would sleep with him. Cassandra demanded the power of prophecy; Apollo quickly granted the wish. But once she had what she wanted, Cassandra coquettishly refused the god's advances. So Apollo wet Cassandra's lips tenderly with his tongue and disappeared.

After that kiss, Cassandra was cursed. Everything she prophesied was true, but was received as falsehood. Her people, the Trojans, thought her crazy. They ignored her when she warned her brother Paris not to go to Greece; they didn't believe that there were armed soldiers in the wooden horse; they ridiculed Cassandra for saying Troy would lose the war.

When Troy did lose, Cassandra was taken captive to Mycenae as a concubine of the Greek king Agamemnon and was murdered with him. Like many dishonored prophets, however, she was respected after death; in Laconia she was worshiped as the goddess Alexandra ("helper of men").

Cassiopeia, Cassiope, Cassiopie   The boastful mother of *Andromeda*, like her daughter, was turned into a constellation. Of the 13 stars that bear her name, five support the queen's seated figure and are familiarly known by the name of Cassiopeia's Chair.

Castalia   The power that resided in a spring on Mt. Parnassus, she was apparently a force of artistic inspiration, for the *Muses* (called "Castalides" in her honor) made her fountain their sacred place.

Cathubodia   Continental Celtic *Banba*.

Cavillaca   The natives of Huarochiri in Peru said that the moon-god rolled his sperm into a fruit that this beautiful virgin goddess ate. It impregnated her; she bore a son. On her son's first birthday, Cavillaca gathered all the gods together and demanded to know the boy's father. None would admit to it, so she set the child down on the ground and he crawled to the moon-god Coniraya. Feeling ashamed, for the moon-god was a poor and slovenly god, Cavillaca ran from the gathering with her child. She fled to the coast of Peru, where she turned herself and her child into rocks. The pursuing Coniraya traveled long and far seeking them, but found them too late to prevent the goddess's transformation.

Ceasg The mermaid of the Highland Scots was said to be half girl, half salmon, and to enjoy affairs with human males, from which sea captains were often born.

Ceibhfhionn Her name, which looks unpronounceable, sounds rather like Yvonne. In Irish legend, she was a goddess of inspiration, who stood next to the Well of Knowledge, constantly filling a vessel with its water and pouring it out without letting wisdom-seeking humans taste it.

Ceiuci Along the Amazon River in South America, the story is told that Ceiuci ("famished old woman"), one of the *Pleiades* come to earth, was having bad luck fishing one day. A shadow fell across her pond; it was a young man. Ceiuci told him to dive into the pool. The young man refused, laughing, and the goddess set a swarm of stinging red ants on him. Quickly, he obeyed her.

Once she had him in the water, Ceiuci snagged the man with her fishing line and put him in her creel. At home, while the goddess was gathering wood to cook her catch, Ceiuci's daughter hid him. When Ceiuci demanded her prey, the girl and the boy ran away, dropping palm branches behind them as they went. These were transformed into animals, the first in this world, which Ceiuci barely stopped her pursuit to taste. Even when all the species had been created, Ceiuci still pursued the runaways. Finally, the girl stopped her flight, but the young man continued through many adventures until he found himself, old and white-haired, at the home of his own mother, who offered the final protection from Ceiuci.

Cer, Ker The Greek goddess of violent death, she was a daughter of *Nyx* ("night") and sister of the *Moirae* ("fates"). This name was also used of the malevolent ghost of any dead person.

Cerberus A hybrid of lioness, lynx, and sow, Cerberus was one of the great Greek monsters. Standing at the entry to Hades, she is a typical "guardian at the gates," who in myth and dream challenges anyone passing between two states of consciousness. Before being incorporated into the Greek map of the underworld, Cerberus was one of the calendar beasts of the great pre-Hellenic earth-goddess.

Ceres "Propitiate the mothers of cultivation, *Tellus* and Ceres," Ovid told his Roman audience, "with their own spelt and the entrails of a pregnant cow. Ceres and Tellus guarantee the same function: one provides the tillages with their origin, the other with their place." The two great earth-goddesses of Rome were thus distinguished by the Roman poet: Tellus was the earth herself, the dark rich soil that lies waiting for the seed; Ceres, however, was the force of vegetable growth personified.

Before Ceres was adopted as the Italian version of the great Greek goddess *Demeter*, she doubtless had her own identity and legend. But what remains of her today is a Hellenized goddess, of whom Demeter's story is told. To determine her original meaning, we can examine her name, which comes from the same root as our word *create*. And we can study her ritual. She was celebrated each April 19 in the Cerealia, when foxes with burning sticks tied to their tails were set loose in the Roman Circus to dash desperately about while the public cheered them on. This exotic rite has given rise to much speculation, some scholars contending that the ritual was to protect the growing crops from disease, others that it was to assure bountiful harvests by increasing sunshine. In either case; the connection of Ceres and the success of the crop is evident.

But the goddess of growth also took responsibility for its inevitable end. Thus Ceres, a goddess of crop-rich August, when women celebrated secret rituals in her honor, was also a funeral divinity. The force of creation, Ceres was also the goddess of the death of plants that makes them edible, the death of human beings that returns them to Tellus Mater, the earth.

Cerridwen The people of Wales said she lived on an island in the middle of Lake Tegid with her two children—the beautiful Creidwy and the ugliest boy in the world, Afagdu. To compensate her son for bestowing such a body on him, the goddess brewed a magical formula that would make her son the most brilliant and inspired of men. For a year and a day, she kept herbs simmering in her caldron, which she left under the care of a little boy named Gwion.

One day, while the goddess was out collecting more herbs for her brew, a few drops of the bubbling liquid splattered onto Gwion's finger. Scowling in pain, he stuck his hand instantly into his mouth. Miraculously, he was able to hear everything in the world and to understand the secrets of both the past and the future.

His enchanted foresight showed him how angry Cerridwen would be when she found a mere mortal had acquired the inspiration intended for her son. So he ran away; the all-knowing Cerridwen realized what had happened and pursued him. Gwion changed himself into a hare; Cerridwen pursued him as a greyhound. So they ran: he as a fish, she as an otter; he as a bird, she as a hawk; he as a grain of wheat, she as a hen.

It was in the final form that she caught and devoured him, bearing him nine months later as a child. She threw the baby into the water where he was caught by a prince and grew into the poet Taliesin, the greatest poet in his language. Thus the Welsh expressed their understanding that death and rebirth were necessary for true inspiration to be brought into this world, showing the *Muse*, the goddess of inspiration, in a somewhat more terrible form than she appears in other cultures.

Cessair, Kesara   After the colonizing Christians arrived in Ireland, the island's ancient legends were altered to incorporate elements from the new tradition. Thus we find some rather strange amalgams of native and imported myth, like the one in which Cessair appears.

She was apparently an early Irish earth-goddess, later called a historical woman, who was "a granddaughter of Noah" and "married to a man of the blood of Seth." With this heritage, it was no small feat to get her to Ireland; the annalists simply defied Judeo-Christian tradition by allowing Cessair to survive the flood, along with three men and 50 women, who in three ships plied the deluge waters from Palestine to Eire.

Ireland, of course, was spared the flood—one of the many miracles in the land's mythic history. Cessair and crew arrived, after 40 days and the loss of two ships, at Corca Guiny in Ireland. There the last ship was wrecked, and Cessair drowned. So did her daughters Birrin and Blama, along with almost everyone from the ship. Cessair leveled mighty curses at Jehovah as she went down.

Cethlion, Kethlenda   "Crooked teeth" was a goddess of ancient Ireland who, as queen of the sea people called the Fomorians, prophesied their doom at the hands of the invading Tuatha de Danaan, the children of the goddess *Danu*.

Cetnenn   Great woman warrior of Irish legend.

Ceto   This vague figure in Greek mythology was probably the Syrian fish mother *Derceto* incorporated into Hellenic legend, where little was said of her except that she was a sea-goddess. Nonetheless, she was said to have produced some of the most fabulous daughters in Greek legend: the *Graeae*, with one eye and one tooth between them; the snake-headed *Gorgons*; the serpent *Echidna*; and the seductive wind demons, the *Sirens*.

Chaabou Semitic name for the earth mother.

Chalchiúhtlicue According to the Aztecs, our world is the fifth in a series; the fourth was destroyed by a great flood sent by Chalchiúhtlicue to punish humanity for its wickedness. Before she did so, the goddess built a multicolored bridge into the Fifth World for the righteous—a bridge that reappears today, sometimes, as a rainbow.

The "jade-skirted goddess" ruled all waters: earth's flowing streams, rain from the heavens, and the nourishing waters used for drinking and baptisms. When painted or sculpted, the goddess was shown decked out in a jade necklace, turquoise earrings, a crown of iridescent blue feathers, and a skirt trimmed with water lilies.

Challalamma Buttermilk-goddess of eastern India.

Changing Woman The Apache called the earth-goddess by this name, for she never grew old. When her age began to show, she simply walked toward the east until she saw her form coming toward herself. She kept walking until her young self merged with her aging self and then, renewed, returned to her home. Among the Chiricahua Apache, the name of this eternal goddess was Painted Woman.

Chang-O, Heng-O In ancient China it was said that this moon-goddess originally lived on earth, where her husband was a famous archer. To honor the man's prowess, the gods gave him the drink of immortality, but Chang-O beat him to the bottle and drank it down. Then she fled to the moon, where she asked the hare who lived there for protection from her (probably righteously) furious husband.

There, some say, Chang-O gained immortality—as a toad. Other legends say that Chang-O's moon was one of the 12 moons, each a different shape, that cross the sky.

Chantico Ancient Mexican fire-goddess.

Charila Once upon a time, the town of Delphi was parching under a terrible drought. The people starved as the crops burned up in the field, and the king grew concerned for his realm. At the height of the disaster, a little girl came to the king to beg for food. Annoyed, the king struck

*See Chalchiúhtlicue, p. 74. Field Museum of Natural History
(Neg# 96688), Chicago.*

Charila in the face; she hanged herself in shame. Later, an oracle told the king that he should have been more kind to the supplicant, and that Delphi must thereafter offer propitiatory sacrifices to Charila's spirit every nine years.

Charybdis This monster daughter of the sea and the earth originally lived on land. But the Greek god Zeus threw her into the ocean, which she afterward constantly swallowed and vomited. Charybdis was the personification of the terrifying whirlpools of the sea, later individualized as the dangerous maelstrom off the Italian coast, opposite the ship-eating rock *Scylla*.

Chelone This nymph, the Greeks said, ridiculed the marriage of Zeus and *Hera* and was metamorphosed into a speechless turtle (*chelonia*) in punishment. But that marriage, scholars argue, was a forced joining of indigenous pre-Hellenic goddess religions with the male-centered theology of the Indo-European tribes. This story, then, may have been a slightly veiled threat to anyone objecting to the enforced religious change; it may also memorialize priestesses who were "silenced" during that era of social upheaval.

Chera The pre-Greek Great Goddess *Hera* in her third aspect, the old wise woman.

Cherubim Hebrew scholar Raphael Patai, examining the legends of the Cherubim, concluded that there were two such beings: one male, one female. A statue of the pair, engrossed in unending intercourse, was the secret held by the sacred Holy of Holies in the Jewish temple. Patai argues that the mating Cherubim originally symbolized a unifying and transfiguring spiritual force, but that later Hebrews failed to understand the intent of the symbol. Unable to integrate the Cherubim into their developing theology, they suppressed descriptions of the temple's sacred precinct.

Chicomecóatl This maize-goddess of the Aztecs had many forms, as many as did the growing corn: she was a maiden decked with water flowers, a young woman whose embrace brought death, a mother carrying the sun as a shield. One of the most popular divinities of ancient Mexico, she was depicted wearing a four-sided headdress and carrying a magic corncob labeled "forgiving strength." It is possible that Chicomecóatl was originally worshiped by the residents of central Mexico who preceded the Aztecs, and that her rites in their era were less bloody than the Aztec sacrifices of young girls in Chicomecóatl's name.

Chih Nu One of the most beloved goddesses of China was the "weaving woman" of heaven, whose task it was to weave the iridescent seamless robes of the divinities. Once, Chih Nu fell in love with the cowherd-god; she spent so much time in his bed that the silk robes of the heavenly ones began to tatter, and there were no new ones in the works. The chief god removed Chih Nu to one side of the heavens, her lover to the other, allowing them one night together annually. On that evening, magpies flew across the sky carrying branches to build a footbridge for the pair's reunion. When it rained, however, the magpies were stranded on earth, and the lovers had to forgo their yearly lovemaking.

Chimera Part goat, part lion, part dragon, this Greek monster was said to have endangered the land of Lycia. Probably she was originally a volcano-goddess like *Pele* or *Fuji* or *Aetna*, for there was a volcano of her name in the very country she allegedly terrorized. See also **Echidna.**

Chinnintamma Household-goddess of eastern India.

Chlaus Haistic Powerful Irish witch.

Chloë "Green," a name for *Demeter.*

Chuang-Mu Chinese goddess of the bedroom.

Chuginadak One of the world's greatest volcano goddesses of the world appears in the myths of the Aleuts, who occupy the islands on the far-north edge of the volcanic Pacific Ocean rim. They say the mountain now called Mt. Cleveland was once a proud woman who refused to marry any man in her village. She had a mate in mind: a man she once knew who shot rosy finches. Because of her disdain for the men there, she became unwelcome in her village and set out to find her chosen mate.

Making magic as she went, Chuginadak walked across impossible waters from island to island on the windy Aleutian Chain. Eventually she came to a village where a dance festival was in progress, and there she saw the man she wanted. She called to him and he came to her. They embraced and fell to the ground in a fever of love.

When Chuginadak arose, the man lay dead beneath her. Disappointed, she retreated to a cave with several birds to mourn her loss. It was not long, however, before the man's father—the village chief—found the body of his son. Angry, he was able to divine, with the help of several old women, who had killed his son, and then he sent armies of warriors and magical spirits against Chuginadak.

None could conquer her, however. A fox spirit finally convinced her to travel to the village and explain her deed. When Chuginadak did so, the chief realized that she had truly loved and desired his son. He sent everyone away. Then, alone in his home, he danced and sang until the body of his son rose up and again embraced his lover. Then the old chief passed on his leadership of the people to his son, and Chuginadak became his wife.

Chup-Kamui Among the aboriginal Ainu of Japan, the sun was worshiped as the highest divinity. Each morning the Ainu greeted Chup-Kamui as though she were a living woman; they were also careful not to step into sunbeams flooding from the window towards the stove, for that was the sun's greeting to the hearth-goddess *Kamui Fuchi*. Originally Chup-Kamui was the moon, but after one night overhead watching illicit trysts on earth, the modest girl asked the male moon to trade places with her. Henceforth, she rose each morning from the mouth of a devil who had spent the night trying to eat her. A magical helper shoved crows and foxes into the devil's mouth while Chup-Kamui escaped; hence, these animals were sacred to the Ainu.

During an eclipse, the Ainu called out "chup rai," meaning the sun was dying, or "chup chikai anu," meaning she was fainting. Then they dipped willow branches in water and cast droplets upwards while calling out "kamui-atem-ka," or "Oh goddess, we revive you!" As soon as the eclipse passed, they drank themselves into a maudlin state with sake, telling tales of their escape from a world without the luminous sun-goddess.

Churalin The Hindus say that a woman who dies in childbirth loses her soul, which melts into the powerful repository of frustrated maternity called Churalin, a monster that roams the countryside looking for pretty infants to kill. See also **Lilith, Kishimogin.**

Chysothenius Homer's name for *Iphigenia;* possibly a historical Greek woman poet.

Cihuacóatl The Mexican goddess of life's trials, Cihuacóatl invented productive labor. She also prophesied doom, wandering through the world decked out in jewels and face paint, moaning in despair over coming disasters.

Cihuateteo, Cihuapipiltin To the ancient Mexicans, these were the roving spirits of women who died in childbirth. See **Churalin, Kishimogin.**

Cipactli, Tlaltecuhtli   Before there was an earth, said the Nahua of ancient Mexico, the goddess Cipactli existed, a monstrous alligator swimming through the waters of primordial chaos. All potential life was contained within her, but it could not be freed until—like *Tiamat* across the oceans in the eastern Mediterranean—Cipactli offered her very body.

Two serpent-gods tore the goddess apart. Her lower body fell through chaos to form the earth, while her upper body rose to form the heavens. Her scaly coat became the mountains; her eyes and mouth turned into caves. Sometimes, the Nahua said, she could still be heard sobbing at night, wishing life to die back into her—a symbolic rendering of death's significance that the Aztecs later took literally, tearing living bodies apart to feed the goddess.

Another legend, in which she was called Tlaltecuhtli, says that this primordial goddess was the most magnificent creature in the universe, a beautiful woman with eyes and teeth at every joint so that she could look everywhere and protect herself. But she could not avoid the two gods who tore her in half, whereupon her hair grew into trees, flowers, and grass, her eyes into rivers, her shoulders into mountains.

Circe   A daughter of the sun and sister of the famous Cretan queen *Pasiphae*, this illustrious witch was said to have gained the rulership of Colchis near the Black Sea by marrying its prince. Then she killed him so that she could rule alone. When Circe's subjects discovered her crime, they rose against her. The enchantress fled, escaping on her father's rays to the island of Aeaea.

There Circe lived in a little stone house set in a clearing, surrounded by lions and wolves. She entertained herself by blending magic potions of herbs that she tried on human subjects shipwrecked in her vicinity. She was most famous for turning Odysseus's men into swine; the wandering Greek king himself managed to escape her spells, but he could not escape her charms and fathered two sons by the witch, who, Hesiod said, became Etruscan princes.

Claudia Quinta   The matriarch of the Claudian family of Rome, she was accused of promiscuity in 204 B.C. At that time, the goddess *Cybele* was traveling to Rome, and her boat stuck fast in the Tiber River. Claudia, proclaiming herself ready for a test of her continence, took hold of the ropes tied to Cybele's boat. Invoking the goddess, she pulled, and single-handedly pulled Cybele into Rome, thus acquitting herself of the false charge.

Cleone   A pre-Hellenic water-goddess who was the divine ancestor of the Cleonae, a tribe who lived between Argos and Corinth.

Clidna, Cliodna The beautiful bird-goddess of the Irish afterlife survives today as a fairy queen of southwest Ireland, ruler of the sacred hill in Cork called Carrig Cliodna. In ancient legend, Clidna was one of the Tuatha de Danaan, the magical divinities subject to the goddess *Danu;* she was said to rule the Land of Promise, where there is no death, violence, or decay.

Legend says that she ruled the ninth wave of every series, which was thought to be larger than the preceding eight; huge swells were therefore called "Clidna's waves." These waves were one of the goddess's forms; she also appeared as a swooping seabird. When she took human form, she was the most beautiful woman ever seen, hence her name, "shapely one."

Like many ancient goddesses, Clidna took mortal lovers. John Fitzjames, for instance, she stole from Eire's mainland. But he already had a human lover, a witty and argumentative Irishwoman named Caitileen Og. This Caitileen was the only woman ever to berate Clidna for her careless ways with human affection. She trailed the goddess all the way to the afterlife, demanding her lover's return. Indeed, she almost prevailed against Clidna's lust. Almost persuaded by the woman's clever speech, Clidna finally decided to keep Fitzjames for herself.

Clymene A common name among Greek heroines. We find at least a dozen in that mythology, including the mothers of *Atalanta*, Prometheus, and *Mnemosyne.*

Clytemnestra The Greek woman *Leda* was raped by—or, some say, willingly mated with—a huge swan, the disguised Zeus. Shortly afterward, she had intercourse with her husband, the king of Sparta. Nine months later Leda laid two eggs. One broke open to reveal the immortal *Helen* (later "of Troy") and her brother Pollux; the other produced two mortal children, Clytemnestra and her brother Castor.

As she grew, Clytemnestra was overshadowed by her immortally beautiful half-sister. It was Helen who attained the crown of the city, raising her consort Menelaus to the throne. Clytemnestra, on the other hand, became part of a foreign family by marrying Helen's brother-in-law, Agamemnon of Mycenae. They had three children: two daughters, *Iphigenia* and *Electra*, and a son, Orestes.

Then Agamemnon was called to Troy to regain Helen—and with her, the crown of Sparta—for his brother. At the town of Aulis on the Aegean coast, the luckless Greek navy was stalled by ill winds. To further their campaign, the brothers decided they needed a human sacrifice. They sent back to Mycenae for Iphigenia, pretending to her mother that the girl was intended as the hero Achilles's bride. But they put Iphigenia to death. The bloody sacrifice pleased the wind deities; the Greeks gained the advantageous winds they needed to sail to Troy. (For variants of this story, see **Iphigenia**.)

Back home in Mycenae, Clytemnestra was stricken with furious grief at her loss. For a decade she planned vengeance. She took as consort Agamemnon's cousin, Aegisthus—also his bitter enemy because of crimes committed in their families' past. The queen and her lover plotted revenge suitable for a man who valued his brother's crown over his own child's life.

When Agamemnon returned, he brought with him *Cassandra*. The doomed Trojan prophet foresaw the results of maternal anger, but the king ignored her warnings. King and captive were quickly murdered by Clytemnestra and Aegisthus. But the queen herself met a violent death, for her own children avenged their father's murder.

This complicated cycle of killings and revenge murders expressed, some interpreters claim, the social upheaval in the Greek city-states when the era of mother right ended and the patriarchal family was established as the base of society. Under a matriarchal system, Clytemnestra acted intelligibly, if brutally, meting out death to her child's killer. Under the new patriarchal system, Clytemnestra's children acted correctly by destroying their father's murderer. Those who favor this interpretation of the myth cite the end of Aeschylus's *Oresteia*: Clytemnestra's son, pursued by the matriarchal *Erinyes*, is absolved of his mother's murder by the supporters of the patriarchy. See also **Erigone**.

Clytie, Clytia   The spirit of the sunflower or the heliotrope, Clytie was once a Greek nymph who slept with the sun. Transformed into a flower, she still worshipfully follows his movement across the sky.

Coatlícue   The earth was a fivefold "serpent-skirted goddess" to the ancient Mexicans, who counted four directions and a central point, up and down, on their compasses. The fivefold earth-goddess therefore sometimes appeared to them as a woman with four sisters; they gathered, it was said, on Coatepec ("Snake Hill") to meditate. There Coatlícue gathered white feathers to adorn her breasts; becoming pregnant while remaining a virgin, she gave birth to the savior-god Quetzalcóatl. In other legends, she was impregnated by emeralds or jade stones.

Sometimes the fivefold goddess was called a moon divinity, wife of the sun-god. She was also called the creator: she was preeminent and pre-existent, floating for eons in a misty world. Even the sun and his magicians did not realize her magnificence. Once they did, however, they brought her love charms, and she suddenly flowered forth as the great mother of all living.

But Coatlícue was the death mother as well. Her most famous images show her as the ruler of life and its end, garlanded with hearts and hands, wearing a skirt of swinging serpents, hung with skulls, vested in a flayed human skin. Coatlícue, honored with spring's earliest flowers, was also rightly attired in claws and snakes, for to the ancient Mexicans the goddess was both Tlaltecuhtli (see **Cipactli**), the ugly earth toad, and *Tonantzin*, the mother redeemer. See also **Coyolxauhqui.**

Coatrischie   Tempest-raising goddess of the Antilles.

Cocomama   The resident divinity of the coca plant was, to the people of the Andes, a goddess who granted healing and happiness to her worshipers. Originally, it was told, she was a promiscuous woman cut in half by jealous lovers; her body grew into the first coca bush, whose leaves men were not to chew until they had satisfied a woman's sexual needs.

Colleda   The old Serbian goddess of the winter solstice, she was the recipient of the ceremonial Yule log that was burned as the year's light drained away. When the daylight was reborn, her devotees served sweet cakes to the children, who went from house to house begging favors for the "sweet maiden goddess" who promised the revival of light and growth.

Concordia   The Roman goddess of peace, her name survives in English as *concord*. In Roman art, she was shown as a heavyset matron, holding a cornucopia in one hand and an olive branch in the other.

Copia   A Roman goddess of plenty, her name survives in the *cornucopia*, which she was often depicted holding, and in *copious*, our word for "abundance."

Corchen   Early Irish snake-goddess.

Corra   In Scotland, the goddess of prophecy appeared as this crane woman.

Cotys, Cotytto, Kotus, Kottutto, Kotyto   In Thrace, far in the north of Greece, this goddess of sexuality was revered. There her servants, the *baptai* ("baptized ones"), celebrated secret festivals in her honor, releasing the forces of life through erotic celebration. The secrecy of the rituals was so treasured that anyone who described them to non-initiates was put to death by other devotees. When the Greeks invaded this goddess's homeland, they saw no religious content to the life-evoking rituals, dubbing the Thracian goddess the "patron of debauchery."

Coventina Among the Celts, both insular and Continental, goddesses were often perceived in the form of flowing water; the "earth-goddess" of a territory was seen, not in the landscape, but in the river that drained it. Best described as "goddesses of the watershed," these divinities included *Boann* of the Boyne, *Belisama* of the Mersey, *Sinann* of the Shannon, and Coventina of the Carrawburgh in England.

At her sacred well in Northumberland, relics were recovered, including portraits of the elegant-looking goddess. In one sculpture, the goddess was shown lying on water weeds, pouring the river from an urn that she carries. In others, she stands holding branches of water plants, while thoughtlessly tipping her bucket.

Many of these goddesses, like *Sulis* at Bath, were considered to be healing divinities, and offerings for good health were dedicated to them at their sacred sites, as to *Mary* of Lourdes today. In addition, the Celtic water-goddesses were also spirits of inspiration and prophecy, rather like the Greek *Muses* or the Roman *Carmenta*.

Coyolxauhqui "Golden bells" was the name of this Aztec moon-goddess, daughter of Mother *Coatlícue*. Some legends say that when the fearful stars tried to kill their mother rather than let her bear rivals to them, Coyolxauhqui was among them. But the traitorous siblings then turned on her, decapitating her and throwing her head into the sky. (Other versions say that she tried to warn Coatlícue of the conspiracy against her so that the sun-god killed Coyolxauhqui to keep her from speaking; her mother, grieving, placed Coyolxauhqui's shining head in the night sky.)

One of the great monuments to Coyolxauhqui was unearthed during construction work in Mexico City in 1978: a 10-ton circle of stone showing her dismemberment, as important a piece of Aztec art as the Calendar Stone found in 1790. The archaeologists were so moved by the stone's discovery that they sang a hymn to the goddess who was buried for more than 500 years but emerged intact. Later excavations have revealed one of the greatest religious centers of Aztec Mexico surrounding the stone.

Cred, Creide This Irish fairy queen of the famous goddess-mountains, "the paps of Anu," promised never to sleep with a man until she found one who could create a magnificent poem for her. Not only did it have to be perfectly constructed but it had to describe in vivid detail her home and its splendid furnishings. But as her palace was heavily guarded and no man had ever entered, it seemed likely she would die a virgin. But the Fionn poet-seer Coll came to her and sang a poem so accurate and so beautiful that she instantly wed him. "Wounded men spouting heavy blood would sleep to the music of fairy birds singing above the bright leaves of her bower," were the words that convinced her to become his *Leanan Sidhe,* or otherworld lover.

Creiddylad   We know this ancient Welsh goddess as Cordelia, daughter of Lear in Shakespeare's play; she was originally a sea queen, daughter of the sea-god Llyr. Geoffrey of Monmouth claimed that Cordelia, the human form of the goddess, ruled the land after her father died. Shakespeare, of course, killed her off along with Lear. By then, the real legend of Creiddylad and Llyr was probably lost.

Crobh Dearg   "Red claw" was an ancient Irish goddess who was sometimes said to be the sister of *Latiaran;* possibly she was a form of *Badb.*

Crocale   The hairdresser of *Artemis.*

Cuba   Roman goddess who guarded infants just out of the cradle.

Cunina   Roman goddess who guarded infants still in the cradle.

Cuvto-Ava   The "tree mother" of the Mordvins was addressed in many charms—probably because she was a haughty deity, always on the lookout for injuries done to her or her tree daughters. If you were to break off branches thoughtlessly or otherwise offend her, Cuvto-Ava would punish you with withering diseases. See **Azer-Ava.**

Cybele, Kubele   Of all the Great Mothers of the ancient Near East, the one whose myth and cult came down to us most clearly was Cybele, for her worship survived in Rome centuries into the Christian era. A mountain-dwelling goddess of holy madness, Cybele's worship originated in Phrygia, in northern Anatolia (modern Turkey); it traveled through the northern Mediterranean, together with her image as a full-breasted mature woman, crowned and carrying corn and keys, arrayed in a robe containing all the flower colors of the earth she ruled.

Here is the story told of her: one day, disguised as the rock *Agdos,* Cybele was sleeping. Zeus, a far younger divinity, came upon her and attempted to rape her. Unable to penetrate her, he was so excited by the contest that he ejaculated onto the ground. But the ground, too, was Cybele the earth mother, and so she conceived.

The child of this unresolved conflict was the hermaphrodite Agdistis, as unpleasant and violent a child as his conception could warrant. The wine-god Dionysus drugged him with alcohol and, to make his life easier, tied his male members to a tree so that, on awakening, he would pull them off. Unfortunately, Agdistis died of the wound, and from his blood sprang up a beautiful almond—some say pomegranate—tree.

From this tree, the nymph *Nana* picked a lovely fruit and placed it next to her skin; it impregnated her with a lovely child whom she named Attis. When he grew into the perfection of young manhood, Attis roused the passion of Cybele. She took him as her lover, bearing him through the world in her lion-drawn chariot, engaging him in ecstatic embraces. This wasn't enough for Attis, though, and he foolishly turned his attentions to another woman. Because his grandmother/lover was the earth itself, there was nowhere that Attis could accomplish his infidelity without Cybele's knowing. He nonetheless tried; Cybele naturally surprised him at it, and in punishment she drove him mad. In an anguish of contrition, Attis tore from himself the cause of all the trouble and, castrated, bled to death beneath a pine tree.

Most interpreters find in this tale a representation of the flowering passage of the short growing season over the face of the constant earth. Indeed, the Cybeline ceremonies focused on springtime. In Rome, they began with the triumphal entry of the young Attis, symbolized by a pine tree, into the city; then followed a day of mourning and fasting for his death; finally, an Easter-like "Festival of Joy" celebrated the arrival of the new growing season. This joyful conclusion is noteworthy in that the myth does not mention Attis's rebirth, although similar stories (*Ishtar*, *Isis*) do show the young lover reborn or restored to Mother Earth's embraces.

Called the "Mountain Mother" in her homeland, Cybele's religion entered Rome in 204 B.C. At that time, the city was threatened by Hannibal, and consultation of the books of the *Sibyl* showed that the Carthaginian would be conquered only if the black stone of Cybele was brought in ceremony to the capital. This stone, apparently a meteorite that had fallen to earth before astonished witnesses, was honored in Asia Minor as the very stone that Zeus had tried to rape. Five distinguished Romans duly sought out the irregularly shaped piece of betyl and brought it ceremoniously into the temple of Victoria. Thirteen years later Cybele is said to have caused the defeat of the Carthaginians.

However, the ritual, which arrived with the sacred stone, was controversial from the start and was sporadically banned. At issue was the self-castration of Cybele's priests, performed as an act of identification with the goddess's beloved, and even today the focus of emotional academic dispute. Amid wild music and throbbing cymbals, the initiate allowed himself to be overcome by mystic abandon and used whatever was near at hand—a blunt knife, a stone would do—to accomplish the act. Ovid described it thus: "His [Attis's] unmanly ministers cut their offending members while they toss their hair." After becoming eunuchs, the initiates would dress in elaborate costumes and serve the goddess in music and dance. All this horrified the masculinity-conscious Romans, who are recorded to have killed slaves in punishment for self-castration, as though death were a fitting retribution for sacrilege of this sort.

But citizens could partake of the goddess's mysteries without such total devotion. Once in a lifetime—or, if one were rich, every 20 years—a worshiper of Cybele could be reborn. In the Taurobolium, one stood in an earth pit under an ox. The beast was slaughtered and drenched the worshiper with its blood. Then, bloody as a babe and spiritually refreshed, the baptized would emerge from the earth-womb, confirmed in his devotion to the Mountain-Mother Cybele. See also **Atargatis, Frigg.**

Cydippe   An Argive priestess of *Hera*, she had two sons to whom she was devoted. She prayed to her goddess to grant them what was best for mortals; that night they died in their sleep.

Cynosura   The Cretan goddess Cynosura leaves us her name in *cynosure,* a word that means "center of attraction" and recalls the navigational uses of her constellation, Ursa Minor or the Little Dipper. Some legends call her the nurse of the Greek god Zeus. See **Adamanthea.**

Cyone   This woman of Syracuse in ancient Greece was raped by her own father. She promptly marched him into a temple and sacrificed him on its altar.

Cyrene   A powerful princess of early Greece, Cyrene entertained herself by wrestling with lions. She was also, Pindar said, excellent with the javelin and sword and hated merely to "pace to and fro before the loom."

Da This seems to have been the original name of the ancient Greek earth mother, who later was *Ge* or *Gaea*. Da's name survives in that of the god Poseidon, whose name means "husband of Da," for the woman-centered culture that preceded the Hellenes saw the ocean as the fertilizing husband of the land. See also **Demeter.**

Dabaiba "Mother of creation," the Great Goddess of early Panama.

Dactyls Ten little women born with no father to the Greek woman Anchiale, they were fabulously inventive and brought to us all we know of metalwork and smithcraft. The Dactyls clearly represent the 10 fingers of the human hands; their legend suggests that women were the discoverers of metal and its working.

Dae-Soon Korean moon-goddess. See **Hae-Sun.**

Dag Early German day-goddess.

Dahut This pagan princess lived in Brittany during the period when Christian monks were destroying the remnants of the old European religion—the worship of maternal nature. These flesh-despising monks ruined the princess's pleasures until Dahut begged her father, King Gradlon, to build her a retreat from the cruelties of the new way.

 Gradlon, seeming not to heed his daughter, was secretly building a magnificent city for her. Called Ys, it was to be hers to do with as she wished. When he presented it to Dahut, the sensual princess was wild with joy at the splendid homes arranged to catch the setting sun's rays.

 Dahut's people were rich and happy, but it soon became clear that Ys had been built too close to the sea. Storms endangered the small fishing craft by which the people of Ys earned their wealth. Dahut asked Gradlon to build them a safe harbor, but the king, threatened with damnation by the monks, built instead a fine new church to the

Christian god right in the center of Ys.

Furious, Dahut rowed that night through dangerous coastal waters to a secret island where women—possibly immortals—continued to celebrate the ancient rites. There she asked them to command the sea spirits, the *Korrigans*, to help her; she offered eternal fidelity to the old ways in return.

But then Dahut's ambition poisoned her. Granted the aid Ys needed, Dahut asked for yet another miracle: that magical powers would raise her palace high above the new Christian church. She was granted that, too, but her selfish desire took its toll.

For many years Dahut and her people lived in splendor and pleasure. But the princess's sickness grew. Eventually she began to take one-night lovers, having them destroyed immediately after they left her. The powers of passion and ambition that Dahut had stirred grew so strong that finally the king of the waters himself came to claim the princess—and he drowned the entire city of Ys when he did.

Dakini, Dagini In Indian Hinduism, these powerful female beings are attendants on the death-goddess *Kali*. Like her, they are of a terrifying aspect, sometimes fish-bodied, sometimes huge as an ogre, often eating raw flesh or drinking blood (from which they are called Asrapas, "blood sippers"). In the esoteric tradition in Tibet, however, they have another aspect, for beneath their horrific guise they carry the power of "the mothers," as Tibetan yogis call them, and grant supernormal powers and insights to the sincere practitioner of yoga, particularly Kundalini yoga.

Damatre Early Italian mother-goddess.

Damatres "The Mothers," a name for *Demeter* and *Persephone* on Sicily.

Dames Vertes The "Green Ladies" of Celtic French folklore were seductive but cruel, luring travelers from the forest paths and holding them upside down over waterfalls, laughing all the while. As wind spirits, they traveled speedily over their chosen countryside, invigorating all the plant life they touched. When visible in human form, the Dames Vertes were said to be tall and seductive, dressed in long green robes, passing so lightly over the grass that it seemed only winds had disturbed it.

Damia An alternative form of the corn-goddess *Demeter*, she was paired with a *Persephone*-like daughter named Auxesia in ancient Greece. In a famous story, a famine struck the Epidaurians that, it was prophesied, would not end until statues of the goddesses were carved of Athenian olive wood. The Athenians gave their neighbors the wood, but afterward demanded heavy tribute. During a rebellion, the Epidaurians stopped payment of the tribute; the Athenians invaded, intent on carrying home the goddesses's statues. But they would not move, and a fierce battle followed. A messenger carrying tidings to Athens of the sacrilege to Damia and Auxesia was murdered by angry Athenian women; the men of Athens used this attack to strip the women of their few remaining rights.

Damkina, in Greek, Daukina In the Akkadian language, this name means "lady of earth," and she was to the Sumerians the earth mother familiar to us in Greece as *Demeter* and in Rome as *Tellus Mater.*

Damona Ancient Celtic cattle-goddess.

Danae, the Danaids There is a Greek story about a woman of Argos who, confined to a tower so that she could not conceive, was raped by the god Zeus, who fell in through the window disguised as a shower of gold. Danae then bore the hero Perseus. And there is another Greek story about 49 Danaid sisters who, forced into marriage, killed their husbands on their wedding night; the 30th sister, *Hypermnestra*, spared her mate and conceived by him the ruling dynasty of Argos.

The names of the Argive heroine and of the husband-slaying sisters are clearly identical, although legends never connect them. In addition, the Argives bore the tribal name of Danai. In Greek times, the excuse was given that the name came from the father of the Danaids, Danaos. Clearly an attempt to disguise the matrilineality of the pre-Hellenic settlers of the Peloponnese, this reveals its bias by assuming that the daughter bears the father's name and her children bear the daughter's.

There is evidence that the Danaids were originally water-goddesses of the region around Argos; Hypermnestra gave her name to a fountain, an odd honor for a mortal woman of that time. If the Danaids were indeed connected with Danae, then she (whose name fittingly means "dawn") would be the ancestor-goddess of the Argive tribe. See **Amymone.**

Danu, Dana The greatest of the goddesses of ancient Ireland, Danu was the ruler of a tribe of divinities called Tuatha de Danaan, the people of Danu, who were demoted to "fairies" called *Daoine Sidhe* in later times. Her name derives from the Old Celtic *dan*, meaning "knowledge," and she was probably the same goddess as the Welsh *Don.* Some scholars see her as the same goddess as *Anu*, while others contend that she is an aspect of *Brigid*. There are no legends of her left to elucidate the search for her meaning, but her preeminence among ancient Irish deities remains clear.

Daphne   A priestess of *Gaea*, this nymph led secret women's rituals in celebration of the earth's femininity. But the mortal Leucippus tried to penetrate their rituals in female disguise. The all-seeing sun, who had ulterior motives for his action, suggested to the women that they conduct their rituals nude, to be certain that there were no male intruders.

So the mortal was found and destroyed for his sacrilege. Then the sun-god's motives became clear. He accosted the beautiful priestess and demanded that she sleep with him. She refused. Apollo grew violent. Chasing her, intent on rape, he overpowered Daphne. But she cried out to the goddess she served, Mother Earth, and instantly was transformed into a laurel tree. The repentant Apollo thereafter wore laurel wreaths in his hair and honored the tree as the symbol of inspiration.

Darago   The volcano-goddess of the Philippines was said to be a warrior woman who lived in fiery mountains and demanded human sacrifices once a year to keep her from angry eruptions.

Daughters of Zelophehad   The individual names of these Jewish heroines are no longer recorded, an ironic aspect of this story of an ancient fight for women's equal rights. When the Hebrews conquered Canaan, they began to divide the country among the males of the tribe. But the Daughters—convinced of their own rights as members of the same tribe and as survivors of the desert exile—waited until a day when Moses was preaching. His subject was the laws of "levirate marriage," the forced marriage of barren widows to the brothers of their dead husbands. Pointing out that their own father was dead and that they, apparently, did not count as offspring, they claimed Moses should demand strict adherence to the Hebrew marriage law by forcing their aged mother into marriage. Shamed, Moses agreed that the Daughters had found a legal inconsistency and thereafter granted them equal land rights with the men.

Davata   Indian fire-goddess.

Dea Caelestis   The name the Romans used for *Tanith*, the Carthaginian sky-goddess.

Dea Dia, Dia   Her ancient name shows that she was one of Italy's original goddesses, but little survived into historical times of Dea Dia. More historically prominent than the goddess's name is that of her servants, the 12 Arval Brothers (Fratres Arvales), a renowned college of priests charged with tending Dea Dia's sacred grove on the Tiber River. So sacred was this laurel and oak grove that whenever a rotten limb fell in a storm or an old tree was blown to the ground, the Fratres had to offer lambs and sows in reparation.

Dea Nutrix   "Nurturing Mother" was the Romanized name given to a Celtic goddess, perhaps a form of *Deae Matres*, whose images were found in central France and southern Germany. The figures were discovered in sacred springs like Vichy and in graves.

Dea Syria   The Romans usually used this name, the "Syrian Goddess," to describe *Atargatis*. Sometimes, however, they lumped together other goddesses of the eastern Mediterranean—*Ishtar, Cybele, Anahita*—under this broad term.

Deae Matres, Matronae   Their names—bestowed by scholars—may be Latin, but the Deae Matres were Celtic, the primary divine image of the Continental tribes. No legends survive of this trinity of earth-goddesses, although hundreds of inscriptions and sculptures attest to the strength of their worship.

Their religion was apparently destroyed early in the Roman occupation, but their names and images survived into the days of the empire. They were then called sorceresses of the early days, thus holding the attention and reverence of their people in ancient Gaul and Germany.

The "mother-goddesses"—for this is what their Latin name means—were always shown as three robed women bearing baskets of fruit and flowers; sometimes they also carried babies. Seated under an archway, they were depicted wearing round halolike headdresses; the central goddess was distinguished from the others by standing while they sat or by sitting while they stood. They were probably ancestral goddesses, rulers of the fruitfulness of humanity as well as that of the earth.

Deborah   A Hebrew prophet, Deborah was married to a man named Barak, called "the ignoramus." She was a high-handed woman who took no commands from her husband, instead ordering him around. A great poet and a judge, she sat in the open air dispensing judgments and composing poems rather than hiding her talents indoors.

Dechtere   The mother of the superhuman Irish hero Cuchulain was herself a magical creature, able to transform herself and her 50 maidservants into birds so that they could travel more quickly through the green hills of the island. Wherever they stopped, they ate voraciously, especially the enormous queen who headed them, for Dechtere was of more than normal height.

Drinking wine one day, she accidentally swallowed a mayfly floating in the cup, whereby she conceived Cuchulain. That, however, is but one of the three versions of the conception: another says that she flew away as a bird with the god Lug; yet another says that Dechtere was miraculously impregnated by Lug with his own soul. She gave birth to the reborn god by vomiting him into daylight, thus retaining her virginity.

Deirdre   The most tragic heroine in all of Irish legend, Deirdre was the most beautiful woman in the world, and one who bore the curse that only sorrow would come from her beauty. The warriors of the Irish north, on hearing the prophecy at Deirdre's birth, demanded her death. But the Ulster king Conchobar, pitying her, sent her into exile in the distant reaches of Ireland.

As she grew into the lovely woman prophecy had foreseen, Deirdre lived happily enough in her exile. One day, though, she saw blood on the snowy ground and a raven nearby. Instantly she remembered an insistent dream of a young man with the same coloring: black hair, white skin, and red lips. She sank into depression until her nurse *Lavercam* told her of Naoise, who lived with his brothers, Ardan and Ainle, nearby. Lavercam arranged a secret meeting, and Deirdre, literally seeing the man of her dreams, demanded that he free her from her woodland exile.

They fled to Scotland, where they took refuge with noble people. But Deirdre attracted the attention of the king, who laid plans to steal her from her lover. To avoid this, Deirdre and Naoise, together with his brothers, fled to the windy coast. There they lived a rugged but happy life, until rumor reached them that Conchobar would welcome them back in Ireland. But the rumor had been deliberately planted; the king, angry at having his captive sprung from his grasp, wanted her back only for evil purposes.

Deirdre knew by intuition that if they returned to Ireland, tragedy would follow. But Naoise was a proud man, loyal to his king, and he overruled his lover. The party of four sailed across to Ireland while Deirdre continued to see gloomy portents, including a blood red cloud. Naoise and his brothers, however, continued to ignore her warnings.

Alas for them all, Deirdre's premonitions proved correct. Through treachery, Naoise and his brothers were murdered by the warriors of Conchobar; Deirdre herself was taken captive. Submitting to her captors, Deirdre saw that she had one way out. So, as she was being transported to the king in a speedy chariot, she suddenly stood up and let her head smash against a tree, splattering her blood and brains across the Irish soil.

Dejanira, Deianira   The Greek hero Heracles had a bad record in relationships. He had countless affairs before, during, and after his first marriage, which ended with his killing his wife *Megaera*. Despite his reputation, a woman warrior, Dejanira, fell in love with Heracles, and he with her. They were married, and she bore him several children. But Heracles soon returned to his usual behavior, even bringing a mistress into Dejanira's home.

　　Desperate to regain Heracles's love, Dejanira wove a splendid garment for her husband and soaked it in what she hoped was an infallible charm: blood and semen from a dying centaur, killed by Heracles. But the centaur had revenge in his heart when he confided the secret potion to Dejanira. His blood burned so terribly on Heracles's flesh that—finding he could not tear the garment off—the hero pleaded to the gods for death. The remorseful Dejanira followed him to the afterlife, dying by her own hand.

Dekla   This sympathetic Latvian fate-goddess watched over infants. When she was forced to witness the birth of a child for whom a tragic life was destined, she wept bitterly. She may be a localized form of the Baltic *Laima*.

Demeter   Once the flowerlike *Persephone*, the lovely daughter of earth, disappeared, her mother, Demeter, could find her nowhere. The weeping Demeter searched and searched through the fields, crying out for the daughter who was so close as to seem her very self, her childhood, her gentle youth. Demeter fretfully clutched her blue-green cloak, then thoughtlessly shredded it into tiny pieces, scattering them as cornflowers in the grasses. But flowers and grasses soon faded, for Demeter was the source of all growth; as she mourned, the goddess withdrew her energy from the plants, which began to wilt and shrivel. So, it was said, Chloë ("green one"), the happy earth, changed for the first time into the yellow-gold, autumnal Demeter.

　　The goddess wandered through the dying earth until she came to a town near Athens. There she took a job as nursemaid to the queen of Eleusis, *Metanira*, whose son Triptolemos she wanted to make immortal by smoking him like a log in the fireplace (see Isis). The frantic queen found her, and the disguised goddess was revealed. Demeter stayed on in Eleusis, however, often sitting sadly by a well as she wept for the loss of her beloved daughter.

One day the queen's daughter *Baubo* (or *Iambe*) saw the sad goddess at the well and tried to comfort her. Demeter refused all her consoling words and so, to make the goddess smile, Baubo exposed her vulva salaciously. Surprised, Demeter chuckled, the first laughter the starving earth had heard from its goddess in many months. Shortly afterward, Persephone was restored to her mother, and spring bloomed again on the earth. In gratitude for the hospitality of the Eleusinians, Demeter taught the arts of agriculture to Prince Triptolemos and thereafter based her mysterious rites at that city.

This Greek story of the Great Goddess is clearly a seasonal metaphor; it contains as well a beautifully tender archetype of the bond between mothers and daughters. A variant of the common Mediterranean myth that explains how the earth loves and consumes its own green growth (see **Ishtar** and **Cybele**), this legend is singular in epitomizing this love, not in a sexual relationship between the ever-dying son and his mother, but in a familial bond between the maternal Demeter and her adored daughter Persephone.

This daughter, the springtime earth, was really only another form of Demeter herself. In Sicily, the identity of Demeter and Persephone was canonical; they were dubbed *Damatres* ("mothers") and were portrayed as indistinguishable. But the most common form of the Great Goddess was a trinity, rather than a pair of deities, and many scholars have sifted through the famous Demeter myths, hoping to find the third part of the feminine triad, the winter earth, the aged crone, the hibernating seed. Speculation has generally settled on *Hecate*, who certainly seems to be the most cronelike of the possible divine figures in the story. In addition, she appears at important junctures; she was, for instance, the only one to witness Persephone's disappearance. Because the omniscient earth, Demeter, could hardly have been oblivious to happenings on her surface, Hecate therefore seems to be an aspect of Demeter as "earth mother."

But "earth mother" is only one of the possible meanings of Demeter's name. The second part of the word unarguably means "mother." The first part, however, translates as easily into "cereal" as "earth," making her the goddess not of the earth's surface but only of cultivated, food-providing plants, parallel to the Roman *Ceres*. If *Damater* derives from the words for "earth mother," the goddess would be another form of *Ge* or *Gaea*. As such, she appears in some legends mated to Poseidon, "the husband of Da."

Whether she symbolized all the earth or just its edible plants,

Demeter was worshiped in fireless sacrifices, demanding all offerings in their natural state. Honeycombs, unspun wool, unpressed grapes, and uncooked grain were laid on her altars. Not for her the offerings of wine, mead, cakes, and cloth, for Demeter was the principle of natural, rather than artificial, production.

Her greatest festival, shared with Persephone, was at Eleusis, where the Greeks annually celebrated mysteries that brought the initiate into a gracious and grateful relationship to the Mother. At the three-day festival, the *mystai* imitated the searching Demeter and rejoiced as, once again, she was reunited with her daughter. In their mimicry, they were at first Demeter Erynes ("angry"), furious and sad at the loss of Persephone; then they acted the happy role of Demeter Louisa ("kindly one"), the mother transformed by reunion. In other places and at other times, Demeter bore other names: Kidaria ("mask"), Chamaine ("soil"), and the powerful Thesmophoros ("lawgiver"), orderer of the seasons of the earth and of human life as well. See **Damkina, Medusa.**

Derceto, Dercetis, Derketo   A Greek translation of *Atargatis*. This word may have originated in *dagitu*, the feminine form of the word for "fish," a symbol of Atargatis.

Despoina   "Mistress," a name for the *Kore* worshiped with *Demeter* at the Greek city of Thelpousa. There, it was said, *Hippia* ("horse-faced" Demeter) took Poseidon as a lover and afterward bore this wild girl, sometimes called *Artemis*.

Devayani   Indian goddess who knew the secret of raising the dead.

Devera   Roman goddess ruling the brooms used to purify ritual sites.

Devi   Hinduism is polytheistic in that it grants many names and forms to the divine force, but it is ultimately monotheistic as well in that all forms of divinity can be reduced to one: Devi ("the Goddess"). True, there are preeminent gods, some of whom have more power than the Goddess. But without her, they would have no power at all, or even a form. For it is Devi, the Hindus say, who gives birth to all force and form, who creates separation out of unity, who is the energy without which all would still be chaos.

All goddesses are Devi, the one goddess; all the myths told of black *Kali*, of golden *Parvati* or *Gauri*, of the fierce *Durga* are myths of Devi. Many of these legends are recounted in the Puranas, Indian religious works created after the indigenous goddess culture was assimilated into the religion of the Indo-European invaders of the Vedas.

What these legends were in pre-Vedic India we have no record. The civilization of the Indus Valley in the 2nd millennium B.C. is known to have been centered on a religion of the Goddess. But generations of invasions and warfare almost obliterated the early worship. Still, followers of the Goddess retained their beliefs and rituals, which erupted in later Indian history in the Shaktic and Tantric movements, heterodox at first but later incorporated into orthodox Hinduism. Almost 3,000 years passed between the heyday of Devi's worship and the Indian Middle Ages, but when she reemerged it was not only as the people's deity, the popular recipient of their devotions, but as the philosophic basis of the perceived universe.

Devorgilla There was a woman of this name in Irish history who, by running off with her lover, Diarmuid, brought ruin to the island by allowing the entrance of Norman warriors. That woman was the namesake of an earlier Devorgilla, an ancient Irish sorceress. Given to the hero Cuchulain by her father, the king of Ireland, Devorgilla was spurned and passed on to another man. Hurt by the slight, she instantly changed herself and her handmaiden into birds; together they flew away. But out hunting one day, Cuchulain brought Devorgilla to earth with a rock; she instantly resumed her human form, to the hero's dismay. The pebble, big enough to stun a bird, was buried deep in Devorgilla's flesh; Cuchulain got on his knees and sucked it out, thereby saving the woman's life. But he swallowed some of her blood in his rescue effort, thereby becoming Devorgilla's blood kin; thereafter there was no possibility of them sharing a bed.

Dharti Mata "Mother Earth" in Bombay.

Dhat-Badan, Dhat-Hami The primary goddess of the Himyaritic Arabs of Yemen, her names mean "she of the wild goats" and "she of the sanctuary." This suggests that she was a goddess of the natural forces of the wilderness, worshiped especially in tree-circled oases.

Dia Griene The daughter of the sun in ancient Scotland was called "the sun's tear" for reasons that remain mysterious. She appears in a long folktale in which, held captive in the Land of the Big Women, she is freed by the *Cailleach*, disguised as a fox, and a helpful young bumbler named Brian.

Diana, Jana Today we confuse Diana with the Greek *Artemis*, seeing both in the familiar picture of the lightly clad, bow-bearing goddess who rides the moon or strides through the forest with her nymphs. And in later

Angwu-shahai-i, Hopi "Crow Mother." Field Museum of Natural History (Neg# 95924), Chicago.

Roman times, Diana was indeed so pictured, but only after the original Italian goddess was assimilated into the powerful figure of Artemis, the goddess of the conquered Greeks.

Diana was originally queen of the open sky, worshiped only out-of-doors, where her domain stretched overhead. Possibly she was ruler of the sun as well as the moon, for the early Italians had no sun-god and had to adopt Apollo for that role. Diana's name comes from the word for "light"; probably she was the original Italian ruler of the sun.

She ruled on earth as well, as bestower of sovereignty and granter of conception; thus she was sometimes called the threefold Diana Trivia. With two other deities she made up another trinity: *Egeria* the water nymph, her servant and assistant midwife; and Virbius, the mysterious woodland-god. The three lived together in the famous Wood of Nemi near Aricia, where runaway slaves competed for the mistletoe—the Golden Bough that would give them a fighting chance for the position of Diana's priest. Not a job a modern man would covet, the priesthood meant continual vigilance against the next contender for the post, and ultimate death at a successful rival's hands.

This fatal kingship was one of the few roles men could play in the worship of Diana. In other cases, the sky queen was entirely a woman's goddess. On her feast day, August 15—today the Catholic feast day of *Mary*'s assumption into heaven—processions of women would journey to Aricia to offer thanks in Diana's grove for her help that year and to implore her continuing aid. The hunting dogs who accompanied them were crowned but kept leashed so as not to disturb the wild creatures who lived under Diana's sky. Eventually Diana's worship moved closer to the population center, to the Aventine Hill in Rome itself, where women continued to flock to her shrine for ritual hair-washing and invocations for aid in childbed.

Dido, Elissa   To most people steeped in European culture, this name evokes the Carthaginian queen who, seduced and abandoned by the wandering Trojan Aeneas, killed herself rather than face public dishonor as a ruler whose wishes could be flouted. But behind this legendary figure is another, for Dido was also the name of the founder of Carthage. It is possible to assume that Dido lived for many centuries and committed suicide twice; this would be necessary to incorporate all the events of "Dido's" life into one story. It seems more probable that the name of a deified ancestor and city founder was adopted, in turn, by each of the Carthaginian queens and that Dido—like *Candace* and *Helen*—was the title that went with the crown. Dido of the *Aeneid*, then, would have been one of a line of so-named Punic rulers.

The first Dido probably took her name from *dida* ("to wander") and was originally Elissa or Alitta ("the goddess") of Tyre or Cyprus. When she discovered that her brother had treacherously murdered her husband, she quitted her homeland with a retinue of 80 women. Dido traveled to North Africa and purchased "a hide's worth" of land, then cleverly cut the hide into strips and claimed all the land they could surround. Her city, Cartha-Elissa ("city of the goddess"), flourished under the more familiar name of Carthage, but its first queen killed herself when a neighboring king threatened war unless she would sleep with him. The sacred grove of Elissa, the divine queen, remained in the middle of Carthage until the Punic city was obliterated by the Romans.

Digne, Digi No Duineach The name given in ancient Irish poetry to the *Cailleach* as Hag of Beare.

Dil Cattle-goddess of ancient Ireland.

Dilbah *Ishtar* as the war-provoking morning star, distinct from her identity as *Zib*, the evening star who provokes desire.

Dinah Mother of the last matriarchal Hebrew tribe, she was the daughter of *Leah* and was changed from male to female in her mother's womb—an inversion of the usual biological development—when her mother, pitying her childless sister *Rachel*, prayed that her child be a worthless female rather than her seventh son.

Hebrew legend tells us that Dinah was kept in a chest by her father Jacob whenever possible suitors were in sight, so concerned was he that she would marry an uncircumcised man. Nonetheless, Dinah went walking one night and stumbled into a joyous group of dancers—one of whom, a prince named Shechem, asked her to come home with him, and slept with her.

Shechem planned to make Dinah his lawful wife, but the Hebrews objected to Dinah's marriage to a man from an uncircumcised tribe. So Shechem's people agreed to forfeit their foreskins and did so. Then, on the third day after the ritual, when all the men were bedridden with postoperative inflammations, the Hebrews fell upon the tribe and massacred them, taking Dinah away, pregnant with a daughter. It is likely this tale holds a political allegory concerning the attempt of the Dinah tribe to ally itself with other, non-Hebrew people of the Near East and an eventual realignment according to blood. Dinah herself was provided with a properly Hebrew mate, suggesting that the matriarchal vestiges were purged from the tribes of Israel.

Dione   She was a very ancient goddess of the territory that became Greece, and what we know of her is confusing and sometimes contradictory. In late Greek legend, Dione is an *Oceanid*, daughter of the ocean, mother of *Aphrodite*. But this is geographically impossible, as the alleged daughter was imported from the eastern Mediterranean long after Dione's worship had faded.

In the invented genealogy of Aphrodite, Dione was said to have been impregnated by Zeus. Zeus appears in another relation to Dione: he was the second ruler of her oracle at Dodona. At that very ancient spot, the rustling of a tree answered questions on personal, never state or religious, matters; only aged women were allowed to interpret the tree's words. Even after Zeus took over Dione's oracle, men were barred from presiding at the rituals.

It is likely, these clues suggest, that Dione was originally an important goddess of inspiration and sexuality of pre-Hellenic Greece. Her name is a cognate of *Juno* and *Diana*, the Roman sky-goddesses; this hints at an early theological preeminence. But the truth about Dione's significance has been virtually obliterated, with rustlings as faint as the Dodona beeches left for us to interpret.

Dis, Disir (pl.)   Originally the deified woman ancestor of a family, this word came to mean any Scandinavian goddess. But the Disir also remained an undistinguished blur of fate-goddesses, worshiped in services called *disablot*. With much drinking and storytelling, a family celebrated "winter nights," the festival that honored these goddesses of heredity, who controlled an individual's talents and defects. See **Norns.**

Disciplina   Roman goddess of discipline.

Diti   If the Indian goddess *Aditi* is "boundless," her counterpart, Diti, is "the bounded one." Many interpreters see Aditi as the endless sky, Diti as the earth. Both apparently come from a non-Aryan source of Hindu mythology, for their children, though recognized as supernatural, were never part of the official pantheon.

Diti's children were *asuras*, non-gods, sometimes called antigods. They were powerful beings, especially the warrior Maruts, who might have conquered the gods. Diti, whose earlier children Indra had killed, practiced magic when pregnant again. So threatened was Indra that he watched her constantly. When Diti fell into a doze, Indra entered her vagina, traveled to her womb, and dismembered the fetus. Even cut to pieces, the fetus was so powerful that it re-formed into 49 separate warriors.

Diuturna, Juterna   A Roman goddess, she ruled healing springs and ponds, one of which was located in Rome near the temple of *Vesta*.

Djanggawul Sisters, Bildjiwuraroju and Miralaidji   Daughters of the sun, these Australian goddesses unceasingly brought forth living creatures from their endlessly pregnant bodies. Plants and animals, sacred articles, and even rituals fell from them as they wandered the world. Their long vulvas broke off piece by piece with these births, producing the world's first sacred artifacts.

But, Australian myth says, the women's power was stolen by their brother. One day as the women were fishing, their brother and a companion sneaked into the camp and stole the women's power objects. Instantly, the women were alerted by psychic alarms, but they returned too late to save their possessions. Bereft of their magic, the women departed to follow the sun's path, continuing to produce new creatures as they traveled.

Djigonasee   A heroine of the Ontario Hurons, Djigonasee was the mother of the peace-bringer Deganiwada, founder of the Six Nations: Seneca, Cayuga, Onondaga, Oneida, Mohawk, and Tuscarora. Like many mothers of heroes, Djigonasee was a virgin when her son was born. A herald from beyond this world announced the birth.

When her son was grown, Djigonasee served the cause of peace by conveying messages and treaties among the nations. In this role, she upheld her woodland people's traditions, for their chiefs were chosen by wise women, who also removed from power chiefs who acted selfishly or foolishly.

Doda, Dodola   Serbian goddess of rain.

Doh Tenagan   Malaysian patroness of women.

Dolya   In Russia, the goddess of fate was said to live behind the stove. When she was in a fine mood, she was called Dolya, the little old lady who brought good luck; when annoyed, she was Nedolya, the shabbily dressed old hag of bad fortune.

Domnu   "The Deep," an Irish sea-goddess.

Don   The ancient ancestral goddess of the Welsh, Don had no real place in their legends except as the mother of all divinities. Most scholars agree that she was the same goddess as the Irish *Danu*—for the Celts of the two islands were related—but there is considerable dispute whether she was related to *Danae* of the Greeks. Irish legend claims that the people of Danu, driven from their Peloponnesian homeland by the Syrians, traveled through Denmark to arrive in the Atlantic islands in 1472 B.C. If this Irish tradition is accepted, then one must see Don as a pre-Hellenic goddess suppressed in Greece who reemerged centuries later in Wales.

Doris   An ancient, probably pre-Hellenic goddess of the waters, she may have been the ancestor-goddess of the Dorians. She was the mother of the *Nereids* and, possibly, *Thetis*.

Draupadi   One of the main heroines of the *Mahabharata*, the Indian epic, Draupadi was a polyandrous woman who slept in turn with each of her five husbands, who were all brothers; she had a favorite, however, named Arjuna.

Druantia   Goddess of fir trees among Continental Celts.

Dryads, Hamadryads   The Greeks believed every tree had an individual soul, an elemental force incarnated in a barky body. They were, as in most cultures, female; they were mortal, dying with the tree. Sometimes, it was believed, a Dryad would punish a mortal for thoughtlessly injuring her by breaking branches.

Dryope   There were a number of Greek heroines by this name. One was a water nymph who, infatuated with a mortal man, lured him into her embrace, and drowned him. Another was a nymph from wild Arcadia who gave birth to that late addition to the Greek pantheon, the lascivious Pan. Finally, there was an unfortunate nymph of this name, raped by the sun-god and turned into a poplar tree. As such a tale often indicates an indigenous goddess suppressed by invading Indo-Europeans, it is possible that Dryope was originally much more than a doomed "nymph," possibly a tree-goddess.

Dubh Lacha   Irish sea-goddess.

Dugnai   This Lithuanian goddess ruled the kneading of dough. Her name, "that which is at the bottom," suggests that she also controlled the lees or dregs of fermenting liquor.

Durga   All goddesses in Hindu belief are ultimately the same goddess, often called simply "the Goddess" or *Devi*. But she appears in different forms with different names. One of the fiercest of Devi's forms is Durga. She was also the eldest: during the primordial war between gods and antigods, Durga was the first manifestation of goddess-energy.

The war was a stand-off; neither side was winning, and the battles dragged on without victory. Almost hopeless, the gods gathered and concentrated their energies. Flames sprang from their mouths and formed Durga, the first female divinity in the universe. Although produced by the gods, the goddess was stronger than any of them, or all of them together, and she was fiercely eager to fight.

Recognizing her power, the gods handed their weapons to Durga. She mounted a lion to ride toward the antigods' chief, the demon Mahisa. That magical being, terrified of this new apparition, used his powers to assume one fearsome form after another. Still the goddess advanced, until finally, as the demon assumed the form of a buffalo, Durga slaughtered him. The demon nonetheless tried to escape through the dying beast's mouth, but Durga caught him by the hair and butchered him, thereby freeing the earth for the gods to inhabit.

The goddess in this form not only symbolizes the fierce power of the combat against evil but also the rule of the intellectual sphere, for Durga ("unapproachable") represents the end of all things; to seek to understand her is to engage in the most powerful intellectual exploration possible. See **Ganga.**

Dzalarhons   The Volcano Woman of the Haida of the northwest Pacific coast was a powerful spirit who ruled the creatures of the earth and punished people who abused them. Once, it was said, Dzalarhons was a mortal woman who migrated into Haida country with her uncle, Gitrhawn the Salmon-Eater. There she fell in love with a Haida man and, according to the matriarchal customs of the indigenous people, had her uncle arrange a marriage.

Bedecked with sea-otter furs and dentalia-trimmed leather, Dzalarhons was escorted across the bays of the Queen Charlotte Islands to the village of her chosen mate. There splendid ceremonies marked the wedding but, when the couple retired to bed, Dzalarhons found she had mistaken the character of her new husband. He demanded that she spend the night, not beside him, but holding a lighted torch above his head. As the torch shrank through the night, the woman protected her arms with her garments, which were singed, then burned.

The next morning the Haida, shocked at the young man's behavior, warned him about bringing Gitrhawn's vengeance on the people. The bridegroom did not care, however, and continued to demand that Dzalarhons hold his torch until all her garments were burned and she was forced to go naked.

Hearing of Dzalarhons's shame, the Salmon-Eater people came to her rescue. They burned the Haida village but found no maiden, only a stone statue from between whose legs a stream flowed. The stream formed a lake; at the lake's head, the stone woman stood, holding a burning staff topped by a copper frog. Thereafter the metamorphosed maiden was a powerful and feared divinity.

Along the Nass River, it was said that Dzalarhons almost destroyed a village because its residents were careless of life. At first, the people lived in comfort, for the land provided them with berries, salmon, and other wild things to harvest. But growing accustomed to the wealth, they began to forget the land's strictures; they killed animals needlessly and left the carcasses for carrion eaters. They even invented a terrible game: they caught spawning salmon, slit their backs and inserted pitch-soaked branches, then lit the candle-fish and set them back in the water. Bleeding and suffering, the shoals of salmon lit up the rivers spectacularly.

This horrible sight roused the fury of the Volcano Woman. Soon the people of the Wolf Clan heard terrible rumblings, like ghostly drums. Fright ran through the guilty village, but it was too late for repentance. Dzalarhons, goddess of the earth's treasures and owner of its metals, poured forth a fiery wrath on the Haida. Few escaped the holocaust, for even the rivers ran hot with the goddess's fury.

Dziwozony   This was the Polish name for the wild women of the woods, whom the Bulgarians called Divi-Te Zeni and the Bohemians, Divo-zenky. They lived in the forest in underground burrows, seeking to understand the secrets of nature, especially those of herbal medicine. The Dziwozony were said to have large square heads, long fingers, and very ruddy bodies.

Eadon   Early Irish goddess of poetry.

Ebhlinne, Ebhlenn   This Irish goddess was worshiped in the southern county of Tipperary; her home was in the Twelve Mountains of Ebhlenn, the highest of which was called Mathair-Shliabh, the Mother-Mountain. In the *dindshenchas*, the geographical poetry of Ireland, Ebhlinne was said to be the daughter of Guaire from the Brugh na Boine. Married to a king of Cashel, she ran away with his handsome son. Until the first part of this century, the ancient goddess behind this legendary woman was honored by midsummer celebrations in her mountains.

Echenais   This Greek nymph fell in love with a mortal, Daphnis, and made him promise sexual fidelity to her. But he got drunk with a priestess and made love to her. Echenais discovered the infidelity and, to assure that Daphnis would never again be tempted by mortal beauty, blinded her lover.

Echidna   This monstrous serpent woman, daughter of the earth, mated with her own brother to produce some of the strangest creatures inhabiting Greek myth: the raging Nemean lion, the dangerous *Scylla*, the many-headed *Hydra*, the ferocious *Chimera*, and possibly even the *Sphinx*.

Echo   An elemental of the mountains, one of the *Oreads*, Echo became an attendant of the sky-goddess *Hera*. But Zeus, ruler of Olympus and Hera's mate, liked to confide in the nymph; he filled her ears with tales of his sexual misadventures. Hera, to prevent her marriage from becoming the laughingstock of heaven, struck Echo mute; Zeus counterattacked by giving her power to repeat anything she heard.

   The beautiful, silent woman was the lover of the wilderness god Pan, but she eventually left him to fall in love with the pretty mortal

Narcissus. The vain young man, however, would not sleep with her. In retribution, Narcissus was condemned to fall in love with his image in a forest pool. He pined away by the pool, eventually becoming a flower. And Echo, still trying to catch his attention, became a rock by the poolside. She still had the power of speech, but could only repeat what was spoken. The pretty story is almost without question a literary invention or fairy tale rather than a real myth.

Echtghe, Aughty Believed to be an ancient form or title of the pre-Celtic goddess *Ana* or Danann, the Mother of the Gods. Until recently, her name was used for a range of mountains in the west of Ireland, Slieve Aughty (Sliabh na Echtghe). Daughter of the god Nuada Silver-Arm, Echtghe was given the hills by her lover. The area surrounding the hills, Feakle Parish, was the haunt in the early part of this century of Biddy Early, the White Witch of Clare, whose magical blue bottle rests beneath a lake somewhere in the hills, its power waiting to be reclaimed.

Edain Born in the southwest of Ireland, Edain married the king of Munster who, a gambler with poor luck, lost her in a chess match to Midir, the fairy king. Fairies in Ireland enjoyed having affairs with humans, whom they kidnapped and held captive in underground palaces; so it was with Edain, who was imprisoned in Midir's crystal mansion.

The human king followed his wife, storming the fairy fort with his armies; that, as anyone versed in fairy strength would know, was foolish as well as useless. The king then persuaded the old gods, the Tuatha de Danaan, to cast magical imprecations against Midir; that too was of no avail.

Finally, the king gathered another army and, joining forces with several powerful Druids, marched to Midir's fort. The fairy king was frightened; unwilling, however, to let his captive go, he sent forth a group of fairies, all magically identical to Edain, who accompanied them.

The fairies stood before the king, who could not distinguish the human woman among them. Despite this lapse in her husband—for true love should have allowed him to see through the fairies' glamour—Edain remained staunch in her love for him and, straining against the enchantment that held her, broke the fairy king's power and returned to her mate. Thus, Irish legend says, did a woman destroy the magical power of the fairies, who thereafter could not capture humans at will.

Edda Her name means "great grandmother," a word also used to describe the great compilations of Scandinavian mythology called the eddas ("tales of great-grandmother"). In the Norse creation story, the dwarf-ish Edda was the first woman to produce offspring; with her husband Ai, or possibly with the fire-god Heimdal, she gave birth to the race of Thralls, the ones "enthralled" to service as food producers. The next great mother was Amma ("grandmother"), who gave birth to the race of Churls, who thenceforth (not always "churlishly") conducted businesses and learned trades. The final mother figure of the story was Mothir herself, who produced the Jarls or leaders, the ones who hunted, fought, and attended school.

Edusa Roman goddess ruling the weaning of infants.

Egeria, Aegeria An early Italian goddess of wisdom and foresight whose name is still used for women advisers. She may have been a form of *Diana*, with whom she shared the sacred shrine at Nemi, from which *Vesta*'s virgins drew water for their rituals. She appeared in Roman legend as a semidivine creature, a water nymph enamored of the Roman king Numa Pompilius; she took him as her husband and thereafter served as his supernatural adviser. Egeria was the one who taught the correct rites for earth worship; she was the one who pronounced the first laws of the city. Later Egeria became a full-fledged divinity, worshiped by pregnant women desirous of easy delivery and (like many midwife-goddesses) responsible for foretelling the future of the newborn.

Egime Sumerian name for the earth mother.

Eileithyia, Ilithyia The Aegean birth-goddess, a spinner who created life's thread, Eileithyia was worshiped in pre-Hellenic Greece; later she was assimilated to the goddess *Artemis*. Though superseded, Eileithyia did not disappear; her name was used even into Roman times. Immeasurably ancient, she was said to have midwived the gods and goddesses of classical Greece. Some legends even call her the mother of Eros—not the frivolous later godling, but the primordial force of creation hatched from the world egg.

Eileithyia could curse a birthing mother by crossing her knees and clasping her hands; until she unfolded her body, the child would not enter the world of light. Dogs and horses were her symbols; the sacrifice of a dog assured that Eileithyia would sit with uncrossed knees during birth. Later peoples used this ancient goddess's name as a title of their own birth-goddess, and so Eileithyia came to be used of *Juno Lucina* and even *Hecate*.

107

Eingana   The people of the oldest continuing culture on the earth's face, the Australian natives, name Eingana the Mother as the creator, maker of all water, land, animals, and kangaroos. This huge snake-goddess still lives, they say, in the ocean, rising up occasionally to create yet more life.

At first, Eingana vomited living beings from her mouth. Then, dissatisfied with this method of birth, she swallowed them again. The primordial snake had no vagina; as her offspring grew inside her, the goddess swelled up. Eventually, tortured with the pregnancy, Eingana began to roll around and around. The god Barraiya saw her agony and speared her near the anus so that birth could take place as all creatures now give birth. From Eingana poured her reborn creatures, which were chased by a dingo and took on their earthly forms as they flew, ran, or hopped away.

The birth mother to these aboriginal people is also the death mother. They say Eingana holds a sinew of life attached to each of her creatures; when she lets it go, that life stops. If she herself should die, they say everything would cease to exist.

Eir   The Scandinavian goddess of mercy was the "best physician" or the "caring one," the youthful goddess Eir who sat upon her hill Lyfjaberg ("healing"), granting health to any woman who could climb to her. See **Frigg.**

Eireisone   The female personification of a Greek ritual object: a branch of olive wood, twined with wool and hung with fruits, which was carried in festivals by children with two living parents.

Ekash-Taka   Indian mother of the moon-god.

Ekhe-Urani   "Colorless one," the Southeast Asian Great Goddess.

Elat, Elath   Same as *Al-Lat* ("goddess"), applied to towns in the eastern Mediterranean where goddess worship was strong in pre-Christian days. See **Asherah.**

Ele, Eile   Pronounced "Ellie," this was the name of the sister of *Maeve.*

Electra   There were many Greek heroines of this name; most were notable for being the mother of someone or the sister of someone else. Most famous was the daughter of Queen *Clytemnestra.* This Electra plotted her mother's murder in revenge for the queen's murder of her father; her name is used to describe young women inappropriately dependent on their fathers. This character was, most scholars agree, a purely literary contrivance with no basis in the original myth.

Embla The first woman on earth was, according to the Scandinavians, an ash tree. (Some say she was an elder and that the ash tree formed the first man.) "Empty of force and empty of fate," Embla lay on the new earth. Into the wooden female form, the god Odin breathed a soul, as he did into her mate.

Emboq Sri "Bride Rice," a food-goddess of Java.

Emer This most desirable of Irish heroines was endowed with everything a woman could possess: wisdom, talent, and wit. Besides all that, she was lovely to look upon, and she pridefully acknowledged her own excellence. "I am," she told one suitor, "a Tara among women, the whitest of maidens, one who is gazed at but gazes not back; I am the untrodden way." That suitor was the hero Cuchulain, of whom she demanded heroic exploits before she would sleep with him, reasoning that her superior endowments warranted them.

Eos The Greek goddess of dawn, Eos was the daughter of two early light deities, Hyperion and *Thea*. The lovely winged creature drove a chariot hitched to four swift steeds, dragging light across the sky; she changed at midday into Hemera ("light of day") and later into the sunset, sometimes called Hesperide.

Eos had many lovers, often kidnapping handsome men to serve her needs. One was the gigantic Orion, a rather brutal human, who, because of his constant mistreatment of his wife *Merope*, was blinded by Merope's father and by the wine god Dionysus. In order to restore his sight, Orion was told to bathe his face in Eos's rays. She saw him standing on a hilltop and not only restored Orion's sight but stole him away for her lover. Orion never did remedy his violent ways, however, and was eventually removed to the stars for an offense against *Artemis*.

Another mortal lover was Tithonus, for whom Eos conceived so lasting an affection that she begged immortality for him. Alas for him, Eos forgot to add a request for eternal youth. Slowly Tithonus wizened, and Eos's love faded. She fled his bed, but took enough pity on her former lover to turn Tithonus into a cricket and install him in a little cage near her door, whence he could chirp good-bye to her as she left on her day's journey. See also **Hekt**.

Eostre, Ostara The early Anglo-Saxon name for spring's goddess survives today in the festival of rebirth, Easter, and in the mood encouraged by springtime, estrus. She was honored among the Germanic people with painted eggs, a tradition that survives today.

Epona, Bubona Epona was the name given to the horse-goddess in Celtic Gaul; her worship, widely popular in territories occupied by Rome, was eventually adopted by the Roman armies as well. Said to be the off-spring of a mare and a man, Epona could take the tangible forms of both parents. Sometimes, too, she appeared as a rushing river, which sug-gests that Epona was a fertility-goddess, often seen in Celtic culture as a water spirit. The sacred mare Epona appeared as the bestower of sovereignty in the ancient Celtic rituals of kingship, which may have included a rite of marriage with the mare-goddess. A few researchers see in the story of *Lady Godiva* a survival of this all-giving powerful goddess.

Erce In Slavic tradition, the earth mother Erce was honored by greeting the newly turned soil each spring and pouring milk, flour, and water into the furrows.

Eri of the Golden Hair A goddess of the Tuatha de Danaan, the magical divinities of early Ireland, Eri found a lover in an unusual way. She was a virgin until the day a silver boat traveling in the path of the sun arrived; it contained a man, shining like his boat, with whom Eri made love almost immediately. But the visitor stayed on shore only long enough to impregnate Eri with the beautiful god Bres, then left to return to his own people, leaving only a golden ring with the goddess as a token of his stay.

Erigone In some versions of the story of Queen *Clytemnestra* of Mycenae, Erigone was the faithful daughter of the queen and her lover Aegisthus: it was Erigone who brought her half-brother Orestes to trial for the mur-der of their mother. When he was acquitted, Erigone hanged herself, rather than live in a world that forgave matricide.

Erinyes Long before the Olympians ruled the territory we now call Greece, the people there recognized three immortal black maidens with ser-pent hair and poisonous blood that dripped from their eyes. Clad in gray, bearing brass-studded whips, baying and barking like bitches, they roamed the pre-Hellenic world in pursuit of those who dared offend the primordial laws of kinship. They were the "strong ones," the force that held a matriarchal world together, for these half-human women waited as punishment for anyone who dared commit the sac-rilege of spilling kindred blood. The dreaded Erinyes, the furious ones,

Javanese goddess; see Emboq. Sri, p. 109; Saning Sri, p. 304.
Field Museum of Natural History (Neg# 44448), Chicago.

hounded to death, like a tortured conscience, anyone who spilled such blood, painfully created by his maternal relatives, for kinship was traced through the mother.

There were three Erinyes, or there was one Erinys with three forms: *Alecto* ("unresting one"), *Megaera* ("envious anger"), and Tisiphone ("avenger"). They were born from the blood of the castrated sky-god Uranus where it touched the earth mother *Gaea*. Standing by the throne of the sun or in the dark world of Tartarus, these implacable goddesses could be stayed by neither sacrifice nor tears once their righteous anger was aroused. Nonetheless, those hoping to avert their gaze from minor misdeeds would lay by their sanctuaries black sheep and honeyed water, white doves and narcissus flowers.

The trinity of goddesses bore many names. As the Semnae, they were worshiped as "kindly ones," although they remained steadfastly just; when guilty conspirators sought their forgiveness by attaching themselves by a thread to the goddesses's statue, the Erinyes miraculously broke free, showing the Athenians that criminals deserved punishment. As the Dirae, they were "curses" personified. As *Maniae* or Furiae, they were the mad ones, the Furies. Most often they were called Erinyes, a force so instinctive and primeval that the Greeks assured each other, "Even dogs have their Erinyes."

The poet Aeschylus identified them with the helpful *Eumenides*, a theologically radical position, the trinities having been originally distinct. In the famous climax to Aeschylus's *Oresteia*, the laws of mother right—of which the Erinyes were the fiercest symbol—are shown giving way to the newer form of social organization imported into Greece by the patriarchal Indo-Europeans. Orestes, son of *Clytemnestra*, killed his mother in a vengeful fury; the Erinyes hounded him until they reached the temple of Apollo, where he took sanctuary. The first trial by jury was then held, with *Athene* presiding; the vote was tied.

Athene cast the deciding vote, against punishment of the matricide. The Erinyes were convulsed with anger at the decision, at having a morsel stolen from their plates. "Gods of the younger generation," they screamed, "you have ridden down the laws of elder times, torn them out of my hand." They threatened to ravage the land in retaliation, but Athene consoled them with promises of sacrifices and honor. Eventually they grew reconciled to the new order and were renamed Eumenides, taking on the name and identity of a triplet of goddesses who originally had little but number in common with the Erinyes. Allowed to keep their original function, the goddesses were thereafter to exercise their calling only at the behest of the Olympian divinities.

Eriskegal, Allatu, Allatum, Ereskigal, Ganzir, Irkalla In Sumerian theology, a vast black-haired woman slept naked in a palace of lapis lazuli in the afterlife, bringing the naked dead into herself. This goddess, Eriskegal, was another form of the earth mother known by so many names in the eastern Mediterranean: *Ishtar, Mami, Inanna*, and others.

Originally Eriskegal alone ruled the wilderness at the world's end, surrounded by rainbow gardens. But then the violent god Nergal invaded her territory. Eriskegal wanted peace. So she had intercourse with Nergal, thus imparting some of her wisdom to him and bringing him closer to equality with her—close enough, at least, that she henceforth shared her throne with him. They ruled together over Kigalla ("dead land"), living in the "House of Dust."

In art Eriskegal appeared as a lion-headed woman suckling lion cubs. She was also shown in a boat, kneeling on the horse of death and traversing the boundary river between her world and ours, gazing toward the offerings that the living place on its shores.

Eriu Ireland is called Erin in Gaelic, a word that means the "land of Eriu," the green isle's ancient earth-goddess. In old Ireland, there were two other goddesses, *Banba* and Folta, and the following story is told of the trinity.

Many tribes had invaded the island, conquered it, and assimilated its indigenous people. Last in prehistory to arrive on Ireland's shores were the sons of Milesius. First, they met Banba ("land unplowed for a year"), the sorceress queen. They promised the goddess that if allowed to pass, they would name the country after her. Banba stepped aside.

Second, they met Folta. They promised her, too, that the island would bear her name; again, the goddess let them pass. Third, the Milesians faced Eriu. As you looked at her, the goddess sometimes appeared as a huge beautiful woman, sometimes as a long-beaked gray crow. A masterful magician, she lived on a hill in Ireland's center; as the goddess aged, her hill grew in size. Eriu could pick up clods from her mountain and fling them at invading armies; the earth turned into warriors and Eriu invariably won the ensuing battle.

But the Milesians, though stunned by the goddess's size and obvious power, were also magicians. They negotiated a truce with Eriu—offering, of course, to name the island after her. This time they were too frightened of her power to break their promise, and Erin remains today the land of Eriu.

Ermutu Egyptian birth-goddess, similar to *Meskhoni*.

Erua "Conception" or "pregnant," a name for *Mami*.

Eshara   The Chaldean goddess of the productive fields, she was also a war-goddess and symbolized the armed defense of property that follows private ownership of land.

Ess Euchen   When the Irish warrior Cuchulain killed Ess Euchen's three sons, this fierce mother turned herself into an aged crone and ambushed the murderer on a narrow mountain path. She asked for the right of passage and Cuchulain, deferring to her sex and age, stepped off the path, clinging to the road with his toes as he hung over the cliff. Ess Euchen immediately stomped hard on his toes, hoping to send him tumbling to his death. However, Cuchulain had been trained by the warrior-goddess *Scathach*; using one of Scathach's magical jumps, he leaped up and killed the woman.

Esther, Ester, in Hebrew, **Hadassah**   It is now well established that this Old Testament heroine was the goddess *Ishtar* in thin disguise. Start from the clues in her name: in Aramaic, Esther is the word for Ishtar; in Persian, it means "star," and Ishtar was the goddess of the morning and evening star. Even the woman's Hebrew name, Hadassah, means "myrtle," a tree with star-shaped flowers.

In addition, the Book of Esther—recorded apparently in the 3rd or 2nd century B.C.—is the only one in which Jehovah's name does not appear. Instead, the book relates the unlikely story that a Persian queen, *Vashti* (coincidentally, the name of an Elamite goddess), and a prime minister, Haman (also coincidentally, an Elamite god), were replaced by a pair of Hebrew cousins, Esther and Mordecai. By this time, it should be no surprise that Mordecai too had a namesake: none other than the Babylonian hero Marduk (Hebrew, Morodach), the cousin of Ishtar. Marduk fought dragons; Mordecai dreamt of them.

In essence, the Book of Esther records the overthrow of the Elamite pantheon and its replacement by that of the Babylonians. Small wonder, then, that for many centuries the book was considered to be of questionable orthodoxy. Doubts somehow were set to rest, however, and the book is now part of authorized Judeo-Christian belief.

Estiu   Warrior and bird-goddess of ancient Ireland.

Estsanatlehi, Ahsonnutli   "Turquoise woman" was the Navaho sky-goddess, wife of the sun; she lived in a turquoise palace at the western horizon, where each night she received her luminous husband. Sister (or twin or double) of *Yolkai Estsan*, the moon's wife, Estsanatlehi was able to make herself young each time she began to age, thus her name, which means the "self-renewing one."

Here is her story: the ancestral goddess *Atse Estsan*, discovering Estsanatlehi on the ground beneath a mountain, reared her to be the savior of the earth's people. When she was grown, Estsanatlehi met a young man; each day they went to the woods to make love. When her parents looked on the ground and saw only one set of footprints, they knew their daughter had taken the sun as a lover.

Delighted at the honor granted their family, they were delighted again when Estsanatlehi gave birth to twins, who grew so miraculously that eight days after birth they were men, ready to seek their father. But when they found his house, the twins found another woman there. Angry at the intrusion, she threatened them with their father's anger as well.

Undeterred, the twins remained and won from their father magic weapons, which they needed to clear the earth of monsters. This they did. After dancing with their mother in celebration, the twins built Estsanatlehi a magnificent home at the sky's end, so that the sun could visit her again.

But the twins' wars with the monsters had depopulated the earth. Estsanatlehi brushed the dust from her breasts. From the white flour that fell from her right breast and the yellow meal from her left, she made paste and molded a man and a woman. Placing them beneath a magical blanket, Estsanatlehi left them. The next morning they were alive and breathing, and Estsanatlehi blessed the creation. For the next four days, the pair reproduced constantly, forming the four great Navaho clans. But the creative urge of Estsanatlehi was not fulfilled. She made four more groups of people, this time from the dust of her nipples, and the women of these clans were thereafter famous for their nipples.

Feeling her creation to be complete, Estsanatlehi retired to her turquoise palace from which she continued to bestow blessings on her people: seasons, plants and food, and the tender sprouts of spring. Only four monsters survived her sons' wars on evil: age, winter, poverty, and famine, which she allowed to live on so that her people would treasure her gifts the more. See **Glispa**.

Etain The "swift one" was one of the early sun-goddesses of ancient Ireland and—like other Celtic solar divinities—was also a horse-goddess, a divine mare no mortal steed could outrun. Her worshipers said Etain lived in the sacred hill of Eochaid Airem, or at the entrance to the underworld, Bri Leith, in a *griane* or house open to the sun.

The most famous story of Etain told how she, though a powerful goddess of the de Danaan tribe, nonetheless fell under the power of the fairy queen Fuamnach, who transformed her into a purple fly. For seven years Etain buzzed bewitched through the world. Then she fell into a cup, was swallowed by a woman, and was reborn in human form. The reborn Etain wed the king of Ireland, then took his brother as a lover. The fairy king Midir, to bring Etain back to the supernatural world, disguised himself as her husband, surprised her with her lover, and demanded that she return home with him. Then, resuming his original form, King Midir flew her off to Bri Leith at the sun's rising point, where they are said to still live happily today.

Another Etain, called Etain of the Fair Hair, was a fairy woman of the hill Ben Edar; married to a mortal, she died of grief when he was killed. Yet another Etain—although possibly all are forms of the original goddess—was the ruler of Beare Island, a well-known ritual spot in Bantry Bay, off the west coast of Ireland.

Ethne, Ethlenn Originally, Ethne was a primitive Irish goddess who lived on nothing but the milk of a sacred cow from India; Ethne was guarded by a demon who staved off any approaching men. She came into later legend as a princess of the Fomorians, the early Irish sea deities; her people offered Ethne to the later gods, the Tuatha de Danaan, in an attempt to unite the peoples. Ethne ("sweet nutmeat") wedded Diancecht of the Tuatha and gave birth to the god Lug.

Another story has it that Ethne was locked in a high tower where no man could reach her because of a prophecy that her sons would kill her father. But a hero, MacKineely, disguised himself as a woman to gain entrance to the tower; he slept with Ethne, but was killed by her father for his rashness. In this variation of the tale, Ethne's sons met a tragic fate, all dying in infancy.

Etugen Ancient name for a Mongol earth-goddess.

Eumenides The "kindly ones" were early Greek goddesses of the underworld, who pushed edible plants through the ground as gifts to humanity. By extension, the Eumenides ruled human reproduction and the establishment of families. Originally distinct from the *Erinyes*, they were later assimilated into that triad of goddesses, and the names became interchangeable. Their sacred cave on the Athenian Acropolis became the preserve of the Erinyes as well. There, in the sanctuary of kindness, a court met in darkness to discuss matters of state. In darkness, too, the rituals of these goddesses were held at low-lying altars, celebrated by worshipers wearing purple robes and bearing torches.

Europa The "wide-eyed one," the moon-goddess after whom the subcontinent of Europe is named, was originally the mother-goddess of Crete.

Europa owned a magic spear that never missed its target and a monstrous brass warrior that protected her island while she rode the night on her servant, the lunar bull. But Europa's guard failed to repulse the invading Greeks, who brought their own gods to Crete and rewrote Europa's legend substantially. As they told it, she was a mere Phoenician princess, and the lunar bull was the sky-god Zeus, who spied the lovely woman bathing and carried her to Crete to rape her. Abandoned there, she married well and bore three famous kings of Crete: Minos, Sarpedon, and Rhadamanthus. That the Greek tale has Europa born in Phoenicia suggests to many scholars a Near Eastern origin for Cretan culture and religion.

Eurydice   There were many Greek heroines of this name, which means "wide-judging," but the most famous was the spouse of the singer Orpheus. When she died, he was so stricken with grief that he followed her to the kingdom of *Persephone*. To reclaim her, he charmed the queen of the dead with a song begging for Eurydice's release. Granted that, Orpheus was instructed not to look behind as he led his lover to the light. But he could not restrain his curiosity and, looking back, saw only the shade of Eurydice disappearing forever. Some scholars, notably Robert Graves, remind us that one Eurydice was an underworld serpent-goddess to whom human males were sacrificed; whether this goddess and Orpheus's beloved were once the same is unclear, though the singer was killed by women shortly after his return to the earth's surface.

Eurynome   The most ancient of Greek goddesses, she rose naked from primordial chaos and instantly began to dance: a dance that separated light from darkness and sea from sky. Whirling in a passion of movement, Eurynome created behind herself a wind that grew lustful toward her. Turning to face it, she grasped the wind in her hands, rolled it like clay into a serpent, and named it Ophion.

Then Eurynome had intercourse with the wind serpent and, transforming herself into a dove, laid the universal egg from which creation hatched. Installing herself high above the new earth on Mt. Olympus, Eurynome looked down on it complacently. But Ophion, her own creation, bragged that he had been responsible for all that was tangible. Forthwith Eurynome kicked out his teeth and threw him into an underworld dungeon.

There was another goddess of this name—or perhaps the later Eurynome was an elaboration of the creator-goddess. Said by the Greeks to rule the sea, she may have been the same goddess as—or part of a trinity with—the great sea rulers *Tethys* and *Thetis*. The "wide-ruling one," Eurynome had a temple in wild Arcadia, difficult to reach and open only once a year. If pilgrims penetrated the sanctuary, they found the image of the goddess as a woman with a snake's tail, tied with golden chains. In this form, Eurynome of the sea was said to have been the mother of all pleasure, embodied in the beautiful triplets, the *Graces*.

Evaki Along the Amazon, people said that this goddess of darkness had a pot with a lid; when she closed the lid of the heavens, the sun was left outside. When she took the lid off the pot again, the sky filled with daylight.

Eve, in Hebrew, **Hawwah** The "mother of all living," also called Ishah. Familiar to us from Hebrew mythology, Eve is called in the Book of Genesis the first man's *'ezer*, usually translated "helper" or "helpmeet." But the masculine word is read, in other biblical contexts, as "instructor." Immediately we know there is more to Eve than the wicked wife of the Bible. And indeed, in folklore and legend, we find another figure, a more complex Eve clearly related to the ancestor-goddesses of the ancient eastern Mediterranean.

Many writers have pointed out that the biblical creation myth actually contains two contradictory stories. In one, Jehovah created Adam and Eve (or possibly *Lilith*) simultaneously. But a second story follows, in which Eve was drawn from Adam's rib—currently the more familiar version.

Slavic folklore—probably merging Eve with a similar goddess from pre-Christian mythology—offers some interesting variants on the conventional tale. In Bulgaria, it was said that Adam and Eve were created, naked and blind, at the same instant; a billy goat told Eve to climb an apple tree and take a bite of the fruit, whereupon her blindness disappeared. In another Balkan story, Eve was created by the devil, who borrowed a quill Jehovah had used to breathe life into Adam and invigorated his female creation; although Satan's breath could not enliven Eve, the remnant of divine breath did so. Similarly, a Turkish and Mongol legend says that Edji (Eve) was naked and hairy but that when she touched the fruit, all her apelike hair fell away.

Turning back to the Hebrew mythology from which Eve sprang, we find again that folklore sheds an interesting light on her character. Jewish folklore says that Adam, certain that Eve was his inferior, did not trust her with the truth about Jehovah's prohibition; instead, over-cautious, he told his companion that Jehovah had forbidden them, on pain of death, even to touch the Tree of Life. The serpent—said to have stood upright and to look just like a man—shoved Eve against the tree.

She brushed against one of the dropping fruits. Satan then argued, convincingly enough, that Jehovah had lied, that the tree was perfectly safe. Seduced by reason, Eve ate the famous fruit. Then she gave it not only to Adam but to all the animals of Paradise, bringing death to all except the phoenix, the magical bird who refused to taste. (See **Gula.**)

This Eve has much in common with the great birth-and-death goddesses of every culture—*Ishtar, Kali, Tlazoltéotl*—and seems, like them, to symbolize the knowledge that woman, by bearing life, brings death into our world as well. But in Jewish legend, Eve brings us rebirth as well. The last part of the tale—rarely included in current tellings—shows Eve traveling from earth to Jehovah's throne while Adam lies near death. She pleads for his life, offering to take half Adam's pain on herself. She eventually draws Jehovah's pity. Although for their sin the first human couple (and their descendants) were still sentenced to die, Jehovah promised Eve that they would be reborn. Thus Eve, like other mother-goddesses of her area, traveled beyond this world to beg the boon of rebirth—and won it.

After Adam died, Eve (like *Demeter* or Ishtar) wept incessantly for days and nights and more days. Finally she rose from her grief to teach her children the first grave rites. A prophet, she foresaw the afterlife clearly and was able to design appropriate passage rituals.

About Eve's children, some Jewish legends say that Cain and Abel, conceived by Eve in intercourse with the serpent, whom she believed to be an angel—an echo of the myths of mother-goddesses impregnated by numinous animals common in Greek mythology. Eve, foreseeing that Cain would kill Abel, named her younger son "born only to die."

And so, behind the shriveled and guilt-laden figure familiar from Judeo-Christian mythology, we find the powerful Great Goddesses of the earth, progenitors of the race and prime divinities of the tribes of the ancient Near East. Like Eve, they were confidantes of the snakes of rebirth; like her, they were the mothers of humanity. Like her, too, they bore responsibility for the downfall of their lovers. And like Eve, they were the saviors of humankind, seeking and winning the prize of resurrection.

Ezili-Freda-Dahomey The *loa* ("spirit") of sensuality in Haitian voodoo, Ezili is generous to the point of extravagance with her worshipers, and expects the same in return.

Fachea   Irish goddess of poetry.

Fama, Pheme   The Roman and Greek goddess of fame.

Fand   The greatest of the fairy queens of Ireland, Fand was the daughter of the sea and ruler of the beautiful Land-over-Wave, from which she flew as a seabird to our world, usually to entrap human lovers.

Fangge   The wood wife of the Tyrol was said to live within trees, rather like the *Dryads* of the Greeks; to kill her, you twisted a tree's branches or sliced off the bark of the trunk. Fangge could be very bloodthirsty, however, if she survived the attempted murder; an assailant would not be safe in the woodlands after such an act. Fangge liked fresh-baked bread and would steal it when possible; of course, loaves could always be filled with caraway seeds, which the forest folk detested.

Feithline   This seer who lived at the hill in western Ireland called the Gateway to Hell, or *Cruachen*, appeared to Queen *Maeve*, attired in a golden crown with seven burnt-gold braids hanging down her shoulders, to foretell the queen's death.

Felicitas   "Good fortune," personified as a Roman goddess in the 2nd century B.C.; distinct from *Fortuna*.

Feng Pho-Pho   Riding herd on the winds of China, Feng Pho-Pho had a tiger for a steed and clouds for her roadway. On calm days, it was thought that the old woman had rounded up the winds and stuffed them into the bag she carried over her shoulder.

Fengi and **Mengi, Fenya, Menya**   When a child in ancient Scandinavia asked "Why is the sea so salty?," her parents had a ready answer. Once, they would say, in the days of the heroic king Frodi, there were two magical female giants who worked a mill called Grotti. Fengi and Mengi were the only beings strong enough to turn the giant millstone that magically produced peace and plenty for Frodi's land.

The king, anxious for endless prosperity, kept them working constantly, letting them rest only as long as it took them to sing a song. One night, angry and exhausted, they sang a magical charm that caused Frodi's death at the hand of the sea king, Mysing. But Mysing set the giants to work again, this time grinding salt—of which they ground so much that the entire kingdom of the sea was filled with it.

Feronia Far from the growing cities of Italy, this solitary goddess made her simple home in woodlands like those at Campania or at the foot of mountains like Soracte. Orchards and fields, volcanoes and thermal springs were her abode, for she was a fire-goddess ruling the heat of reproductive life as well as the fires beneath the earth's crust (see **Maia**). At her festivals on the Ides of November, great fairs were held and first fruits offered; freedom was bestowed on slaves; men walked barefoot across coals to the cheering of crowds.

The energy of Feronia could not be contained within cities, and her sanctuaries were therefore in the open country. So unsociable was she that when her Campanian forest shrine once burned and her worshipers planned to remove her temple to the safety of a town, the goddess instantly restored the charred trees to leafy greenness.

Fideal The water demon of the Highland Scots, Fideal was one of those seductive maidens who, after luring their lovers into the water, dragged them under to drown.

Fides Often dismissed by modern writers as a personified abstraction, "good faith," this goddess was in fact one of the most ancient divinities of Rome and, like the Greek *Themis*, personified the very basis of human community. Without her influence, no two people could trust each other long enough to cooperate; Fides was the guardian of integrity and honesty in all dealings between individuals and groups.

Once each year, on October 1, Rome's three major priests gathered at her sanctuary to offer sacrifice, their right hands wrapped in white cloth. The solemn ritual was carefully guarded from ill omen, for there was no feast more sacred than that which sanctified the bonds of trust among the worshipers of Fides.

Finchoem Irish goddesses often had unusual ways of conceiving, and Finchoem was no exception: she swallowed a worm from a magic well, hoping it would impregnate her with a hero. Indeed it did; his name

121

was Conall, and he figures in Irish heroic legend.

Findabar   Her name derives from the same word as *Guinevere* in English; this Irish heroine was the daughter of the fiery Queen *Maeve* and her consort, the king Aillil. Aillil opposed Findabar's choice of a husband, but Findabar simply overruled him and married the beautiful mortal named Froach.

Finncaev   "Fair love," a powerful fairy queen of Ireland.

Fiongalla   The "fair-cheeked one" lived in the far southwestern corner of Ireland, where legend says that she was held in enchantment by the powerful Druid Amerach from Ulster, who grew no older as years passed. She made Fiongalla vow never to sleep with a man until one brought magical yew berries, holly boughs, and marigolds from the earthly seat of power. Amerach lost her power over Fiongalla when a hero named Feargal actually managed to perform the almost-impossible task.

Fionnuala, Finda   The story of Fionnuala, one of the most famous of Irish myths, began when the woman Aebh married the Irish king Lir. She died in childbirth, after bearing Fionnuala and three brothers. Lir married again: the sorceress *Aife*, who, jealous of her stepchildren's claim on Lir's affections, decided to kill them. Aife feigned illness in order to hatch her plot, then sent the children on the long trek to Connaught, their mother's wilderness home. While they were traveling, Aife cast her spell on them. The children, shedding their human forms, rose into the air as swans.

Aife's magic was so strong that there was no one in Ireland who could free the children of Lir for 900 years. But King Bobh, Aebh's father and Fionnuala's grandfather, discerned what had happened and vowed to punish Aife. He trapped her and asked what shape she hated most. "That," Aife responded, "of the demon of the air." Instantly she was changed to one, and in that form—or, it is said, as a crane—she still haunts the Irish countryside.

Meanwhile Fionnuala and her brothers, who sang so sweetly that people fell enchanted to the ground as they flew overhead, remained trapped. Once, separated from her brothers by a fierce storm on the Sea of Moyle, Fionnuala thought she had lost the enchanted boys. Her lament—written in English in Thomas Moore's "Silent, O Moyle"—was one of the saddest and most lovely laments in Ireland. But it proved happily unnecessary, for the siblings were reunited on the northern Irish coast.

Fionnuala ("fair-shouldered one") nurtured her brothers during almost a millennium of banishment from human form. Finally, during the reign of Queen Decca, they were freed from enchantment and, crumpling into impossibly aged people, died almost immediately. As old Irish tradition demanded—though the countryside had been Christianized during their enchantment—Fionnuala and her brothers were buried standing upright together in the grave, as they had been in the sky.

Fithir   The younger daughter of an Irish king, Fithir drew the attention of the king of Leinster, in southeastern Ireland. But her older sister Darine was still unmarried, and their father refused to let the younger girl wed before her. The king of Leinster then kidnapped Darine and trapped her, together with nine handmaidens, in a tower in the woods. He returned to the palace at Tara, claiming Darine was dead. Fithir was then, although mourning for her sister, free to wed.

Years later, while she was wandering in the woods, Fithir happened upon her beloved, sorely missed Darine. The shock killed Fithir; Darine, seeing her sister dead, killed herself with weeping.

Flidais   Almost every old European culture had a goddess who roamed the woodlands, owned all animals, and embodied the fruitfulness and freedom of the wilderness. Among the Irish, she was called Flidais, the Stag-Mistress who roamed the earth in a chariot drawn by supernatural deer. She possessed a cow whose milk supplied 30 people in one night; she also called the wild creatures of the countryside her cattle. Flidais had one daughter, Fland, a lake maiden who sat beneath her waters and lured mortals to herself—and death.

Flora   Apparently forgetting that flowers are the sex organs of plants, most mythographers express shock and puzzlement that the blooming Flora was the patron of prostitutes, worshiped in public orgies from April 28 to May 3. But this very ancient Roman goddess was the embodiment of the flowering of all nature, including human nature. Thus it was presumed that the best way to honor Flora was to pass obscene medallions around, scatter beans and lupines, and make love to passersby.

The female body was especially honored at the Floralia, the festival of nude women celebrated until the 3rd century A.D., when Roman authorities grew prudish and demanded garments on the revelers. This Floralia was not frivolous partying, for Flora was the queen of all plants, including edible ones—for flowers lead to fruit as intercourse to conception, a basic truth that the Romans recognized by calling Flora the secret patron of Rome, without whose help the city would die

Fons   Roman goddess of fountains.

Fornax   In ancient Rome, where every action had its divinity, this goddess ruled a vital act: the baking of bread.

Fortuna   In early Italy, this was the name of the goddess who controlled the destiny of every human being. No mere "Lady Luck," she was the energy that drove men and women to reproduce themselves, a truly irresistible Fors (her later Latin name). Fortuna was originally "she who brings," the goddess who permitted the fertilization of humans, animals, and plants; thus was she worshiped by women desiring pregnancy and gardeners seeking bumper crops. Even when she grew into the monumental figure of Tyche, the destiny of the human community, she still retained her earlier reproductive function as Fortuna Virilis, the goddess who made women irresistible to men, who was worshiped by a regular invasion of the men's public baths by luck-seeking Roman women.

Frau Holle, Frau Holda   Throughout German, Austrian and Swiss folktales we find this former goddess demoted, together with her twin *Perchta*, to a witch-woman. Frau Holle was the more pleasant of the two: sunshine streamed from her hair when she combed it, snow covered the earth when she shook a feather comforter, and rain fell when she threw away laundry water. She was a splendid white lady who appeared each noon to bathe in the fountain, from which children were said to be born. She lived in a cave in the mountain or in a well, and people could visit her by diving into it.
   She rode on the wind in a wagon. Once she had to have a broken linchpin repaired, and the man who helped her later found that shavings of wood from the project had turned to gold. In addition to gold, she rewarded good people with useful gifts, such as the invention of flax and spinning.
   Her feast day was celebrated on winter solstice, the Jul, when she checked the quality of each spinner's work. A good spinner would wake to find Frau Holle had left her a single golden thread, but sloppy ones found their work tangled, their spinning wheels shattered or burnt.
   The period between December 25 and January 6—the "twelve days of Christmas"—were sacred to Frau Holle; during that time she traveled the world in her wagon. No rotary actions were allowed; sleighs were used instead of wagons, and all meal-grinding had to cease. Her twin Perchta was, if not welcomed, at least acknowledged at the same season. See **Perchta.**

Fraud Roman goddess of treachery.

Freya, Frejya Far from the ancient Near East, home of the lustful warrior *Anat*, we find a goddess who is virtually her double: a Scandinavian mistress of all the gods who was also the ruler of death. Leader of the *Valkyries*, war's corpse-maidens, this goddess was also the one to whom love prayers were most effectively addressed. The goddess who gave her name to the sixth day of our week, Freya was one form of the "large-wombed earth," another version of which her people called *Frigg* the heavenly matron. Here was how Freya appeared to her worshipers: the most beautiful of all goddesses, she wore a feathered cloak over her magical amber necklace as she rode through the sky in a chariot drawn by cats, or sometimes on a huge golden-bristled boar who may have been her own brother, the fertility god Frey.

When Freya was in Asgard, the home of the deities, she lived on Folkvangr ("people's plain") in a vast palace called Sessrumnir ("rich in seats"). She needed such a huge palace to hold the spirit hordes she claimed on the battlefields, for the first choice of the dead was hers, with leftovers falling to Odin. Like *Persephone,* the Greek death queen, Freya was also the spirit of the earth's fertility; like Persephone too, Freya was absent from earth during autumn and winter, a departure that caused the leaves to fall and the earth to wear a mourning cloak of snow. And like *Hecate,* an alternate form of Persephone, Freya was the goddess of magic, the one who first brought the power of sorcery to the people of the north.

Despite her connection with death, Freya was never a terrifying goddess, for the Scandinavians knew she was the essence of sexuality. Utterly promiscuous, she took all the gods as her love—including the wicked Loki, who mated with her in the form of a flea—but her special favorite was her brother Frey, recalling Anat's selection of her brother Baal as playmate. But Freya had a husband, too, an aspect of Odin named Odr; he was the father of her daughter *Hnossa* ("jewel"). When Odr left home to wander the earth, Freya shed tears of amber. But she soon followed Odr, assuming various names as she sought him: here she was Mardol, the beauty of light on water, there Horn, the linen-woman; sometimes she was Syr, the sow, other times Gefn, the generous one. But always she was "mistress," for that is the meaning of her own name, and a particularly appropriate double-entendre it proves in her case. See **Gollveig, Gondul.**

Frigg Scholars and mythographers still argue whether Frigg was the same as, or different from, the goddess *Freya* (the same argument would probably not rage over the god Jehovah and his son). Whatever the understanding of the people who worshiped them—whether the Scandinavians distinguished the two goddesses from each other or saw them as aspects of the same female energy—Frigg unquestionably embodied a different aspect of womanhood from Freya. They were as alike, and as different, as mother and daughter; if they were identical, it was in the way that Frigg was identical to her mother, the great earth herself, Fyorgyn.

And who, really, could confuse the White Lady of Midsummer, the flaxen-haired matron Frigg ("bearer") with the promiscuous battle maiden Freya? The goddesses were distinct in their symbols and in the images of womanhood they reflected. Freya may have been the favorite goddess of lovers, but the overall rulership of Asgard, the home of the gods, was granted to the motherly Frigg, named as the primary goddess in the famous compilation of Scandinavian mythology called the eddas. "Frigg," claimed the compiler, Snorri Sturluson, "comes before any." He described her as a quiet but knowing goddess, dressed in the plumage of hawks and falcons, who spent her days in her home Fensalir ("sea-hall"), surrounded by the goddesses who were actually forms of herself: the physician *Eir*, the wise *Saga*, the virginal *Gefjon*, the secretive *Fulla*, and others.

The story told of Frigg is strikingly like that of *Ishtar*, *Cybele* and other Near Eastern earth-goddesses whose son, the vegetation-god, dies through his mother's will. In the Scandinavian story, Balder was not the lover of his mother, Frigg, as Attis was to Cybele; rather, he was said to be married to *Nana*, a goddess with no identity of her own whose name resembles that of Attis's mother. (Some scholars believe that the entire story migrated north from its original home in the Mediterranean, so similar is the Scandinavian tale to the southern version.) Frigg, the story goes, loved her son Balder so much that she extracted a promise from all earth's creatures that they would never harm him. The most loved god became the source of great sport at Asgard; the divinities used to gather and throw darts and rocks and arrows at Balder and were entertained by the way the weapons glanced off without harming the beautiful god.

But wicked Loki was disgusted with the sport. His envy of Balder made him sick with fury. So he disguised himself as an old woman and approached the spot where the gods were throwing darts at Balder. Spotting Frigg, who sat calmly watching, he asked if she was not concerned for his safety. Frigg answered, of course, that she'd seen to it: nothing on earth would hurt her son. Nothing? Loki inquired carefully. Well, the goddess admitted, there was that little sprig of mistletoe. It had been just a baby when she'd been extracting promises, too small to hurt anything . . .

Loki was off like a shot, gathering the mistletoe and forming it into a sharp arrow. This he placed in the hand of the blind god Hoder, convincing him to take part in the sport. The arrow found its way to its mark, and Balder dropped dead. He went off to the realm of *Hel*, accompanied by Nana, who died of heartbreak at her husband's death. Frigg organized a rescue effort, which meant convincing every creature on earth to weep for Balder's return. And all did, save a strange female giant who turned out to be Loki in disguise. And thus Frigg lost Balder, not to be freed until a son of *Rind* had been born and had matured into a hero. See **Gna, Hlin.**

Fuji   On all continents, people have seen volcanoes as female forces, hailed them as goddesses: *Aetna* in Italy, *Pele* in Hawaii, and *Chuginadak* in the Aleutians are among the many female divinities of earthly fire. The aboriginal Japanese Ainus, too, saw volcanic fire as female, naming their chief divinity Fuji, goddess of the famous mountain that bears her name.

Now the highest mountain in Japan, Fuji was once almost the same height as nearby Mt. Hakusan, wherein a god lived. A dispute arose about which was, in fact, the higher mountain, and the Amida Buddha invented an ingenious way to measure: he connected the two peaks with a long pipe and poured water in one end. Alas for the proud goddess, the water fell on her head. Her humiliation didn't last long, however. Fuji forthwith struck Mt. Hakusan eight blows, creating the eight peaks of today's mountain.

Fulgora   Roman goddess of lightning.

Fulla, Volla   From her name we get our word for abundance, and this Scandinavian goddess embodied the fullness of the fruitful earth. She was a servant of *Frigg* (and probably another version of that Great Goddess), the one who carried the coffer in which Frigg kept her riches. She was pictured as a young woman with long, full hair bound at the temple with a golden band.

Fu-Pao   It is customary in most countries to ascribe a miraculous conception to culture heroes, and the Yellow Emperor of China was no exception. His mother, a well-traveled intellectual, sat outdoors one spring night watching an unearthly light play across the sky. Soon Fu-Pao found herself pregnant. Her child Huang-Ti gestated for two years—another common phenomenon among heroes.

Furrina   The prominence of this ancient Italian goddess is obvious from the fact that—although by Cicero's time no one knew what Furrina represented—one of the 12 Roman priesthoods was dedicated to her. She had a feast, the Furrinalia, on July 25; some conjecture she was one of the Furies, goddesses of vengeance. See **Erinyes.**

Fylgja, Fylgukona (pl.)   A family's guardian spirit was called by this name in Iceland and other parts of Scandinavia; sometimes the spirit was called Haminga. Though in some senses the Fylgukona resembled the goddesses called *Disir*, the former were never actually worshiped. The Fylgukona rarely appeared to human sight; when they did, it betokened misfortune; some scholars contend that they were external souls, visible only when death was nigh. (See **Banshee**). But some legends consider them to be protective as well as ominous spirits of the future in either good or unfortunate form.

·G·

Gaea, Gaia, Ge   In the beginning, the Greeks said, there was only formless chaos: light and dark, sea and land, blended in a shapeless pudding. Then chaos settled into form, and that form was the huge Gaea, the deep-breasted one, the earth. She existed before time began, for Time was one of her children. In the timeless spans before creation, she existed, to herself and of herself alone.

But finally Gaea desired love, and for this purpose she made herself a son: Uranus, the heaven, who arched over his mother and satisfied her desire. Their mating released Gaea's creative force, and she began to produce innumerable creatures, both marvelous and monstrous. Uranus hated and envied Gaea's other children, so the primeval mother kept them hidden from his destructiveness.

Eventually, however, her dark and crowded womb grew too heavy to endure. So Gaea created a new element: gray adamant. And from it she fashioned a new tool, never known before in her creation: a jagged-toothed sickle. With this Gaea armed her offspring. Cronos, her son Time, took the weapon from his mother's hand and hid himself.

Soon Uranus came, drawing a dark-sky blanket over himself as he approached to mount his mother-lover. Then his brother, his son Cronos, sprang into action, grasping Uranus's genitals and sawing them off with the rough blade. Blood fell in a heavenly rain on Mother Gaea. So fertile was she that even the blood of the mutilated sky impregnated her. The *Erinyes* sprang up; so did Giants; and so did the ash-tree nymphs, the *Meliae*, humanity's ancestors.

This was the familiar creation story that the ancient Greeks told their children. Even after the earth mother had been supplanted as the primary divinity by the invading Olympians, the Greeks worshiped Gaea's power with barley and honey cakes placed at sacred openings in her surface. At such fissures, too, gifted people would read the will of the Great Mother, for she was through all ages the "primeval prophet" who inspired the oracles at Delphi, Dodona, and elsewhere. And it was to Gaea—even in the days when Zeus ruled the pantheon—that the

Greeks swore their most sacred oaths, thus recognizing her theological sovereignty. See **Demeter.**

Galatea   There were two figures by this name in Greek mythology, one of whom was a minor sea-goddess whose legend revolves around the two men who desired her. The more familiar Galatea appeared in the story of Pygmalion, a man afraid of the desires of mortal women but devoted to the static beauty of statuary. He especially lusted after the pale marble form of a statue of *Aphrodite* herself and carved an ivory statue of the goddess, with which he used to sleep. Such unnatural love was distasteful to Aphrodite, who encouraged the free and generous sharing of physical love.

Aphrodite cursed Pygmalion by constantly increasing his desire for the ivory statue. It could not, of course, return his affection, neither could his love find satisfaction against its hard thighs. Driven to despair, Pygmalion finally threw himself upon Aphrodite's mercy. Touched, the goddess breathed life into the statue, which came alive as Galatea. The lovers quickly produced a child, a daughter whom they named *Paphos* in honor of the promiscuous Aphrodite, who bore this name and shared it with her most active worshipers.

Galiana   This Etruscan heroine saved her city—today called Viterbo—from a Roman invasion by the simple expedient of appearing naked on the battlements. Her appearance had a magical effect on the Roman legions, which fell back in disarray at this vision of female courage.

Gamlat   Babylonian goddess of whom little is known except that she was assimilated into the mighty figure of *Ishtar.*

Gamsu   Wise Chaldean sea-goddess which merged with *Zarpandit.*

Ganga   The Hindu mother of rivers once lived in heaven with her sister, the virginal Uma. When sea-dwelling demons harassed the earth, the sage Agastya swallowed the ocean where they hid. Agastya got rid of the demons, but the earth was left parched and dry; such was the heat in the sage's stomach that the waters evaporated immediately.

Because of the prayers of her people, the heavenly water-goddess Ganga threw herself down to earth. Unbroken, Ganga's power could have washed away the world; but the god Shiva received her torrent on his head and saved the earth. Henceforth the goddess, embodied in the sacred river Ganges, flowed through India.

Some said that Ganga remained in heaven as well, as the celestial river we call the Milky Way; another part of the Ganges flowed under the earth. The intersection of the three Ganges at Benares was considered to be Ganga's most sacred spot. There people daily washed themselves in the purifying waters. Once a year pilgrims traveled—still travel—to avail themselves of Ganga's promise to wash away 10 sins from each of a bather's last 10 lives. And many a devout Hindu seeks to die immersed in Ganga—for the goddess, who has no human form, actually lives in her river—and the goddess then ensures instant freedom from both punishment and reincarnation.

One of the greatest of Hindu goddesses, Ganga appears often in groupings with other powerful divinities: as a pair with Uma; as a trinity with the other river-goddesses, *Sarasvati* and Yauni; as a fivefold group with Sarasvati, *Laksmi, Durga, Savitri,* all as aspects of *Devi* ("the Goddess") of *Prakriti* ("earth"). Her role in any of these groupings is as bestower of health, happiness, fertility, and material wealth.

Ganymeda   Originally the goddess who served ambrosia and nectar at Olympian feasts, she was later split in two. Her name and her position as bearer of immortal food and liquid were granted to an invented figure, Ganymede, a mortal boy elevated to heaven to replace her. But her other attributes remained in Greek theology under the guise of *Hebe.*

Ganzir   Semitic name for *Eriskegal.*

Gatamdug   The mother-goddess of the Tigris area, counselor to kings and interpreter of dreams, eventually assimilated into *Gula.*

Gauri   Because Hindu philosophy recognizes that divinity is ultimately indivisible, all goddesses are called aspects of *Devi,* or simply "the Goddess." Despite this philosophy, however, Indian culture provides innumerable goddess names that seem remarkably like separate divinities. To explain away this apparent contradiction, Gauri ("golden one") is said to be a form of the mighty *Durga;* before she made her reputation as a warrior, Durga was Gauri, the golden sky virgin. But sometimes Gauri is called *Parvati,* Shiva's dark lover, after she underwent magical skin-lightening beauty treatments. Yet again, some say Gauri is another name for Varuni, goddess of golden liquor.

In any case, Gauri is the name used for the goddess worshiped in August festivals; this is said to be the best time to arrange marriages and to name babies. Gauri's particular day is August's new moon, when bedtime sweets are eaten to bring Gauri's honeyed grace into the soul for the year.

Gauri-Sankar An Indian mountain-goddess embodied in the world's highest peak, the one we call Mt. Everest.

Gefjon, Gefjun It is difficult to determine whether or not the Scandinavian giant Gefjon and the virgin goddess of the same name were identical. The former Gefjon was a trickster-creator; a vagrant, she was promised as much land as four oxen could plow in a day. So she conceived four ox-shaped sons by a resident of Giantland; when her sons had grown, Gefjon brought them back to Sweden, plowed off a part of that country and dragged it south, where it became Seeland. The other Gefjon, a goddess, sold her hymen for a jewel but miraculously retained her virginity. She was an attendant upon *Frigg* and possibly a form of that earth-goddess as the "generous giver." All women who die maidens were said to pass into Gefjon's possession.

Gendenwitha The Iroquois called the morning star by this name, which translates as "she who brings the day." Their religion recalled the time when the great hunter Sosondowah ("great night") was stalking a supernatural elk. The hunt brought him to the heavens where the jealous goddess Dawn snared Sosondowah as her doorkeeper.

But the new slave could not remain faithful to his duties. Down on earth he saw Gendenwitha, then a mortal woman, and daily left his duties to court her. While Dawn was busy coloring the sky, the hunter was singing to his beloved: in spring as a bluebird; in summer, a blackbird; in autumn, a hawk. And it was as a hawk that he tried to carry Gendenwitha to heaven with him. But Dawn, angry at his disappearance from her doorstep, turned the woman into a star and set Gendenwitha just above Dawn's door, where she shines today, just out of reach of her dark hunter-lover.

Genea Phoenician mother of all humans.

Genetaska "Maiden peace queen" of the Iroquois was a human woman so wise that lawsuits were brought to her for settlement. Genetaska was, for a long time, impartial, but eventually fell in love with a defendant; when she married him, her office was abolished.

Gentle Annie The pleasant aspect of *Black Annis* was said to bring good weather to the English countryside, as well as to the nearby waters. Sometimes the weather-goddess—thought by some to be descended from *Anu*—turned on those she had recently favored, ravaging their boats and crops with high winds. In many cultures, weather-goddesses were similarly perceived: beautiful but dangerous maidens, alternatively seductive and treacherous.

Gerd A Scandinavian deity of light, Gerd was said to live in a house ringed by fire and to shoot flames from her hands. She was the most beautiful of creatures, the daughter of a female giant and a mortal man. The fertility-god Frey became infatuated with Gerd and sent his servant to bring her to him. Gerd refused, but Frey kept sending gifts and, finally, threats. A spell in runes finally won Gerd, and she traveled to Asgard, the home of the gods, to live with Frey. Some interpreters, tracing Gerd's name to a word for "field," see the legend as an allegory of the springtime earth ready to produce fruit under the god of fertility's influence, but still living in the grip of winter, symbolized by the Frost Giants.

Gestinanna, Geshtinnanna Around the figure of the dying god Dumuzi we find one of the great trinities of eastern Mediterranean religion: the lover *Inanna*, the mother Ninsun, and the sister Gestinanna ("Lady of desolation"). Tortured by nightmares, Dumuzi brought the dreams to his sister for interpretation. Skilled in such matters, Gestinanna immediately realized her brother was under attack by demons. Warned, Dumuzi fled, swearing Gestinanna to secrecy. The demons arrived as predicted, attacking Gestinanna to force her to reveal her brother's whereabouts. But she remained steadfastly silent. Nevertheless, the demons found Dumuzi, hiding in the form of a gazelle in his sister's sheepfold. He was carried to the underworld; Gestinanna set off in pursuit, and the siblings were eventually reunited. The goddess then persuaded the underworld divinities to grant Dumuzi half her own life; henceforth, each was allowed to live on earth six months of each year.

Ggigantia The massively fat goddess of the megalithic temples on the island of Gozo off Malta.

Ghar-Jenti "Light of the house" was what this Assamese spirit's name meant; she was the spirit of good fortune within the home who manifested herself by making ticking noises at night—only the sounds of nails pulling out of wood, so we're told. She walked around the house at night, and residents felt her passing like cats' paws in their dreams.

Giane In Sardinia, this was the name of the woodland spinning spirit, an average-size woman with steel fingernails and long disheveled hair. Giane also had long, pendant breasts that, as she was working her magic loom, she threw over her shoulders. As she wove, Giane sang plaintive love songs. If a human man should respond, Giane would have intercourse with him. The man, overcome with the spirit's force, would die, and his child, a half-breed brute, would be born only three days later.

Gidne   Long-tailed forest-goddess of the Saami.

Gillagriene   Daughter of the sun in Irish legend.

Glas   "Blue one," a magical milch-cow in Irish legend.

Glispa   This great Navaho heroine who brought the healing beauty chant to her people may have been a form of the Great Goddess *Estsanatlehi*, for she was a turquoise woman, while her sister (like Estsanatlehi's sister, *Yolkai Estsan*) was associated with white shells. The two girls were lured away from their village by young men; when dawn came, however, the men were withered and old. Her sister was too terrified to escape, but Glispa fought her way through venomous snakes to freedom.

At the center of the world, the place of emergence from the lower worlds, Glispa stopped to drink. Snake people appeared and lifted the magical lake so that Glispa could travel beneath it. There she met her lover, again firm and handsome. He was, he explained, a shaman of the snake people. To keep her with him, he taught Glispa the healing chant called Hozoni and its rituals. Glispa was quick to learn; she instantly memorized the information.

After many years, Glispa grew homesick for the surface world, and the snake-god allowed her to return. Once on earth, she tried to teach the song of beauty to her brother, but he was slow-witted and could not remember the elaborately beautiful song. With magic and maize she taught him then so that when she returned to the lower world the Navaho were left with the gift of healing, performed in four-day ceremonies in honor of Glispa.

Gna   Riding her horse, Hoof-Tosser, this goddess was the messenger of heaven and of heaven's queen, *Frigg*; a wind deity, Gna's name was used as a synonym for *woman* in Scandinavian poetry.

Gnatoo   Tapa-making moon-goddess in the Friendly Isles.

Gnowee   The sun-goddess of the Wotjabaluk, aboriginals of southeast Australia, she once lived upon the earth at a time when the sky was always dark and people walked around carrying torches in order to see. One day while Gnowee was out gathering yams, her child wandered away from camp. She set off to search for him, bearing a huge torch, but never found him. She still climbs the sky daily, trying to find her son.

Godiva, Lady Godiva   Late form of the Celtic horse-goddess *Epona*.

Goga   In Melanesia—Papua-New Guinea and nearby islands—the primal being was an agelessly old woman. In her body, Goga nurtured fire, which a human boy stole from her. She pursued the boy; he dropped the burning branch he was carrying onto a tree, which caught fire; inside the tree was a snake, whose tail caught fire. Though Goga deluged the world with rain, hoping to quench the stolen fire, the snake's tail continued to smolder, and humans used it to light the first earthly blaze.

The Kiwai of Papua said that the primal woman was the first to kill an earthly creature. Hunting down a wallaby, she left it to rot; human beings emerged from it like maggots, and the old woman taught them the necessary rituals and regulations of earthly life.

Gollveig   The story of "Gold-Might" is a mysterious part of Scandinavian mythology. Many interpretations have been offered to explain why this mighty witch entered the halls of divine Asgard demanding vengeance for an injury, why she was killed three times but still lived, and why she possessed the power of the Vanir, a group of divinities distinct from the Aesir of Asgard.

Some see her simply as a symbol of the corruption of wealth, interpreting her name as "drunkenness of gold." Others say that the Vanir were an invading people's gods and that Gollveig (also called Heid, the Volva, or sibyl) embodies a historical combat. Among the latter scholars are some who see Gollveig as a disguise for the mightiest of the Vanir, *Freya*, who possessed a golden necklace and the power of prophecy.

Gondul   One of the most famous *Valkyries*, Gondul was sent to earth to bring back the spirits of famous kings who fell in battle. She figured prominently in the legend of *Hild*, for she was the creator of the everlasting battle involving that woman's lover; for this reason, some legends say Gondul was *Freya*, the queen of the Valkyries, in disguise.

Gonlod, Gunlad   The mother of poetry, she was a giant in Scandinavian mythology who owned the caldron of inspiration that the god Odin took by trickery; she was also said to be the mother of Bragi, god of poets.

Gorgons   Their faces and figures were beautiful, and above their shoulders arched golden wings. But they were as terrifying as they were lovely, for these three sisters were covered with lizardlike scaly skin and hair of hissing serpents. The Gorgons had huge boarlike tusks and brass fingers, and their gaze was so powerful that a single glance could petrify the onlooker.

The three sisters lived together beyond the sea, almost at the end of night, and their triplet sisters, the *Graeae* guarded the way to their preserve. Of the three, two Gorgons were immortal; they were Sthenno ("strength") and Euryale ("wide sea"). But they were less prominent in Greek legend than their mortal sister *Medusa* ("ruler").

The poet and scholar Robert Graves saw the Gorgons as priestesses of the triple moon-goddess, mask-wearing women who guarded the secrets of the women's mysteries. Graves pointed out that the moon's face was called "Gorgon's head" by the Orphics and that Greek bakers mounted Gorgon's heads on their ovens to warn the inquisitive not to pry and ruin the bread. A different interpretation is offered by Helen Diner, who argued that Gorgon was the name of a tribe of Libyan *Amazons*, who, conquered by the Greeks, were thereafter described by their murderers as monsters.

Graces   The most common English name for these three goddesses comes from the Latin *Graciae;* in Greek these divinities were called Charites. Both words mean the same thing: the grace of movement, for they were dancing goddesses; the grace of manners, for they were always gentle and polite; and the greatest grace, the gift of love itself, which these goddesses ruled with *Aphrodite.*

The goddesses themselves were called Thaleia ("abundant, overflowing, flowering one"), Aglaia ("radiance" or "splendor," the glow of youth and love), and Euphrosyne ("joy and merriment and delight"). In the early days in Athens, there were two, Auxo ("waning one") and *Hegemone* ("mastery"); they were probably moon-goddesses, like the Laconian Graces named Cleta ("invoked") and Phaenna ("brilliant"), goddesses said always to dance by moonlight. But the ancient triple goddess could appear as easily as a single or a double goddess; thus we find Charis, the single Grace, called the double of Aphrodite and, like that goddess, said to be the mate of the smith-god Hephaestus.

Single, double, or triple, Grace or the Graces represented the delight in living that produces art, dance, music, and love. Agelessly young, they nonetheless were older than Aphrodite, whom, some say, they met as she rose from the sea; for the love-goddess they provided fitting garments and thereafter always accompanied her, dressing her, arranging her hair, massaging her with sweet oils. They were always

See Goga, p. 135. Field Museum of Natural History
(Neg# 98211), Chicago.

pleasant and charming, bringing to human encounters a wistful long-ing. The Greeks described the difference between the Graces and other goddesses in the proverb that the first cup of wine at a banquet was theirs; the second belonged to the lustful Aphrodite, while the third was ruled by the argumentative *Até*. See also **Eurynome.**

Graeae   The three sisters of the *Gorgons* were swan maidens who lived at the world's edge, guarding the path to their sisters' sanctuary. The Graeae were beautiful although gray-haired from birth; some tales say they were also deformed, having only one eye and one tooth among them.

Their names were Pemphredo ("wasp"), the beautifully clothed one; Enyo ("warrior"), who always dressed in yellow; and Deino ("terrible"). Their shared name means "the gray ones" or "the crones," and they may have given their name to the Greeks themselves, if *Graeci* is translated "worshipers of the crone."

Grainne, Graine, Grania   Her name means "hateful goddess," suggesting that she was originally divine. However, Grainne comes into Irish mythology as the heroine of its most famous romance in which the strong-willed beauty chose her own lover and traveled the entire island with him, sleeping out of doors and sanctifying the countryside (like a goddess) with their love.

A princess of Ulster, Grainne was promised by her father to the hero Finn MacCool. But at their wedding feast, a sudden breeze lifted the long bangs of the handsome Diarmuid (in English, Dermot). On the man's forehead was a magical love spot that, if any woman saw it, left her helplessly in love with him. And so it was with Grainne.

Some versions of the legend claim that Grainne offered herself to first one, then the next, of the assembled heroes, and that only Diar-muid was foolish enough to accept her advances. Another version says that Diarmuid refused Grainne, unless she came to him neither clothed nor unclothed, ahorse or afoot, in daylight or at night. Grainne went to a wise fairy woman to borrow a cloak of mountain mist, then came to Diarmuid just at sunset mounted on a goat. Thus avoiding his pro-hibitions, Grainne won Diarmuid.

But the most familiar tale was that of Finn's wedding feast and the magical love spot that enraptured her. She quickly slipped soporific drugs into the drinks of the company, and when everyone else was sleeping, demanded that Diarmuid escape with her. At first, afraid of Finn MacCool's anger, he demurred, but Grainne prevailed. She knew that Diarmuid had once pledged never to refuse aid to a woman, so Grainne cleverly enforced the *geasa* and, to maintain his honor, Diar-muid had to do as she demanded. They fled together to the Shannon

River, to the Wood of the Two Tents—so called because for their first few nights together Diarmuid refused to sleep with Grainne. Again, however, Grainne prevailed. This time a gigantic monster accosted her and Diarmuid rescued her; Grainne sarcastically remarked that at least *something* was interested in touching her, and Diarmuid, humiliated, moved into her tent.

The new lovers were found by the pursuing Finn and his band, the Fianna, but Diarmuid gave Grainne a cape of invisibility in which to escape while with superhuman strength he leaped from the pursuers' grasp. A god then appeared to the pair, saying they could never again sleep in a cave with one entrance, land on an island with one approach, eat a cooked supper, or sleep two nights in one place.

And so the lovers began their travels, sleeping in rocky alcoves called even today "the beds of Diarmuid and Grainne." Eventually, tired of constant travel, they took refuge under a magical rowan tree guarded by a giant named Sharvan the Surly. He let Diarmuid and Grainne hide in the tree, provided they did not eat the berries. Grainne, again, had other ideas, and on her urging Diarmuid killed the giant and they feasted on the magical food.

The screams of the dying giant gave the couple's location away to Finn, who had continued to pursue them. Grainne and Diarmuid quickly climbed the tree; Finn, suspecting that they were hiding there, sat down to a game of chess with the poet Oisin and challenged him to guess the winning move. Three times Diarmuid—proud of his chess-playing skill—tossed berries from the tree to signal the correct move to Oisin. Finn, sure that Diarmuid was nearby, called his name and Diarmuid, like a good Irish hero, had to answer.

Grainne wrapped herself in the cloak of invisibility and fled, while Diarmuid took a mighty leap and landed beyond the reach of the Fianna. And so the pursuit began again, until the poets' god, Aengus, appeared to Finn to plead the lovers' cause. Finn's heart was touched, and Grainne and her beloved were allowed to return to the company. And thus did the "hateful goddess" have her will.

Grainne ni Malley The Irish pirate queen from County Galway was a contemporary of England's Elizabeth I. Trying to convince Grainne to stop harassing the British fleet, Elizabeth invited her to the English court and presented the Irishwoman with a lapdog and embroidered gifts. Grainne scoffed at the useless trinkets and left the court without making Elizabeth the desired promises. Grainne returned to Ireland and promptly kidnapped the Englishman who lived in Dublin's Howth Castle, holding him hostage until her point was made: that she acknowledged only her own sovereignty.

Grainne was as strong-willed about men as she was about rival queens. Each year she took a new lover and, on the first day of the second year, maintained the right to evict him by standing in the castle yard and loudly announcing that she wanted him out. If the man refused to leave, she would kill him. At last, however, Grainne found a man who satisfied her—an Irish nobleman with whom, when the first day of the second year arrived, she could not bear to part.

Grian Her name means "sun," which this early Irish goddess ruled. As her daughters, Irish women lived in open homes called "sun houses," or *griannon*, after their goddess. There are no surviving legends of Grian, just her name, but some researchers think that she was the twin of *Aine*, another Irish solar deity. One goddess might, in that case, represent the weak winter sun, the other the more powerful sun of summer.

Groa In the Scandinavian mythological books, the eddas, this wise woman combined the attributes of sorcery, healing, spell-casting and house-keeping.

Guabancex Goddess of wind and water in the Antilles.

Guatauva Messenger-goddess of Antilles.

Guinevere, Gwenhyfar This ancient Welsh triple goddess came almost undisguised into Arthurian legend. In some tales, King Arthur was said to have married three women, all named Guinevere; this recalls the ancient tradition that the king must "marry" the earth's triple goddess to be fully invested with kingship. In another recollection of the ancient tradition, Guinevere betrayed Arthur by sleeping with a younger man; this was a common part of stories of such goddesses who, like *Blodewedd* or Delilah, both made and unmade kings and heroes.

Gula, Gula-Bau During the slow process whereby similar goddesses were assimilated into one grand figure, this Near Eastern goddess took over the attributes of *Bau* and *Gatamdug*, emerging as one of the primary divinities of the Akkadian and Babylonian peoples. She was the mother-goddess as the "great physician," with the power both to inflict and to cure disease; she was shown with the eight-rayed orb of vital heat, the heat of the body that sustains life and, as fever, can destroy it. Sometimes in recognition both of the goddess she assimilated and of her own duality, she was called Gula-Bau.

Gula lived in a garden at the center of the world, where she watered the tree that forms its axis. The moon-man, her mate, stood in the sky over the tree, from which Gula plucked fruit to offer her worshipers. (See **Eve**.)

In art, Gula was shown accompanied by a dog, for she defended the boundaries of her people's fields as a hound might. At other times, Gula was depicted with both hands raised in the air, showing humans the proper position to assume when entreating her aid.

Gumshea   Vegetation-goddess who merged with *Ishtar*.

Gwyar   The story of this ancient Welsh goddess, the wife of the god of heaven, is virtually lost. All that is left is the meaning of her name ("gore"); the fact of her relationship to King Arthur, said to have been her brother; and the information that she had two sons, one good, the other bad.

Gwyllion   Wandering alone in the Welsh mountains, you might, it was said, come face to face with this fierce spirit of wilderness, an old woman who spitefully told you the wrong road, whereupon you would lose your way in the hills and die. Of course, carrying an object of iron would be protection against her enchantment.

Gyhldeptis   "Lady hanging hair" was a kindly forest spirit of the Tlingit and Haida in southeastern Alaska; they saw her in the long, hanging mossy branches of the great cedars of the rain forest. A protector of Indians and other humans, Gyhldeptis was disturbed by the activities of Kaegyihl Depgeesk ("upside-down place"), a tremendous whirlpool that devoured entire ships of travelers. To break this power, Gyhldeptis staged a huge feast and invited all the coastal powers: the ice, the forest fire, the wind, and others. Magically feeding them in her underwater Festival House, Gyhldeptis convinced the forces that human beings needed more protection from Kaegyihl Depgeesk. Thereupon, all the well-fed natural powers set to work rearranging the coast so that the whirlpool was smoothed into a gentle river.

Habetrot One of the most famous English spirits was the spinning-goddess Habetrot, who was a goddess of healing as well; the wearer of her handmade garments would never suffer from ailments.

Habondia, Abunciada, Dame Habondia, Habonde This goddess of "abundance" was celebrated, particularly in medieval times, as the special divinity of witches. Apparently she was, or was descended from, an ancient Germanic or Celtic earth-goddess.

Hada Bai An Assamese goddess of wealth, she was also invoked when one wished to financially ruin an enemy.

Hae-Sun In the *yennal-yaegi*—Korea's "old tales"—this is the name of the sun-goddess. Originally a girl on earth, she lived with her mother and two sisters in an isolated valley. One morning the mother went to market, warning the girls not to open the door until she got home, for the land was full of tigers. And sure enough, the woman was eaten by a tigress, who then tried to pass herself off to the children as their mother.

They were too smart, however: they ran out the back door and climbed a tree. The tigress followed them out but couldn't find the girls. As she stood there looking around in bewilderment, the girls began to giggle. "Get down," the tigress ordered. But they refused. "Then I'm coming to get you," the tigress said. But she couldn't climb the tree.

When she demanded to know how the girls had gotten to the treetop, they told her to pour oil on the trunk. The tigress did and slid down to the ground to the children's laughter.

Furious, the tigress got an axe and began to carve steps into the tree. Terrified, the children called to heaven for help. They grabbed the magical golden chain that swung down to them just as the tigress reached the treetop. She too called for help, but a rotten straw rope was all that descended. She grabbed hold anyway, only to be smashed to death when the rope broke. Meanwhile, in heaven the girls were given duties: Hae-Sun, to ride the sun, *Dae-Soon*, the moon, and *Byul-Soon*, a star.

Behind this tale of "Grandaunt Tiger" is an ancient cosmological myth of the destruction of the great cosmic mother. (See **Tiamat**.) The tigress-mother, an aboriginal goddess in many Asian lands where this widespread folktale occurs, was connected with water, the sun, and the seasons.

Hagar   In the Old Testament, Hagar was Abraham's slave and mother of his son Ishmael. But originally she was a desert mountain-goddess; her son's name means the "goddess's favorite," and the Ishmaelite people were goddess worshipers. The Christian Paul distinctly linked her with Mt. Sinai in Arabia, an interesting connection in view of Yahweh's decision to bestow the Hebrew commandments there. Some traditions say that Hagar had, in all, six sons for whom she built a city and to whom she taught the black arts.

Hainuwele   West of Papua-New Guinea on the island of Ceram, this supernatural woman was the source of food plants. It was said that Ameta ("night"), hunting with his dog, pursued a wild pig into a deep pool. The animal drowned, and Ameta tried to pull out the body for meat. What emerged from the water was a coconut, stabbed with a boar's tusk.

Ameta planted the coconut, which grew miraculously and flowered within a week. From one of its leaves, fertilized by a bit of Ameta's blood, a nine-day gestation led to the birth of Hainuwele. Like the tree from which she sprang, Hainuwele grew swiftly. Less than a week after her birth, she led her father's people in the world's first ritual dance. Around and around the people spiraled, with Hainuwele at the procession's head until she began to sink into the ground. Around and around the people danced, over her head, until Hainuwele was completely buried. And from her place of descent grew wonderful food plants, never before seen on earth.

Halcyone, Alcyone   The faithful human lover of the fisherman Ceyx, Halcyone was warned by a dream of his death at sea. She stood watch thereafter by the seashore and eventually caught Ceyx's body as it washed to shore. Transported by grief and unquenchable longing, Halcyone burst out of human form into the shape of the first kingfisher, and her dead mate magically revived and joined her in the same shape. So kindly did the Greek divinities look on this loyal love that they blessed the couple. Now, when the kingfisher is ready to lay its eggs, a calm descends on the sea until they hatch, called by the ancient name of the loving mortal—the halcyon days.

Halmasuit A Hittite throne-goddess, she represented divine legitimation of earthly rulership. Her name is Hattian, suggesting that she descended from a goddess of that pre-Hittite culture. She is addressed in prayers as "the friend behind the mountains," which has suggested to some that she was a primary Hattian divinity adopted by the invading Hittites who wished to keep their new subjects at a safe distance.

Haltia This was the name among the Baltic Finns for the house-goddess, called Holdja in Estonia. She was said to live in each room's roof beam, bringing good luck and health to the residents if they greeted her on entering. Haltia was so attached to her domicile that she would call down mournful curses on a family who destroyed her home to move to a new one; the only way to assure her continued goodwill was to bring a log from the old house to the new (Haltia moved in as soon as three logs were crossed) or to bring a bit of ash from the old hearth to the new one.

Hanata *Ishtar* as a warrior.

Hannah, Anna The name of a Jewish prophet, she was the mother of *Mary*, and according to apocryphal legend was married three times and produced three daughters of the same name.

Hannahanna Once, Hittite legend says, the fertility-god Telipinu disappeared, and with him disappeared all happiness and fruitfulness from the earth. Water ceased to flow; animals ceased to bear; even the milk of human mothers dried up within the breast. Everywhere gods and humans searched for the missing divinity, and everywhere they found him absent. Food became scarce. Even the wind-god, blowing through the universe, could not find Telipinu.

But the queen of heaven, the mother of all the people, knew what to do. While other gods mocked, she instructed a tiny bee to fly out in search of Telipinu. When she found him, the bee was to sting the god awake, for it was clear that he must be sound asleep indeed to have missed the commotion of the search parties.

Fly the little bee did, until almost exhausted. And in a village so tiny that previous searchers had overlooked it, the bee found Telipinu fast asleep. She stung him mightily, and mighty was his fury as he awoke.

Telipinu flew into a destructive rage, destroying everything animate or inanimate within reach. But Hannahanna was ready for this. Quickly she sent a huge eagle to fetch the god. Then, with the help of lovely maidens bearing sesame and nectar and accompanied by the enchantments of the magician *Kamrusepas*, Hannahanna cleansed all fury from the god. Thus was fertility restored to the earth, all happiness, all celebration, and all growth.

Hanwi The moon-goddess of the Oglala originally lived with Wi, the sun-god, but another woman tricked Hanwi into giving up her seat next to Wi. Coming late to a banquet, Hanwi saw Ite in her place and hid her head with shame. As a judgment on the sun-god for allowing another woman to take the moon's place, Hanwi was allowed to leave Wi's residence and go her own way; to compensate for her humiliation, she was given rulership over dawn and twilight, but henceforth always hid her face when near the sun.

Hariasa Germanic war-goddess.

Harimela Germanic war-goddess.

Harmonia The "uniter" was the daughter of love (*Aphrodite*) and war (*Ares*), and from her the legendary *Amazons* claimed descent. Harmonia was also said to have founded the dynasty of Thebes and to have borne the famous Dionysian women *Semele, Agave,* and *Autonoe*, as well as their sister *Ino*. At Harmonia's marriage ceremony, all the Olympians bore magical gifts, including a famous necklace bestowed by Aphrodite that gave irresistible sexuality to its wearer.

Harpies Originally they were aspects of the death-goddess, who came to snatch away the living. Death appeared to the people of the ancient Aegean as a seabird, so they left food offerings for her. Later Greek legend shows the goddess transformed into the Harpies ("snatchers") three fair-haired winged maidens, swifter than birds or winds, daughters of the earth mother *Gaea*. They had the pale faces of beautiful starving women, the bodies of vultures, sharp claws, and bear's ears. Many names were given them, but the most common were Aello ("howler"), Celaeno ("screamer"), and Ocypete ("swift"). See also **Sirens.**

Hastseoltoi Navaho goddess of hunting.

Hatai Wugti, Spider Woman Among the people of America's southwestern desert, the earth-goddess was most familiar as a spider, big-bodied like the desert spiders who lived near the Zuni and Hopi. Another name for this earth-goddess was *Awitelin Tsita*. See also **Unelanuhi.**

Hathay In South India, this goddess ("grandmother") was originally a girl who refused to marry the man her father selected for her. She went to the pool in the center of the village and drowned herself there. When she appeared in dreams to people, announcing that she had been an incarnation of *Parvati*, her worship was assured.

Hathor One of the prime divinities of Western civilization, Hathor was worshiped for more than a millennium longer than the life, to date, of Christianity. For more than 3,000 years her joyful religion held sway over Egypt. Small wonder, then, that a profusion of legends surrounded her, or that she was depicted in so many different guises: at once mother and daughter of the sun, both a lioness and a cow, sometimes a woman, and sometimes a tree. Goddess of the underworld, she was also ruler of the sky. Patron of foreigners, she was mother of the Egyptians. Like *Ishtar* to the east, she was a complex embodiment of feminine possibilities.

One of Hathor's most familiar forms was the winged cow of creation who gave birth to the universe. Because she bore them, she owned the bodies of the dead; thus she was queen of the underworld. Again, she appeared as the seven (or nine) Hathors who materialized at a child's birth and foretold its inescapable destiny. Then too, she was the special guardian spirit of all women and all female animals.

"Habitation of the hawk and birdcage of the soul," Hathor was essentially the body in which the soul resides. As such, she was patron of bodily pleasures: the pleasures of sound, in music and song; the joys of the eye, in art, cosmetics, the waving of garlands; the delight of motion in dance and in love; and all the pleasures of touch. In her temples, priestesses danced and played their tinkling tambourines, probably enjoying other sensual pleasures with the worshipers as well. (Not without cause did the Greeks compare her to *Aphrodite*.) Her festivals were carnivals of intoxication, especially that held at Dendera on New Year's Day, when Hathor's image was brought forth from her temple to catch the rays of the newborn sun, whereupon revels broke out and throbbed through the streets. (In this capacity she was called *Tanetu*.) She was a most beloved goddess to her people, and they held fast to her pleasureful rites long into historical times. See **Isis, Meri.**

Haumea Originally, Hawaiian myth tells us, human women could not give birth. They swelled with pregnancy and, when it was time for delivery, they were cut open—a dangerous procedure. But the goddess Haumea came to their rescue, teaching women how to push the child out between their legs.

*See Hathor, p. 146. Field Museum of Natural History
(Neg# 108052), Chicago.*

Haumea was not so much ageless as ever-renewing. Frequently she grew old, but as often she transformed herself into a young woman. Generations went by and still she lived among humans, sleeping with the handsome young men even when they were her grandchildren and distant descendants. One of her favored mates was named Wakea. Once, it was said, the people intended to sacrifice him. Taking him to the forest, which was her domain, Haumea ran directly through the tree trunks, leaving shreds of her skirts blooming as morning glory vines, and carried her lover to safety.

Because she owned all the wild plants, Haumea could withdraw her energy, leaving people to starve. This she did when angry, but most often Haumea was a kindly goddess. Some say she is part of a trinity whose other aspects are the creator *Hina* and the fiery *Pele*.

Hawwah "Life" or "life-giver," the Hebrew name for *Eve*.

Hebat, Hepatu Originally the presiding goddess of the Hurrian pantheon, she merged with *Wurusemu*, the Hittite sun-goddess; this, as well as her title of queen of heaven, suggests that she was a solar figure. She was depicted as a distinguished, well-dressed matron, wearing a crown, jewelry, and fancy shoes, standing on a lion.

Hebe Her ancient name was *Ganymeda* and under that name she was the Olympian cup-bearer, refreshing the divinities with the ambrosia and nectar of immortal youth. The "downy one" who represented spring's young herbiage, Hebe was reverenced with ivy cuttings at her sanctuary in Phlius. The incarnation of all that is young and fresh, she could renew youth magically.

The young spring-goddess was the younger, maiden self of the great heavenly matron *Hera*, the primary deity of pre-Hellenic Greece. But just as Hera's preeminence gave way to that of Zeus, so did Hebe lose her position to a male divinity: Ganymede, a homosexual youth kidnapped from earth by Zeus to bear the Olympian cup of immortality. Greek legend recorded an excuse for replacing the goddess with a deified mortal: Hebe, it was said, had been clumsy enough to fall while serving, embarrassing the divine assembly by exposing her genitals as she fell. From the maiden form of the Great Goddess, she was demoted to the daughter of Hera and was eventually just a shadowy pale goddess with little legend and no cult practices.

Hecate, Hekate At night, particularly at the dark of the moon, this goddess walked the roads of ancient Greece, accompanied by sacred dogs and bearing a blazing torch. Occasionally she stopped to gather offerings left by her devotees where three roads crossed, for this threefold goddess was best honored where one could look three ways at once. Sometimes, it was even said that Hecate could look three ways because she had three heads: a serpent, a horse, and a dog.

While Hecate walked outdoors, her worshipers gathered inside to eat Hecate suppers in her honor, gatherings at which magical knowledge was shared and the secrets of sorcery whispered. The bitch-goddess, the snake-goddess, ruled these powers and she bestowed them on those who worshiped her honorably. When supper was over, the leftovers were placed outdoors as offerings to Hecate and her hounds. And if the poor of Greece gathered at the doorsteps of wealthier households to snatch the offerings, what matter?

Some scholars say that Hecate was not originally Greek, her worship having traveled south from her original Thracian homeland. Others contend that she was a form of the earth mother *Demeter,* yet another of whose forms was the maiden *Persephone.* Legends, they claim, of Persephone's abduction and later residence in Hades give clear prominence to Hecate, who therefore must represent the old wise woman, the crone, the final stage of woman's growth—the aged Demeter herself, just as Demeter is the mature Persephone.

In either case, the antiquity of Hecate's worship was recognized by the Greeks, who called her a Titan, one of those pre-Olympian divinities whom Zeus and his cohort had ousted. The newcomers also bowed to her antiquity by granting to Hecate alone a power shared with Zeus, that of granting or withholding from humanity anything she wished. Hecate's worship continued into classical times, both in the private form of Hecate suppers and in public sacrifices, celebrated by "great ones" or Caberioi, of honey, black female lambs, and dogs, and sometimes black human slaves.

As queen of the night, Hecate was sometimes said to be the moon-goddess in her dark form, as *Artemis* was the waxing moon and *Selene* the full moon. But she may as readily have been the earth-goddess, for she ruled the spirits of the dead, humans who had been returned to the earth. As queen of death she ruled the magical powers of regeneration; in addition, she could hold back her spectral hordes from the living if she chose. And so Greek women evoked Hecate for protection from her hosts whenever they left the house, and they erected her threefold images at their doors, as if to tell wandering spirits that therein lived friends of their queen, who must not be bothered with night noises and spooky apparitions. See also **Baubo, Eileithyia, Iris.**

Hedrun In Valhalla, the hall of heroes where the *Valkyries* brought those slain in battle but not selected for *Freya's* retinue, a magical nanny goat lived. Every day Hedrun stood on her hind legs nibbling needles from a magical pine tree, possibly the very tree that held up the world. She converted this nourishment not into goat's milk but into intoxicating mead, which she produced so copiously that all the heroes spent every day getting roaring drunk, and would do so until the world's end.

Hegemone   An ancient goddess of the soil whose name survives in a word for sovereignty, Hegemone appeared so early in Greek history that we have no real record of her independent worship. As wave after wave of invaders reached the Aegean, they assimilated this early goddess to various deities of their own: to *Artemis*, to the horse-goddess *Despoina*, and to the *Graces* as a double goddess. In this last identity, she was honored at Athens with her sister Auxo, their names signifying "increase" and "mastery." The power of her original identity, as the force that allows humankind to produce foodstuffs from her land, is indicated only by the power her name still evokes, for no legend survives of her.

Heith   Scandinavian witch giantess.

Hekoolas   The body of this Miwok sun-goddess was completely covered with shining abalone shells so that she glowed in the sky. But she did not always live in this world, which was dark and cold, with only the faint glow in the east from her reflection. Oye the Coyote sent two men to bring the sun to our side of the earth, but she refused. Then Oye sent enough men to tie her up with ropes and drag her back across the world. Once here, she made her home above us and provided the sunlight our world needed.

Hekt, Heket, Hiquit   The frog-headed goddess, the "great magician" of Egypt, Hekt represented the embryonic grain that apparently dies, rots, and then sends forth roots and sprouts. One of the most ancient of Egyptian divinities, Hekt was midwife at the birth of the sun and continued each day to help it into the sky. (Other dawn-goddesses were *Eos, Ushas*, and *A*[*Aja*].) It was she who gave the Egyptians—indeed, all people—life, for at the original creation she touched the lifeless humans with the *ankh*, causing them to breathe and move.

Hel   The goddess who gave her name to the Christian place of eternal punishment was the Scandinavian ruler of the misty world under the earth. Her name means the "one who covers up" or the "one who hides," and the ones Hel hid in her nine-circled realm were those who died of disease or old age. Those who died heroically, in battle or by other violence, were carried off by the *Valkyries* to the heavenly halls of *Freya* or Odin.

Hel was the daughter of the giant woman *Angerboda* and was thought to be an ugly pinto woman, half black and half white, who rode to earth to fold the dying in her horrible arms and to rest her drooping head against theirs. Down in her nine-ringed realm, where the inhabitants kept up a constant wail, Hel lived in a miserable palace called Sleet-Cold, eating with a knife and fork called Famine from a plate named Hunger. Her slave, Senility, served her, as did her maidservant, Dotage. When she slept, it was on her cot, Bedridden, covered by curtains named Woefully Pale.

The entry to her queendom was guarded by the hellhound, Garm; before you reached the threshold you had to travel Helveg ("Troublesome Road") to Hel, past the strange guardian maiden, *Modgud.* Some scholars say the conception of Hel is more ancient than the heroic myth of Valhalla, the hall of dead heroes—old, perhaps, as the grave itself.

Helen, Dendritus, Helena, Helene   Before the Dorian Greeks invaded her territory in the Peloponnese, Helen was a full-fledged goddess whose second name was Dendritus ("she of the trees"). A vegetation deity, she was depicted with two mates, the Dioscuri, later said to be her "brothers" Castor and Pollux. All were born of an egg laid by the mother-goddess *Leda*, possibly a recollection of a tradition that connected the tree-dwelling goddess with birds.

Her name means "fair" or "bright one," and some see her as a form of the moon-goddess. There was a folk tradition that, in her human form, Helen was so perfect that when the potters of Greece learned their art, they molded the first bowls upon her breasts.

As a goddess, Helen had several famous sanctuaries. In Rhamnus she was worshiped as the daughter of *Nemesis*; at Argos, in the temple of the goddess of childbirth, *Eileithyia*. And in Sparta, home of the heroine who bore her name, Helen was honored in a shrine of trees; figurines of her were hung in orchards as votive offerings for a good harvest.

The goddess of the land's fertility gave her name to the queens of that land. Thus the most familiar Helen, the queen of Sparta who figured so prominently in the epic struggle of Greeks against Trojans. Raped by the Athenian king Theseus when she was but a girl, Helen grew into a strong-minded ruler who took Menelaus as her spouse, thereby granting him the right to her city's throne. But soon Helen left Menelaus for the beautiful Trojan prince, Paris. To regain his throne, Menelaus had to regain the queen. He chased Helen to Troy and fought for years to win her back. But there is a persistent tradition that—

because the queen was so necessary to the seasonal cycle of her land, Lacedaemon—Helen could not be removed from it. Only a ghost, therefore, accompanied Paris to Troy, and the famous war was fought over a specter. See **Helle, Selene.**

Heliades   The daughters of the sun, these seven sisters were poplar-tree goddesses who cried amber tears at the death of their beloved brother Phaëthon. Some of their names were Aegilae, Aegle, Lamethusa, *Lampetia*, and Phatusa.

Helle   Once, it was said, King Athamas of Boeotia and the cloud queen *Nephele* had two children, Phrixus and Helle. But the king turned his attentions to another woman, *Ino*, who conspired against Nephele's children by urging the Boeotian women to parch the seed corn, inducing a famine when the burned seeds did not germinate and grow.

According to custom, someone had to be sacrificed to restore the earth's fertility, and Ino bribed an oracle to claim that the earth spirits demanded Nephele's children. But a golden, winged ram magically appeared and took Helle and her brother northeast to the land of Colchis. Helle grew dizzy and fell into the narrow strait that separates Europe and Asia, even today called Hellespont in her honor. Her brother arrived safely in Colchis and sacrificed the ram, whose golden fleece figured in the later legend of the sorceress *Medea*.

Scholar and poet Robert Graves saw in this myth the residue of an earlier one in which Helle was the moon-goddess who ruled the sea and its tides. He identified Helle with *Helen* and *Selene* and called her the ancestral goddess of the pre-Ionian residents of Boeotia, who persuaded the invading patriarchal tribes to adopt the "bright" goddess Helle. The invaders made her a male ancestor, Hellenus of the "Hellenes," and scrambled the goddess's legend together with their own religious tales to produce the hybrid and complex stories about Helle and Helen known today.

Henwen   In British mythology, this magical sow-goddess came forth early in creation to give life to the world. As she roamed the hilly countryside, she gave birth to litter after litter. But instead of piglets, Henwen produced a grain of wheat and a bee; a grain of barley and a bee; a wolf cub, an eaglet, and a kitten, each strange litter in a different part of the country.

Hera   Many generations before Zeus was known in Greece, the people there worshiped as their chief divinity the cow-eyed sky queen whom we call Hera, although that title means only "Our Lady" and may not have been the goddess's actual name. Magnificent of form and feature, ruler of the earth and its dwellers, Hera was particularly the goddess of women and their sexuality. Like the women who worshiped her, she was the daughter of flesh and time, *Rhea* and Cronos. Also like human women, she passed through three life stages: youth, prime, and age.

First, she was the maiden *Hebe* or Parthenia, called virginal not because she avoided intercourse but because, having no children, she was free of responsibility. In this stage, she was also called *Antheia* ("flowering one"), symbol of both the flower of human youth and the budding earth. Second, she was revealed as the mature woman, *Nymph-euomene* ("seeking a mate") or *Teleia* ("perfect one"); she was then the earth in summer, the mother in the prime of life. Third; she grew into Theira ("crone"), the woman who has passed through and beyond maternity and lives again to herself.

In honor of the three phases of Hera, the ancient residents of Greece celebrated the Heraea, a competitive festival that dates to earlier times than the Olympics. Every four years, or perhaps annually, women came to a field near Hera's town of Argos for the 160-yard races. They ran bare-breasted and with hair unbound in three age groups to honor the goddess's three stages. There were three winners, each receiving identical olive crowns and a share in the cow sacrificed at the festival. Each winner—young, mature, and old—had the right to leave a statuette of herself in Hera's shrine.

Another part of her religion was Hera's annual revival. Her worshipers bathed her image, renewing her youth and preparing her again for the seasonal cycle of maturation and death. Carrying the goddess's statue to the water to cleanse the winter from her marked how they, too, like the earth, would forever be reborn. As goddess of birth and death, of the tender spring and the weary autumn, Hera held the emblems, respectively, of a cuckoo and a pomegranate.

Originally Hera had no consort, but when the patriarchal tribes of the north descended on Greece, they brought with them their sky-god Zeus. Because Hera's religion was too strong to destroy, a marriage of convenience was forged between the two predominant divinities. From this melding of the pre-Hellenic goddess of women and the newly arrived thunderbolt wielder, the Hera of classical times emerged.

This new Hera was not a very attractive figure, a jealous and petulant wife who hounded her unfaithful husband and his lovers. Of course, legend says, she never wanted the marriage to begin with. Zeus so desired the statuesque goddess that he transformed himself into a cuckoo—the bird for which Hera had a special fondness—and flew bedraggled into her lap. Taking pity on the bird and soothing it, Hera found herself being raped by Zeus. Shamed by the violation, the goddess agreed to restore her dignity by joining in marriage with Zeus. But it wasn't long, the stories say, that she wearied of his ceaseless pursuit of other women and goddesses—probably a mythic recollection of the destruction of indigenous goddess cults by Zeus's worshipers—and Hera organized a heavenly revolt against the tyrannical Zeus. She and other Olympians tied him to his bed and gathered to mock him. Freed by one of the deities, Zeus took his revenge on the instigator of the palace revolt by stringing Hera from the sky, her wrists tied to golden bracelets and her ankles weighted by anvils. When freed, Hera resumed her persecution of *Io, Semele,* and other paramours of Zeus, siding against him in the Trojan War and otherwise making a mythic nuisance of herself to the father symbol of the patriarchy. Eventually, little remained of the ancient threefold goddess of dignified womanhood except the insistence of Greek mythology on the periodic retreat of Hera into solitude, a remembrance of the days in which that was her honored third phase, the prophetic crone, the distinguished wise one, the woman alone.

Hero   A priestess of *Aphrodite* at Sestos, she took a young man named Leander as a lover. Each night he swam across the waters that separated them, made love with her, and swam back at dawn. One night, however, Leander dove into stormy waters, so great was his passion for Hero. He drowned, and the priestess joined him in death.

Hertha, Aertha   No legends survive of the Germanic goddess from whom we get our word for *earth.* It is known, however, that she was worshiped into historic times, when plows were carried in Christian Shrovetide processions in honor of the earth's fertility. Hertha was also frequently invoked by medieval witches as their special patron. The Scandinavian earth-goddess, *Fyorgyn* (also called Erda, see **Jord**), was similar to Hertha.

Hervor   One of the few Scandinavian heroines to whom a saga—the *Hervarar Saga*—is devoted, Hervor was a warrior maiden. Needing a magical sword for her campaigns, Hervor dared to enter the rocky grave of her father and uncles. There, battling their violent spirits, she claimed her prize.

Hesperides   Far to the west of the world, at the edge of night, lived the evening stars, the sweet-singing daughters of *Njx,* the night-goddess. The Greeks said that they and a majestic serpent guarded the golden-fruited apple tree that the earth-goddess, *Gaea,* gave to the sky queen, *Hera.* Sometimes legend said there were three Hesperides, sometimes four. Sometimes they were said to be like *Harpies*, at other times like *Sirens*. But consistent in their legend was their stewardship of magical objects. Thus they might have been embodiments of the guardians of secret rites held at nightfall to soft music, conducted by goddess worshipers long after the conversion of Greece to patriarchal worship.

Hestia There were never statues of this most ancient Greek goddess, for she took no human form. Hestia was seen only in the fire of the hearth, living in the center of every home, an honored guest and helpful to her hosts. As the hearth-goddess, Hestia symbolized family unity; by extension, as goddess of the public hearth, she embodied the social contract.

According to Greek legend, Hestia was the firstborn of the Olympian goddesses. Her antiquity is attested by the Greek proverb "Start with Hestia," meaning "Begin things at the beginning." In the beginning of her worship, matrilineal succession seems to have been the rule, and traces of it survived in the custom of classical Greece whereby a new home was not considered established until a woman brought fire from her mother's hearth to light her own. In the same way, Greek colonists brought fire from the mother-city's public hearth to assure the cohesion of their new communities.

Het, Heh To the Egyptians, a serpent-goddess, "maker of invisible existences apart," who ruled fire.

Hiedo-no-Ame, Hiyeda-no-Are A court woman of phenomenal memory, she was assigned by the empress Gemmyo to memorize all the tales of Japan's primordial goddesses and gods, for the invasion of Buddhism had threatened the survival of Shinto. For 32 years Heido kept the ancient tales in mind until a scribe was finally assigned to take dictation from her. The written compilation of her tales, called the *Kojiki*, has served as the Japanese scripture for more than a thousand years.

Hiera A famous woman warrior, general of the Mysians, she fought in the Trojan War but was edited from Homer's account because, Philostratus says, "this greatest and finest of women would have outshone his heroine *Helen*."

Hikuleo The underworld-goddess of the Tongans of Polynesia owned a land called Pulotu, to which several men traveled to seek food for their people. Drinking, diving, and surfing contests were held; the men performed admirably. But the gods did not really want to share the precious food. So Hikuleo chased the humans out of her realm, not realizing that they had hidden the seeds of yam and taro in their clothing.

Hild Scandinavian legend said that when this heroine's father refused to make peace with her lover—declaring war on him instead—Hild used magic nightly to raise the dead warriors. Then the battle could never end with capitulation to her father. Hild's fight, legend said, would go on forever, to the doom of this world called Ragnarok.

Himiko "The great child of the sun," this Japanese empress never left her palace and governed by means of messages received while in a trance. It is possible the name is a title held by all shaman queens of early Japan.

Hina, Ina The greatest Polynesian goddess was a complex figure of whom many myths were told. Like other major divinities, she was associated with many aspects of life and had many symbols: she was the tapa-beating woman who lived in the moon; she was Great Hina, the death mother; she was a warrior queen of the Island of Women. An all-inclusive divine archetype, Hina appeared in many Polynesian legends, some of which—not surprisingly, for such a complex and long-lived goddess—contradicted others.

In some legends, Hina was said to have been created of red clay by the first man. But others—in Tahiti, for instance—knew Hina as the pre-eminent goddess, for whose sexual pleasure the first man was created. This goddess had two faces, one in the front as humans do, one at the back of her head. She was the first female being on earth, from whose fertile womb fell innumerable others, many bearing her name.

One of these was the dawn-goddess Hina-Titama, who was seduced by her own father, while unaware of his identity. Furious and ashamed on discovering this trickery, Hina ran away to Po, the Polynesian underworld; this was the first death in creation. Her fury was so unquenchable that she announced her intention of henceforth killing any children begotten by her father, thereby assuring that death would remain a force on earth.

How the goddess Hina reached the moon—she who had originally lived on earth and populated it—was a matter of numerous myths. In Tahiti, Hina was a canoeist who enjoyed the sport so much that she sailed to the moon, which proved to be such a good boat that she stayed there, guarding earthly sojourners. Others told of Hina being sent to the moon by violence. Her brother, hung over from indulgence in kava, became infuriated at the noise Hina made while beating tapa cloth. When she would not cease her labors for her brother's convenience, he hit her, sending her sailing into the sky. Because tapa beating was thought to be like the process by which the human body is slowly beaten down into death, this Hina of the moon, the tapamaker of

*See Hina, p. 156. Field Museum of Natural History
(Neg# 76567), Chicago.*

the sky, was closely related to the Great Hina of the underworld. Finally, a Hawaiian variant of these legends said that Hina, a married woman, grew tired of constantly picking up after her family and she simply left the earth to pursue a career as the moon's cloth-maker.

One guise Hina wore was as a warrior of the Island of Women, a place where no men were allowed, where trees alone impregnated the residents. A man was washed up on the shore and slept with Hina, the ageless and beautiful leader. He stayed for some time. But every time she began to show her years, Hina went surfing and came back renewed and restored. At the same time, her human lover gradually bowed under the years. Hina returned the man to his people on a whale, which the humans impudently and imprudently killed. The whale was Hina's brother, and she sent terrible sufferings on the people as a result.

One story told of Great Hina, the queen of death, says that this aspect of the goddess slept eternally, a huge naked woman snoring through an open mouth. Maui, the Polynesian hero, tried to be reborn by slipping into the vagina of Great Sleeping Hina, then working his way through her body and out her mouth. A bird traveling with him found the entire proceeding so amusing that it giggled, waking up the goddess and bringing death to all within her—and all thereafter.

Among all the many stories of Hina, however, probably the most commonly known one was that of the goddess and her lover, the eel. Living on earth as a mortal woman, Hina bathed in a quiet pool where, one day, she had intercourse with an eel. Her people, afraid of the power of the serpent, killed him, only to find that Hina had been mating with a god. Furious and despairing at having her affair so terminated, Hina took the eel's head and buried it. Five nights later the first coconut grew there, a staple product thereafter to Hina's folk. See **Haumea.**

Hindi, Hindira *Durga* as a pomegranate-carrying death queen.

Hippia The "horse-headed" *Demeter* was worshiped in rural Arcadia, where the story was told that the Greek Earth mother was once pursued by the sea-god Poseidon. She changed her shape several times, but he changed shape as well. Finally she became a mare, and he a stallion, in which form he was able to mount her and engender the marvelous horse Arion and, possibly, the young goddess *Despoina*.

Hippo Her name means "horse," a word found in many *Amazon* names. She was a general who, with *Marpesia* and Lampado, inaugurated the worship of the Amazonian *Artemis* at Ephesus; that city became one of the goddess's most famous shrines. After conquering Asia Minor and Syria, the warrior women set up a wooden image of Artemis near a beech tree at Ephesus. There they performed a shield dance. Then they circled in a second dance, one in which they stamped the ground rhythmically and shook their arrow-filled quivers as pipes played a wild, warlike melody.

Hippodamia She was originally a goddess of pre-Hellenic Olympia honored annually in secret rites of women, but she passed into Greek legend merely as the ancestral queen of the tragic house of King Atreus.

Hippolyta, Hippolyte The "stamping mare" was one of the greatest queens of the *Amazons*. One of the most beautiful and strongest women of her time, she wore the golden belt of Amazonian queenship, a gift from her father, Ares, the war-god. The fabulous treasure was coveted by the Greeks to the south, who sent a raiding party to despoil the women warriors. The burly Heracles ("glory of *Hera*") led the raid.

A fight ensued, although the legends that surround the event are confused and sometimes contradictory. Apparently Hippolyta found Heracles attractive but, as was customary, wished to wrestle with him before she would sleep with him; thus she tested the strength of her potential lovers so there was no chance that she might bear a weak child. Her loyal retainers, however, thought that the Greek champion was attacking their queen and sprang to arms. Alas, the women were defeated.

Here the legend becomes almost hopelessly confused, with Hippolyta merging with her sister *Antiope* and with Queen *Oreithyia*. Sometimes the tales say Hippolyta died in the first battle over the golden belt. Then again, it was said she was carried off as hostage and granted to the Athenian king Theseus as a concubine. (Some versions even have Theseus leading the raid on *Amazonia*.) Finally, there were stories that Queen Antiope was carried off to Athens and that her sister Hippolyta led the women warriors to regain her. Defeated by Theseus, Hippolyta led her decimated legions north again, dying of grief en route. Her mourning comrades, these stories say, buried her in Megara under a tombstone shaped like an Amazon's shield.

Hit In the Caroline Islands of Micronesia, this name was given to an octopus-goddess. Hit's daughter was sleeping with one of the gods, who already had a wife in heaven. The sky woman followed her husband, trying to drag him away from his mistress, but Hit began dancing lewdly. So erotic was her performance that the sky woman fainted from excitement and had to be carried back to heaven. Each time she tried to stop her husband's intercourse with the octopus's daughter, Hit began dancing again, thus allowing for the conception of the hero Olifat.

Hlin, Hlyn Either a minor Scandinavian goddess or an aspect of the Great Goddess *Frigg*, Hlin's name means "protector," and her role was to defend Frigg's favorite humans. Sometimes she was invoked as "mildness" or "warmth," possibly a reference to the Scandinavian summertime as a "servant" to the earth.

Hlodyn "Protectress of the hearth" may have been a title of the Germanic earth mother *Hertha* or a distinct goddess whose special province was the human home.

Hnossa, Hnos The youthful goddess of infatuation in Scandinavia, she was the daughter of the goddess of sensuality, *Freya*. Her name means "jewel" and was used of precious stones by her worshipers.

Ho Hsien-Ku In Chinese mythology, there were, in addition to divinities, a number of "immortal beings" or apotheosized humans. One of these Eight Immortals was Ho Hsien-Ku, who dreamed at puberty that, by eating mother-of-pearl, she could gain eternal life. She did so, and soon her body began to fade away; she could pass through solid objects and travel at impossible speeds. While she still dwelled on earth, Ho Hsien-Ku spent all night wandering the hills gathering flowers and herbs. Eventually she simply faded away, but was seen a half-century later floating on a cloud, whereupon it was recognized that she was living with the goddess *Hsi Wang Mu* in the heavens.

Hokkma, Chokmah, Hokmah The Hebrew god Jehovah had Hokkma ("wisdom") from the first, and almost from the first this quality isolated itself in female form and became a demigoddess. Some contend that Hokkma was merely allegorical, but she speaks from the Bible in terms that make such a reading difficult to support. In two books—Proverbs and Ecclesiasticus—she makes particularly strong claims to a separate identity.

The earliest creation of Jehovah, Hokkma was also his favorite. "At the first, before the beginning of earth," she brags in Proverbs, "when he established the heavens, I was there, when he drew out a circle on the face of the deep" (8:23, 28). Having established her temporal seniority, she further claims, "I was daily his delight" (8:30). It was Hokkma who cast her shadow on the primeval waters, stilling them so that creation could continue. It was Hokkma who gave consciousness to humankind, for humans crawled like worms until she endowed them with spirit. Hokkma goes so far as to call herself the playmate, even the wife, of Jehovah. Allegorical or not, this figure and others (*Shekinah*, Sabbath) undercut and softened the patriarchal religion of the Jews with their semidivine femininity.

Holika   Goddess of a famous Indian fire festival.

Holzweibel, Hozbrauen, Holzfraulein   *Buschfrauen* in the form of owls.

Horae   Also called the "hours" or the "seasons," they were a group of Greek goddesses and, like other groups, appeared in various numbers. Sometimes there were two of them: Thallo ("spring") and Carpo ("autumn"). Sometimes there were three: Eunomia ("lawful order"), Dike ("justice"), and *Irene* or *Eirene* ("peace"). They were the goddesses of the natural order, of the yearly cycle, of plant growth; they ruled the varied weather of the seasons. By extrapolation they became the goddesses who ruled the order of human society.

    Few legends were told of them, although they made cameo appearances in Olympian celebrations and myths of other goddesses—clothing the newly born *Aphrodite*, for example, dancing with the *Graces*, or opening the gates of heaven for *Hera*'s escapes to solitude. Only Dike had an actual myth to her name. The younger self of her mother—*Themis*, as *Hebe* was of Hera and *Persephone* of *Demeter*—she grew so weary of the constant wars of humankind that she withdrew to the mountains, to await a more peaceful order. Ages passed, and conditions grew worse instead of better. Finally Dike, losing hope in humanity, ascended to heaven to become the constellation Virgo.

Horephoros   Title of *Demeter* as bringer of favorable weather.

Hrede, Rheda   Bede, writing of the Anglo-Saxons, mentions her as one of their goddesses; no trace of her name is found among their Germanic cousins on the continent, however. Little is known of her except that the month of March bore her name in that land; presumably she was a spring-goddess.

Hsi Wang Mu, Wang-Mu Niang-Niang, Weiwobo   The highest goddess of ancient China was the Queen of the West, who lived in a golden palace in the Kun-lun Mountains, where once every 3,000 years, she threw a birthday party for herself. It was a special day for all the gods, for on that occasion the peach tree, *p'an-t'ao*, ripened, providing the fruit of immortality. Also on the menu for the party were such delicacies as dragon livers and monkey lips.

    Like the Roman *Juno*, Wang Mu was the goddess of female energy, the essence of *yin* and the ruler of individual female beings. In her most ancient form, she was a monster-mother, a wild-haired human-faced female with tiger's teeth and a cat's tail. She lived, in those days, not in a palace but in a cave, where magical three-footed birds fed her and from which she sent forth disease and death. Later Wang Mu took a gentler form as a beautiful ageless woman dispensing peaches that, mixed with the ashes of mulberry trees, cured rather than caused disease. Clearly, these forms were two sides of the same archetype.

Hsian Fu-Jen   Chinese double water-goddess.

Hsi-Ling Shih   This ancient and legendary Chinese empress was said to have invented silk and the culture of silkworms and to have taught it to her people.

Huitaca, Chia   The moon-goddess of intoxication and joy to the Chibcha, residents of what is now Colombia, Huitaca was the rival of the industrious male preacher Bochica. In the Chibcha legends, Bochica wandered through the countryside teaching not only useful crafts but a puritanical attitude toward life. Following him, and undoing his efforts, was the owl woman Huitaca, whose reckless delight in life was contagious.

Sometimes this goddess was called Chia and was said to be the wife of Bochica. The story of their conflict remained the same in this version, except that the "woman" became so angry at Bochica's influence that she raised a great flood by magic, drowning Bochica's followers; her husband then threw Chia into the sky, where she became the moon.

Huixtocíhuatl   The sister of the Aztec rain-gods quarreled with them one day and left home to live by herself in the ocean, where she became the goddess of salt. Her June festival celebrated Huixtocíhuatl's invention of salt extraction by exposing ocean water in pans; she was thus considered to be the patron goddess of saltmakers.

Huldra   Huldra ("hill lady") was the queen of the Germanic hill fairies, and her people were thus the Huldra-folk. Elegant mountain dwellers, they were addicted to dancing and music making. Unfortunately for humans, the mournful melodies of Huldra's people were hypnotic, none more so than the harping of Huldra herself. She was a tall being who seemed from the front like a beautiful human woman; her back, however, was hollow like other fairies' backs, and she had a long tail.

Huligamma   Obscure Indian goddess with transvestite priests.

Hulla   Daughter of the Hittite sun-goddess *Wurusemu*.

Hulluk Miyumko   The star chiefs of the California Miwok were beautiful women who lived beneath a whistling elderberry tree, which kept them awake so they could work all the time. They include the Morning Star and the *Pleiades*.

H'Uraru, Atira   To the Pawnee, the omniscient earth was the mother of life and death; she both fed the living and embraced the dead. Uniting with the god of heaven, H'Uraru brought forth life in the form of a daughter, *Uti Hiata* ("Mother Corn").

    So sacred was H'Uraru that the heroic Smohalla, supporting traditional Pawnee values under pressure from white invaders, asked rhetorically: "You ask me to dig for stone—shall I dig under her skin for her bones? Then when I die I cannot enter her body to be born again. You ask me to cut grass and make hay and sell it—but how dare I cut off my mother's hair? It is a bad law, and my people cannot obey it."

Husbishag   The ancient Semitic name for the underworld-goddess. She kept the secret book in which the hour of death was written for every living thing; she was possibly an aspect of the underworld queen *Eriskegal*.

Hu-Tu, Hou-T'u   As did all other recorded cultures except the Egyptian, the Chinese saw the earth as a female divinity ("Empress Earth"), patron of fertility, worshiped until this century on a square marble altar in the Forbidden City, whereon the ruler offered sacrifices each summer solstice.

Hybla   The name of the greatest goddess of ancient Sicily still appears in Italian place-names; she was an earth-goddess and ancestor of humanity.

Hydra   The beast of *Hera*, daughter of the serpent-goddess *Echidna*, guarded the entrance to the underworld at Lerna. There, her many heads hissed at any mortal who tried to enter death's kingdom; if a head was chopped off another—or two, or seven, more—took its place. The dangerous swamp of Lerna was also a sanctuary where murderers could purify themselves of spilled blood, giving rise to the Greek saying, "a Lerna of evils."

    The blood of the Hydra was so poisonous that, touched by it, the immortal centaur Chiron begged to die to escape its torture. And in some Greek tales, it was Hydra blood that destroyed Heracles—a bit of mythological irony, for the strong man had previously killed the serpent. Hydra's blood, these tales say, was the poison imbued in the robe that *Dejanira* wove for Heracles, the robe that burned him to death.

Poet Robert Graves saw in the Hydra myth a memory of the patriarchal Greek tribes' extermination of the worship of the pre-Hellenic divinities. Meeting in secret groves, these religious groups grew through persecution: for every goddess-honoring group destroyed or converted, another sprang forth in its place. Even the ancients, finding the Hydra a puzzling figure, offered their own explanations. One early scholar, for instance, thought that the Hydra was an underground river whose waters, if stopped up in one place, would burst forth in another.

Hypermnestra Oldest of the *Danaid* sisters, she was worshiped in Greek Argos as the founder of its royal dynasty. It is theorized that she was originally not a Danaid but a water-goddess. She did not join her husband-murdering sisters but spared her mate in order to give divine sanction to the Argive monarchy.

Hyrrokin After *Frigg's* son Balder was killed, the earth mourned so much that his death ship could not travel to the underworld. But this giant, strongest of a strong race, was brought to heaven to throw her weight against the ship. She arrived riding a wolf, using snakes for a bridle, and performed the near-impossible task of launching Balder into *Hel's* world.

Ia In one version of the story of the goddess *Cybele* the hermaphrodite Agdistis did not die from the trauma of castration, but survived as a woman. The discarded penis and testicles bled into the earth, which engendered a tree whose fruit impregnated *Nana*, who in turn gave birth to the lovely youth Attis. Attis, meeting the womanly Agdistis, fell instantly in love, as did the former hermaphrodite with the handsome boy. But King Midas, opposed to the union, arranged a marriage between Attis and his own daughter Ia. At the wedding supper, the jilted Agdistis burst upon the scene in fury. She drove all the guests mad, most notably Attis, who castrated himself on the spot, throwing his genitals aside and condemning them as "the cause of all evil." Then he died, and the newly widowed bride, Ia, killed herself.

Iahu Anat According to some scholars, this was the most ancient name of the Hebrew divinity a goddess who, over the ages, was changed into the god Yahweh, later called Jehovah.

Iambe "Abuse" or "indecent speech" this Greek princess was called, for her talk was bawdy and full of raillery. She brought the first smile to Great Mother *Demeter's* face after the loss of her precious *Persephone* by telling salacious jokes. When Demeter smiled at these obscenities, Iambe offered her a cup of wine. The goddess refused, asking instead for water mixed with barley meal and pennyroyal. Some say Iambe was the same as *Baubo*; in any case they both signified the crude humor that invariably accompanied the solemn Eleusinian mysteries of the earth mother.

Iarnvithja Scandinavian troll wives.

Iaso Greek goddess of healing, sister of Hygia.

Ida, Idaean Mother The name for *Rhea* as goddess of Mt. Ida, also a name of the Cretan nurse of Rhea's son Zeus; this suggests that an embodiment of the goddess's own nurturing energy protected the newborn godling.

Idem-Huva This harvest-goddess of the Cheremis, a Finno-Ugric people of northern Europe, was said to haunt the threshing area in early morning to ensure all was in order; she was shy, however, and fled if approached.

Idothea, Eidothea A minor Greek sea-goddess, she was daughter of the multiformed Proteus; a favorite of sailors, she was so disrespectful of her father that she revealed Proteus's weather tricks to humans.

Idunn In the Scandinavian eddas, this goddess performed the same function as *Hebe* did for the Greeks: she fed the gods magical food that kept them young and hale. The Norse gods and goddesses were not immortal; they relied on Idunn's magical apples to survive. But once the evil Loki let Idunn and her apples fall into the hands of the enemies of the gods, the giants who lived in Jotunheim. The divinities immediately began to age and weaken. Charged with reclaiming the goddess of youth and strength, Loki flew to Jotunheim in the form of a falcon, turned Idunn into a walnut, and carried her safely home.

Igirit Jewish demon queen better known as *Agrat Bat Mahalat.*

Ikutamayorihime From the *Kojiki*—Japanese myths and folktales compiled in the sixth century by the noblewoman *Hiedo-no-Ame*—comes the story of this woman who conceived a child from a mysterious unknown lover. To discover the man's identity, Ikutamayorihime's parents told her to sew a thin, long hemp thread to him to follow it after his departure. Next morning, oddly, the thread was not found to go under the door but through the keyhole. Then it led straight to the snake-god's shrine on Mt. Miwa. The child in the girl's womb became the ancestor of the shrine's priestly family. In this tale Carmen Blacker, noted scholar of shamanism, detects a link with a matrilineal tradition of an ancestral human mother and an unearthly father. See **Tamayorihime.**

Ila, Ida Apparently a very ancient name for the earth-goddess, Ila appears in ancient Indian scripture in several contradictory stories that attest to her antiquity while disguising her original form. (In some stories, indeed, she is said to be male, or to have changed sex several times, not an uncommon circumstance among goddesses whose people were

*See Ishtar, p. 174. Field Museum of Natural History
(Neg# A88034), Chicago.*

overcome by patriarchal Indo-Europeans.) In the oldest Indian scripture, the Rig Veda, Ila was said to be the goddess-progenitrix of humanity, the earth as producer of living intelligence; in addition, she invented all the food and milk to feed her children. She also invented speech—which streams forth like food—and the first religious rituals.

Ilma, Ilmater   Finno-Ugric sky-goddess.

Imd   Scandinavian water-goddess, daughter of *Ran*.

Inaba   Japanese heroine with a similar story to the tale of *Andromena*.

Inanna, Innini, Nana, Nini   The Sumerians knew how civilization had come to the ancient Near East, and here is how they told the tale. Across the immeasurable distances of the sweet-water abyss lived Enki, god of wisdom, and with him were the Tablets of Destiny and other magic civilizing implements. These were his treasures, and he kept them from humankind. But his daughter, the crafty queen of heaven, took pity on the miserable primitives of earth and fitted her boat to travel to her father's hall. There she was grandly welcomed with a banquet of food and wine. Wise he may have been, but Enki loved his daughter beyond wisdom, so much that he took cup after cup from her at table and then, drunk, promised her anything she desired. Instantly Inanna asked for the Tablets of Destiny and 100 other objects of culture. What could a fond father do but grant the request?

Inanna immediately loaded the objects onto the boat of heaven and set sail for her city, Erech. Awakening the next day from his stupor, Enki remembered what he had done—and regretted it. But he was incapacitated by a hangover as massive as the previous evening's pleasure, and he could not pursue his daughter until he recovered. By then, of course, Inanna had gained the safety of her kingdom, and even the seven tricks Enki played on her did not regain him his treasures.

And the Sumerians knew how the various seasons came to the desert in which they lived. It started long ago, when the lovely queen of heaven had two suitors, the farmer Enkiddu and the shepherd Dumuzi. Both brought her gifts; both wooed her with flattery. Her brother urged the farmer's suit, but the soft woolens that Dumuzi brought tipped the scales of Inanna's heart. And so Dumuzi became the goddess's favorite, in a tale like Cain and Abel's that must have recorded a common dispute in the days when the new agricultural science was gaining ground from the nomadic culture of the cattle and sheep herders.

It was not long before Dumuzi grew arrogant in his favored position. But that leaps ahead in the story, for first Inanna—compelled, some say, by curiosity, while others accuse the goddess of ambition—made plans to descend from her sky throne and visit the underworld. She arranged with her prime minister, Ninshuba, that if she did not return within three days and three nights, he would stage mourning ceremonies and would appeal to the highest deities to rescue her. And then Inanna began her descent.

At the first of the seven gates of the underworld, the goddess was stopped by the gatekeeper, Neti, who demanded part of her attire. So it was at each gate. Piece by piece, Inanna gave up her jewelry and clothing until she stood splendid and naked before *Eriskegal*, the naked black-haired goddess of death, who turned her eyes of stone on the goddess from the upper world.

At that Inanna lost all life and hung for three days and three nights a corpse in the realm of death. When Inanna failed to return to her sky kingdom, Ninshuba did as instructed. Enki, the goddess's father, came to her aid. Fashioning two strange creatures, Kurgurra and Kalaturra, from the dirt beneath his fingernails, he sent them into the wilderness of the afterlife with food and water to revive the lifeless Inanna.

But no one can leave the underworld unless a substitute be found to hang forever naked in the land of doom. And so demons followed the goddess as she ascended to her kingdom. One after another, the demons grabbed the gods they met. Each in turn Inanna freed, remembering good deeds they had performed for her. But when Inanna reached her holy city, Erech, she found that her paramour Dumuzi had set himself up as ruler in her stead. Angered at his presumption, the goddess commanded that he be taken as her substitute to Eriskegal's kingdom. Luckily for Dumuzi, his loving sister *Gestinanna* followed him to the underworld and won from Eriskegal her brother's life for half each year—the half of the year when the desert plants flower, for Dumuzi was the god of vegetation.

In some versions of the tale it was Inanna herself, not Gestinanna, who freed Dumuzi. But Gestinanna's name incorporates that of the other goddess, and Inanna herself was sometimes said to be Dumuzi's mother, while Ninsun claimed that role in other versions. All these apparent contradictions cease to be problematical, however, if one extends the "three persons in one god" concept to this trinity of Sumerian divinities. Then we see that the mother, the lover, and the sister were all aspects of a single grand figure: the queen of heaven, who may have been the life-giving sun itself, as able to parch the earth into a desert as to reclaim vegetation seasonally from beneath the earth's surface. For a similar tale, see **Ishtar**. See also **Eve, Inaras.**

Inaras, Inara In the Anatolian or Hittite embodiment of the heavenly queen *Inanna*, Inaras went to the rescue of the earth's people when they were threatened by the great dragon Illuyuksa. The goddess filled vessel after vessel with liquor, inviting a man to set them as bait for the dragon. That night Inaras rewarded the human's industry by sleeping with him. The next morning the pair found the dragon and her children unconscious from intoxication, easy to slay.

As a reward for service in battle and bed, Inaras installed the man in a splendid house on a high cliff, and there they lived in pleasure until the goddess was called on a journey. Inaras instructed her paramour not to gaze out the window while she was away, but after 20 days he disobeyed. Seeing his human wife and children in the sands outside, the man grew suddenly homesick for mortal company. His complaints angered Inaras when she returned, and she dispatched him to the underworld for his disobedience.

The story of the destruction of the dragon of darkness was celebrated each new year by Inaras's worshipers. A man enacting the part of the goddess's human helper seems to have met his death after spending the night with the goddess, who for the occasion took the form of a priestess. He could not continue to live, for should he ever have intercourse with a mortal woman after sleeping with the goddess, he might transfer some of Inaras's magical power to her and thereby weaken the goddess.

Inari The Japanese rice-goddess liked to wrap herself in a fox's body. Sometimes, too, she took the shape of a human woman in order to sleep with men, who had excellent crops as a result. One of these men, it was said, realized he was sleeping with the goddess when he saw a long, furry red tail sticking out from beneath the blankets. He said nothing of it, and she rewarded his discretion by causing all his rice to grow upside down, thus bearing a full harvest that was exempt from the rice tax.

The legendary woman Tamamo-no-Maye, possibly an incarnation of Inari, lived at court and could change at will into a flying fox. An enemy, however, ended her power of transformation (and her life, some say) by confronting her with a mirror, which was powerful medicine against her magic.

Indara Her name means "maiden"; she was the creator-goddess of the people of central Celebes, forming human beings from stone and awakening them to life with her winds.

India Rosa A form of *Kuma*, Great Goddess of the Yaruros of Venezuela, she was the inventor of women's culture, teaching pottery skills and

*See Isis, p. 176. Field Museum of Natural History
(Neg# 98430), Chicago.*

basket weaving. She also gave birth to the sun and the moon, the snake and the jaguar. In some myths, she is the ancestor of all humanity as well.

Ingebord, Ingebjord   A magical maiden of Scandinavian mythology, she took a mortal for her lover and after spending three nights with him, blinded him so that he would never love another woman.

Inghean Bhuidhe   The Yellow-Haired Girl, sister of *Latiaran*, was honored in ancient Ireland on May 6, which was considered the first day of summer. Until recent times that day was celebrated in her honor with rituals around a sacred well. See **Latiaran.**

Ino, Leucothea   The daughter of *Harmonia*, "she who makes sinewy" was originally a goddess of orgiastic agricultural rites in pre-Hellenic Greece, to whom human victims apparently were sacrificed in a magical attempt to make rain fall as freely as blood on the soil. When later tribes brought their own pantheon into Boeotia, the religious conflict that ensued was recorded in the legend that Ino was a rival of the Boeotian king Athamas's wife *Nephele*. Ino brought on a famine and in punishment was pursued into the sea bearing her son Melicertes. Both were then "transformed" into sea deities by Greek legend, although Leucothea ("white goddess") had always ruled the sea, as the moon controlling the tides.

Intercidona   After birth of a Roman child, this goddess was invoked as the "ax" or "cleaver" that separated the newborn from evil and danger.

Io   The first king of Argos, the Greeks said, was a river-god who voted against Poseidon and for *Hera* when the two divinities contested ownership of the city. To punish the Argives for refusing him, Poseidon cursed the area around Argos with dry summer streams, for the sea-god could withdraw nourishing water from the land at will.

But the Argives were not concerned. They worshiped the moon as the heifer Io, or the "cow-eyed" Hera, and the moon was the maker of rain. The king's daughter Io, named for the moon, led them in rainmaking dances, in which priestesses mimicked the desperate actions of cattle driven mad by gadflies in the scorching heat.

Then came the invasions by Zeus-worshiping tribes. The indigenous cow-goddess of the moon found her legend grafted onto that of the patriarchal sky-god. And so it was told that Hera, jealous of the love of Zeus for Io—who was originally her servant or an aspect of herself—accused her husband of infidelity. He transformed Io into a heifer and denied the accusation, but Hera was too smart to be taken in by the ruse. She asked for the cow, and Zeus could hardly refuse. Hera tied Io to a tree in her own sanctuary, setting the 100-eyed Argos to guard her. Hermes, on order of Zeus, freed the heifer; Hera then sent a gadfly to torment her. Io ceaselessly wandered the world, a vestige in later legend of the original portrait of the moon-cow wandering restlessly across the sky.

Iphigenia   The daughter of *Clytemnestra*, she was sacrificed by her father to bring favorable winds for the Greek voyage to Troy. Some legends say that she was miraculously saved from sacrifice by *Artemis*, who replaced Iphigenia with a stag and wafted the girl off to live in Asia Minor as her priestess. There, after his trial for matricide, Iphigenia's brother, Orestes, came to steal the statue of Artemis, which an oracle said would relieve his tortured conscience. Iphigenia was supposed to sacrifice all noble strangers to the goddess, but when she discovered her brother's identity, she spared him and assisted him in moving the statue from its sanctuary. See **Chysothenius.**

Iphis   A Cretan woman, she was reared as a boy because her father planned to kill any daughters he begot. Iphis grew into a beautiful youth with whom the woman Ianthe became infatuated. Iphis too fell in love; she begged *Isis* to be changed into a man. The goddess answered her prayer and the lovers were wed.

Irdlirvirisissong   The crazy cousin of the Yupik and Inupiat sun-goddess *Akycha*, this clownish dancer lived in the sky with the sun's brother, the moon. Sometimes she danced through the sky to make people laugh; she was probably the ruler of the northern lights.

Irene, Eirene   The Greek goddess of peace, she was worshiped with bloodless sacrifices at Athens. Some legends named her as one of the *Horae*.

Iris   The rainbow-goddess Iris was *Hera*'s messenger, a winged maiden who—when not delivering messages for her mistress—slept under Hera's bed. It was Iris too who, when her mistress slept with Zeus, prepared their bed with sanctified hands. She was one of the few Olympians who could journey at will to the underworld, where she fetched water for solemn oaths; for this reason, she was sometimes called a form of the witch-goddess *Hecate*.

Irkalla   *Eriskegal*, the Sumerian queen of the afterlife.

Irnini   The patron goddess of the cedar-tree mountains of Lebanon; she was originally distinct from *Ishtar* but later merged with her.

Iro Duget   Melanesian death queen.

Ishara, Asakhira   Semitic goddess of promiscuity, originally distinct from *Ishtar* but later merged with her.

Ishikore-Dome   Stone-Coagulating Old Woman was the smith-goddess of ancient Japan who created the first mirror from copper-bearing stones of the Isuzu River. Three times she tried, working in the darkness that befell the world when the sun-goddess *Amaterasu* hid herself in heaven's Sky-Rock-Cave; twice she failed to create a perfect reflection of the sun's beauty, but when at last she succeeded, her mirror became the most sacred relic of Japanese Shinto. It is kept to this day in the Imperial Shrine at Ise, south of Nagoya. So sacred is this mirror that every 20 years the shrine buildings are rebuilt according to elaborate 1500-year-old plans. When the new shrine is completed, a complex ceremony is held to apologize to the mirror for the inconvenience and possible harm that accompanies moving.

No one can see the mirror, for it is hidden in brocade coverings and carved boxes, but tradition has it that Ishikore's creation is eight-sided or shaped like an eight-petalled flower. Each of the more than 90,000 Shinto shrines across Japan have as their most sacred object a similar mirror. See **Amaterasu.**

Ishtar, Ashdar, Astar, Istar, Istaru   As the process of assimilation of similar goddesses took place in the ancient Near East, the mighty Ishtar slowly emerged from a throng of lesser divinities (*Anatu, Anunit, Gumshea, Irnini, Ishara*) to become a complex image of the multiple possibilities of womanhood. She was the mother holding her massive breasts, symbols of her benevolence. She was the ever-virgin warrior, never giving her essence to anyone, warring with any who tried to take it. She was the wanton, constantly plotting to find a new lover—divine, human, bestial, it did not matter. And she was judge and counselor, the old wise one whom women emulated in the courts and the homes of her lands.

The Babylonian Ishtar was a later, more complex form of the Sumerian *Inanna*, and their myths were similar in many respects. Both loved a vegetation-god who died constantly and was constantly reborn; both were responsible for the death as well as the rebirth of the beloved. Like Inanna, Ishtar descended to the underworld in search of Tammuz, the lover whose death she had caused. But unlike the timid Inanna, the moon-goddess Ishtar ("light-giving") demanded entry at the gate of death, threatening to smash it open and set the dead loose on the earth's surface if her request were denied.

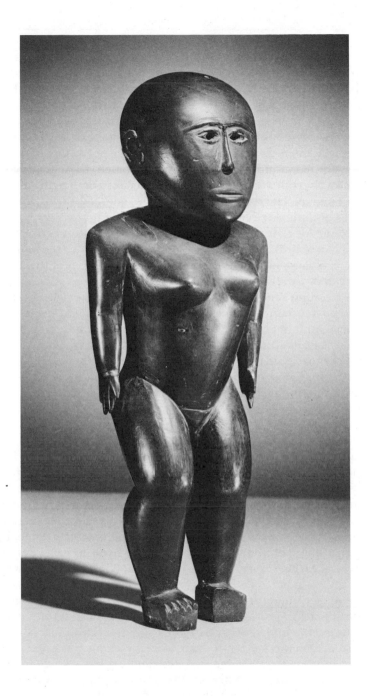

Ibibio headdress; see Isong, p. 178. Field Museum of Natural History (Neg# 97009), Chicago.

But even a divine visitor to the hell queen, *Eriskegal*, must go naked, so Ishtar was forced to give up her jewels and clothes as she descended. As the moon darkens, so Ishtar too was stripped: her crown taken from her at the first gate, then her earrings, her necklace, her diadem, her belt, her bracelets, and finally—at the seventh gate—her very garment. All these were courting presents from Tammuz, and Ishtar was loath to part with them. But to gain her desire—the resurrection of the vegetation-god Tammuz for whom earth's women were wailing—Ishtar allowed herself to be stripped and stood naked before Eriskegal to beg for Tammuz. Her wish granted, Ishtar reemerged slowly through the gates of darkness, regaining her attire as the moon regains its white light, until it glows full in the sky as *Sharrat Shame* ("queen of heaven").

Not only did she rule the moon, but Ishtar owned the morning and evening stars, invariably the symbol to the people of the Tigris and Euphrates of the alternately warlike and lustful energies of the feminine. As the morning star, *Dilbah*, the goddess arrayed herself in armor and hitched her chariot to seven lions before setting off in the dawn to hunt animals or humans. As *Zib*, the evening star, she was served by promiscuous temple women who adored the "glad-eyed Ishtar of desire, the goddess of sighing," the one "who turns the male to the female, and the female to the male," the goddess "whose song is sweeter than honey and wine, sweeter than sprouts and herbs, superior even to pure cream."

Sometimes these two energies were combined into a figure of threatening sexuality. Thus the hero Gilgamesh spurned the goddess, claiming that her lovers came to naught (for all who live, who love, will die), then fell into a terrible sickness, his body's self-punishment. The hero's comrade Eabani similarly rejected the honor due the goddess and died miserably, his final agony lasting 12 days. For Ishtar was life itself, which leads to death and (so her devotees would say) to a new birth. And who denies sex denies life, who denies death denies life, and such a one will find neither life joyful, nor death easy. See **Astarte, Cybele, Esther, Frigg, Hanata, Isis, Nana, Nintur,** and **Sarbanda.**

Isis Isis of the winged arms, first daughter of *Nut,* the overarching sky, and the little earth-god Geb, was born in the Nile swamps on the first day between the first years of creation. From the beginning, Isis turned a kind eye on the people of earth, teaching women to grind corn, spin flax, weave cloth, and tame men sufficiently to live with them. The goddess herself lived with her brother, Osiris, god of Nile waters and the vegetation that springs up when the river floods.

Alas for Isis, her beloved was killed by their evil brother, Set (see **Nephthys**). The mourning goddess cut off her hair and tore her robes to shreds, wailing in grief. Then she set forth to locate her brother's body. Eventually Isis arrived in Phoenicia, where Queen *Astarte*, pitying but not recognizing the pathetic goddess, hired her as nursemaid to the infant prince. Isis took good care of the child, placing him like a log in the palace fire, where the terrified mother found him smoldering. She grabbed the child from the fire, thus undoing the magic of immortality that Isis had been working on the child. (A similar story was told of the mourning *Demeter*.)

Isis was called on to explain her action, and thus the goddess's identity was revealed and her search explained. And then Astarte had her own revelation: that the fragrant tamarisk tree in the palace contained the body of the lost Osiris. Isis carried the tree-sheltered corpse back to Egypt for burial. But the evil Set was not to be thwarted; he found the body, stole it, and dismembered it.

Isis's search began anew. And this time her goal was not a single corpse, but a dozen pieces to be found and reassembled. The goddess did find the arms and legs and head and torso of her beloved, but she could not find his penis and substituted a piece of shaped gold. Then Isis invented the rites of embalming, for which the Egyptians are still famous, and she applied them with magical words to the body of Osiris. The god rose, as alive as the corn after spring floods in Egypt. Isis magically conceived a child through the golden phallus of the revived Osiris, and that child was the sun-god Horus.

There was another tale told of the magician Isis. Determined to have power over all the gods, she fashioned a snake and sent it to bite Ra, highest of gods. Sick and growing weaker, he called for Isis to apply her renowned curative powers to the wound. But the goddess claimed to be powerless to purge the poison unless she knew the god's secret name, his name of power, his very essence. Ra demurred and hesitated, growing ever weaker. Finally, in desperation, he was forced to whisper the word to her. Isis cured him, but Ra had paid the price of giving her eternal power over him. (A like tale was told of *Lilith* and Jehovah.)

When she was born in Egypt, the goddess's name was *Au Set* (Auzit, Eset), which means "exceeding queen" or simply "spirit." But the colonizing Greeks altered the pronunciation to yield the now-familiar Isis, a name used through the generations as the goddess's worship spread from the delta of the Nile to the banks of the Rhine. Like *Ishtar* (of whom a similar tale of loss and restoration was told), Isis took on the identities of lesser goddesses until she was revered as the universal goddess, the total femininity of whom other goddesses represented only isolated aspects.

She became the Lady of Ten Thousand Names, whose true name was Isis. She grew into Isis Panthea ("Isis the All-Goddess"). She was the moon and the mother of the sun; she was mourning wife and tender sister; she was the culture-bringer and health-giver. She was the "throne" and the "Goddess Fifteen." She was a form of *Hathor* (or that goddess a form of her). She was also *Meri*, goddess of the sea, and Sochit, the "cornfield."

But she was everlastingly, to her fervent devotees, the blessed goddess who was herself all things and who promised: "You shall live in blessing, you shall live glorious in my protection; and when you have fulfilled your allotted span of life and descend to the underworld, there too you shall see me, as you see me now, shining . . . And if you show yourself obedient to my divinity . . . you will know that I alone have permitted you to extend your life beyond the time allocated you by your destiny." Isis, who overcame death to bring her lover back to life, could as readily hold off death for her faithful followers, for the all-powerful Isis alone could boast, "I will overcome Fate." See also **Cybele.**

Ismene　A daughter of King Oedipus and Queen *Jocasta*, she was the sister of the noble *Antigone*, the Greek heroine who gave her life for her brother's eternal happiness. In today's society, such dedication would be eccentric at best, but in matrilineal societies—such as early Greece seems to have been—a woman's closest male relation was her brother, the man who had shared her mother's womb; thus Antigone's devotion was a social duty. Ismene felt this tie of blood as strongly as her sister, but Antigone denied Ismene's claim of equal guilt and went to her death alone.

Isong, Eka Obasi, Obasi Nsi　The tortoise-shell goddess of the earth's fertility, she was one of the primary divinities of the Ibibio and Ekoi peoples of West Africa.

Istehar　A "maiden" with a name suspiciously like *Ishtar*'s, she appeared in Jewish legend as the prey of the angel Shemhazai, who planned to rape her. Instead, Istehar agreed to sleep with him if the angel would reveal the secret name of Jehovah. He did so, and she, breaking the bargain, used it as a magical charm to ascend to heaven, where she became one of the stars we call the *Pleiades*.

Istustaya and **Papaya**　Hittite spinning fate-goddesses.

Itiba Tahuvava　Among the Taino, a pre-Hispanic people of Cuba and other Caribbean islands, this woman was the great ancestor, who gave birth to four sons by Caesarian section; these boys accidentally created the sea.

Guatemalan goddess; see Ix Chel, p. 180. Field Museum of Natural History (Neg# 71170), Chicago.

Ituana "Mother Scorpion," the Great Goddess of the Amazon River people, was said to live at the end of the Milky Way. There she ruled an afterworld, where she reincarnated each soul to new life, nursing earth's innumerable children from her innumerable breasts.

Itzpapálotl The goddess of the soul was symbolized by an obsidian butterfly among the Nahua of Mexico. She was, if you could see her, a beautiful goddess who wore the symbols for death tattooed on her face; however, most humans saw only jaguar claws, her material aspect. Once, it was said, Itzpapálotl came to earth to pick roses. Pricking her finger on a rosebush and starting to bleed, she became angry. Ever afterward, she made sure that humanity paid well for its pleasures, just as she had to pay for her rose with blood.

Ivithja Scandinavian female forest monster.

Iwa-Naga-Hime Rock-goddess of Japan, sister of *Kono-Hana-Sakuya-Hime*.

Ix Chebel Yax Among the Maya people, this name was given to the daughter of the moon, the goddess who taught weaving, dyeing, and spinning to the women of the Yucatan, Guatemala, and Honduras.

Ix Chel Among the Maya of the Yucatan peninsula, this was the name of the snake-goddess of water and the moon, of childbirth and weaving. Once, it was said, she took the sun as her lover, but her grandfather hurled lightning to kill her. Grieving dragonflies sang over Ix Chel for 13 days, at the end of which time she emerged, whole and alive, and followed her lover to his palace.

But there the sun grew jealous of the goddess, accusing her of taking a new lover: his brother, the morning star. He threw Ix Chel from heaven; she found sanctuary with the vulture divinity; he pursued her and lured her home; immediately, he grew jealous again.

Ix Chel, weary of the sun's behavior, left his home and his bed to wander the night as she wished, making herself invisible whenever he came near. The night-riding goddess spent her energies in nursing the women of earth through pregnancy and labor, taking special care of those who visited her sacred island of Cozumel.

Ixtab This Mayan goddess cared for the souls of suicides.

Izanami Before this world, there was only a chaos of oil and slime, which slowly congealed to produce unnamed and innumerable divinities. Finally, said the Japanese, two emerged distinct: Izanami, the inviting woman, and her consort, Izanagi, the inviting man. Standing on the rainbow, they stirred chaos with a spear until a bit of matter formed. Placing this island on the oily sea, they descended to create and populate the earth.

But they did not, at first, know how. It was only after watching two water birds mating that they understood the necessary procreative act. So they, too, mated, and Izanami gave birth to the islands of Japan, to its waterfalls and mountains, and then to the animals and plants that live there.

Last to be conceived was fire, which virtually exploded from Izanami's body, leaving her retching and bleeding. From all her excretions—from her blood, her vomit, her urine—new creatures sprang up and established themselves on the new land. But Izanami herself died.

She traveled to the underworld—Yomi ("gloomy land"). Izanagi, however, desperate without her, traveled to Yomi to ask her to return. She, however, had already established herself in the world of death and refused. But she suggested that he speak to the lord of death, asking for her release. Izanami warned him, though, not to enter the palace.

Heedlessly curious, Izanagi approached the dark building; then he took a broken comb and broke off its last tooth. Lighting it, he looked inside, where the body of Izanami was decomposing. Her spirit attacked him, humiliated at having been seen that way; she drove him from the underworld and, as they parted, claimed his actions constituted a final divorce. Some say that Izanami rules still as queen of death from her home in gloomy Yomi.

Iztaccihuatl   A volcano-goddess of central Mexico.

Izushio-Tome   "Grace maiden," a divine Japanese heroine.

Jaki The Persian menstruation spirit, she was perceived as a demon who urged men to evil deeds.

Ja-Neba The Samoyeds of Siberia invoked Mother Earth under this name; she was mother of animals and ancestor of humanity. Among the nearby Udegeis, the same goddess was Sangia-Mama; among the Nasnai, Sengi-Mama. Statues of these goddesses were covered with blood of animals killed in the hunt in order to encourage her to bring more game. Usually the heart and head were sacrificed as well if the prey were reindeer; if elk, the tongue and nostrils were the gift to the goddess.

Janguli, Jangulitara Three-mouthed, six-handed golden Tantric snake-goddess of Bengal, she is shown holding a sword, a thunderbolt and an arrow with her right hands, while her left held a noose, a blue lotus and a bow. Invoked as "remover of poison, born of a lotus," for as a snake-goddess she could remove venom, she may be the same goddess as *Manasa.*

Jeh The Indo-Iranian first woman, called the "queen of all whores" because she arrived at the creation with the devil already in tow and had intercourse with him immediately.

Jezebel This famous queen was one of only two women who ruled the Hebrew tribe; the other was *Athaliah.* Jezebel, famous today as a "harlot," was in reality a devoted follower of the goddesses of her region, some of whose religious rites sanctified sexuality. Even the Hebrews who murdered her could not help but admire their victim, whom they remembered as having "a capacity for sympathy with others in joy and sorrow."

Jezenky In Czechoslovakia, these spirit women were said to travel the night looking for human children to kidnap and cage as pets, feeding them with morsels through the bars. They could also be more violent, putting out human eyes as they traveled the night.

Jingo There seems to be no evidence that this Japanese warrior queen's name formed the base of the current term *jingoism*, but it is known that she was a magical being who remained pregnant for three years, rather than stop her war on Korea to give birth to her son. Jingo utterly devastated the three Korean kingdoms, which pledged undying loyalty to her sovereignty; some credit not her battle prowess but her supernatural control of the tides for the victory.

Jocasta Thanks to Sigmund Freud, the story of Oedipus of Thebes is undoubtedly the most familiar Greek legend in the 20th-century West. But the myth on which the Austrian psychoanalyst based his theories was unfortunately not so universal as he believed; rather, it was a late and literary record of a historical event in Greek religious history.

Scholar Robert Graves has suggested this reconstruction of the original tale: Oedipus successfully besieged Thebes, but he had no real claim to the throne until he married the local priestess, Jocasta, whose earlier consort, Laius, was first dragged to death in a ritual slaughter. Then Jocasta ceremoniously "gave birth" to the new king, who immediately announced his intention to overthrow Theban traditions and replace them with those of Corinth. Jocasta committed suicide in protest; the land rose up against him; and Oedipus was forced from the throne. The dead priestess's nearest male relative, her brother Creon, took over the Theban throne as regent. But the tide of which Oedipus had been the first wave—the patrilineality already practiced in Corinth—was rising, and the sons of Oedipus again put the town under siege, demanding the throne that was rightfully theirs under the new social order.

Jocebed The mother of *Miriam*, her name means "divine splendor" and was thought to refer to the unearthly light that surrounded her body. She seems to be a vestige of the ancient mother-goddess who appeared in the legends of the patriarchal Hebrews.

Jord, Fyorgyn, Hloldyn, Iord The goddess of the primeval earth—the world before the creation of humankind—had this name among the Scandinavians. The daughter of *Nott* ("night"), she was worshiped on high mountains where she was thought to have mated with the sky.

Judith   The great Jewish war heroine is held by many to be a fictional creation of the 4th century B.C., a sort of "Miss Liberty," useful as a symbolic
figurehead of rebellion. But other scholars claim that there actually was
a historical woman who lived in that era and who braved the battle lines
to butcher the oppressive general Holofernes. Yet others claim that
Judith was originally a barley-goddess, for her husband died during the
harvest, like a ritual king of vegetation.

Juks-Akka   The daughter of *Madder-Akka*. Among the Saami, the "old lady
of the bow" was also called the "Gun-Woman" (apparently a later
name) and was a symbol of fierce motherhood who guarded children
from harm.

Julunggul   The rainbow snake-goddess of Australia was able to be male, to
be neuter, or to be androgynous. She was said to be embodied in the
ocean and waterfalls, in pearls and crystals, and in the deep pools in
which she lived. A goddess of initiations, Julunggul was approached in
Arnhem Land by boys who, symbolically swallowed and regurgitated
by the mother snake, were vomited out again as men. See also **Wawalag
Sisters.**

Junkgowa   The great ancestor-goddess of the Yulengor of Australia's Arnhem Land lived during Dreamtime in the spirit-land of Buraklor. It was
she—in multiple form, as female ancestors—who created the food-
producing zones of the earth, as well as forming the waterholes which
link humankind with the spirit world. The Junkgowa Sisters made the
sea so that they could build the sea-going canoe. Setting off, they sang
the world's first songs to accompany their rowing. As they passed over
the sea, they created fish and ocean mammals. Finally, when they
realized how slowly they progressed, they created wind to blow them
along. But a long black rock, far out in the ocean, overturned their boat
and forced them back to land. There they established sacred zones and
constructed necessary crafts so that their descendants would have a
spiritual life: they invented the dilly bag, amulets, yam sticks and
feather belts; they designated tribal totems and bore their first children;
they invented fire to keep their babies warm.

   The Junkgowa Sisters invented and managed all ceremonial life.
But some of their sons, jealous of their power and magical skills,
decided to steal the sacred totems. And so they did. The Junkgowa Sisters then vanished into the sea, never to return to the Yulengor.

Juno   A vestige remains of her worship in today's culture: brides still
choose to marry in the month of June, thus assuring themselves of the

beneficence of the goddess after whom the month is named. Indeed, under her different names Juno ruled not only marriage but the entire reproductive life of each woman: she was called Pronuba, arranger of appropriate matches; Cinxia, ruler of the first undressing by the husband; Populonia, goddess of conception; *Ossipago*, who strengthens fetal bones; Sospita, the labor-goddess; and *Lucina*, who leads the child to light, the birth-goddess (see also **Eileithyia**).

Juno ruled these uniquely feminine occasions because she was herself the ruler of femininity, its very essence. To the Romans, each man had a "genius," the spirit that made him alive and sexually active; in the same way, each woman had her "juno," not so much a guardian spirit as an enlivening inner force of femaleness.

A very ancient Italian goddess, Juno was originally quite different from the Greek *Hera*; both, however, were essentially goddesses of women. When the Greek sky queen came to Rome during the days of cultural assimilation, she merged with the Roman goddess and her legends were told of Juno. Juno's separate mythology was lost, except for the tale that, impregnated by a flower, Juno bore the god Mars—a story never told of Hera.

Not only was she ancient but she was long recognized as one of the predominant Roman divinities. Juno, with *Minerva* and Jupiter, made up the Capitoline triad, the trinity that ruled Rome. As such she was *Regina* ("Juno the queen"); she was also *Moneta* ("warner"), who warned her people of encroaching danger (and women of bad marriages), although because her temple contained the Roman mint, Moneta came to mean "money."

Most important, Juno was the goddess of time. Daughter of Saturn, she was a symbol of the menstrual cycle as time's indicator; goddess of the new moon, she was worshiped by Roman women on the Calends, or first, of each lunar month. In addition to these monthly celebrations, Juno was honored in two festivals: the unrestrained Nonae Caprotinae on July 7, when serving girls staged mock fights under a wild fig tree; and the more sedate Matronalia on March 1, when married women demanded money from their husbands to offer to the goddess of womanhood.

Juras Mate The Latvian sea mother may be the same goddess as the Lithuanian mermaid *Jurate*.

Jurate Mermaid-goddess of the Baltic, she lived in an amber castle at the bottom of that sea. Spurning the love of the thunder-god Perkunas, she selected her own mate from among the fisherman who worked her shores.

Jyestha "The elder," a form of *Devi* or *Kali*.

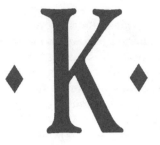

Kadi The Babylonian-Assyrian goddess of justice, she symbolized the earth itself upon which solemn oaths were sworn because she was witness to all that happened on her surface. Kadi was shown as a snake with human head and shoulders.

Kadlu The Eskimo thunder-goddess was originally a little girl who played so noisily that her parents told her and her sisters to go outside to play. So they did, inventing a game in which Kadlu jumped on hollow ice, causing a thunderous sound; Kweetoo rubbed flint stones together to create lightning; and an unnamed sister urinated so profusely that she created rain.

   Transported to the sky, the goddesses lived in a whale-bone house far in the west, away from the sea, where the sisters wore no clothing but blackened their faces with soot. For food, they went hunting for caribou, striking them down with lightning.

   Some legends said that Kadlu made thunder by rubbing dry sealskins together or by singing. In some areas, women were said to be able to avert thunderstorms, or to create them, by leaving offerings for the trinity of weather-goddesses: needles, bits of ivory, old pieces of sealskin.

Kadru Sometimes called *Aditi*, she was an Indian one-eyed goddess who also went by the name Sarpamatar or "Mother of Serpents." She wagered with her sister *Vinata* as to who could see farthest. But then she attempted to cheat and, as a result, had to forfeit one of her eyes. Kadru prayed to become the mother of a thousand snakes, while her sister prayed for two children more powerful than all her sister's. And sure enough, Kadru laid a thousand eggs, Vinata two. For 500 years they rested together in a jar of water. Then Kadru's eggs hatched into a thousand splendid snakes. Anxious, Vinata broke open one of her own eggs to see if anything was alive within. She found a son, but the lower half of his body was malformed from hatching too early. He cursed his mother

African sacred spoon; see Kla, p. 191. Field Museum of Natural History (Neg# A99149), Chicago.

to serve her sister for another 500 years, at the end of which time the second egg hatched into the giant snake-eating bird Garuda, which avenged his mother by eating Kadru's offspring.

Kaguya-Hima   "Brilliant lady," a Japanese mirror-goddess.

Kait   Hittite grain-goddess.

Kakia   The Greek "goddess" of vice was merely a personified abstraction, invented as a foil to *Arete*, goddess of virtue. In legend, the two fought over the champion Heracles, whose teacher was Arete and whom Kakia attempted to seduce with promises of love, ease, and riches.

Kali, Kalika   In Hindu India, all goddesses are ultimately one: *Devi*, whose name simply means "the goddess." But she takes different forms— perhaps a way of allowing limited human minds to fix on first one, then another, of her multiple possibilities. One of the most powerful, most common, and—to Western eyes—most terrifying of these forms is Kali ("Black Mother Time"), the goddess who perpetually transforms life into a fascinating dance of death.

Her tongue juts out of her black face; her hands hold weapons; her necklace and earrings are strung with dismembered bodies. She seems at best a stern mistress, this *Shakti* ("animating power") of the creative-destroyer Shiva, the dancing god. As *Durga*, Devi is personified as a just warrior, purging the world of evil; as *Parvati*, the same energy exemplifies passionate attachment to sexuality. But as Kali, the goddess is uncompromisingly alone, the mother of death, which swims in her womb like a babe; she is the force of time leading ever onward to destruction. And then, when she has destroyed everything, Kali will be the timeless sleep from which new ages will awaken.

Kali first manifested herself when the demon Daruka appropriated divine power and threatened the gods. The powerful goddess Parvati knitted her brows in fury, and from her sprang three-eyed Kali, already armed with her trident. This emanation of Parvati quickly dispatched the demon and made the heavens safe again. Once born, this goddess remained in existence, beyond the control of even Parvati (of whom, it must be remembered, she is an aspect).

Several famous myths tell just how uncontrollable is Kali's energy. Once, it was said, she dared to dance with Shiva, the Lord of the Dance. They grew wilder and wilder, more competitive in their dancing, until it seemed the world would shake itself to pieces—and so it will, for beneath all appearances that dance continues. Once again, it was told that Kali fought and killed two demons and celebrated her victory by draining their bodies of blood. Then, drunk with slaughter, she began to dance. Thrilling to the feel of lifeless flesh beneath her naked feet, Kali danced more and more wildly—until she realized that Shiva himself was underneath her and that she was dancing him to death. The god's tactic slowed Kali's wildness, but only for the moment, and eventually she will resume the dance that ends the world.

It may seem surprising that Kali is still one of India's most popular goddesses: her picture hangs in many homes, her name is familiar in Calcutta (Anglicized from Kali-Ghatt, or "steps of Kali," her temple city). Served at one time by murderers called *thuggee* (from which derives the English word *thug*), the goddess of cemeteries was thought to thrive on blood; most often, however, goat rather than human blood was sacrificed to her, and it is still poured out in some parts of India today.

So terrifying do these bloody rites seem that few understand Kali's spiritual significance. As a symbol of the worst we can imagine, as the most extreme picture of our fears, she offers us a chance to face down our own terror of annihilation. Ramakrishna and other great Indian poets sang rapturously of Kali, for they understood that she is a blissful goddess. Once faced and understood, these mystics say, Kali frees her worshipers of all fear and becomes the greatest of mothers, the most comforting of all goddesses. See also **Dakini, Eve, Rati.**

Kalisha "Purity," an ancient Arabian goddess worshiped, as most other female deities of that culture, in the shape of a stone.

Kalma "Corpse odor," the Finnish death-goddess.

Kalwadi An old woman with the human name of Mujingga, this Australian goddess worked as a baby sitter. Unfortunately, she had a powerful craving for infant flesh, and occasionally one of her charges would mysteriously disappear. People—in fact, her children, for she had been minding her own grandchildren—were understandably upset by the babies' disappearance. Then Kalwadi too disappeared after one of these incidents. They tracked the goddess to an underwater lair and—regretfully, for they loved her dearly—killed Kalwadi and released the children, who were still alive within her. But the children were not in Kalwadi's stomach, but in her womb, awaiting rebirth. Australian aborigines celebrated this second birth in their initiation rituals. Some scholars feel that Kalwadi was known elsewhere in Australia as *Kunapipi.*

Kamala One of *Lakshmi's* most famous names.

Kamrusepas   The Hittite goddess of magic who assisted the heavenly queen *Hannahanna* in restoring the earth's fertility by purging the god Telipinu of wrath. She ruled chanting, healing, and ritual purification.

Kamui Fuchi   Ainu goddess of the hearth, visited each morning by the sun-goddess *Chup-Kamui* as she rose. It was extremely impolite to walk through sunbeams as they streamed across the floor each morning, for this was the sun's greeting to the hearth-goddess.

Kandiu   Great mother of Sri Lanka.

Kanene Ski Amai Yehi   The Cherokee Grandmother Spider brought the sun to our world, the only creature able to do so after Possum had burned off his tail and Buzzard, his claw-feathers, trying. She wove herself a little basket and then, spinning out a web to carry her, she traveled to the other side of the world. Then she reached out one of her many arms and grabbed the sun out of the sky. Popping it into her basket, she fled back across the waiting web to light our sky.

Kapo   Hawaiian midwife-goddess of childbirth and abortions.

Karaikkal-Asmmaiyar   This Vaishnava Hindu saint and poet was a renowned ascetic honored by those who wished to conquer bodily appetites.

Karpophoros   "Lady of wild things," a name for *Artemis* or *Demeter*.

Kasum-Naj-Ekva, Tetetka   The ancestral goddess of the Siberian Mansi, who lived on the Kasym River, she was called Great Woman (Kasum-Naj-Ekva) or Greybird (Teterka). Daughter of the highest god, she wore bird-pendants, which jingled as she walked, in her hair. Massively powerful, she was a fighter known to kill six opponents at one blow; she was also a magician known for the strength of her curses.

  Two suitors wooed her. She lived with one for a time, then abandoned him and their daughter, whom she turned into a mountain. Then she lived with the other, but discovering that they were siblings, she left him as well and settled on the Kasym River to become ancestor of all the people there. She was honored as a bird-goddess by them; they embroidered her image on baby pillows as a plea that she protect the newborn. See **Vut-Imi.**

Katau Kumei   "Queen of women," the Great Goddess of Cambodia.

Kathirat The "wise goddess" of the Ugaritic religion, she set the bride-price for every woman, including the mighty *Ishtar*. As she who decides the proper order in which all things must be done, she corresponds to the Greek *Graces*.

Kaya-Nu-Hima Japanese goddess of herbs.

Keca Aba, Ketche Avalon Mother Sun, to the Cheremis of Russia, was worshiped by bowing in the direction of the east each morning as she rose. She was also called Os Keca Aba, "White Sun Mother." Huge festivals were held annually in a sacred grove in which horses and other animals were sacrificed if they wished to be, signified by their shuddering at a certain moment in the ritual.

Khala Kumari Water-goddess of Bengal.

Khon-Ma A kind of *Hecate*-figure, Khon-Ma was the "ancient mother" of Tibet, a ghostly queen who rode on a ram through the night, dressed in golden robes and carrying a golden noose; she sought unguarded doors to enter, bringing her earth demons with her to attack the household. She was easily thwarted, however: one merely placed a ram's skull and food outside the door, along with pictures of the inhabitants; should Khon-Ma pass, she would mistake the pictures for reality and eat them.

Ki, Kirisha, Kishar The Chaldean primeval earth-goddess who was the original female principle of matter.

Kikimora In Russia, this little woman lived behind the oven in every home. She was thought to be tangible to the family she haunted—usually in the form of mysterious night sounds—but only if danger threatened; otherwise, she was an invisible pest who particularly sought to torment women while they were spinning.

Kilili *Ishtar* the promiscuous, the bringer of tremendous anxiety to the men who desired her. She was symbolized by windows and birds.

Kishimogin In Japan, a spirit similar to *Churalin* and *Lilith* once ate children, but she was converted by a saint and now works as a kind of infants' guardian angel.

Kla In West Africa, there are two types of "souls," a male Kla and a female. The male Kla, the Ashanti say, is full of evil, but the female Kla is the force of goodness in this world.

Koevasi Although she was suffering from a bad cold, the creator-goddess of Melanesia walked through the world creating humanity. Because her speech was so difficult to understand through her stuffed-up nose, all the different islanders did their best to approximate it—which is why they all speak in different dialects.

Kongsim In a variant of the Korean legend of *Pali Kongju*, this heroine became insane—perhaps suffering from *shin byong* or "spirit sickness" that precedes shamanic initiation—and was thrown out of her palace. She wandered through Seoul towards the magical South Mountain, but the king banished her further to distant Mt. Diamond in Kangwon province. There she dreamed that a blue-winged crane flew into her mouth and caused her to conceive. Her twin sons each became the fathers of four daughters, all of whom became healers. Through their efforts, the princess became an honored ancestor.

In another myth attached to this name, Kongsim was a desperately ill princess confined to a dark-curtained room. Through her own prayers, and those of the maid she'd inspired to pray, Kongsim cured herself and was honored as the originator of the *mundang* or spirit religion.

Kono-Hana-Sakuya-Hime The Japanese cherry-tree-goddess had a name that means the "lady who makes the trees bloom." Daughter of the mountain-god, she was sister to the rock-goddess Iha-Naga. Both desired the man Ninigi, who chose the younger flower-goddess; for that, Iha-Naga cursed their children with lives only as long as a blossom, while hers would have lived as long as the rocks.

All did not go well with the couple, however, for Kono-Hana gave birth nine months to the day after their marriage. As she swelled with pregnancy, her new husband began to suspect she had conceived before they met. Angered at his doubt, Kono-Hana built a magic house that, when labor began, she set afire, saying any children born who were not Ninigi's would die in the blaze. Triplets were born, all safe, disproving the man's doubts. As the same story was told of Sengen Sama, a goddess of Mt. Fuji, it is probable that Kono-Hana was the same goddess under a different name or title.

Kore, Cora The most familiar "maiden" goddess (for that is the meaning of her name) to bear this title in Greece was *Persephone*, but the term was also used of such nubile deities as *Despoina, Athene,* and *Artemis*. Kore was the youngest form of the threefold goddess, the others being matron and crone. As such, she represented the youthful earth, the fresh season of buds and flowers, and the fragrant breezes of springtime.

*See Kore, p. 192. Field Museum of Natural History
(Neg# A101791), Chicago.*

Kornjunfer Germanic corn-goddess.

Korobona With her sister Korobonako, this Warrau divinity from South America's tropical forests was said to live beside a sweet-water lake that the girls were forbidden to enter. However, the rebellious Korobona went swimming in the lake one day. Colliding with a stick in the middle of the pond, she released a captive divinity who dragged her down into the water and had intercourse with her.

Korobona soon gave birth to a wholly human child. She decided to visit the water deity again; this time she returned pregnant with a half-serpent baby that, though she tried to hide it, was killed by her brothers. Korobona offered the dead babe her breasts, and it revived. Discovered again by Korobona's brothers, the baby was this time not only killed but dismembered. The grieving mother gathered the pieces, planted them deep in the earth, and kept watch until, fully armed, the first Carib warrior sprang forth and drove the brothers, the Warrau, away. Scholars believe that Korobona was a local name for Kururumany, the creator-goddess of the Antillean Arawak.

Korrigan In France, especially in Brittany, this was the name of the goddess of underground springs near dolmens and other ancient monuments; some legends said that Korrigan was the granddaughter of a great female Druid of ancient Gaul. A beautiful, translucent, and tiny spirit, she seemed to be a young maiden at night, when her power was at its height; during the day, she looked like a wrinkled crone.

Like other ancient goddesses who survived in the form of fairies, Korrigan was said to be dangerous. Women were not at all endangered, even if they should stumble upon Korrigan bathing or performing ancient rituals; men who saw her, however, were either killed or forced to marry Korrigan and never return to human society. The most dangerous time was the spring festival, when the Korrigans all met to pass the crystal goblet of inspiration and wisdom; a man who happened on the rite would instantly die. See **Dahut.**

Kostrubonko This Russian goddess was impersonated each spring by a young woman who would lie on the earth as though dead. People of her village would form a ring around her, singing mournfully that "Kostrubonko is dead, our loved one is dead." Then the girl enacted the resurrection of the spring-goddess, accompanied by the joyful songs of her friends and family.

Kottavi, Kotta-Kiriya This popular aboriginal South Indian mother-goddess was later assimilated into *Durga*. She was shown nude, with

*See Kuan-Yin, p. 196. Field Museum of Natural History
(Neg# 86356), Chicago.*

mussed hair, sometimes with the upper part of her body covered with armor. Her name is found in many places in the south and west of the continent, suggesting that her worship was widespread.

Kou-Njami The sun-goddess of the Tvagi Samoyeds of Siberia was sent away into her winter absence each year with a sacrifice of white reindeer hung on a south-facing tree. Among the related Nenets, she was the eye of the heavens; because of her, no arrows or guns were ever shot into the air, lest the goddess be blinded.

Kualchink Tree-goddess of Tierra del Fuego.

Kuan-Yin, Kwannon Just as Catholic Christianity has provided an antidote to pure theological patriarchy by encouraging the reverence of the Virgin *Mary*, so Chinese Buddhism evolved a feminine bodhisattva, or Buddha-to-be, named Kuan-Yin. And just as Mary captured the hearts of Catholic worshipers, so Kuan-Yin far outstripped the male bodhisattvas in popularity. Both in Japan (as Kwannon) and in pre-revolutionary China, this semidivine being was honored in virtually every home; she was the most powerful being in the entire Chinese pantheon.

It was said that Kuan-Yin was so concerned for humanity that, upon receiving enlightenment, she chose to retain human form rather than transcend it as pure energy. And so she would stay until every single living creature attained enlightenment. Her name translates "she who hears the weeping world"; Kuan-Yin sat on her paradise island P'u T'o Shan answering every prayer addressed to her. The mere utterance of her name in prayer was said to assure salvation from physical and spiritual harm. Even better was the observance of Kuan-Yin's own testimony of peace and mercy; her most devout worshipers ate no flesh and lived entirely without doing violence to other beings.

Sometimes it was said that Kuan-Yin originally lived on earth as Miao Shan, a young woman of unearthly virtue. Although her father wished her to marry, Miao Shan decided to visit a monastery, which, contrary to her expectations, was a hotbed of vice. Her father, hearing of her presence in the convent and suspecting the worst, burned it to the ground. A rainbow carried her to heaven, where her innocent death earned her transmutation into the divine world (see **Pi-Hsia Yuan-Chin**).

On the other hand, it was sometimes said that the bodhisattva emerged directly from the light of Amitabha Buddha's eye. As this story is also told of the male Indian bodhisattva Avalokita, some scholars believe that Kuan-Yin represents a merger of that compassionate figure with the playful Tibetan goddess *Tara*.

In either case, the feminine Kuan-Yin has for centuries been the chief symbol of human compassion in the Orient. Her statues show her dressed in flowing garments and often hung with golden necklaces, attended by the dragon-girl Lung Nu and the male child Shan Ts'ai. Often she holds willows or jewels; she makes symbolic gestures of generosity and the banishment of fear and hardship. Such statues were designed as guides to meditation, but the most effective meditation was the constant repetition of Kuan-Yin's name. That continual inner reminder of Kuan-Yin's peace and generosity brought such qualities into every aspect of her worshiper's life.

Kuma Among the Yaruros of Venezuela, the creator-goddess was mother of the sun and of all people on earth. She always appeared dressed as a shaman, but with beautiful gold jewelry.

She was the first living being to appear on earth; afterwards came the gods. Desiring to become pregnant, she asked the god Puana to have intercourse with her thumb. Convincing her that she would become too productive that way, he impregnated her internally.

After she had thus produced the gods, she sent them scurrying about the earth looking for people. After a lengthy search, they found them in a hole in the ground. Kuma gave the gods a rope and hook, with which they pulled forth human life from under the earth. See **India Rosa**.

Kunapipi, Gunabibi Eternally pregnant, the great mother-goddess of northern Australia was worshiped into this century as the creator of every living being. Sometimes represented (like *Julunggul*) as a rainbow snake, Kunapipi was the overseer of initiations and puberty rituals. She came, it was said, at the beginning of time from a sinking land to reestablish herself and her worship in Arnhem Land.

Along the Roper River, people said that Kunapipi had several daughters whom she used as bait for her favorite meal: human men. Kunapipi ate so many men that it attracted the attention of a hero who, catching her in the act, destroyed her. But the moans she made while dying struck into all the trees in the world, and still can be heard if the wood is carved into bullroarers, which cry out "Mumuna," Kunapipi's ritual name. See **Kalwadi**.

Kunti An ancient Indian mother-goddess was Kunti ("woman"), the ever-virginal lover of the gods who, like the earth, could take innumerable men into herself without changing her essence. Although replaced in Hindu worship by later goddesses, Kunti figured in the epic, the

Mahabharata, as well as giving her name to a north Indian people and their territory.

Kupalo The Russian goddess of midsummer, Kupalo was honored in effigy by a well-dressed straw woman; in the Balkans the same figure was made from birches stripped of their lower branches, leaving a topknot of leaves, and dressed in women's clothing.

   The Russian Kupalo took part, with her worshipers, in the annual fire ritual: young men and women leaped over a huge bonfire, dragging the straw maiden with them. The next day, everyone joined in ritual bathing. Again Kupalo's image accompanied them, and she magically removed all evil from the village when her straw figure was allowed to float away in the stream.

Kupapa, Kubaba, Kubabat A very ancient Hattian goddess, the "mountain mother," from whom the better-known *Cybele* derives her name.

Kurukulla Tibetan form of *Kali.*

Kusumamodini Mountain-goddess of the Himalayas.

Kuzu-no-Ha Japanese fox-goddess.

Kveldrida "Night-rider," a Scandinavian witch name.

123131

*See Kurukulla, p. 198. Field Museum of Natural History
(Neg# A100408), Chicago.*

La Reine Pedaque "The flat-footed queen," a jeering name for the Germanic spinning-goddess *Perchta* because one of her feet had become oversized from vigorously pushing the pedal on the spinning wheel.

Lada In Lycia, in southwestern Asia Minor, this word means both "woman" and "goddess." Although there is no myth left to say who she was, Lada's name seems to have made its way into Greek legend as *Leda*.

Lahar Babylonian goddess of sheep and flocks. See also **Ashnan.**

La'i-la'i Among the Hawaiians, this was the name of the first goddess born after chaos settled into form; mating with the sky, she produced humanity.

Laima, Laima-Dalia The Baltic goddess of fate sometimes appears as three or seven goddesses to symbolize the many fates possible. Laima, like the *Norns* and Fates, measures the length and happiness of a person's life. Sometimes called Laima-Dalia, "happy fate," she was invoked in prayers: "Oh, Laima, thou art healthy; give me thy health." Often mentioned in the same prayer was the sun-goddess *Saule*, for Laima measured the length of the sun's day as well as a woman's life.

Laka, Rata Patron of hula dancers, this Hawaiian goddess was said to rule the islands' uncultivated areas; her dancers also represented the untamed element of human nature. Originally, hula troupers were satirists and puppeteers as well as performers of the now-familiar dances; they worshiped Laka in the shape of a piece of wood covered with yellow cloth and decked with wildflowers.

Lakshmi, Kamala, Padma, Shri, Sri Laksmi Ancient India did not erect temples to this goddess, for why try to contain the one who embodies herself in all forms of wealth? Lakshmi is everywhere: in jewels, in coins, in rare shells, in every child born to welcoming parents, and particularly in cows.

The well-known reverence for cows in Hindu India is based on the worship of this goddess, called the *Shakti* of life-preserving Vishnu. Hindu philosophy defined male godhead as passive and abstract, distant and powerless, unless activated by the goddess. In Vishnu's case, his power to maintain and enrich life only functions when Lakshmi inspires it. Therefore it is thought good policy to bestow reverence on those embodiments of wealth—the cows who in some parts of India are simply called "lakshmi" after their owner.

Some myths say that Lakshmi existed from all time, floating before creation on a lotus; for this she is called Padma ("lotus-goddess"), whose symbol became the sign for spiritual enlightenment throughout Asia. Some stories say that Lakshmi sprang up from the ocean when it was churned by the gods, emerging like a jewel in all her beauty and power, covered with necklaces and pearls, crowned and braceleted, her body fat and golden. Many interpreters see the variant legends as recording Lakshmi's preeminence in pre-Aryan India, where she was goddess of the earth and its fructifying moisture, and her later incorporation into Vedic theology when her worshipers would not abandon their devotion to the lotus-goddess. Once established in the religious amalgam called Hinduism, Lakshmi grew to symbolize not only the wealth of the earth but of the soul as well, becoming a magnificent symbol of the delights of spiritual prosperity. See also **Ganga**.

Lalal, Losna, Lucna Etruscan moon-goddess.

Lalita, Lolita The divine essence of the universe is sometimes said by the Hindus to take the form of this adolescent woman, delighting both in girlish play and in womanly intercourse. Lalita is a symbol of the carelessness of the divine energy; to her, creation is merely another pleasant toy.

Lamamu, Lakhamu The daughter of *Tiamat* the sea-goddess, she derived her name from the Chaldean word for "primeval sediments" and apparently symbolized the first bits of created matter. This primal matter was invoked at the completion of human creations, especially buildings.

Lamasthu Almost every culture produced a figure like her: the lion-headed "daughter of heaven," desperately covetous of human beings and their offspring. She was *Lamia* to the Greeks, *Lilith* or Gilou to the Hebrews, *Kishimogin* to the Japanese, *Baba Yaga* to the Russians. The Sumerians named her Lamasthu, a plague-bearing woman who carried double-headed serpents and suckled dogs and pigs. She infected children with disease whenever possible, but she would attack adults as well, drinking their blood and consuming their flesh.

It was possible to avoid this demon of destruction, however. One merely hung on all the doors of the household plaques or amulets bearing Lamasthu's name. (Women hung them on their breasts.) The demon, thinking them greetings or signs of reverence, reacted in her usual perverse way: she went elsewhere, somewhere she was not wanted.

Lamia To the Greeks, she was a nursery bogey, useful for scaring children, as *Lilith* was to the Semitic tribes. "Be good, now," Greek mothers would say, describing how the beautiful features of Lamia's face grew twisted, how her eyes detached themselves from their sockets. Lamia was, they said, originally a mortal woman who lived in a cave; she bore Zeus several children. The jealous *Hera* destroyed all her offspring but *Scylla*, and Lamia went crazy with grief. That is why (this was most effective in silencing toddlers) the "greedy one" started stealing other women's children and sucking out their blood.

Some scholars contend that Lamia was a case of one people's goddess becoming the next culture's demon. They find in this half-snake figure the vestige of a Cretan snake-goddess, in turn an image of the death mother, the earth who ultimately devours all who walk on her. This Lamia seems to have been honored at mystic rituals similar to those of *Demeter* at Eleusis. But the children of classical Greece were no scholars, and they doubtless grew silent with fright at Lamia's name. See also **Lamasthu.**

Lampetia The English word *lamp* comes from this Greek goddess's name. The sun's daughter, she was his chief herdswoman as well, guarding his fabulous cattle. The *Odyssey* tells how the Greeks arrived on the island of Trinacria (modern Sicily), where this goddess and her sister Phathusa lived. King Odysseus warned his men not to touch the sacred cattle, but a few disobeyed.

The immortal cattle suffered greatly: the hides walked around by themselves; the spitted flesh groaned over the fires. Lampetia reported the sacrilege to her father, who sent a punishing storm to destroy the Greek boats. Only Odysseus was saved from the sun-god's anger; he was washed ashore on the island of *Calypso.*

Lan Ts'ai-Ho Among the Eight Immortals of ancient China was this androgynous being who dressed as a woman but had a male voice. She was the singing Immortal, originally an earthly street musician who wandered about bringing joy until she was lifted to heaven on a stork's wings. Afterward, she brought delight to the heavenly gatherings, always carrying her flute and a basket of fruit to any party.

Lara, Larentia, Mater Larum   Roman sources mention this goddess passingly as "mother of the dead," an underworld-goddess who may have been the same one who granted Rome prosperity as *Acca Larentia*. She was sometimes called Tacita or Muta ("deadly silent one"); she was invoked by that name in magical attempts to stop the mouths of detractors, in which women would tie the mouths of dead fish so that gossips would suffer the same fate.

Lasa   An Etruscan goddess who supplied comfort to her worshipers when they invoked her in times of need.

Lat   Another form of *Al-Lat*, the Arabian goddess.

Latiaran   An Irish goddess who had two sisters: the eldest Lasair ("flame") and the middle sister *Inghean Bhuidhe* ("yellow-haired girl"). They survived into the Christian era disguised as saints, Lasair ruling the first spring; Inghean Bhuidhe, the beginning of summer; and Latiaran, the beginning of harvest-time. Originally, it can be assumed, they were seasonal goddesses.

   The story that survives of Latiaran is that each morning she carried a "seed of fire" from her nun's cell to a nearby forge. One morning the smith complemented her on her beautiful feet, and she, vainly, looked down. As she did, her apron caught fire, but though her clothes burned she remained unharmed. Then she sank into the ground under a heart-shaped stone and was never seen again. See also **Inghean Bhuidhe.**

Latis   Ancient water-goddess of Celtic Britain.

Latona   "Queen Lat" was the Latinized form of this goddess's name, the same birth-goddess as *Al-Lat* in the Near East and *Leto* in Greece.

Laugo-Edne   A Saami laundry-goddess.

Laumes   These Lithuanian spirit women with long hair and long breasts lived in wild areas of the country. Because they loved children, they often captured human offspring, but never failed to treat them well, dressing them in lovely clothes. Generous but easily angered, they might do all the farm work and then, at a wrong word, destroy their handiwork and disappear.

Lavercam   This Irish poet made an appearance in the famous tale of *Deirdre* of the Sorrows, but she was more than the tragic heroine's nurse and companion. Born a slave, she was so brilliantly witty—though uncommonly ugly—that she rose in society, right to the court of Irish nobility. She was exceedingly strong and so fleet that she would run Ireland's entire length in a single day, gathering news. Lavercam would return to the court of King Conchobar by dinnertime to relate the tidings of his realm.

Once assigned to care for the doomed Deirdre, she transferred her loyalty from the king to the woman. When, after escaping with her lover, Deirdre was foolish enough to return to Ireland, Lavercam warned her and prophesied death if she should stay; Naoise, Deirdre's beloved, would not heed the poet's words. So Lavercam went to the king and lied about Deirdre's appearance, saying her beauty had been ruined by hardship; the deceit might have worked, had Conchobar not chanced to see the tragic heroine again.

Laverna   Roman goddess of thieves and impostors.

Leah   The sister of *Rachel*; both were part of Jacob's harem. Like her sister, Leah gave birth to founders of the great Hebrew tribes; her sons were Reuben, Simeon, Levi, Judah, Issachar, and Zebulon.

Leanan Sidhe, Lhianna-Shee   The sister and opposite of the dreaded *Banshee*, this Irish goddess was the spirit of life and muse of singers. One of her forms was the poet Eodain who wooed her human lovers with beautiful compositions. One of these, a king of Munster, so attracted Eodain that she granted him victory in war and wealth in peace. Ungrateful as he was, the king took his riches to Spain and spent nine years squandering them. He finally returned to a kingdom in ruins. Eodain, however, was loyal to her love. She restored him to the throne and, henceforth, was the power behind it, making sure the king did not slip into dissolute behavior again.

Leanan Sidhe ("fairy sweetheart") was sometimes thought destructive to her chosen mate; a man, once witnessing her unearthly beauty, would find mortal life dull and meaningless. Through no fault of the beautiful spirit, he would pine away whenever she was not with him, eventually dying of depression.

Leda   Originally she was probably *Lada* ("woman"); her name may also be related to that of the goddess *Leto*. In her most familiar Greek legend, she was raped by Zeus, who took the form of a swan for the occasion; Leda slept with her husband the same night and laid an egg. Out hatched two sets of twins, male and female, mortal and immortal. The mortal children were *Clytemnestra* and Pollux; the immortal ones, *Helen* and Castor. Leda was then raised to heaven, the legends say, as the goddess *Nemesis*.

Other variants say that Zeus raped the avenging goddess Nemesis herself. She fled from him, changing shape as she ran, but finally overpowered in the body of a bird, Nemesis laid an egg that the woman Leda found and cared for. Another tale says Zeus tricked Nemesis as he had *Hera*: disguising himself as a swan, he hid in the goddess's bosom and then turned on her in violence. The egg that resulted was laid between Leda's legs so that she was the foster mother of the four children. The complexities of these variations indicate that, hidden in the dim pre-Hellenic past, Leda was important in her own right, not merely as a mortal victim of Zeus. But it is currently impossible to assign her a character and myth unbiased by Greek influences.

Le-Hev-Hev Before a departing soul could pass to the afterlife, the Melanesians said, it had to confront this goddess, who tried to trick the soul with games. Drawing on the sand in front of her, she challenged the soul to complete her diagram. Should the dead one be unable to do so—or did so incorrectly—Le-Hev-Hev had the soul for dinner.

The Malekulans who honored Le-Hev-Hev considered her a goddess, not a monster, offering her boars so she would not eat human corpses. Her earthly forms were the spider, the crab, and the rat; she was also embodied in female genitalia. Her name has been roughly translated as "she who smiles so that we draw near and she can eat us."

Lemkechen Among the Berbers, the polestar was a black woman who held the reins of a camel (Ursa Minor) while its mother (Ursa Major) was milked. Fearful of her life, for she believed the other stars wished to kill her, she stood motionless in the sky in fright.

Lemna, The Lemnian Women The little island of Lemnos is in the far north of the Aegean Sea—near the land of Amazonia, if that country existed where the ancient Greeks believed it did. The people of Lemnos had other connections to those women warriors, for they claimed descent from *Myrine*, one of the greatest *Amazon* queens. And the tiny isle was the setting for one of the most amazonian of Greek myths.

The women of Lemnos—worshipers, probably, of an earth-goddess named Lemna—were so confident of their renowned beauty that they began to neglect proper sacrifices to the goddess of desire, *Aphrodite*. In punishment she put a curse on them, a curse appropriate to their neglect. They were stricken with a terrible odor, some legends say;

other stories say they became sexually repulsive. In either case, the men began consorting with slavewomen, conceiving children upon their concubines. In revenge, the proud Lemnian women killed the men. They also killed the slavewomen and the children born of the illicit unions.

Only their queen, Hypsipyle, broke the women's covenant by hiding her father from death. Later, the Greek hero Jason and his Argonaut companions stopped at the island. To repopulate their land, the women had intercourse with the strangers, Hypsipyle choosing Jason himself. It was said that the women—realizing that their murders had changed their society utterly—thereafter called the children begotten by the Argonauts by their fathers' names, rather than by their own.

Leto The Greeks said that she was a paramour of Zeus who bore the sun and moon, Apollo and *Artemis*, despite the persecutions of *Hera*. But Apollo was an immigrant god said to have traveled from the north, the realm of the Hyperboreans ("people beyond the north wind"). And Artemis existed in Greece before her twin, a circumstance recorded in the legend that says she was the first child born, with no labor pains, to Leto. She then sprang up and aided her mother in delivery of the later god, a long and difficult birth.

Who, then, was the "mother" of these unrelated deities? Her name means "darkness" and she was invoked as the "nocturnal one," suggesting a parallel to the Greek *Nyx*, the primordial night that also gave birth to light. In matriarchal symbolism, many scholars point out, night is said to precede day and winter precedes summer, while in patriarchal societies the opposite is usually the case. Leto may therefore have been part of the substratum of Greek religion shared with Hera and other pre-Hellenic women's goddesses. She may also have been an imported goddess, for some researchers argue that she was the same as *Lat*, or *Al-Lat*, the Near Eastern goddess.

Leucippe The daughter of a Greek king, she jeered at the women who participated in the rituals of Dionysus. In punishment she was stricken mad and, while entranced, ripped her sons to pieces in an action worthy of the most frenzied *Maenad*.

Leviathan The snake-shaped monster of the Old Testament, she was said to have been a daughter of Adam's first wife, *Lilith*. Thus she was probably an ancient dragon-goddess (see **Tiamat**) in disguise; Jehovah's victory over her may have symbolized the successful Hebrew campaign against their region's indigenous goddesses.

Liban   This early Irish goddess was the daughter of the god Eochaid who, because he eloped with his stepmother and neglected the sacred rites, angered the other divinities. A punishing flood was sent on his household, and everyone save Liban was drowned; the only other living survivor was the goddess's lapdog.

For the next 300 years Liban and her dog lived beneath the lake formed by the flood. Eventually they changed into sea creatures, Liban into a salmon, her lapdog into an otter. But Liban finally grew curious about happenings on earth and allowed herself to be caught in a net. Hauled to land, the goddess looked like a *berooch*, or mermaid, clinging to an otter.

The two were exhibited as curiosities until a cruel man killed the otter without reason. The goddess, deprived of her lifelong companion, turned herself back to human form and died. Liban still haunts the sea, however, in the form of a seabird.

Libera   With *Ceres* and the god Liber, this goddess composed a triad of Roman agricultural divinities worshiped at the Liberalia on March 17. At that time, to celebrate the return of vegetation to the earth's surface, old women would serve as Libera's priestesses, sitting at little portable street stands selling fried honey pancakes. Romans bought the lucky cakes from the ivy-decked old ones, offering a bit to the goddess and devouring the rest. When Greek influence modulated the Roman pantheon, Libera was assimilated to *Persephone*, and the same stories were told of both.

Liberalitas   Roman goddess of generosity.

Libertas   Roman goddess of personal liberty.

Libitina   Roman goddess of funerals.

Lignaco-Dex, Liganakdikei   The early Italians knew that the forest had laws of its own, and Lignaco-Dex was their name for the goddess who pointed out which trees were acceptable for human use. Before chopping down a tree for fuel, the Italians invoked this "inmost-forest-revealing" goddess, who threatened appropriate punishment if her orders were ignored.

Ligoapup, Ligoububfanu   In Micronesia, the creator-goddess made all land in the form of islands. Some legends said that she drank water from a hollow tree, swallowing invisible animals who fertilized her. She bore a girl as humans do, but also produced three other children from unusual organs: a son from her arm, another from one eye, and a second daughter from the other eye. These four beings were the ancestors of the human race we know.

Ligoband   In the Carolina Islands, a name for a goddess similar to *Lorop*.

Lilith   "Male and female he created them," proclaims Genesis in its first version of humanity's creation. But the Bible later changes its mind, explaining the creation of woman as Jehovah's afterthought. Jewish tradition outside the Bible understood the disparity: there was a female created simultaneously with Adam, and her name was Lilith. (There were variants: she was created before him; or after him, from the slime of the earth; or much later, as the twin of the evil Samael.) When the first man suggested intercourse to the primal female, she enthusiastically agreed. Adam then instructed Lilith to lie down beneath him. Insulted, she refused, pointing out that they had been created equally and should mate so.

Lilith then went to Jehovah and tricked him into revealing his secret name, his name of power. (See **Isis** for a similar tale.) Once she had power over him, Lilith demanded that Jehovah give her wings; she then flew from Eden to the western deserts. There she happily had orgies with elemental spirits and sand demons, producing demon children by the score. (Here, too, there were variants of the story: perhaps Lilith was banished from Paradise; perhaps she was born with wings; maybe she flew off to the Land of Nod. Again, some say that Jehovah cursed her with sterility.)

Adam was provided with a new mate, but he and *Eve* fell from Jehovah's favor. As penance for his sin, Adam vowed to avoid the pleasures of marriage for a century. Then Lilith had her revenge. Each night she came to Adam and had intercourse with him (in her preferred positions, one assumes), capturing his emissions to form little demon babies. One of these, some say, was Samael the evil prince, whom Lilith then took as her playmate and companion.

You would think her beautiful, Lilith of the luxurious hair and the arching wings—until you saw the talons she had instead of feet. Her unearthly beauty was dangerous to young men, who lusted after her and pined away, never aroused by mortal women. Lilith threatened children as well, for she had power over all infants in their first week, all babies on the first of the month and on Sabbath evenings, and all children born of unmarried people. Mothers could protect their young, however, by hanging an amulet marked "Sen Sam San"—for the protective angels Sensenoi, Samangalaph, and Sanoi—around the child's neck.

When Lilith came to steal a child, it was usually at night, when the babe was tucked in crib or cradle. Because she liked her victims smiling, she tickled the infant's feet. It giggled; thereupon Lilith strangled it. Mothers hearing their children laughing in dreams, or noticing them smiling as they slept, hit the baby's nose three times, crying out, "Away Lilith, you have no place here." Mothers were also wary of kites, pelicans, owls, jackals, wildcats, and wolves, all disguises favored by Lilith, who went as well by 40 other names and represented a terrifying power that the Sumerians called *Lamasthu*, the Greeks *Lamia*, and other people Gilou, *Kishimogin*, or *Baba Yaga*. See **Agrat Bat Mahalat, Eve, Mehitabel,** and **Naamah.**

Lilwani, Lilwanis   The Hittite earth-goddess, at whose shrine near Babylon the festival of *Inaras* was celebrated.

Limnades, Limoniades   These Greek nature spirits never attained immortal status but, like English fairies or Celtic *Banshees*, were part of the daily lives of unlettered folk. The Limnades haunted lakes, marshes, and swamps; they sang soft songs to passing strangers, luring them to a watery death, or called out desperately as though they were drowning women, luring passersby into mire and mud. The Limoniades were more gentle folk, nymphs who lived in open meadows and entertained themselves by dancing with the flowers.

Liomarar   Creator-goddess of Yap Island; see **Lorop.**

Litae, Litai   Innumerable sweet-natured goddesses, they represented penitential prayers, which—light as the frail bodies of the Litae—wafted to Olympus to be answered by the Greek gods and goddesses.

Lla-Mo   One of the Great Goddesses of Tibetan Llamaism whose rule encompasses life, death and regeneration.

Lo Shen   Chinese goddess of rivers.

Lofn   This Scandinavian love-goddess had a special purpose: she was charged with smoothing over love's difficulties. Lofn ("mild") received the prayers of those separated from their lovers and was empowered to bring together those she favored.

Logia   Goddess of the Lagan River in Ireland.

Lohasur Devi   Goddess of iron forgers in India.

Loo-Wit The goddess of the volcanic Mt. St. Helens. Loo-Wit was said by the Multnomah and Klickitat to be an old woman who, because of her generosity, was granted one boon by the sky spirit. She wished for eternal youth and beauty.

Granted, said the sky father. He told Loo-Wit to build a fire on the magical bridge that separated the Multnomah and the Klickitat. These selfish and greedy people had been stricken with killing weather; all their fires had gone out. So when the now-magnificent woman appeared on the magic bridge, bringing them fire, they made peace between the tribes.

But trouble soon started. Loo-Wit was courted by both Chief Wyeast of the south and Klickitat of the north; she could not choose between them. The men started a war over Loo-Wit, breaking the magical bridge in the battle.

Finally, the sky father intervened, turning Wyeast and Klickitat into the fiery peaks of Mt. Hood and Mt. Adams (the latter sometimes said to be a goddess) and Loo-Wit into Mt. St. Helens. Long after they were raised into mountains, the chiefs continued to make war, shooting fire at each other and spilling rocks—the Columbia Cascades—into the space where the magical bridge once stood.

Lorop The creator-goddess of the Micronesian islanders of Yap, Lorop was the daughter of an earlier creator named *Liomarar*, who tossed sand into the ocean to form the first islands, then squatted on one to bear her daughter. Lorop herself had three sons whom she fed with miraculous food. They did not know where Lorop got the plentiful rations, and two did not care. But the third, the youngest, stayed home one day, curious to see where his mother gathered dinner. Seeing Lorop dive into the sea, chanting a spell, he followed her to the underworld. There he saw her filling baskets with food—a discovery that meant she must remain below the earth. But Lorop continued to provide for her offspring, sending them many fish each day, and occasionally even a new island on which to live. A similar goddess was called Nomoi or Mortlock in other parts of Micronesia.

Lotis In Greek legend, this nymph was pursued by Priapus, intent on rape. She called out to her mother the earth and her father the sea; they transformed her into the first lotus tree.

Louhi The fierce and magical queen of the Arctic in the Finnish epic, *Kalevala*, Louhi was the great antagonist to the hero Vainamoinen. He tried to steal her treasured *sampo*, a charm that brought prosperity to her country. Louhi raised a huge ocean storm to prevent the thief from

See Lla-Mo, p. 209. Field Museum of Natural History (Neg# 39516), Chicago.

escaping; she called down her son, Winter, to freeze the sea to restrain Vainamoinen's flight. But all she managed to do was shatter the *sampo*. Vainamoinen escaped with the fragments, which were still powerful enough to bring abundance and wealth to his country.

Luaths Lurgann "Speedy foot," the fastest runner in Ireland, was the aunt of the hero Finn. At birth, Finn was threatened by those fearful of his eventual power, but Luaths Lurgann, who had been his midwife, swiftly carried the child away. Deep in the woodlands, she raised the boy, teaching him all the physical arts. But Finn accidentally killed his aunt. An enemy was pursuing them; Finn picked up the aging athlete and ran as fast as he could—so fast that the wind he created tore the woman's body apart, leaving only her thighbones. The mourning Finn planted these in the earth, where they formed Ireland's Loch Lurgann.

Lucina The little red ladybug was the emblem of this Roman goddess, later merged with *Juno* and *Diana*, and even later converted to Christianity as "St. Lucy." The early Italic Lucina was a goddess of light and there-fore—because birth is the first time we see her—of labor and childbed as well. She was variously honored in September and in December—still the times for festivals of Lucina as the candle-bearing saint; her holidays were enforced by the superstition that any work done on those days would be undone by the morrow.

Luminu-Ut The ancestor of humanity, among the people of the Minahassa peninsula in the South Pacific, was Luminu-Ut, a goddess born of rock sweat. She constructed the earth from a handful of soil foraged from primeval chaos; then she opened her legs to the wind and conceived a son. The boy, when grown, was sent off by his mother and instructed that his wife should be shorter than Luminu-Ut's staff. The son circled the world but did not find a mate. When he returned to his starting point, Luminu-Ut had so shrunk with age that she fit her own descrip-tion. The son did not recognize Luminu-Ut and had intercourse with her, and she gave birth to all the gods.

Luna Minor Roman moon-goddess.

Luonnotar The "daughter of nature," Finnish myth recalls, floated in the sky for serene ages, content and virginal. Eventually, however, Luon-notar grew lonely and threw herself into the ocean. For seven centuries, she floated there.

One day, as Luonnotar rested near the turbulent surface of the water, another creature appeared—a duck, seeking a place to nest.

Luonnotar's knee was breaking through the water; the duck, seeing this, built a nest on it and laid her eggs. But Luonnotar could not remain still long enough for the eggs to hatch. After three days, she felt a cramp in her legs and suddenly twisted involuntarily so that the eggs fell into the primeval slime.

There the eggs were transformed into the universe: the lower part into the earth, the upper part into the overarching sky, the yolk into the sun, the white into the moon. Luonnotar afterward took a hand in the emerging creation, forming islands and peninsulas, building the earth.

Luot-Hozjit, Luot Chozjik   The reindeer virgin of the Russian Saami was a friend to humanity who watched the roaming cattle in the summer forests. Although a wild spirit, she cooperated with human hunters in locating untamed reindeer herds. Luot-Hozjit was said to look just like a human girl, except that she was covered with reindeer fur.

Luperca   Roman goddess of pregnancy.

Lygodesma   Bound with twigs and sexually thwarted, *Artemis* in Sparta.

Lysippe   In a Greek legend of Amazonia, this queen had a lovely young son, Tanais, who found no woman so beautiful as his mother. Some say he drowned himself in despair at his hopeless love, while others say that death was accidental. In either case, Lysippe lost her sorrow in work consolidating her queendom, building the city of Themiscyra and raising temples to *Artemis* with the spoils of her many victories. "She who looses the horses" led a force of women (for by law her men lived at home and kept house, contrary to tales that all *Amazons* lived without men); those ancient warriors were the first to use cavalry in battle. Dressed in wild animal skins and bearing brass bows, Lysippe's warriors expanded her empire throughout Asia Minor. Even after Lysippe was slain in battle, her Amazons advanced under the leadership of *Marpesia* and other renowned generals.

Lyssa   "Canine madness" was the name of this Greek underworld-goddess, who drove her dogs through the world, spurring the divine intoxication of the *Maenads* to destructive fury.

·M·

Ma Tsu-Po   Chinese goddess of waters.

Maat   The Egyptian goddess of truth, she took the form of an ostrich feather in the second pan of the underworld balancing scales, where the deceased's heart was weighed. If the dishes balanced—if the heart of the dead one was light with justice—the judge, Osiris, said, "Let the deceased depart victorious. Let him go wherever he wishes to mingle freely with the gods and spirits of the dead." Alas for the soul if the dishes did not balance, for if his heart was heavy with evil, the dead man was instantly eaten by the monstrous goddess *Ahemait*. Sometimes dividing into two identical goddesses, Maat had no temples but was worshiped in the rhythm of truth, wherever it was perceived.

Mabb   A close relative in Celtic Wales of the Irish warrior, Queen *Maeve*, she descended into English fairy lore as a nightmare-bringing little sprite described by Shakespeare at length in *Romeo and Juliet* as Queen Mab, "the fairies' midwife."

Macaria   The "blessed one" was the only daughter of the champion Heracles and the warrior woman, *Dejanira*. During a siege of Athens, an oracle announced that the city would be overrun unless a child of Heracles should die; to save her home, Macaria committed suicide. The city was saved, and a spring was named in Macaria's honor.

Macha   Many Celtic goddesses were threefold, and Macha was an Irish triple goddess. The "three Machas" were in reality one deity: athlete, queen, and warrior, named "Macha, wife of Nemed, Macha, wife of Cruchchu, and Macha the Red" to distinguish the legendary exploits of the goddess's different aspects.
   The most famous Macha was the "wife of Nemed, the sun of women," the magnificently beautiful queen of northern Ireland. She lived with a mortal king and became pregnant with his twins. But he

proudly boasted that the goddess could outrun any horse; Macha warned him against arrogance, but he ignored her. Placing her in a horse race, he made his point when the hugely pregnant goddess handily won. But at the finish line Macha gave birth to twins, then died—for Irish goddesses were not immune to death—and, as she did so, cursed her husband's people.

The "curse of Macha" figured importantly in Irish legend. Because of her humiliation, the goddess caused all Ulster men to be stricken in time of danger with labor pains lasting five days and four nights. Only one man, the hero Cuchulain, was ever immune to the curse.

Some legends said that Macha was a form of the *Morrigan* or of *Badb*, both war-goddesses. Certainly, like Badb, she took the form of a hooded crow; conversely, her three aspects were similar to the three-fold Morrigan. As an independent figure, Macha especially ruled the *mesred machae*, the pillars on which, following Celtic tradition, the severed heads of those who died in battle were displayed.

Macris The daughter of Autonoe and cousin of Dionysus, she helped raise the infant wine-god in a cave where she spoon-fed him with honey.

Madalait Creator-goddess of Arnhem Land aboriginals; see **Walo**.

Madder-Akka The Saami birth-goddess had three daughters: *Sar-Akka, Juks-Akka* and *Uks-Akka*, a trinity of fate-goddesses who lived with their mother beneath the earth's surface. While Madder-Akka had general control of fertility, her daughters were more directly involved with human reproduction. Sar-Akka opened the womb; as magical assistance for her, wood was chopped outside the birthing tent so that the woman's flesh would divide as neatly as cleft wood. The new mother also drank brandy in Sar-Akka's honor before giving birth; afterward, her first meal was of Sar-Akka porridge, in which three magical sticks had been cooked. Whether you found the white one (good luck), the black one (death), or the cleft one (success) was important in determining how Sar-Akka saw the child's future.

Juks-Akka ("old lady of the bow") was also honored in the porridge ceremony; if the newborn were a boy, she assured him successful hunting, provided a tiny bow was placed in the porridge and fished out by one of the diners. The third sister ("old lady of the door"), Uks-Akka, was charged with receiving the newborn into the world of light. She, however, was said to live away from daylight, just beneath the tent's entry. There she blessed and protected anyone leaving home, just as she protected those crossing out of the womb into daylight.

Ma-Emma, Maa-Ema   The Estonian earth mother was one of the great divinities of that Baltic people, reverenced wherever an old tree stood alone in a meadow or where a pile of stones marked the foundation of a long-since burned-down house. Because Ma-Emma controlled all the earth's creatures, human beings depended on her for food; in thanksgiving for what she offered, they returned to her the first fruits of milk, butter, wool, and other products.

One of her favorite feast days was midsummer, when fires were lit in celebration of her fruitfulness; animals were herded around these fires so the sacrificial smoke could bless them for the year. Flowers and grasses were carried through the smoke by children and then fed to the cattle. The evening ended when the village's most distinguished woman led three processions around the fire, then placed food on the earth, thanking Ma-Emma with these words: "Mother, you gave to me, now I give to you. Accept from me what I have accepted from you."

Maenads, Bacchantes, Thyiades   The ecstatic worship that overtook the women of Greece, descending from wild Thrace in the 8th century B.C., is still the subject of scholarly conjecture. What was this mania, this religion of madwomen? Was it transcendent or pathological? The women in question followed the wine-god Dionysus, a late-comer to the Olympian pantheon, who, myth says, was born of Zeus and *Semele*. Hidden from other gods, Dionysus grew to young manhood nursed only by women, then began his triumphal procession across Greece. With him came the intoxication of unity with the divine, as well as throngs of women, entranced and transformed by communion with the spirit he represented.

They gathered, these Maenads, dressed in wild-animal skins, bearing ivy-wreathed staffs of fennel, erecting altars to their god in the wilderness. And they flung themselves into their religion with such fury that it often seemed terrifying to men—who were forbidden to witness, much less to join, their secret rites. The Maenads ran through forests and mountains, heads flung back and hair unbound, in a strange wild dance accompanied by flutes, drums, and tambourines. Sometimes they hunted, killing with bare hands and devouring raw flesh in a primal communion, drinking warm blood to sustain themselves in their sleepless rituals.

An intruder on these secret festivals was subject to terrible punishment, for it was sacrilege to spy on women transformed by "the rage" or mania of their ecstasy. Many are the stories of men who, like *Agave*'s son, Pentheus of Thebes, ignored these strictures and met death; there are stories as well of women who mocked the sacred religion of "the women's Zeus," as Dionysus was called, and who were driven mad in

216

punishment. Attempts to jeer at or persecute the religion out of existence failed, and the ritual procession marched through Greece, with Dionysus recognized as a full-fledged god by the 7th century B.C.

At the head of his women he marched, this intoxicated god, clad in women's robes, beautiful to see. Perhaps Dionysus was once "the shoot" (the meaning of one of his names), a god of vegetation destined to be destroyed as a human symbol of growth and death. In that interpretation, the Maenads embodied the goddess of life and death, the "nurse" of life and then its devourer.

Not all women participated in the all-night wilderness revels, but it was said that all Greek women honored the rights of their sisters who chose this magical, dangerous form of worship. Once, it was said, the Maenads descended to their village from the mountains where they'd spent the night running beneath the moon. They collapsed beside the central fountain, unable to drag themselves to their homes. When they awoke, they saw ringed about them, silently holding hands, all the town's matrons, solemnly guarding the women from assault.

Scholars of religion offer various and conflicting interpretations of the motivations that drove the Maenads wild. Some agree with Bachofen that the women were possessed, insane, or criminal. Others suggest that the oppression under which Greek women lived was such that their anger erupted in occasional furious orgies; Philip Slater suggested that the killing of boy children was a direct attack on the children's fathers. Still others believe the Dionysian religion to have been an essentially female form of spirituality, a chance for women to enact the divine and horrible roles of goddesses.

Eventually the Dionysian religion suffered the same fate as the other woman-centered religions of the ancient Aegean: it was reinterpreted by men and taken from the hands of the original priestesses. The singer Orpheus, calling men to become homosexual rather than indulge women's lusts, created a substitute religion for Greece. Though the singer himself was torn to death by Maenads seeking to preserve their religious independence, there was no stopping the singing of Orpheus's head or the progress of the Orphic religion. See **Sphinx.**

Maeve, Meave, Mebhdh Of the great female figures of Ireland, Queen Maeve was probably the most splendid. Originally a goddess of the land's sovereignty and the goddess of Tara, the island's magical center, she was demoted in myth, as the centuries went on and Irish culture changed under Christian influence, to a mere mortal queen.

But no mortal queen could have been like this one, this "intoxication" or "drunken woman" (variant meanings of her name), who ran faster than horses, slept with innumerable kings whom she then discarded, and carried birds and animals across her shoulders and arms. If there was ever a woman named Maeve who reigned as queen of Ireland, it is probable that she was the namesake of the goddess; the goddess's legends may have attached themselves to a mortal bearer of her name.

Maeve is the central figure of the most important remaining old Irish epic, the *Tain Bo Cuillaigne,* or Cattle Raid of Cooley. The story begins with Maeve, then ruling the Connaught wilderness in the Irish west, lying abed with her current consort, King Aillil. They compare possessions, Aillil attempting to prove he owns more than she does. Point for point, Maeve matches him. Finally, Aillil mentions a magical bull—and wins the argument, for Maeve has no such animal.

But she knows of one, the magic bull of Cooley, and so Maeve gathers her armies to steal it. She rides into battle in an open car, with four chariots surrounding her, for she is glamorously attired and does not wish to muddy her robes. She is a fierce opponent, laying waste the armies of the land, for no man could look on Maeve without falling down in a paroxysm of desire.

The armies of Ulster, stricken with the curse of the goddess *Macha,* fall down in labor pains upon the arrival of Queen Maeve's army in their land. Only the hero Cuchulain resists, killing Locha, Maeve's handmaiden, as well as many male heroes of Connaught. Maeve tries to buy victory with her "willing thighs," stops the battle whenever she is menstruating, and otherwise shows herself to be an unusual warrior. After much bloodshed, she does indeed win her bull—but it and Aillil's bull fling themselves upon each other, tear each other to bits, and die in the bloodiest anticlimax in world literature. See also **Feithline.**

Mafdet   The Lady of the Castle of Life was an early (1st Dynasty) Egyptian goddess whose totemic animals were the cat and the mongoose; she was invoked against snakebite.

Magna Mater   "Great Mother," the Roman name for *Cybele.*

Magog, Ma Gog   With Gog, her consort, this ancient goddess of England was honored with chalk-cut effigies. A mountain-goddess, she was honored on hills still called Magg's or Megg's Hills, which became Christianized as St. Margaret's. At Wandlebury near Cambridge, the Gogs or Gogmagogs (or even Hoggogamagog Hills) were incised with massive images of two or three divinities; one was a four-breasted woman mounted on a horse. Her name may mean "Mother God."

*See Mahakala, p. 220. Field Museum of Natural History
(Neg# A86276), Chicago.*

Mahakala   One of Tibet's many names for the Great Goddess named *Kali* in nearby India.

Mahakh   Aleut dog-goddess.

Mahalat   In Jewish legend, Queen Mahalat commanded 478 bands of dancing demons. On the day of judgment, she will march them into the desert to meet her rival *Lilith* in fierce combat. Mahalat, a compulsive dancer, will whirl and gyrate in an attempt to terrify her enemy. Legend does not predict the outcome of the conflict.

Mahui-Iki, Mahuea   The underworld, the Polynesians said, was a fiery realm whose queen was Mahui-Iki. Her grandson was the trickster-hero Maui, who one day decided to extinguish her power despite the warnings of his mother *Taranga*.

   Maui traveled to Mahui-Iki's domain, where he found her stirring a cooking pot. Begging for help, Maui said he needed fire to cook some food. Mahui-Iki pulled out a fingernail and gave it to him; he secretly quenched the half-moon's fire. Then Maui asked for another, then another, until Mahui-Iki had given all her fingernails and nine of her toenails. Just as Maui was asking for her last toenail, Mahui-Iki's fury exploded and, pulling out the nail, she flung it on the earth, causing a massive fire. Maui called down rain from the heavens to extinguish the blaze, but what landed in the trees remained there, so that humans could thereafter kindle fire from wood.

Maia   We derive the name of our most beautiful springtime month from this ancient goddess who appeared in both Greek and Roman legend. In Greece, she was "grandmother," "midwife," or "wise one" (variant meanings of her name). Originally the goddess of the night sky and later the oldest of the *Pleiades*, the only surviving myth about her claims her as mother of the phallic god Hermes. The Romans identified the Greek Maia with their fire-goddess of the same name; she, like *Flora* and *Feronia*, ruled the forces of growth and warmth, including sexual heat. Maia's festival was held on the first day of her month, a rite that still survives in the Christian dedication of May to *Mary*, queen of flowers.

Maitreya   This divinity of Indian and Tibetan Buddhism appears sometimes as male, sometimes as female. Sex changes in divinities may indicate that a force is seen as essentially nonsexual; the changing sexual identity alerts the viewer not to limit the divine essence to its human form. This seems to be the case with Maitreya. In other cases, however, as with *Amaterasu* in Japan and the *Dactyls* in Greece, sex change comes with political or social change; a powerful goddess transmuted into a god can indicate that the power represented by that divinity has been transferred from human women to men.

Makore-Wawahiwa   "Fiery-eyed canoe breaker," one of *Pele's* sisters.

Ma-Ku   Chinese maiden goddess of springtime.

Mal   The old goddess of Hag's Head, the most famous of the Cliffs of Moher in Ireland's far west, she was an over-eager lover who died pursuing a much younger man along the Irish coast. The village of Miltown Malbay was named for her.

Mala Liath   "Grey eyebrows" was the name given to the *Cailleach* in Ross and Cromarty in Scotland. She was said to tend a herd of pigs, which included the wild boar of Glen Glass.

Malophoros   Greek goddess of the underworld.

Mama   The great smallpox-goddess of Korea leaves spirit footprints, which appear as little pimples, on the bodies of those she visits. If her children talk while in the grip of fever, it is believed to be her voice. The ritual to send away Mama begins five days after infection, when the poxes appear; clean drinking water ritually welcomes the spirit of Mama, then prayers are offered that family members taken by her should not return. Conducted by a woman shaman, the ceremony is called Skimun or "gate of sickness." This preventive rite continues through the twelfth day, when the patient is no longer in danger; then Mama is sent away on a mugwort mount. Called Sangma, this is made of three pieces of mugwort formed into a horse and saddled with baskets of steamed rice, cakes and money.

Mama Allpa   Peruvian mother-goddess of the harvest.

Mama Cocha   The eldest divinity of ancient Peru was the ocean ("Mother Sea"), worshiped not only by the Inca but by all the tribes of South America's Pacific Coast. Mountain dwellers would regularly descend to her, carrying their infants, for Mama Cocha was the source of health. Indeed, as the fish provider, the whale-goddess, Mama Cocha was also the source of all food.

Mama Ocllo   When the Spanish invaded South America, they found a variety of names given to the foremothers of their race by the Incas. There were four—or six—of them, and they bore the names of Mama Ocllo or Mama Ocllo Huaca, Mama Huaco, Mama Coya, and Mama Rahua; or Topa Huaco, Mama Coya, Cori Ocllo, and Ipa Huaco. Coming, with their brothers, into time at the creation, these women populated the world.

Of Mama Ocllo, it was said that she was the most intelligent sister and that she found inhabitable land for the group by scouting until she came to where the city of Cuzco rose. She killed a passing Poque Indian, cut his chest open, and removed his lungs. Carrying the bloody organs in her mouth, Mama Ocllo entered the area's impoverished towns. The residents, terrified at this murderous apparition, instantly fled, leaving the region to the people of Mama Ocllo.

Mama Quilla   In ancient Peru, this was the name of the moon-goddess, imagined as a silver disk with a woman's face. "Mother Moon" was honored at regular calendar-fixed rituals, especially held during eclipses, when a supernatural jaguar was said to try to devour her.

Maman Brigitte   A *loa* (spirit) of death in Haitian voodoo, she owns all cemeteries, particularly those in which the first body interred was a woman. Her children are the spirits who outline, dig, and mark graves.

Mamapacha, Amara, Pachamama   Among the Inca, the earth was seen as a dragon-goddess who lived beneath the mountains; occasionally she quivered, sending earthquakes through the world. Mamapacha was also the deity of agriculture; rituals in her honor had to be performed daily to assure a sufficient food supply. During planting and harvest, women would travel to the fields to talk softly to Mamapacha, sometimes pouring a thank-offering of cornmeal on her surface.

Mami, Amadubad, Aruru, Ma, Mah, Mama, Ninmah   Just as the Hebrew creation legend described mankind's creation from the earth's clay, so did others in the ancient eastern Mediterranean tell the tale. But the Sumerians said that the creator was not a god but the almighty All-Mother Mami, the lapis-crowned ruler of earth.

A potter, the goddess mixed clay over the cosmic abyss to form 14 images of herself, placing them in two rows, seven on her right hand and seven on her left. Between the rows, Mami set a baked brick. She uttered life-giving incantations over the clay images, and they sprang to life: those on her right hand as men, those on her left as women, both in the goddess's image, hence her title *Nindum* ("lady of procreation").

Delighted with her creations, Mami called together the other gods for a celebration. It was not long before the goddess, now drunk, began playing with the remnant clay of creation. In her intoxication, she created barren women, eunuchs, and four other unrecorded human types. This excited Enki, the god of wisdom, who decided to display his creativity. He was too drunk: up from the ground wobbled a crippled, retarded man. Horrified at the creature, Enki begged Mami to correct it, but the creator-goddess had no power to change what already existed.

Mami's symbolic brick was a pillow to Sumerian women as in labor they partook of the All-Mother's power. They also called her name during childbirth; she was especially kind to those birthing second children. Any woman's work was an image of the mother's creativity; when men served her, they did so as *fanatici* eunuchs who danced in wild ecstasy to trumpet and tambourine, wounding themselves in Mami's honor.

As Mami's worship traveled across the Mediterranean, she became less and less a gentle earth mother, more and more a warrior-goddess of private property, protector of the rich field. As owner of the earth, she demanded that a corner of every tilled field be left wild in her honor; if this were done, she would protect the entire holding against bad crops and covetous neighbors. In these later times, Mami was portrayed standing or riding on fierce lions, bejeweled with the riches of her people. By the time she reached Rome, she was the image of that people's warrior, *Bellona*, and so the gentle earth mother of the East passed into Western history as Mah-Bellona. See also **Eriskegal, Mawu, Nagar-Saga.**

Mamitu The Chaldean divine ancestor responsible for all that happens to her descendants, this destiny-goddess seems to be a sort of deified chromosome.

Manasa Snake-goddess of Bengal who inspires women.

Mania We use her name to describe an obsession, possibly a reminder of the days when her ghost came back to earth to drive the living mad. To the Romans, Mania was the mother of ghosts. Her spirits were penned in Rome's center, in a deep well capped with a stone that was removed several times annually. Those nights when the dead roamed in search of victims, woolen effigies were hung on doorposts, one for every free person in the house, a different style of doll for every slave—all in the hope that Mania's hosts would leave the house in peace. See **Erinyes.**

Manto   We still call prophetic words *mantic* speech after the name of this Greek heroine, daughter of the seer Tiresias and a gifted prophet. A Theban woman, she was captured by the people of Argos who, impressed with her gifts, carried her off to become an oracle at Delphi.

Marahi Devi   Indian cholera-goddess; see **Sitala.**

Marcia   Ancient agricultural goddess of Italy.

Marcia Proba   A legendary Celtic queen of Britain, she ruled in the 3rd century B.C. Her people's law, notably fair in its treatment of women, was inscribed into the Marcian Statutes; the same law in Ireland became the Brehon Laws, which provided legal equity for ancient Irish women. Many provisions of the Marcian Statutes became part of the later Magna Charta, although the legal equality of the sexes was virtually ignored.

Mardeq Avalon   The wind-goddess of the Cheremis of Russia was worshiped in sacred groves that included both oak and birch. Eighth in order of precedence among divinities, she was honored even more than the earth-goddess.

Maria   In Lithuania and Latvia, this Christian-seeming name was used to disguise goddess imagery. It is thought that the main goddess hiding behind this title was *Perkuna Tete*, the mother of thunder and lightning.

Mari-Ama   This Scandinavian death-goddess was invoked as "Mother Death" by her people, who depicted her with four hands holding a trident, a skull, a rope, and a drum.

Marici   Tantric Buddhist goddess connected with the sun and masculined into a god in China and Japan.

Marinette   A powerful *loa* ("spirit") sorceress, Marinette "of the dry arms" is a screech-owl demon who, when she possesses Haitian voodoo worshipers, causes them to move their arms like wings and hook their fingers into claws. Like *Hecate* among the Greeks, Marinette is a night-goddess who searches the woodlands for offerings left for her. Special services in her honor are held far out in the country, under a tent beside a huge fire fueled with salt and oil, where chickens, pigs, and goats are sacrificed.

Marpesia One of the great *Amazon* military queens, she began her victorious campaign, the Greeks tell us, at the Black Sea and soon conquered Thrace and Syria. Then, with Queen *Hippo* she marched through Ephesus and Cyrene, finally reaching the Aegean Sea. Marpesia then settled back to rule her empire. But she was called back to the battlefield to defend it, losing her life putting down an uprising of her subjects.

Marpessa Homer called this Greek heroine, the lover of the mortal Idas, the "fair-ankled daughter." When the immortal Apollo tried to rape her, Marpessa appealed to Zeus for aid. He gave her a choice of mates: the god or the man. Not surprisingly, she chose Idas rather than her assailant.

Maruwa, Marwe Among the Wachanga and Chaga of Kenya, this ancient story is told: Maruwa and her little sister were set to guard the family bean garden. Thirsty, Maruwa walked to a nearby pond for a drink, leaving her sister to watch the beans. While Maruwa was gone, a baboon troop descended and devoured the entire crop in front of the frightened little girl.

Maruwa, ashamed of losing her family's food supply, threw herself into the pond. Sinking to the bottom, she found a village where she was welcomed and given hospitality. Wise in the ways of spirit people, Maruwa refused to eat their food, claiming that people above the waters lived on bitter foods, unlike the tasty meals served beneath.

The old woman with whom Maruwa was staying gave her daily instructions, which she disobeyed every day. This drew a little girl to her; she told Maruwa to ask to go home, and then to obey the old woman's orders. The old woman told Maruwa to jump into a pile of manure. She did, and instantly she found herself at home, covered with silver chains and expensive beads.

Another village girl, envious of Maruwa's new wealth, imitated her actions. When she arrived beneath the waters, she followed the old woman's orders to the letter—including leaving all the housework to Maruwa's helper, the little underwater girl. This child told the visitor to ask to go home, but reversed the advice she'd given Maruwa. The girl returned home, indeed, but full of poisonous fire that drove her to drown herself in waters that remain bitter to this day.

Mary There is a time-honored tradition among goddesses: a people never truly gives up its own. So, when the early Europeans were slowly Christianized as Roman imperial power grew, they faced conversion—

often forcible—to a faith that denied a major portion of their traditional beliefs.

What Christianity denied was the possibility of divine femininity, that force worshiped in ancient Europe as *Epona, Freya, Hertha, Mokosh,* and under countless other names. More than just a nominal change was entailed when the utterly nonfeminine Christian theology was introduced to these goddesses' devotees. Christianity provided no image of the mother-goddess to substitute for the ones they revered so highly.

It was not long, however, before the people located within Christian mythology a female figure that could serve quite adequately. The Virgin Mary (daughter of *Hannah*), who lost and regained her divine son, later reigning as queen of heaven, had the necessary qualifications. Try as the church might, it could not stop the spread of Mariolatry, an extreme reverence toward the power of the Mother of God.

Many scholars have traced the spread of the Marian devotions; some contend that from the first, Christianity contained female-oriented rituals that, like the all-women feasts of the Roman *Bona Dea,* honored the mother above the son. Whether or not that was so, the excesses of Mary's devoted followers brought warning after warning from church officials that she was not a goddess—despite bearing all the titles and attributes of one. Even today, long after other goddesses have been forgotten, Mary remains a threat to patriarchal Christianity; the greater proportion of churches are dedicated to her, not her son, and she is the one to whom many Catholics prefer to address their prayers.

Marzana   This was the Polish name for the goddess of winter and death, called Marena in Russia. Each spring an effigy of "Old Woman Winter" was carried through the village and thrown, amid rejoicing, out of town.

Masaya   The ancient Nicaraguan goddess of volcanoes and earthquakes was the source of oracles; she was described as having black skin, thinning hair, and long sagging breasts.

Matariki   The *Pleiades* among the Maori, seen as an ancestor and her six children.

Matergabiae   "Womanfire," Lithuanian goddess of the household. To her the house mistress offered the first loaf from each bread-baking; ornamental markings were molded into the dough with the fingers to designate the loaf as belonging to the goddess, a custom still used by some Lithuanian women. The last loaf was offered to the baker herself,

*See Ma-Ku, p. 221. Field Museum of Natural History
(Neg# 35931), Chicago.*

as a representative of the goddess; she ate it at her pleasure as a communion with her productive energies.

Mati   It was a grave sin in the Slavic culture to strike the earth with iron implements before March 25: Mati ("Mother Earth") was pregnant until that time, and one does not strike a pregnant woman. Mati's full name was Mati Syra Zemlja ("moist Mother Earth"), and she was the great source of power and strength to her people. When they swore oaths, they did so by eating soil or placing lumps of dirt on their head; when they married, each party swallowed a bit of earth.

Among the Russians, who also honored Mati as supreme, her prophetic powers were acknowledged; to know how the harvest would turn out, you only had to dig a hole in the ground and place your ear to it. The sound of a full sleigh meant a good harvest; the tinkling of an empty one meant trouble ahead. The Russians also cared for their Mother's honor by demanding that anyone who spit on her apologize immediately.

The Matronit, Makhut, Matronita   In the Cabala's esoteric Judaism, we find two demigoddesses formed by analyzing the mystic name of god, YHWH. Each letter was given a human character: thus, the *Y* of Yahweh became the Father and the first *H* the Mother, who proceeded from the Father. These two produced *W*, the Son, the King, and finally a second *H*, the blameless Daughter, the essence of kingship, Makhut or the Matronit.

However abstract the analysis that produced her, the Matronit soon became a livelier personage than uplifting allegory should permit. The lowest of the 10 mystic emanations of the male godhead, she was the one that human senses could perceive. Jacob, for instance, perceived her, as did Moses. She not only took the latter's soul to heaven when he died, but she apparently took human form in order to sleep with him. But her usual lover was her brother, the king, with whom she regularly cohabited in the temple on Friday nights. (Jewish couples were encouraged to have intercourse then, in emulation of the sacred couple.)

Whenever the children of Israel fell into sin, however, the Matronit and her king were separated; the king mated instead with *Lilith* while the demon king Samael was allowed to have intercourse with the pristine Matronit. All this—even read as allegory—is rather seamy and melodramatic material; it seems that Judaism, in denying the possibility of female divinity, left itself open to this kind of overblown and seductive quasi-mythology.

Matuta, Mater Matuta   To the Romans, Dawn was not the reckless, lustful goddess that many other people saw. Instead, she was a matron, the mother bringing day to her frightened children. They worshiped her in a touching ceremony on June 11, when women held their sisters' children in their arms and begged Dawn's blessings for them. At the same rite, the Matralia, the women drove from the temple a slavewoman who symbolized night, thereby incarnating their divinity's own activity in human form.

Mawu   The creator-goddess of Dahomey in northwest Africa, Mawu not only made the earth but created human beings as well. At first (like *Mami* in Mesopotamia), she used clay mixed with water, but running short of materials, Mawu began to re-enliven the bodies of dead people, which explains why people sometimes look like their forebears.

But her experiment in creation was not entirely successful, for humanity began to grow arrogant. Annoyed with her earthly creation, Mawu retreated to her home in the sky. Things did not go well on earth after her departure, so Mawu sent her son Lisa to teach useful arts to humanity, then instructed him to watch the people each day to ensure obedience to her rules. Because Lisa was sometimes identified with the sun and because of the proverb "When Lisa punishes, Mawu forgives," the goddess was sometimes assumed to be a moon spirit.

Maya, Mahamaya   Like *Shakti* ("energy") and *Prakriti* ("nature"), Maya is less a goddess than one of the great philosophic concepts of Indian Hinduism embodied in female form. In Hindu thought, the male energy is essentially passive, while the female is the force of action. Maya is one of those active powers: the constant movement of the universe, pervasive to the atomic level. There is no life—no existence, even—without Maya, but she is so powerful that we cannot see the essence of things and mistake her movement for reality. For this reason, Maya is often called "the veil of illusion," the dance of multiplicity that distracts us so that we cannot see all matter as essentially identical. Illusion, however, as the sages have stressed, is not the same as falsehood. Maya is not a negative force, but can be a mesh through which we perceive the ultimate reality of existence—if we are not distracted by her magnificent creativeness and complexity.

Mayáhuel   There were two major myths told by the ancient Mexicans of the Great Goddess whose name means the "strangling one," ruler of the earth and the night sky as well as of hallucinations and drunkenness. The 400-breasted goddess was said to nurse the stars, the fish in the oceanic heaven; in art Mayáhuel was shown sitting naked on a throne of tortoises and snakes, offering a dish of intoxicating pulque to her worshipers.

The Nahua, who lived in central Mexico before the Aztec, said that Mayáhuel originally lived in the heavens, where she slept constantly, guarded by the stern goddess Tzitzimitl. But the god of winds blew across her, caressing and arousing her until she awoke. To consummate their desire, they descended to earth where, as soon as their feet touched the ground, they melted together into a beautiful tree with two branches— one of which, the goddess, instantly flowered.

But the chaperone Tzitzimitl, who had been dozing, awoke to find the maiden goddess gone. Furious, she gathered an army of gods and started in pursuit. Finding the heavenly tree rooted in the earth's soil, she cursed the divinities it held. The tree cracked in two and Tzitzimitl fed the flowering branch to the young gods, who ate their former friend.

When the gods had departed, the wind-god resumed his own shape and gathered the few bits and bones of his lover, burying them with care in the earth. There they sprouted into the maguey plant, which gives forth a winy sap that can be fermented into pulque, then distilled into mescal or tequila.

The other version of the story says that Mayáhuel lived on earth as a peasant woman. One day she passed a merry mouse who not only refused to shy at her approach but actually danced and scurried about under her gaze. Mayáhuel noticed that the rodent had been nibbling the maguey plant; she put a pot under the broken stem and caught some of the sap. This she took home with her, discovering the basis of intoxication, which she introduced to the gods, a gift so popular that they welcomed her as one of them and her earthly husband as the god of gambling and of flowers.

Mayi-Mayi   The Australian *Pleiades,* star-goddesses.

Medea   Without the aid of the "cunning one," the Greek hero Jason would have been unable to obtain the golden fleece from the kingdom of Colchis. The princess Medea, adept in magic, first led the Greek through dangers surrounding the well-guarded treasure; then she sailed off with him on the *Argo,* bringing her brother with her so that, when pursued and in danger of capture, she could kill him and cast him piecemeal overboard. The people of Colchis, stopping to catch for burial the members of their prince, eventually let the Greeks escape.

When they reached Greece, Medea found that nothing could hold the wandering attentions of Jason. Though Medea had borne him several children—14, some sources say—he married again, a well-endowed princess. He seemed, however, to have forgotten the temperament of his first spouse, who promptly killed his children and new wife, mounted her serpent chariot, and flew away.

An ancient version of the tale says that Medea, far from slaying her offspring, placed them under the protection of *Hera* and left Jason's city. But a plague broke out, and the Corinthians killed the children as a sacrifice; thereafter they offered 14 children each year as servants to the goddess. In this version, Medea is not only connected with the goddess of womanhood, Hera, but is herself considered divine.

Jason ended poorly, wandering homeless through Greece until he wretchedly slumped beneath his old ship, the *Argo*, pitying himself and his aimless life. A piece of the rotting hulk suddenly detached itself and brained him.

Medea did better. Flying to Athens, she married King Aegeus. But she grew jealous of the attention he lavished on his son Theseus, whom he favored over Medea's son Medus. So she mounted her chariot again and flew home to the north, to Colchis, where she continued her magical practices until deciding to leave earth. So great a sorceress did not need to pass through death's portals; she went straight to the Elysian Fields, where she became a goddess, worshiped in Italy as the snake divinity *Angitia*.

Meditrina   Roman goddess of medicine.

Medusa   Once she was a beautiful woman who took the sea-god as a lover. Often Medusa would lie with Poseidon in the spring grass, the heavy fragrance of blossoming trees around them. But once, the Greeks said, the pair made their bed within a chapel of *Athene*. The offended goddess turned Medusa into a *Gorgon*, later engineering Medusa's murder.

As she died at the hand of Athene's servant, Medusa gave birth. From her neck sprang the magnificent winged Pegasus and the hero Chrysaor as well. Drops fell on the desert, and there engendered snakes. The Gorgon's remaining blood was caught in vials; it had such power that a single droplet from the left side could raise the dead, and the same tiny amount from the right could instantly kill.

Behind this eerie figure seems to be an early goddess, possibly similar to the corn mother *Demeter*, also said to have mated in the form of a mare with Poseidon, a name that merely means "husband of earth." Medusa is also believed to derive from an Anatolian sun-goddess. The fierce snake-haired head of late legend probably was originally the mask worn by priestesses when they impersonated the goddess; later peoples, not remembering the old rites, explained the image as a decapitated woman.

Megaera This Greek word named the cleft in the earth into which sacrificial pigs were driven during the festival of Thesmophoria; the bodies of the sacred animals restored the fertility of the earth mother. Megaera ("anger") was also the name of one of the *Erinyes* and of the first wife of Heracles, whom he murdered and for whose death he was sent to perform 12 near-impossible tasks.

Mehit A double of *Tefnut*, worshiped in Egypt as a lion-headed woman.

Mehitabel In the Cabala, a mysterious figure, the mother of *Lilith* the younger.

Mehurt, Mehueret The Egyptian goddess *Neith* as the sacred cow of creation, the mystic animal mother of the world. She was shown as a pregnant woman with huge breasts, or as a cow-headed woman holding the lotus of the world.

Meilichia The name of this obscure underworld-goddess, companion of Zeus in his snake form, may have been a title for *Demeter* as the mate of Zeus.

Melanippe The "black mare" was one of the most illustrious *Amazon* warriors and one of three queens of the Thermodon empire. When the Greek hero Heracles sacked the Amazons' capital, he took Melanippe captive, but later released her when he acquired the women's most priceless treasure, their golden belt of sovereignty. In some legends, she accompanied the Amazon forces in their raids on Athens.

Meliae One of the Greek creation stories claimed that when Mother *Gaea* arranged the castration of her oppressive son-lover Uranus, drops of his blood fell on her fertile body. In those spots, Gaea conceived. Among her daughters by that strange and brutal mating were the ash-tree spirits called Meliae. The world's original women, they were the mothers of humankind, for people rose from the earth at their roots.

Melissa This name, meaning "bee," was applied to the priestesses of the earth-goddess *Demeter* and of *Artemis* of Ephesus. It was also said that one Melissa was a Cretan princess who learned to collect honey as food

for the infant Zeus, who, when he grew into a supreme god, turned his
nurse into a bee.

Mellonia   Roman goddess of bees.

Melusine   In Celtic France they tell of a water spirit, Pressina, who married
a mortal king but made him promise never to visit her when she was in
childbed. But when their first children—the triplets Melusine, Melior,
and Palatina—were born, the king forgot himself and rushed into the
queen's chambers. Angrily reminding her husband of his promise, Pressina gathered the children and disappeared to a miragelike coastal
island.

There Pressina brought up her children. The oldest girl, Melusine,
was infected by her mother's disappointment at the marriage's outcome. She organized her sisters for a magical raid on their father and
encased him in a mountain, together with his castle and servants.
Returning, they found their mother angry, for this revenge had gone
too far. Pressina, unable to contain her vengefulness, cursed Melusine
to become part-serpent each Sunday.

Melusine wandered across the continent, hoping to find a man
who would agree to a marriage contract with a "never on Sunday"
clause. Finally she fell in love with Raymond of Poitou. They lived
passionately together until Raymond grew curious about Melusine's
prohibition and spied on his wife. She discovered the oath-breaking
and fled from him, becoming a *Banshee*-like creature who afterward
haunted his family.

Mem Loimis   Among the Wintuns of the Pacific Coast, this underworld-
goddess was said to control the earth's water supply.

Menalippe   Because she could so accurately predict the future, the Greek
gods hated this daughter of centaurs. So they sent the wind-god Aeolus
to rape her, then transformed her into a horse, the mare Ocyrrhoe.

Menat, Manat   With *Al-Lat* and *Al-Uzza*, this goddess of fate and time was
the third member of the ancient Arabian religious trinity. The three
goddesses seem a single woman, passing through the three parts of her
life: in youth, the virgin warrior Al-Uzza; in the prime of life, the fertile,
benevolent Al-Lat; and as an aged woman, Menat, a force of fate and an
embodiment of death.

The religion of Menat stretched across most of ancient Arabia. Her
principal sanctuary was located on the road between Mecca and Medina.
There she was worshiped in the form of a black uncut stone (see

Cybele), destroyed by Mohammed as he struggled to establish his own male-centered religion. Despite the destruction of her shrine, this goddess's worship long continued. But her people, impressed by the success of the masculine religions around them, changed Menat slightly: from a goddess into a god.

Meng-Po Niang-Niang "Lady Meng" was said by the Chinese to live just inside the exit door of hell. There she brewed a secret broth that, forcibly administered to those departing for a new incarnation, caused them to forget not only where they lived between lives but also their previous lives—and even the words of their last human language.

Menrva The Etruscan thunderbolt-goddess was originally distinct from *Athene*, but shared with her patronage of commerce and industry. She was the special goddess of artisans, doctors and musicians. See **Minerva.**

Mens "Menstruation" does not, as some women fear, include the English word for the other sex within it. Instead, it derives from the name of the Roman goddess of the "right moment."

Mentha, Minthe The spirit of the mint plant was said to be the beloved of the Greek underworld ruler; she may have been an aspect of Hades's other "wife," the spring-goddess *Persephone.*

Mere-Ama The "sea mother" of the Finns and Saami was also called Vete-Ema or Mier-Iema, according to the language of her worshipers. But she was conceived identically by all of them: as the spirit of water. Her most powerful manifestation was, of course, the ocean, but she resided as well in streams and brooks.

At ceremonies in honor of this goddess of silky, silver-streaked hair, her people were sprinkled with water, an embodiment of Mere-Ama. When a bride moved into a new home to start a family, one of the first things she did was to make the acquaintance of the "water mother" of the area, walking to the stream nearest the new house and offering bread and cheese, or cloth and thread, to the goddess. The bride would then wash her face and hands, or at least sprinkle herself with water. Those married in winter, when Mere-Ama was distant beneath the ice, would gather after the ice broke up for a general ceremony of friendliness; all who participated were blessed with healthy children, for the water mother controlled human, as well as animal and vegetative, reproduction.

Mere-Ama also ruled sea creatures, especially the fish on whom her people depended for food. To woo her good nature, humans only had to pour liquor into the sea; then many fish would bite when fishing began, for Mere-Ama loved brandy.

Meri An ancient name for *Isis* as goddess of the sea; used for *Hathor* as well. It may be etymologically the same as *Mary*.

Meroe This Greek witch could lower the sky, extinguish the stars, raise the dead, and send the gods to hell. When angry, she could turn people into beavers, snakes, or rams; she also teleported them hundreds of miles from home. Whenever Meroe needed human blood, she simply selected someone, stole his heart, and substituted a sponge; the man died as the sponge drank his blood. Like other witches of Thessaly in the north of Greece, she was renowned for her magical craft.

Merope Of the seven starry sisters called the *Pleiades*, one of them—the shy sister or Lost Pleiad—is virtually invisible to stargazers. In Greek times, she was sometimes called *Electra*, crying for the loss of Troy. At other times, she was Merope, wife of the criminal king Sisyphus who stewed his children and was sentenced to eternal punishment; in embarrassment and shame, his star wife faded from human sight. The name Merope was also used of a victim of rape; Orion, her assailant, was blinded by Merope's father in retaliation.

Mertseger, Merseger "Friend of silence," she lived on the pyramidal peak of the burial ground at Egyptian Thebes. Benevolent and punishing by turns, she was sometimes shown as a snake with three heads—one its own, one human, one that of a vulture—and sometimes as a snake with a human head. See **Ta-Dehnet**.

Meskhoni, Meskhent Like the Sumerian *Mami*, this Egyptian birth-goddess was symbolized by a brick, but a human-headed one in her case. On such a goddess image an Egyptian woman crouched during labor. Meskhoni appeared—usually in company with *Ermutu*—at the precise moment when contractions began and remained through the delivery to predict the future of the newborn. In Egyptian bas-reliefs, Meskhoni appeared as a woman wearing palm shoots on her head.

Meta, Mestra In Greek legend, she was the daughter of the mortal Erysichthon, whom *Demeter* afflicted with insatiable hunger. The sea-god Poseidon, who desired Meta, offered her the power of metamorphosis in return for sexual favors. She concurred, and her father—discovering her new talent—afterward regularly sold her at market, spent the money for food, then sold her in another animal form.

Metanira, Megaera This queen of the Greek town of Eleusis was kind to the mourning corn mother *Demeter* after the abduction of young *Persephone*. As a reward for the queen's hospitality, Demeter taught Metanira's family the arts of agriculture.

Meter The oldest of Greek goddesses, her name means simply "mother" and survives in that of *Demeter* ("corn mother" or "earth mother"). Statues of Meter were half-carved: the top a stately maternal figure, the lower half uncut rock.

Metis "Prudent counsel" was a Titan, daughter of the ocean queen of early Greece. When the new pantheon headed by Zeus arrived in her territory, Metis's priority was noted by the invaders, who named her as their sky-god's first wife. They said that Metis told Zeus what emetic would make his father, Cronos, disgorge the other gods; ironically, Zeus later swallowed Metis. Afraid, as his own father, Cronos, had been, of being surpassed by his offspring, Zeus devoured his pregnant spouse and gave birth to her daughter *Athene* through his head. This legend is a pastiche of elements from different tribal myths and eras, consistent only in its attempt to disguise the early mother-oriented religion, of which both Metis and Athene seem to have been part—a legend that is less a true myth than what Jane Ellen Harrison called a "theological expedient."

Metsannetsyt Among the people of western Finland, this forest woman was said to live in the woods where she exposed herself to passing men, hoping to seduce them. However, if they were to take her in their arms, they would embrace a tree stump.

Metsarhatija Finnish goddess of the forest.

Metzli Aztec moon-goddess who sacrificed herself to bring back sunlight.

Mictecacíhuatl In pre-Columbian Mexico, this goddess ruled the nine rivers of the afterlife to which evil souls were condemned. There, however, they did not suffer torments or pain; instead, they led afterlives of boredom and monotony, while better souls enjoyed the colorful existence of heaven.

See Marici, p. 224. Field Museum of Natural History
(Neg# 49491), Chicago.

Mielikki   Finnish goddess of game.

Minachiamman, Thurgai   Local goddess of Madura in India, she incarnated as a little girl to revenge herself on a king who dared to close her temples. She appeared miraculously in the palace, wearing a tiny bracelet that duplicated a favorite diadem of the queen's. Astrologers warned the king not to adopt the babe, so he cast Minachiamman into the river from which a merchant plucked her. He raised her to be a fine young woman, who attracted the eye of Shiva, incarnated as a poor man in a village on the River Kaveri. They were so poor that Shiva took the bracelet from his wife's arm and attempted to sell it. But, alas, he was accused of stealing the queen's jewel and was put to death. The goddess, taking her demon form, under which she was called Thurgai, immediately killed the king in retaliation.

Mindhal, Mindhal Devi, Bhagvati   In Himachal Pradesh, this was the name given to a goddess who emerged from the ground in the form of a huge black stone. The woman from whose yard Mindhal issued tried to push the stone back into the earth by pounding on it, but to no avail. Converted to awareness of the goddess's intent, the woman tried to convert her friends. When they laughed, she transformed herself and her seven sons into standing stones around Mindhal's image.

Minerva, in Etruscan, **Menrva**   Familiar though her name is, the origin and descent of this Roman goddess are vague. Some scholars claim the figure of Minerva fused Etruscan and Italian deities of handicrafts and war, respectively; some claim she was always the artisans' patron and that the imposition of the Greek figure *Athene* on her meant the addition of war to her domain. (The Latins already had a proper war-goddess, *Bellona*.)

It is clear that the goddess's name derives from the ancient root for "mind," and her domain was—even more than Athene's—intellectual. She was wisdom incarnate in female form, the goddess therefore of the application of intellect to everyday work, thus of commerce and crafts. She was also said to be the inventor of music, that most mathematical of arts.

The Romans celebrated her worship from March 19 to 23 during the Quinquatrus, the artisans' holiday. The "goddess of a thousand works," as Ovid called her, was pleased to see scholars and schoolmasters join in spring vacation with those who labored with their hands.

Minerva Medica   If her name seems Roman, it is only because of the imperial legions' policy of *interpretatio Romano* whereby Celtic goddesses were assimilated to those from their homeland. Many local and tribal goddesses lost their identities this way; many became *Minervas*, perhaps because they were originally connected with household industry, war, or healing—all of which fell under the dominion of the Italian original. At least one "Minerva" was strong enough to resist renaming; see **Sulis.**

Minu Anni, Minu Ulla "She who apportions men into sanction or denial," an Assyrian fate-goddess.

Miriam The greatest woman prophet of Jewish tradition, she began to foretell events at the age of five, at which time she also began working with her mother, *Jocebed,* as a midwife. She foresaw the birth of her brother Moses, and it was Miriam who knew the babe could be saved from death if placed in a reedy basket and hidden in a river. Her prophetic gift was matched by her genius for poetry; it was Miriam's song that celebrated the Hebrew escape from Egypt's pharaoh.

Like many prophetic females, Miriam was associated with water. Her name seems to be derived from *marah*, the "bitter water," and she sang her most famous poem after crossing the Red Sea. Most important, she gave her name to the miraculous spring that burst forth from the desert rock struck by Moses; Jewish legend says that it was an ancient spring, brought into existence at twilight of creation's sixth day and rediscovered by Miriam.

But even a great woman prophet and poet can overreach herself in a patriarchal society. Miriam did so by siding with her sister-in-law *Zipporah* when the latter complained that Moses's divine revelations had led to his abandoning conjugal duties. (Miriam herself continued to cohabit frequently with her husband, leaving her inspirational work outside the bedroom.) Jehovah, furious at Miriam's condemnation of Moses, spit in her face, and the poet grew leprous. But the father-god then cured her, demanding only a seven-day infection as punishment; during that time the Hebrew people would not leave the spot of Miriam's confinement.

Miru Throughout Polynesia the queen of the last three circles of the underworld was a goddess, with Miru being one of her common names. The soul, departing earthly life, was supposed to take a great leap, landing safely in the arms of ancestors. But standing nearby with a net, hoping to catch weaklings and evildoers, was Miru; she threw captured souls into her oven. There they did not suffer, but were instantly consumed, while better souls lived calmly in a world identical to earth but eternal.

Mnasa   Little is known of this Mycenaean goddess but her name, which means "memory" and is related to the Greek *Mnemosyne*. Mnasa was part of a trinity of goddesses worshiped in Pylos, far in the west of the Peloponnese. Her companions were the young woman Potnia and Posidaeia ("wife of the husband"), the woman of childbearing years. This would make Mnasa, the third member of the traditional female trinity, an old woman wise in her years.

Mnemosyne   The daughter of earth and sky, she was to the Greeks "memory" personified. She was mother of the *Muses*, goddesses of art, whom she conceived in nine days of continual intercourse with Zeus. In Boeotia, she was worshiped in the form of a spring, and a fountain bearing her name was said to flow in Hades.

Modgud   The servant of *Hel*, the Scandinavian queen of death, this maiden guarded the path to the underworld. To reach her realm, the newly dead had to cross Hell-Ways, the yawning caverns surrounding the World Tree Yggdrasil, at whose roots Hel lived. Spanning the abysses where the roaring River Gjoll flowed was a gold-paved bridge where Modgud stood her watch.

Moirae, Moira   In Homeric times, there was just one "fate," and her name was Moira ("strong one"). Then, as often happened in antiquity, the Greek goddess began to multiply herself. Soon there were two Fates, one of birth and one of death, or for good and evil fortunes; in the Olympian gods' war with the Titans they appeared, brandishing brass pestles. Later there were four Fates. But most commonly, the original goddess triplicated into the three Fates, the spinners of destiny.

   Sometimes the goddesses were said to be the daughters of *Nyx* the night queen; in other tales, they sprang from the womb of *Themis* the lawgiver. They were named Clotho ("spinner"), she who bore the distaff and spun the thread of life; Lachesis ("measurer"), to whom the thread was passed as it came off the spindle; and Atropos ("inevitable"), who snipped it with her shears. Among the most ancient pre-Hellenic Greek goddesses, they never lost their authority; even Zeus could not countermand them. Once Apollo got the Fates drunk, in an attempt to save a friend's life; they bargained with him, agreeing to cut another person's thread instead.

Mokosh   The ancient Slavic culture worshiped the Great Goddess of earth under this name, and her religion survived into Christian times. As late as the 16th century, Christian chronicles complained that Slavic women still "went to Mokosh" ceremonially.

Mokosh was represented by stones, particularly those breast-like in shape; rain was perceived as Mother Mokosh's milk, so she was invoked in time of drought. In the 19th century in the Ukraine, archaeologists moved some of Mokosh's stones during a survey; a drought ensued; the people of the area blamed the scholars.

At the stones of Mokosh, people came on pilgrimages to pray for health and prosperity. The crippled and handicapped particularly brought offerings of grain and animals, begging for the restoration of wholeness.

In Russian folklore, Mokosh survived as Mokuskha, female haunts who live in each house and spin every night.

Momu   An ancient Scottish goddess of wells and hills.

Moncha   Druid priestess of Irish legend.

Moneta   Originally this was a title of the Roman goddess *Juno*, indicating her tendency to warn against ill-fated marriages. But the temple of Juno Moneta contained the Roman mint, so her name evolved into the word for money.

Mora, Mahr, Mara   When you go to bed at night, German and Slavic lore said, you should beware of stray pieces of straw lying around the bedroom, for they could be Mara in disguise. Her name lives on in our language as "nightmare," for she was the night-riding witch who entered bedrooms as a white shadow to strangle her victims and suck their blood. Alternatively, she tormented them with bad dreams, appearing in these visions as a leather band, a mouse, a cat, a snake, or a white horse. She did not confine her activities to the torture of humans, however; she was just as happy persecuting animals and plants.

Morgan Le Fay, Fata Morgana, Morgain   *Mor* meant "sea" in several Celtic languages, and Morgan was a sea-goddess whose name still survives in Brittany where sea sprites are called morgans. The most famous sea-goddess was surnamed Le Fay; in Welsh mythology, she was said to be a queen of Avalon, the underworld fairyland where King Arthur was carried—some said by Morgan herself—when he disappeared from this world. In some legends, Morgan was Arthur's sister, whereas in other tales she was immortal, living with her eight sisters in Avalon, where she was an artist and a healer.

Some scholars claim she was the same goddess as the one called, in Ireland, Great Queen *Morrigan*. That crow-headed goddess was a battle divinity, which suggests that Morgan might also have been a goddess of death. Indeed, there is dispute over whether her surname means "the fairy" or "the fate." If Morgan were not a mere sea sprite but the goddess of death, that would explain her unfriendly character in Malory's *Morte d'Arthur*, where Morgan appears as the king's dreaded foe, constantly plotting his death, and in *Sir Gawain*, where she seems similarly bent on the destruction of the king and his Round Table. If Morgan were once the queen of death, ruler of the underworld and of rebirth to the early Britons, a cultural shift could easily have seen her reinterpreted as a powerful demonic force bent on destruction.

Morgay   North English harvest-goddess.

Moriath, Moriath Morca, Muiriath   Her name means "sea-land," and she was an Irish princess who, finding a man named Labraid irresistibly attractive, set herself to win him with music and flattery—and succeeded.

Mormo   A Greek female boogie like *Lamia*.

Morrigan, Morrigu   There was a trinity of goddesses of war and death in ancient Ireland, and scholars argue about which one was the preeminent figure. Was Morrigan a form of *Badb*, or the other way around? Was *Nemain* the same as, or different from, *Macha*? Was the overall name Morrigan, with the component parts being Macha, Badb, and Nemain; or was there no overall name, with Macha being a completely different goddess?

   The disputes are probably unresolvable. And the goddesses involved are difficult to distinguish; here one appears as the *Bean Nighe* or Washer-at-the-Ford, there the same figure bears a different name. All the goddesses could take the shape of a crow. All were giants when they took human form.

   The only thing that distinguished Morrigan from the others was her association with magic; she sang runes and cast charms before battles to strengthen her favorites. Otherwise she was, like Badb, seen before battle washing the armor of the doomed; she was seen flying over the battlefield as a crow hoping for carrion; she could turn into a snake to observe the slaughter from that angle. From our point of view, this "great queen" is hardly a cheerful female image, but *Anahita*, the *Valkyries, Bellona,* and many other warrior-goddesses show that other cultures and eras have not been so squeamish.

Moruadh, Moruach   The brandy-drinking sea maiden of Ireland was said to have a red nose, green teeth and hair, and a pig's eyes. Like other sea spirits, she made a very good wife for a human man—if he could keep her, which entailed stealing her magic *cohuleen druith*, the cap that allowed her to breathe beneath the sea. Of course—like swan maidens and other enchanted lovers—should she ever find her cap, Moruadh would leave home, husband, and human children to return to freedom.

Mother Friday   The Russian and Slavonic harvest-goddess was very particular about her people's keeping her feast days sacred. If, on the goddess's favored days, any woman worked on her spinning wheel or loom, or even mended cloth, the offending woman would be blinded by dust that rose from the earth.

Mou-Njami   Among the Uralic speakers of Siberia, this was the name of Mother Earth, a goddess who carried eyes within her as other creatures carried eggs. When females became pregnant, Mou-Njami provided the eyes for the offspring, thus allowing them to see her. Because of their sacredness, hunters were forbidden to injure their prey's eyes, which had to be carefully cut out and buried as an offering to Mother Earth.

Mou-Njami looked like a huge green animal, for the grass was her fur. Every year, she shed her coat and grew another one. Because the soil was the Mother's skin, her people never cut into it with metal knives or spears. Even needless digging or driving of fence posts was forbidden out of concern for the earth's skin.

Mu Olokukurtilisop   Among the Cuna of the Isthmus of Panama, this was the name of the great preexistent goddess who parthenogenetically produced the sun, took him as her lover, birthed the moon and mated with him, and thus produced the entire skyful of stars. Still full of energy, Mu Olokukurtilisop took all the stars as lovers, thus producing the plants and animals of our world.

Muime Chriosda   "Foster mother of Christ," a title given to the Christianized form of *Bridget* which emphasizes her maternal qualities.

Muireartach   Her name means "eastern sea," and this Irish goddess was the embodiment of the storm-torn ocean; she was so turbulent that the only way to kill her was to drown her in a calm sea or bury her up to her shoulders in soil. The one-eyed crone lived beneath the waves with the seasmith, loving only him and the sea merchants who massaged her

243

surface. "Ill-streaming, bald-red, white-maned," Muireartach was eventually killed by the Irish warrior Finn MacCool.

Muk Jauk "Black lady," the Cambodian form of the Great Goddess of earth.

Mulhalmoni The Korean goddess of water is invoked when women shamans wish to cure eye disease or blindness. Coins are dropped in sacred springs, and rice steamed in a *nok* (sacred caldron) is offered to the goddess. The dedicated rice is eaten by the patient, whose eyes are bathed in spring water. Sometimes this ritual is performed not to cure but to protect the eyes; then it takes the form of a family outing or picnic in the mountains.

Munanna In Irish legend, this woman was married to a man whom she found tedious; she took a lover, a Scandinavian sea pirate with whom she plotted her husband's death. After the killing, the pair left for Norway. But the pirate, terrified of the power the woman had over him, pushed her into a lake, where she drowned. Even then, Munanna remained a powerful spirit, flying around the cliffs of Inishkea, crying "Revenge, revenge" at anyone who saw her cranelike figure.

Muses, Mousae The Greek goddesses of art and inspiration are probably the most familiar ancient divinities today. Daughters of *Mnemosyne*, they were born near Mt. Olympus in a place they later made their dancing ground. There they were raised by the hunter Crotus, who was transported after death into the sky as Sagittarius.

Usually there were nine Muses: Clio or Kleio ("fame-giver"), ruler of history, depicted with an open scroll or a chest of books; Euterpe ("joy-giver"), the flute-playing lyric Muse; "the festive" Thalia who wore the comic mask and wreaths of ivy; the singing Melpomene, Thalia's opposite, who wore the mask of tragedy and vine leaves; Terpsichore ("lover of dancing"), who carried a lyre and ruled choral song as well as dance; another lyre-bearer, Erato ("awakener of desire"), ruler of erotic poetry; Polyhymnia or Polymnia, the meditating one whose name means "many hymns" and who inspired them; *Urania* ("heavenly"), the globe-bearing Muse of astronomy; and Calliope ("beautiful voiced"), ruler of epic poetry, shown with a tablet and pencil.

Sometimes, however, there were fewer than nine Muses. Three named by Hesiod were obviously symbolic: Melete ("practicing"), Mneme ("remembering"), and Aoide ("singing"). When there was only one Muse, she was called by any of the names of the nine. The group as a whole had many alternative names, derived from places sacred to them: Carmentae, Pieriades, Aganippides, Castalides, Heliconiades, and Maeonides. See also **Coventina.**

Mut, Maut   Originally from Nubia, this bisexual world mother was sometimes a vulture, sometimes a crowned woman, to the Egyptians. Her name means "mother," but her character is now vague, for her ancient worship was slowly supplanted by that of such goddesses as *Isis* and *Hathor.*

Mutyalamma   The pearl-goddess of eastern India.

Muzulla   Little is known of this daughter of the Hittite sun-goddess *Wurusemu.*

Mylitta   Actually the name of this goddess was Mulitta or Mu'Allidtu, but it was Hellenized by Herodotus when he described her worship in ancient Phoenicia. The ancient writer tells us how Babylonian priestesses of Mylitta, burning incense and wearing wreaths around their heads, awaited strangers with whom to perform the sacred rites of love. Mylitta's worshipers bobbed their hair at puberty and offered her these youthful locks; afterward they could offer themselves more totally. At her shrine beside the sacred spring of Afka—a name sometimes used of the goddess herself—these women set up booths or camped in the green groves, enjoying intercourse with those who came to them.

At the great spring of Afka, fire was said regularly to fall into the water, renewing the youth of its goddess. Thus Mylitta combined the force of flowing water and the force of heavenly fire into a highly sexual energy personified as a nude, bearded woman riding a tortoise or a he-goat. Ancient travelers from Greece and Italy, coming upon this image, called Mylitta the goddess of desire, *Aphrodite* or *Venus.*

Myrine   In addition to the huge *Amazon* queendom north of Greece, there was another one, possibly earlier, in Libya, where Myrine ruled. The "swift-bounding one," she invaded Atlantis and subdued it with 30,000 mounted women warriors supported by 3,000 infantrywomen, all armed with bows and protected by heavy snakeskin armor. Defeating the Atlantians, Myrine executed all the men and enslaved the women and children. Then she established a city in her name and signed a truce with the remaining Atlantians to protect them against the fierce neighboring tribe of Gorgons—not, presumably, the immortal ones the Greeks mentioned in other tales. When the Amazons relaxed, confident in their victory, the Atlantians concluded a secret alliance with the

Gorgons and overthrew the women warriors.

Myrine escaped and pursued her military career eastward, conquering Lesbos, Samothrace, and Lemnos. Caught in a storm in the Aegean, she sacrificed to "the Mother" and was spared, thereafter setting up shrines in the goddess's honor. She died in battle in Thrace, when an alliance of kings invaded Amazon-held Asia Minor; her grave was covered by a huge hill built by women and called Baticia ("thorn hill").

Myrkrida "Dark-rider," a Scandinavian witch name.

Myrrha Across the ancient Near East the same story was told in various ways: how the earth fell in love with a beautiful youth in his springtime years, how he betrayed her and was punished by death, and how the kindly goddess brought him back to life again—the story of the springtime that flowers and fades on the face of the ageless earth. Sometimes the legend told, too, of the magical conception of the beloved vegetation-god, and this was the case with Adonis, the young lover of Asia Minor's mother-goddess, *Aphrodite*. At an autumn festival, white-robed women who had endured nine days of fasting and chastity offered the first fruits of the fields to the goddess who provided them. After this offertory, a communion: a public orgy during which the princess Myrrha mated with her own father and conceived the child whom the goddess would love. The tale, it seems clear, was allegorical, for Adonis was a tree spirit and thus his mother was a personified tree, the myrrh tree whose blossoms are fertilized by nearby, probably kindred, trees.

·N·

Naamah In ancient times this word, which means "pleasant," was used of the Canaanite goddess of sexuality, *Astarte*. But one people's deities are often their enemies demons, and so the name Naamah was given by the Hebrews to one of their demon queens, a being so beautiful that mortal men—even angels—could not resist her. She seduced them with her sweet cymbal music, but once they became aroused she stole their semen to form demon children. Like *Lilith*, Naamah also entertained herself by strangling sleeping babies, but she much preferred to endanger the human race by luring men from their appropriate mates. She is alleged to be still alive, living in the sea, where even the monsters of the deep, infatuated with her beauty, pursue her constantly through the waves.

Naenia Roman goddess of funerals.

Nagar-Saga "Framer of the fetus," a title of the Sumerian mother-goddess *Mami*.

Nahab A snake-headed goddess of Egypt.

Nahkeeta The goddess of Lake Sutherland in the Olympic Mts. was originally a delicate maiden, gentle as a water bird, with hair like a stream and a voice like a waterfall. She was beloved of her people, and she herself loved the dense forests where they lived.

One day while Nahkeeta was gathering wild plants, she lost her way in the thick rain forest. As the light dimmed beneath the great trees, she wandered until exhausted, then fell asleep beside a fallen tree.

There, the next day, her family found her bloodied body, marked with the claws of a wild beast. They had loved her so much that their sorrow was unceasing—until the day that she reincarnated herself in a soft blue lake, a lake filled with water birds and the slow sound of wind, like a voice, on her surface.

Naiads   To the Greeks, everything on earth had a resident spirit, often perceived in female forms called nymphs. The Naiads, nymphs of water, were not so long-lived as oceanic *Nereids* or rocky *Oreads*, but did live longer than the tree women or *Dryads*. As long as the streams and rivers embodying them did not go dry, the freshwater Naiad lived.

Naila   An Arabian goddess of great antiquity whose name means the "blue"—suggesting a sky-goddess—but whose character is vague.

Naina Devi   The Bilaspur goddess of eyes was brought to earth by a supernatural cow, who gave great floods of milk at her sacred spot.

Nakineitsi   Finnish and Estonian water-goddess.

Nambi   The first woman of Uganda lived in the sky as princess of heaven, but she desired an earthly man and descended to have intercourse with him. Then Nambi returned to the sky.

Her family was appalled that she would lower herself to make love with an earthling. Nambi's father stole her lover's only cow, taking it to the sky and forcing it to feed on wild plants. Nambi returned to earth and told her lover, Kintu, where his cow was hidden, suggesting that he reclaim it—and her. Kintu traveled to heaven, where the sky father presented him with vast herds of identical cattle, demanding that he find his own cow. With Nambi's help he identified the beast, but the sky father subjected Kintu to other tests before allowing his daughter to live on earth with the man.

The sky father also warned Nambi that her brother, Death, might follow them to earth. The couple left in haste, taking the first animals with them. Halfway down, Nambi realized they had no seeds for edible plants; she stole back to heaven to get some. Death spied her and followed her to earth. Now, although humans have food to eat, they also have the unwelcome presence of Brother Death.

Nammu   An early Sumerian goddess of the formless waters of creation, Nammu assisted *Mami* in forming the human race. She was also the one who—when *Lahar* and *Ashnan* failed to provide food and drink for the deities because they were drunk—tattled to the high god Enki; the result was the creation of humankind.

Nana, Nata, Nina   The nymph who conceived Attis, beloved of *Cybele,* by carrying a ripe almond or pomegranate next to her skin, Nana may have been—like *Myrhha*, mother of Adonis—a tree spirit, for she gave birth to a tree-god. Before being incorporated into the major seasonal myth of Asia Minor, however, Nana starred in a similar one of her own. For Nana ("queen") was one of the old Babylonian names for *Ishtar* as patron of Lagash and Ninevah, used at the same time as the similar name *Inanna*. Ishtar's worship as Nana was long-lived, for the Assyrian conqueror Assurbanipal, while sacking the Elamite capital of Susa in 636 B.C., discovered an image of the goddess that the Elamites had carried off from Erech 1,635 years earlier.

Another Nana was the wife of the sacrificed Scandinavian god Balder; she had no other mythic role than accompanying Balder to the underworld. Her name, obviously, is identical to that of the mother-lover of the young vegetation-god of the eastern Mediterranean. Some scholars believe that the story of Nana migrated northward to become part of Scandinavian tradition; there the mother was distinguished from the vegetation-god's lover, the former being named *Frigg*, while the latter retained the name Nana.

Nana Buluku The world-creator was, to the Fon people of Dahomey in west Africa, the mother of the Great Goddess *Mawu* and her twin brother-lover Lisa. The source of divinity, Nana Buluku retired from active participation in this world after Mawu's birth.

Nanshe This Babylonian water-goddess was honored each year with a flotilla of boats sailing on her canals. At the city of Lagash, the flotilla joined a sacred barge bearing the goddess's image, and the procession floated about as Nanshe's worshipers reveled. A wise goddess, she was an interpreter of dreams and omens; she served each New Year's Day as the judge of each persons' activities during the preceding year.

Nar, Nair Any Irish king who slept with this goddess died, says a legend that many scholars believe records a period of so-called ritual kingship, when a king "married" the earth-goddess and was ultimately sacrificed to assure her fertility. Save for a suspicious repetition of kingly names at regular intervals and a coincidentally similar length of residence on the throne, there is scant evidence for the practice of sovereign murder in Ireland, but such ancient myths as this suggest it.

Naru-Kami, Kami-Naru The Japanese thunder-goddess was the protector of trees and the ruler of artisans. Wherever she threw a bolt, that place was afterward considered sacred to her.

Nasa In Persian mythology, this female dragon disguised herself as a fly in order to devour corpses.

Natosuelta "Winding river" was this Celtic goddess's name; she was a raven-goddess worshiped in Gaul as creator and destroyer of this world.

Nausicaa The princess who welcomed Odysseus back to human society was really the author of the famous Greek epic. So argued Samuel Butler (1835-1902) in *The Authoress of the Odyssey*, calling Nausicaa a Sicilian noblewoman who created the work from shreds of legend. He supported his argument by asserting that the writer was clearly more familiar with homelife than the sea and contending that Nausicaa used the story to frame portraits of the great Greek heroines: *Calypso, Circe,* and *Penelope,* for instance.

Navky In Slavic-language areas, children who drowned or babies who died in infancy haunted their survivors for seven years, half-naked and crying. Then they were transformed into lovely water-dwelling women who called out to passing travelers. When the passerby approached, the Navky (Mavky in Russian) leaped on him and tickled him to death.

Neb-Ti The "two-mistresses," the ruling goddesses of north and south Egypt, *Uadgit* and *Nekhebet,* respectively.

Necessitas Roman goddess of human destiny; mother of the Fates.

Nehalennia Celtic dog-goddess of sea traders.

Neith, Net One of Egypt's most ancient goddesses, Neith was originally the essence of the tribal community perceived in its totems, two crossed arrows and a mottled animal skin. Later, as her worshipers politically dominated those of other Egyptian goddesses, Neith assumed the attributes of the conquered deities, becoming a complex figure who could boast (as Plutarch recorded her temple inscriptions), "I am all that has been, that is, that will be, and no mortal has yet been able to lift the veil that covers me." Despite accretions, however, Neith remained bascially the mistress of handicrafts and industry—a warlike mistress who could protect her worshipers' property against invasion. (In this, the Greeks saw an image of their own *Athene.*) Wearing the double crown of unified Egypt, Neith eventually commanded the reverence of all Egyptians from her temple city of Sais.

In the beginning of time, it was said, Neith took up the shuttle, strung the sky on her loom, and wove the world. Then she wove nets and from the primordial waters pulled up living creatures, including men and women. Finally, in the shape of a cow, Neith invented child-birth by bringing forth Ra, who grew to be the mightiest of the gods. During their lives, she was responsible for her worshipers' health—for her priests were doctors and healers—and after death, she guarded their remains while welcoming their souls into the afterworld. See **Mehurt.**

Nekhebet   The vulture-headed goddess of the Nile's source, she was called the "twin" of *Uadgit* after Egypt's political unification; together they formed the *Neb-Ti*, the "two mistresses." Nekhebet, the patron of labor-ing women and called by the Greeks *Eileithyia*, combined political and motherly roles in her mystic task of suckling the pharaoh-to-be.

Nemain, Neman, Nemon   Her name means the "venomous one" and is a cognate of the British goddess *Nemetona*; she was one of the powerful battle-goddesses of ancient Ireland and was related to the crow-god-dess *Morrigan.*

Nemesis   In late Greek mythology, she was monstrous, a fierce figure of revenge and anger. But in earlier days she was one of a pair of Great Goddesses worshiped with *Themis* in Attic Rhamnus. The white-garbed, winged Nemesis tormented those who broke the social rules that Themis represented. Although sometimes said to be one of the *Erinyes*, her power was less narrow; hers was more the force of justice than retaliation.

When Zeus arrived in Greece with his worshipers, he conquered Nemesis in the same way that legends show him overcoming other goddesses. Intent on rape, Greek legend says, Zeus chased Nemesis across the land. The powerful goddess changed shape once, twice, a third time, but the god transformed himself as well. Finally he over-powered her in bird form, and she laid an egg that hatched into the god-dess *Helen.*

Nemetona   The British "goddess of the sacred grove" was one of the di-vinities worshiped at Bath, where *Sulis* was also honored as patron of the thermal springs. She was depicted as a seated queen holding a scep-ter, surrounded by three hooded figures and a ram.

Nephele   Originally a Semitic goddess whose name means "cloud," she came into Greek legend as wife of a Theban king and mother of *Helle.* A cloud spirit, she became identified with the sky queen *Hera.*

Nephthys, Greek for **Nebthet**   The ancient Egyptian goddess was *Isis*'s sister and opposite: Isis was the force of life and rebirth; Nephthys, the tomb-dwelling goddess of death and sunset. They had similarly opposite mates. Isis's consort was the fertility-god Osiris, while her sister's mate was the evil god Set.

Set was not only wicked but sterile. So Nephthys, who wanted children, plied Osiris with liquor until, forgetting his loyalty to Isis, the god tumbled into bed with Nephthys; that night she conceived the god Anubis. Set, possibly out of jealousy, then killed and dismembered Osiris. This proved too much for Nephthys, who left Set to join in her sister's lamentations and helped to restore Osiris to life.

Nereids   The daughters of *Doris*, the sea-goddess, the 50 Nereids were famous for their rosebud faces and their oracular powers; not only could they predict shipwrecks but they could avert them. In their honor, the Greeks danced, imitating the ocean journeys of the demon-riding maidens, sometimes clad and sometimes naked. Some famous Nereids were *Amphitrite, Clymene, Galatea,* Glauce, *Panope,* and *Thetis.*

Nerthus   One of the most famous passages from the Roman writer Tacitus described the common form of worship among the Germanic tribes dwelling north of the empire. Their primary deity, he said, was Earth, called Nerthus. Her major sanctuary was on an island in the ocean, where a statue of her sat on a cloth-covered cart until the moment her priest divined the presence of Nerthus herself in the statue.

She then began a solemn procession among her people, drawn by oxen from tribe to tribe. All fighting ceased; all weapons and, indeed, all iron tools were locked away until the goddess's journey was completed. Festivities accompanied her, all doors were open in hospitality, and prosperity came to the countryside.

Eventually the accompanying priest realized that the goddess was tired of human company, and the procession started back to Nerthus's island sanctuary. In a hidden lake, the goddess and her chariot were bathed by slaves who, apparently unable to live a normal life after contact with the goddess's effigy, were offered to her in death.

Nessa   Originally she was Assa ("gentle one"), a princess of Ulster in northern Ireland. But the evil Druid Cathbad murdered the tutors who made life pleasant for this studious girl, and she changed her nature utterly, becoming Nessa ("ungentle"). A warrior rather than a scholar, she defeated king after king and kept a strong hand on the reins of government.

But Cathbad still had designs on her. One day, while Nessa was bathing in a quiet spring and her armor was just out of reach, Cathbad surprised her. Weaponless, she could not resist him. He raped her and then demanded her friendship. "Better," she said diplomatically, "to consent than to be killed, and with my weapons gone."

Although he kept her hostage as his concubine, Nessa refused to bear him children. Knowing, however, that she would eventually give birth to a hero, she watched for omens. One day when she was sent to draw water for the Druid from a magical well, Nessa spied in the pail two tiny worms. She drank some water, swallowing the worms; they fertilized her; soon she gave birth to the famous king Conchobar. Lest anyone think that he was the spawn of the Druid, the hero came from the womb clutching a worm in either hand, evidence of his miraculous conception.

Nevinbimbaau   Melanesian goddess of initiation.

Niamh, Neeve of the Golden Hair   Her very name means "beauty," this daughter of the sea, the fairy queen of Tir-nan-Og, the Irish Land of the Blessed far away in the western ocean, almost beyond human reach. Like many fairy goddesses, Niamh had a fondness for mortal lovers.

Once, legend says, she stole the poet Oisin from the Fianna, the band of heroes with whom he lived. For a long time—human speech has no words for the length of time, but the Fianna aged and died while Oisin lived young and blissful with Niamh—Oisin was happy in Niamh's domain. Finally, homesickness for the mortal world stirred the poet. The longing grew until, finally, Niamh could no longer stand his complaints. She put him on a magic horse and set the horse's head east, toward humanity, but she warned her lover not to dismount. Poor Oisin—when he landed on earth, the buckle on his fairy saddle broke, and he fell to the ground. The moment his young body touched the earth, all its accumulated human years fell on it. Instantly Oisin grew old, died, and turned to dust, never again to enjoy Niamh's embraces. See **Oto-Hime**, the sea-goddess of Japan, for a similar tale.

Nicnevin   "Bone mother," a Scottish name for the *Cailleach* in the Lothian and Border counties.

Nike   The Greek winged "victory" was the daughter of the fearsome river-goddess *Styx* and the sister of Zelos ("zeal"). She was honored throughout Greece, especially at Athens, as a companion—or form—of *Athene*.

Nimue This is the Welsh name for the supernatural sorceress called the Lady of the Lake in Arthurian legend. She lived, surrounded by beautiful fairylike immortal maidens, in an island realm where there was neither winter nor pain nor death. She was one of the mighty goddesses who took King Arthur to Avalon at the end of his earthly reign, a particularly appropriate action, for it had been Nimue who had invested Arthur as king.

Ninazu Naked Death who, sleeping herself, holds the sleeping dead in the perpetual embrace of a mother; identical with, or assimilated to, *Eriskegal.*

Nindum "Lady of procreation," a title of the Sumerian *Mami.*

Ningal, Nikkal, Ningul The "Great Lady" of the fruitful earth was courted by the moon-god, the Sumerian and Ugaritic people said. He brought her necklaces of lapis lazuli and—for he was the rain provider—turned the deserts into orchards to win her heart.

Ningyo This Japanese goddess looked just like a fish, but she had a woman's head, and when she cried her tears were pearls. Women tried to capture her, to take a bite out of her; this would guarantee them eternal youth and beauty.

Ninhurra, Ninkurra Granddaughter of *Ninhursag* and mother of *Uttu*, the Sumerian goddess of plants. For the full story of how her grandchildren were eaten, see **Ninhursag.**

Ninhursag, Ninkhursag, Ninkkarsagga Long ago in a fine fair town, the serpent-goddess of birth and rebirth lived with the god of wisdom. In Dilmun, where Ninhursag and Enki made their home, there was no age or death, no sickness and no barrenness; not even the animals harmed one another.

One day Ninhursag's belly swelled up. Nine days later the goddess *Ninsar (Ninmu)* was born. The lascivious Enki seduced his daughter, who bore *Ninhurra.* Then Enki slept with his granddaughter, who bore *Uttu*, the goddess of plants. Of course Enki wished to sleep with his great-granddaughter, but Ninhursag whispered to her that she must first demand a bride-price of cucumbers, apples, and grapes. The lustful Enki granted them, and Uttu agreed to occupy his bed.

From their affair sprang eight different kinds of plants, living things the world had never seen before. But Enki ate his offspring as quickly as they appeared, even before the mountain mother Ninhursag could name them. Furious with the greedy god, Ninhursag leveled so terrible a curse at him that he immediately fell down, stricken in eight parts of his body with eight different diseases.

The other gods grew concerned as Enki weakened and grew thin. But the Great Goddess, still angry at the god, refused to heal him. Finally—when Enki was a breathing corpse—the congregation of heaven prevailed on Ninhursag to cure him. Still unwilling, for fear he would resume his upsetting behavior, the goddess agreed to a compromise: she would not heal him directly but would create eight tiny goddesses (among them *Ninti*) to control the health of Enki's afflicted parts; they could do the healing if they chose. Indeed, the little goddesses set to work, and soon Enki was well again. Some say, however, that Ninhursag did finally cure Enki herself and that she did so by placing him within her vagina, whence he could be reborn whole.

Ninkasi "Lady horn face," a Sumerian wine-goddess whose name became a title of the all-embracing *Ishtar.*

Ninkharak "Lady of the mountain," a dog-goddess of healing who was assimilated into the figure of *Ishtar.*

Ninkigal "Lady of dead land," a name for *Eriskegal.*

Ninlil, in Babylonian, **Belit-Matate** One day the young Sumerian goddess Ninlil was bathing in the stream Ninbirdu, a lonely spot far from all eyes. The god Enlil, happening by, took full advantage of the solitude: he raped the virgin goddess. The other deities, horrified at the deed, swiftly banished Enlil to the underworld. But Ninlil had conceived; she followed Enlil to the kingdom of the dead, her huge belly a reminder of his crime.

This development disturbed heaven even more, for in their omniscience the deities knew that the child in Ninlil's belly was the moon. If born in the underworld, he would have to remain there for eternity, for not even divinity grants freedom from the hell queen *Eriskegal*'s laws. When her time came, Ninlil performed magic: she bore three shadow children, one each for herself and Enlil, one for their child, each to remain a perpetual hostage to Eriskegal. Then, still pregnant, she climbed to earth with Enki. Thus was the moon-god Sin born, on the horizon from which he can mount the sky.

"Mistress of winds," Ninlil was the ancient goddess of the city of Nippur, a mother figure whose emblems were those of all the great earth rulers of the ancient Near East: the serpent, the heavenly mountain, and the stars. Because she was the earth, Ninlil had to approve any ruler of her surface. Thus each prince gained his throne by mating with the goddess, incarnate in one of her priestesses; then he ruled as Ninlil's consort. As the worship of *Ishtar* spread across Babylonia, Ninlil was identified with her as "Ishtar of Nippur," eventually losing her identity entirely, while her name became a title of Ishtar.

Ninmah   "Lady Mother," a Babylonian name for the mighty mother-goddess *Mami*.

Ninsar, Ninmu   Sumerian plant-goddess. See **Ninhursag**.

Nin-Si-Anna   "Lady eye of heaven," a name for *Ishtar*.

Ninsikilla   The "pure queen," a title of the Sumerian all-mother *Mami*.

Ninti   One of the eight healing-goddesses whom *Ninhursag* created to spare herself the annoying task of curing the greedy Enki, this goddess ruled the ribcage. Her name is a pun, meaning both "lady of the rib" and "lady of life." See also **Eve**.

Nintur, Nintu, Sentu   "Lady of the womb," or "Lady life-giver," this ancient goddess of Shirpurla later became identified with the Babylonian *Ishtar*.

Niobe   Early Greek legend named her as the mother of humanity; her seven daughters, the *Meliae* or ash-tree nymphs, produced human beings as fruit. Often called a goddess rather than a woman, Niobe was noted for her fruitfulness; some say her children were without number.

Later Greek legend said that she bragged of the number of her children and mocked *Leto*—once her friend, Sappho said—for having only two offspring. Those, however, were the powerful *Artemis* and Apollo, and they avenged their mother by slaughtering all but one of Niobe's children. (Her daughter Chloris survived to become one of Greece's great beauties.) Overcome by grief, Niobe was so transfixed by weeping that the gods took pity on her, transforming her into a stone from which a fountain eternally sprang.

Nirriti   In Hindu India, humanity's misfortunes are embodied in this goddess: a weary old woman, starved and leprous, always holding out her hand for alms. All born into poverty and crime who, nonetheless, attempt to live righteously are protected by Nirriti; as the goddess who endures earth's misfortunes, she is naturally the one to whom those

*Soyok mana, Hopi "Ogre Woman." Field Museum of
Natural History (Neg# 96009), Chicago.*

wishing for a change of luck would pray. Wearing black garments and ornaments, priests offer sacrifice to her, then put a stone into a pot of water and toss it to the southwest, transferring more disease and ill fortune to the already heavy shoulders of Nirriti. See also **Surabhi.**

Nisaba   "She who teaches the decrees" of divinity to humans, this goddess brought literacy and astrology to a Sumerian king on a tablet inscribed with the names of the beneficent stars. An architect as well, she drew up temple plans for her people; she was also an oracle and dream interpreter. The most learned of deities, this snake-goddess also controlled the fertility of her people's fields. See also **Sheshat.**

Nish-Kan-Ru Mat, Kamui Katkimat   An Ainu sky-goddess or star-goddess worshiped at the Festival of Falling Tears.

Nixies   The Germans—like many other peoples—considered the prophetic spirits of water to be feminine. Like the rivers they inhabited, the Nixies were changeable in nature: sometimes charming and peaceful, sitting in the sun to comb their long blonde hair; sometimes fierce and hungry, drowning people for food.

They could assume human form to go to market or to dance on the riverside; in this form, they were long-breasted young women about four feet tall, who might pass for completely human except for the wet hems of their skirts and aprons. Mortal men often fell in love with them, wasting away because of their beauty; sometimes a Nixie would agree to marry a human, making him vow never to ask her origin. Excellent dancers, they would dance with human men, but should one steal her glove it meant the Nixie's death; the next day the river where she lived would be red with her blood.

No-Il Ja-Dae   The Korean goddess of the toilet was said to be perpetually angry, perhaps because her clitoris had been cut out and thrown into the ocean, where it became a seashell. She was especially hostile to women who tried to use the outhouse at night; she might make them sick or strike them blind. In some areas of Korea, she was called Nam-Sa Kui, the ghostly maiden, and was said to be a lovely woman dressed in bright silks.

Nokomis   This word, meaning "grandmother," was the Algonquin name for the goddess called Eithinoha ("our mother") by the Iroquois. She ruled the earth and its produce; she created the food for the people and animals who dwelled on her land. But she did not only create it: she fed herself to her people, for the woodland Indians recognized that life continues only if it devours life.

They said that earth had a daughter, *Onatah*, the corn maiden. When the thirsty Onatah was wandering through the land, looking for dew, an evil spirit abducted her and held her under the earth; the sun eventually found her and led her back to the surface. The similarities between this North American myth and the Greek legend of *Demeter* and her daughter are obvious; both are expressions of a similar profound understanding of the vegetative cycle on which humanity depends.

Nona, Decima Roman goddesses of the most important months of fetal gestation.

Noogumee Whale-mother of the Canadian Micmac.

Norns At the foot of the World Tree, Scandinavian religion said, lived three sisters, the most powerful of all deities; not even the gods, the Aesir, could undo what they had done, or do what they did not wish. Urd, Verdandi, and *Skuld*, the three Norns, drew water each day from Urd's well and, mixing it with gravel, carefully sprinkled the World Tree. They never overwatered, causing the tree to rot, neither did they allow the tree to parch, for on it not only human life but the universe itself depended.

Although these three were most familiar, there were innumerable Norns—one for each person born, for they were the Fates that ruled each life. Some legends said that each person had one Norn, who taught life's rules; your luck depended on the talent of your Norn, whom you were to honor at each meal by setting an extra place for her. Other legends said that each person had three Norns, two who promised good, one bringing evil.

The latter belief may represent the influence of Mediterranean culture, which also affected the Scandinavian conception of the three most powerful Norns. Urd, the eldest sister, may at first have stood alone, with Verdandi and Skuld joining her later. As finally perceived, each member of the trinity had distinct powers: Urd (whose name became "weird") ruling the past, Verdandi the present, and Skuld the future.

Nortia To the Etruscans, who occupied Italy before Rome conquered the peninsula, each entity had a preordained life span—each human being, and each nation or state as well. To them Nortia was a preeminent goddess, the force of time-linked destiny. In her temple in Volsinii, a nail was pounded into the wall at the close of each year; in this way people could know exactly how many years had passed, how many were to come, in their individual lives and in the collective life of Etruria.

Norwan   The "dancing porcupine woman" of the California Wintuns was a goddess of light who brought food to earth. A daughter of earth and sun, Norwan danced, light as warm air, above growing plants; she kept dancing each day until sunset. Once, it was told, she slept with a new man, angering her usual lover; this brought on the first war in human history.

Nott   The Scandinavian primeval goddess Nott ("night") was the mother of the earth (*Jord*) and of the day as well. She rode forth each evening on her horse Frostymane, from whose foaming mouth the dew fell.

Nsomeka   The culture heroine of the Bantu of southern Africa brought riches to her people by boldly visiting the jungle home of the great mother-goddess Songi, who taught a magical tooth-filing ritual that created prosperity. When Nsomeka returned to earthly life, Songi caused cattle and fowl and other domestic animals to crowd out through her tooth notches; entire villages of well-built houses and shade-producing trees appeared, too. Because of wealth produced by women, the Bantu men lived peacefully with their mates, treating the women with utmost respect.

Nu Kua   The creator-goddess of ancient China made the first human beings from yellow clay. At first, she carefully molded them. At length, finding this too tedious, Nu Kua just dipped a rope into slip-like clay and shook it so that drops splattered onto the ground. Thus were two types of beings born: from the molded figures, nobles; from the clay drops, peasants.

Later this serpent-bodied goddess quelled a rebellion against the heavenly order and, when the dying rebel chief shook heaven's pillars out of alignment, she restored order by melting multicolored stones to rebuild the blue sky. Finding other problems on earth, Nu Kua set about correcting them: she cut off the toes of a giant tortoise and used them to mark the compass's points; she burned reeds into ashes, using them to dam the flooding rivers. Order restored, Nu Kua retreated to the distant sky—her domain and her attribute.

Nuliayoq, Nuliajuk   On the western coast of Hudson Bay, the Inuit people consider the world's primary divinity to be this goddess who is similar to *Sedna*, the preeminent deity of other Eskimos. There are differences between the tales told of Nuliayoq and of Sedna, however. Nuliayoq was an orphan girl who, when her village moved to another place, had no one to watch out for her safety. She would have been abandoned, had she not jumped onto one of the departing boats. But she missed her footing and drowned in the sea, where, like Sedna, she became the controlling spirit of marine life. Nuliayoq was said to have a home in a warm heavenly land, where souls of good people and of suicides traveled to play ball with a talking walrus skull; these games flitted across the sky, visible as the aurora borealis. When not in her heavenly home, Nuliayoq guarded her animals and fish, waiting at the entrances to inlets and rivers to punish anyone who flouted her fishing and hunting regulations.

Numma Moiyuk Ocean-goddess of the Yulengor of Arnhem Land in Australia, she created herself in the form of a very fat woman—full of the unborn children who would someday populate the entire continent. Though she came from the sea, she knew the need for fresh water and created the first pools and wells. Then she gave birth to humankind and taught her descendants the necessary crafts to survive on earth, including the weaving of fishnets and the painting of sacred designs. Finally she died, offering her body as food to her children.

Nut Once, long before our earth existed, the great sky-goddess Nut lay across the body of her small brother the earth, holding him in constant intercourse. But—so said the ancient Egyptians—the high god Ra disapproved of their incessant incest, and he commanded the god Shu to separate the pair. Shu hoisted Nut into a great arch, but—such was the goddess's desire for her little brother Geb—he was forced to remain forever holding them apart, supporting the star-spangled belly of the sky queen. And that is how we see Nut in Egyptian art: a woman standing on her toes and bending forward in a perfect arch, her fingers touching the earth opposite her feet, her hair falling down like rain. So she stood, on the inside of sarcophagi, where as mother of the dead she stretched her long body protectively over the mummy.

Ra cursed Nut for her love, forbidding her to bear children during any month of the year. But the god Thoth outwitted the curse, playing draughts with the moon and winning from him five intercalary days, days not attached to any month, which float between the years. And in these five days, from her brother's seed already within her, Nut produced five children: the sister goddesses *Isis* and *Nephthys*, their mates Osiris and Set, and the sun-god Horus.

Sometimes Nut took the form of a huge cow; such was the shape she wore when the god Ra decided to abandon the earth. She kneeled so that he could climb on her. Then up, up she strained, bearing the god upon her back until she became dizzy from the weight. Four gods instantly rushed to hold up Nut's vast body, remaining thereafter as the world's four pillars.

Nyapilnu   Ancestral goddess of the Australian Yiritja people, she was the one who invented household crafts when, stranded in a storm with her sister Wurdilapu, she discovered that tree bark could be used to build shelters.

Nympheuomene   "She who takes a mate," *Hera*'s second phase.

Nyx, Nox   In mother-ruled cultures, theorists contend, night was given precedence over day, the moon over the sun. The interpretation is arguable, but it is unarguable that the pre-Hellenic creation myth calls the goddess Nyx ("night") the first daughter of unruly Chaos, and these pre-Hellenic Greeks were matriarchal or at least matrilineal.

Nyx gave birth to Erebus and mated with him to produce the first light ever seen, the *Hesperides*. Unfortunately, she did not stop there, spewing out many other often dreadful creatures like Age and Death and Fate. (Perhaps the light she birthed balanced the horrors.) She lived, like her daughter Hemera ("day"), beyond the horizon in Tartarus. Twice each day Hemera and Nyx passed at the brass gates of the other world, waving from their chariots as one went home and the other mounted the sky. There were few worshipers of this elderly goddess, but upon them Nyx bestowed one gift: that of prophecy, of seeing beyond the night of the present. See **Leto.**

Oanuava　Celtic earth-goddess worshiped in Gaul.

Oba　Jealous Santeria river-goddess who is the mate of the god Chango.

Obatallah　This creator-goddess is among the pantheon of four great female divinities of Brazilian Macumba, the others being *Oshun, Oya* and *Yemanja.*

Oceanids　There were 3,000 of them, these elder sisters of the *Nereids.* Early Greek water-goddesses, they were daughters of the sea queen *Tethys* and eventually were replaced in mythology by the latecomers. See **Dione.**

Ochumare　Yoruba and Santeria goddess of the rainbow, sometimes Catholicized into "Our Lady of Hope."

Ocrisia　One of the great Roman matriarchs was originally a servant of Queen *Tanaquil.* One day, as Ocrisia was laying out the day's offerings by the hearth, a penis-shaped flame stretched out toward her. Tanaquil, skilled in reading omens, knew that the fire-god lusted for the young woman and instructed Ocrisia to dress in bridal attire and lie near the fireplace. Apparently the fire demon's desire was satisfied, because nine months later Ocrisia gave birth to the child who grew to be Servius Tullius, the sixth king of Rome.

Oddibjord　In Scandinavia, prophets were women called Volvas or *Voluspas.* The one by the name of Oddibjord was very famous; she traveled about telling stories and fortunes, and the fortune you got depended on how well you fed her.

Oddudua　Primary mother-goddess of the Yoruba, she is called "Saint Claire" in Santeria.

Odras   In Irish legend, this human woman was strong enough—or foolish enough—to demand her rights from the queen of death, the *Morrigan*. Odras had a cow that the goddess wanted to mate with her bull, Slemuin the Smooth. The Morrigan simply stole the animal and carried it beneath the world.

Angry at her loss, Odras went to wild Connaught, to Hell's Gate in the Cave of *Cruachen*. But there enchantment overtook her, and she fell asleep under magical oak trees. The Morrigan came again to the earth's surface and, to punish the girl for her presumption, sang a spell over her that turned Odras into a pool of water.

Ogdoad   In the primordial abyss, said the Egyptians, there were four female frogs—Naunet, Kauket, Hauket, and Amaunet—and four male snakes. Out of their random movements a pattern began to emerge, which grew increasingly more regular until they had brought order out of chaos.

Ognyene Maria   "Fiery Mary," a Serbian prophet.

Ohoyo Osh Chishba   "Unknown Woman" was the name of the Cherokee vegetation-goddess. The people of what is now southeastern America told the following story. Ohoyo Osh Chishba lived alone, an old woman full of wisdom but set in her ways. One day, as she walked along a familiar path, she saw blood on the ground. She covered it with a jar.

A few days later, she picked up the jar and found an infant boy, whom she raised to be a hunter, teaching him what animals to seek and how to kill them. But Ohoyo Osh Chishba taught him nothing of plants, for she provided all the maize and beans they could eat. And she gave him one caution: that he should never pass a certain blue mountain, visible from her home.

As he grew, the boy became curious. One day, peering in Grandmother's window, he saw her disrobe and scratch herself over a pot. As she did so, cornmeal and beans ran down her legs and into the pot, for she herself was food and she was creating meal for her child.

When he entered and refused his dinner, Grandmother knew instantly that he had spied upon her. She sent him away with instructions that, as he left, he should set fire to her house. Sadly, he did so, and followed her dying instructions by seeking a wife from a distant tribe. When at last he brought his bride back to Grandmother's land, he found all the food plants of the world growing, enough to feed all their descendants.

Olosa   Santeria crocodile-goddess who assists fisher-folk.

Olwen   The Welsh sun-goddess's name may mean "leaving white foot-prints" or "golden wheel"; she was the opposite of the "silver-wheeled" moon-goddess *Arianrhod*. Olwen was mentioned in early Arthurian legend as a princess who, attired in many rings and a collar of red gold, married a man named Culhwch, despite the knowledge that this marriage would kill her father.

   The father, whose name translates as the "giant hawthorn tree," tried to prevent the consummation of her love for Culhwch by placing 13 obstacles—possibly the 13 lunar months of the solar year—in her path. But Olwen survived the tests by providing the 13 necessary dowries.

   That Olwen was specifically the summer sun seems clear from descriptions of her: she had streaming yellow hair, anemone fingers, and rosy cheeks; from every footstep a white trefoil sprang up. The "white lady of the day," she was called, the flower-bringing "golden wheel" of summer.

Omamama   The ancestral goddess of the Crees of Ontario, Omamama was endlessly beautiful, although old as the earth herself; she was also endlessly loving to her children, the spirits and the divinities of the world. Her firstborn was the thunderbird; her second, the sorcerer frog; her third, the Cree hero Weesakayjac; and finally the wolf and beaver. After these firstborn powers, rocks and plants fell from her almighty womb until the earth was furnished and populated as we know it today.

Omecíhuatl, Citlalinicue   One day the Great Goddess—the female half of divinity who, together with her consort, formed an androgyne called Ometeotl—squatted down to give birth. Her child was a stone knife, which she instantly threw down to the vacant earth, where it miracu-lously shattered into 1,600 heroes.

   The heroes could have become gods and rejoined their mother in her heaven. But, both lazy and ambitious, they wished to remain on earth and be served by men. There were, however, no men then in exis-tence. Turning to Omecíhuatl ("star-skirted goddess"), they asked her to create some. She suggested instead that they improve their spiritual condition and seek eternal reunion with her.

   The 1,600 heroes then sent the hero Xólotl to the underworld to gather ashes and bones. These they formed into the bodies of the first man and woman, destined ever after to serve the goddess's children.

Omphale   This *Amazon* queen was said by the Greeks to rule the southern empire of Libya. As was customary, Omphale ("navel") purchased slavemen of attractive appearance and sensual manners; the Amazons knew no man could equal a queen, much less be superior, so their rulers enjoyed men as kings of other lands enjoyed female concubines. When the brawny Heracles came up for sale, in punishment for the murder of his wife and children, Omphale brought him home.

Omphale kept Heracles for three years. For amusement, she ordered him to wear transparent purple dresses. When not engaged in other duties, Heracles had to weave and spin and card wool. If he made mistakes at these unfamiliar chores, Omphale beat him with a golden sandal. Eventually growing bored with him, Omphale sent Heracles back to his homeland.

Onatah   Daughter of the American Indian *Nokomis,* her myth was similar to that of *Demeter.*

Oniata   Once the daughter of the sun came to live among the Iroquois people, legend says, being born with a beauty exceeding that of all other human women combined. Not only a beautiful girl, then woman, she was compassionate and noble in spirit. But the men around her, alas, were far from either. They left their wives and children to linger about the camp where Oniata lived; they fought each other at the least pretext, claiming they fought for Oniata's favor. When, finally, the Iroquois women complained bitterly and angrily about Oniata's presence among them, she explained sadly that she had never wished for the men's attentions. In order to ensure that the men would return to their families, she left the earth for good. She did, however, leave a trace of her beauty behind: the spring wildflowers.

Oona, Onaugh   The most beautiful of Ireland's fairy queens, she was said to have golden hair so long it swept the ground; she flew through the earth robed in gossamer silver bejeweled with dew. Oona lived with the fairy king Finnvara, who was constantly unfaithful to her with mortal women; she retained, nonetheless, an even, benevolent temperament.

Ootonobe-no-Kami   The goddess of the female element of primitive life forms, she emerged from primordial chaos shortly before the creator-goddess of Japanese Shinto.

Ops   Her name survives in our word *opulent,* and she represented the opulence of the earth's fruiting. Worshiped at harvest festivals on August 25 and December 19, she was associated with the god Consus, ruler of the "conservation" of the grain that Ops brought her people. She was a very ancient Roman goddess, identified in later days with the Greek *Rhea*.

Oreads The sweet-singing nymphs of mountains and rocks, they were slender, pale women who wore thin robes, woven in caves on fine looms visible to the second-sighted. To honor these elemental spirits, the Greeks used to anoint rocks with fragrant oils, hang attractive belts on rocks, and leave offerings in caves. See **Echo.**

Oreithyia, Orithyia The daughter of Erechtheus and Praxithea, she was dancing by the River Ilissus one day when the north wind, Doreas, snatched her up, carried her to Sarpedon's rock in Thrace, and raped her. From this crime, two daughters, Cleopatra and Chione, were conceived, as were the winged Argonauts, Calais and Zetes.

Orore To the Chaldeans, there was nothing before creation except a goddess—an insect with a hugely pregnant abdomen and a giant eye—and her bull-headed fish-tailed consort; they were the male and female principles of creation, the original egg and sperm.

Orthia *Artemis* in Sparta was the "upright one" or "she who causes erections," a thirsty goddess particularly pleased with blood and semen released by the young male initiates whipped at her shrines.

O-Ryu A willow-tree-goddess of Japan.

Oshun One of the four great divinities of the Brazilian Macumba religion, the goddess of waters is depicted wearing jewels, holding a mirror, and wafting a fan. She derives from a goddess of the Niger River in Africa, where she was the consort of the thunder-god Chango. She rules love, beauty and flirtation. In Santeria, Oshun is revered as "Our Lady of La Caridad," patron of the island of Cuba.

Ossipago *Juno*, as strengthener of infants' bones.

Otiona An Athenian patriot, she offered herself as a sacrifice when her father, King Erechtheus, was waging war on the Eleusinians. Her death was apparently effective, because her side won.

Oto-Hime Of the sea-goddess of Japan, almost the same story was told as of the Irish *Niamh*. Once a young fisherman met Oto-Hime; impressed with his charm, she took him to her castle beneath the waves. There they lived for a little while, making love and enjoying court life. The young man, however, grew worried about his family and spoke of his homesickness to Oto-Hime. She agreed to let him go, but gave him two conditions: that he carry a tiny box, and that he never open it.

He left immediately, box in hand. But when he reached his home island, he found nothing he remembered: the faces and names were different, the clothes of a new style, the houses in a different shape. Puzzled, he finally found an ancient resident who had heard the name of his family. He said they had been dead for hundreds of years. Baffled and sad, the young man sat down and, forgetting his promise, opened the little box. Out swept the years he had lived with Oto-Hime. Surrounding him like smoke, they withered his body, and he fell instantly into dust.

Otrere "Nimble" was the name given in some tales to the ancestral goddess of the *Amazons*; it also was a title of distinction bestowed on women leaders.

Ovda A violent wanderer of the Finnish forests, the mightily powerful Ovda was almost always in ill humor. She had long breasts, which she threw over her shoulders, and long ragged hair; she wore no clothing as she wandered through her property, looking for trespassers to tickle to death. Those who encountered her tried to take advantage of a hole in her left armpit: if you could stick your finger in, Ovda would fall helplessly to the ground.

Oya A warrior storm-goddess who also rules fire, she is one of the great divinities of Brazilian Macumba. In Santeria she is the nine-headed mate of the lightning-god Chango. Patron of justice and memory, she is pictured holding a flame.

·P·

Pa Chinese goddess of droughts.

Pahto A mountain-goddess of the Yakima and Klickitat, she was embodied in a mountain in southwestern Washington, today called Mt. Adams. Once, it was said, she was a wife of the sun. But he had four other mountain-wives, and two of them stood in the way of the sun's rays each morning. Plash-Plash (Goat Rocks) and Wahkshum (Simcoe Mountain) received caresses of sunshine long before the god even noticed Pahto.

So Pahto killed the other wives; she exploded and dashed off their heads. Then she happily accepted the first rays of the sun on her wooded sides each morning.

But she grew restless and greedy. Having once felt her power, she decided to improve herself further. She went south, where she stole everything she could from other mountains, all the berries and ferns and trees and animals, the salmon and the trout, and she took them all back to her own hill.

The other mountains grew furious. Klah Klahnee (Three Sisters) urged Wyeast, goddess of Mt. Hood, to do something. First she offered Pahto a truce, if half of the stolen goods were returned; Pahto refused. So Wyeast blew her head off, leaving a pile of rocks on the north face, once Pahto's head. Then Wyeast took back what had been stolen, leaving only a few berry bushes and some elk and fish for the haughty mountain.

The sky spirit, seeing how Pahto had been humbled, offered her a new head: a great white eagle, a cap of snow that shone in the sunlight. This eagle was the law of generosity and freedom, the law that—in the shining of the sunlight on mountain snow—stood forever to remind Pahto's people to share the resources of her earth.

Pais "Girl," a name of *Persephone*, also used of *Hera*.

269

Paivatar   In the *Kalevala*, the classic compilation of Finnish tradition, this was the name of the spinning sun virgin who wove daylight from a rainbow arch. "Competent maid," she was called, "resplendent on a shaft-bow of the sky." She held a weaver's batten, a heddle, and a golden shuttle. The cloth she wove was gold; her moon-sister's was silver.

One of the epic events of the *Kalevala* is the freeing of the captive sun from a dark cave where the witch *Louhi* had hidden her. As in the Japanese myth of *Amaterasu*, a mirror image of the sun was first forged from metal. But when hoisted into the sky, it proved unsatisfactory. So the poet Vainomoinen demanded that Louhi say where the goddess was hidden. "The sun got into the crag, the moon vanished into the rock, and they will never get free, never, never at all!" the witch taunted.

But Vainomoinen, undeterred, lopped off the heads of Louhi's henchmen as though they were turnip tops, and set out to free the sun. He went to Ilmarinen, the smith, and ordered a three-tined hoe, a dozen ice picks, and many keys. Louhi, seeing all the activity at the forge, disguised herself as a bird and flew over to spy on Ilmarinen. When she saw that it would be impossible to win over the determined heroes, she set the sun-goddess free.

Paive   Among the Saami of Norway, this is the name of the goddess called *Beiwe* elsewhere.

Pales   For many years mythology texts called her a god, but recent scholarship confirms that the Roman divinity of cattle was indeed a goddess. Although there was a god of this name among the Etruscans, all other tribes of Italy knew Pales as a goddess. There is some evidence, indeed, that she was not only one goddess but two: the goddesses of small and of large cattle. At her festival, the Parilia on April 21, the stock-keeping farmers purified their animals by driving them between blazes of fragrant woods; then they offered a long prayer to Pales begging forgiveness for any unintended slight against nature committed in the previous year. Without such careful ceremony, the Romans were convinced, the animals would not bear healthy offspring and the farmers would suffer even for minor offenses like burning the wrong dead tree.

Pali Kongju   This princess, according to Korean myth, was the ancestor of all shamans. Her story began when her father, King Upbi of Sam, decided to marry despite predictions of misfortune for his children. A large part of that misfortune came from their father's rejection of them, for he would have preferred a single son to all his first six daughters.

When the queen birthed a daughter for the seventh time, the king ordered the child thrown into the ocean—whence her name, meaning "princess thrown away."

Unable to save her child, the weeping queen put her in a jewel box with a bottle of milk. Rough soldiers tore the box from her arms and threw it into the sea. But then, from beneath the waves, a horde of golden turtles slowly rose until they bore the little box above the water. Thus she was brought to shore where she was adopted by a peasant couple who, from the time they took her in, had great good fortune. She grew to be a happy, loving daughter.

Meanwhile, the king and queen had been stricken with a wasting illness from which diviners said they could only recover if Pali Kongju would aid them by fetching the medicinal water from the Western Sky. The desperate king repented his infanticide and begged his other daughters to get the water. They refused, claiming they were unable to bear the arduous journey.

But the god of the mountains found Pali Kongju and told her of her duty. Sad though she was to leave her foster parents, the princess returned home to the palace where the king and queen greeted her with disbelieving relief. She did not stay long; taking a pair of iron shoes and an iron stick, she set off.

She had to pass the North Pole Star and the South Pole Star, playing at their interminable games of chance; she had to pass the Old Farming Woman of Heaven, who made her plow and sow an immense field; she had to find the Laundress of Heaven and wash her clothes from black to white. Finally, she reached the Western Sky, where she was met with glittering golden turtles who formed a bridge to the beyond for her.

Nearly falling to hell from the cliffs above it, Pali Kongju struggled on until she found the ugly Guardian Armed Guard at the well of heaven. Of course he would give her the water, the god said, in return for money. Alas, though, the princess had not thought to bring money with her.

So she agreed to marry the god and bore him seven sons. Finally, he gave her a bottle of the water, and with her children she set off for home.

But she came too late, for the funeral was already underway for her mother and father. Desperate with grief, she sprinkled them nevertheless with the healing fluid. There was a stirring of life—then her parents sat up and embraced her. They wished to shower her with gifts and love, but she realized that her duty was to return to the world beyond so that she could help others in need. Taking her seven sons, she disappeared from this world.

Because of her sacrifice, she became the patron saint of the *mudang,* the women shamans who still practice in great number in Korea. During the *kut,* the danced ritual that is the heart of their religion, the *mudang* often don a stripe-sleeved multicolored robe and tell the tale of Pali Kongju as an incantation and an inspiration.

Pallas   "Great maiden" was the name of this pre-Hellenic goddess whose independent identity became submerged in the great *Athene.* She survived in the myth that said she was an early friend of Athene and was accidentally killed by her, whereupon Athene took her friend's name as her own. (An almost identical story is told of *Callisto* and *Artemis.*)

Pallor   Roman goddess of fear.

Pamphile   This great Greek sorceress could bring the moon into her garden with her spells, so powerful were they. Mistress of metamorphosis, Pamphile rubbed herself with ointment by a magic lamp's light to change her shape. Often she became an owl and flew through the night, bathing in spring water with anise and bay leaf when she returned to regain human form. But even her fabulous magic had its limitations. Once, it was said, she was infatuated with a young man and needed only a hair from his head or body to enchant him forever; never able to procure the hair, she never satisfied her love.

Panacea   Roman goddess of health.

Pandia   It is not known whether this goddess was a powerful one whose legend was lost or merely a local form of the moon-goddess *Selene.* Some Greek tales called her Selene's daughter, the "entirely bright one," probably the full moon; she was also said to be the mate of Zeus Pandion, the full-moon god.

Pandora   Originally she was "rich in gifts," the "all-giver," the earth in female form, endlessly producing food for people and animals; the goddess was also called *Anesidora* ("sender-forth of gifts") and shown as a gigantic woman rising from the earth while little men opened her way with hammerblows. Later, as Greek society changed, she became the evil *Eve* of their legend, the one who brought all sorrow to earth.

Panes   A bird-goddess of the Acagchemen of California.

Pani   A plant-goddess of the Polynesian Maori, she was impregnated by a man who had sweet potato seeds in his loincloth. Pani gave birth

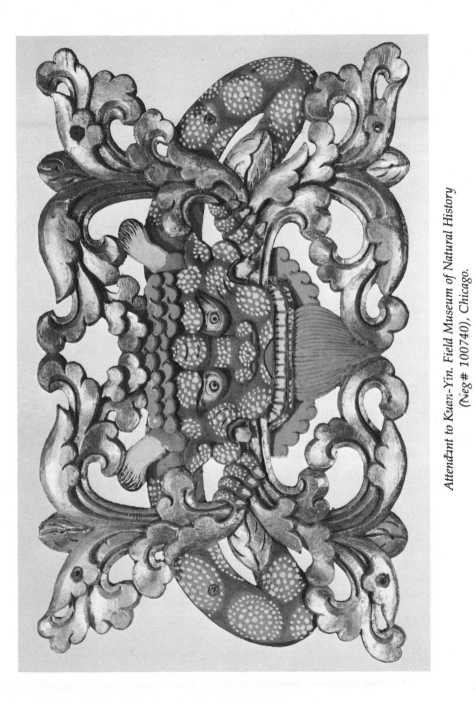

Attendant to Kuan-Yin. Field Museum of Natural History (Neg # 100740), Chicago.

(naturally enough) to a plant and, realizing her duty, retreated to the underworld, where she tended the magical sweet potato patch in the divine garden.

Panope, Panopea   The best loved of the *Nereids*, "she who gives assistance" was invoked by storm-tossed Greek sailors.

Pantariste   This heroic *Amazon* was on the scene when the Greeks attempted to steal the belt of queenship from the royal *Hippolyta*. She left the palace to track the Greek Tiamides, who was on his way to alert his shipbound countrymen of the women warriors' resistance; she killed the messenger with her bare hands.

Pao-Yueh   "Precious mouth," a heroic Chinese queen.

Papa   The word we use for *father* was used by the Polynesians to summon Mother Earth, who existed from the beginning in perpetual intercourse with her lover, the sky-god Rangi. They left no room between them, creating darkness everywhere, which stifled the gods that resulted from the divine union. Finally, the young gods decided to separate their parents. Although apart, the pair remained lovers still; the earth's damp heat rose lustfully to the sky, and the rain fell from heaven to fertilize beloved Papa.

Paphos, Paphia   *Aphrodite* at Paphos, where she was said to have risen from the waves; this name was applied to all women who devoted their bodies to the goddess's service. It was also the name given the daughter of Pygmalion and *Galatea*.

Parca   Roman Fate or *Moira*.

Pare   Some Polynesians used this name for their volcano-goddess, but among the Maori, Pare was said to have been a flirtatious young woman who led on, and then rejected, a young man named Hutu. He exploded in fury at her; ashamed of toying with his desires, she hanged herself.

Hutu was so anguished at the news of Pare's death that he decided to convince her to return to life. He traveled to the underworld but could find no traces of her. Hoping to lure her from hiding, Hutu began to play island games, Pare's favorite sports. Secretly she began to draw near. Then Hutu pulled saplings down to his height, soaring with them as they snapped upward. Pare found this new sport irresistible. As soon as she joined Hutu, he swung a tree so high that he dragged Pare back into the light.

Parewhenua-Mea   Maori rain-goddess.

Parooa   Among the Assam in India, this female spirit lurked where three roads met, hoping to lure wayfarers astray with her *taka*, a flutelike instrument made of bamboo with which she imitated the moan of a lost person. When the helpless traveler left the road, the Parooa enveloped him in a thick fog from which he could see no way out. Similar forest entities are *Fangge, Dames Vertes,* and *Vila.*

Partula   Roman goddess of parturition.

Parvati   One of the greatest goddesses of India is the daughter of the Himalayas, known also as Uma, *Gauri,* and sometimes as *Shakti* ("energy"). She was the consort and enlivening force of Shiva, the lord of life's dance, and many myths surround her.

She gained Shiva's attention by practicing magical asceticism until she had such power that he could not resist her. Thereafter he spent his time sexually pleasing the goddess. Once, when interrupted before she was satisfied, Parvati cursed the gods so that their consorts were barren but they themselves were pregnant. They were most miserable with the affliction, until Shiva allowed them to vomit up the semen that had impregnated them.

Parvati had one son of her own. It was no thanks to her spouse, for Shiva did not want to be bothered with children. As they argued about it one day, Parvati cried out that she wanted a child to hold and caress. Shiva teased her, ripping a piece of her skirt and handing it to her, telling her to fondle that. Hurt and betrayed, Parvati grasped the red cloth to her breast, and—touching the nipples of the mother-goddess herself— the cloth took form and began to nurse. Thus was Ganesha, the benevolent god, born. But Shiva, angry and jealous, found an excuse to behead the child, saying that he had slept in a ritually incorrect way. Parvati was desperate with grief, and Shiva, ashamed, told her he would find the boy another head. The only one he was able to locate— Parvati must have received this news suspiciously—was an elephant's. And so Ganesha was reborn half human, half elephant.

Shiva's Shakti is also called *Kali* and *Durga,* for she is at times a fierce form of femininity. One legend explains how the goddess divided herself. Originally, it seems, she had dark skin, about which Shiva teased her once too often. Furious at him—for she felt less than beautiful, wishing that her skin were golden like his—she set off for the mountains, intending again to practice asceticism until she gained her desire. Ganesha accompanied her; she left Viraka, Shiva's attendant, to guard his bedroom so that he didn't enjoy other women's company during her absence. But a demon disguised as Parvati attempted to kill Shiva. He lured the god to bed after loading his illusory vagina with real nails. Shiva, recognizing the deceit, put à sword on his penis and dispatched the demon.

Parvati's informants spread the word that a woman had been seen entering Shiva's bedroom, and Parvati exploded in anger. Her anger shot out of her mouth in the form of a lion; she cursed the false guardian Viraka to become a rock. Then she continued practicing yoga until Brahma took pity on her and asked her what she wished. When she said she wanted a pure golden skin, he blessed her. From her body sprang her darkness in the form of another goddess, usually named Kali.

Now golden and beautiful, Parvati started home. Viraka, still on guard, refused to let her enter, not recognizing the goddess in her new skin. Realizing that she had made a mistake in cursing him—but unable, so powerful are a goddess's words, to recall her ill wish—Parvati mitigated it by allowing him to be reborn as a girl named Rock.

Pasiphae "She who shines for all" was a Cretan goddess, daughter of sun and moon; she mated with a magical bull who rose from the sea, as another Cretan goddess, *Europa*, mated with Zeus in bull disguise. Later, the Greeks made Pasiphae's story both more and less realistic, calling her a Cretan queen, who, conceiving an unnatural passion for a bull, satisfied her desire by having the artisan Daedalus build her a wooden cow in which she could have intercourse with her beloved. By this means, she conceived the bull-man, the Minotaur; her other children were *Ariadne* and *Phaedra*, who also figure in Cretan and Greek myths. See also **Circe**.

Pavor Roman goddess of fear, similar to *Pallor*.

Pele, Madam Pele Even today, visitors to Hawaiian volcanoes report seeing a wizened old woman who asks for a cigarette, lights it with a snap of her fingers, then disappears. Others say that a red-robed woman dances on the rims of the fiery mountains, although it is not certain whether this figure is an incarnation of the goddess or only one of her worshipers. Of all the world's goddesses, Pele is one of the few still living in the belief of her people, not as metaphor but as metaphysical reality, to whom offerings are still made when volcanic eruptions threaten Hawaiian towns.

A bright daughter of the earth-goddess *Haumea*, Pele spent her girlhood watching fires and learning how to make them, thus revealing her temperament early. This did not please the sea-goddess Namaka, who prophesied an unpleasant future for the fire-loving girl, but she, who lived in the ocean, may have been biased. But Namaka had a point: Pele did cause a conflagration in her mother's homeland once, toying with underworld fires.

The mother, knowing that Namaka would persecute Pele on her return, suggested that it was time for Pele to find a home of her own. So she set off in a canoe with several siblings including her sister Hiiaka ("cloudy one"). They were *malihini*, goddesses who migrated to Hawaii after human settlement there began. Hawaii was only an atoll when they arrived, so Pele used a divining rod to locate likely places to build islands.

Namaka trailed her sister, furious at the destruction Pele had wrought in their original homeland. Ocean and fire met in a terrific brawl, and Pele got the worst of it, rising like a steamy spirit from the fray. No longer embodied, she disappeared into the Hawaiian volcanoes, especially Kilauea, said today to be one of her favorite haunts.

There she was honored by the Hawaiian people as the essence of earthly fire. Into her craters, offerings were cast: cut hair, sugar cane and flowers, white birds, money and strawberries. Some say that human beings were also tossed into the lava; others deny this, claiming there is no evidence for such rites.

There is one famous legend, however, that suggests that some were, if not sacrificed literally, at least consecrated to the goddess. This is the tale of the young Hawaiian man named Lohiau. Pele, it was said, sometimes dozed in her crater, sending her spirit wandering through the islands. One night, hearing the sweet melodies of flutes, she followed the sound until she came upon a group of sacred hula dancers.

Among them was Lohiau. Instantly attracted to him, Pele embodied herself in beautiful human flesh and seduced him. They spent three days making love before she decided that it was time to return to her mountain. Promising to send for him, Pele disappeared, awakening far away on Kilauea.

Not one to break a promise—and immediately desiring the young man again—Pele endowed her sister Hiiaka with magic and sent her off to fetch Lohiau. Hiiaka was a kindly goddess, given to singing with the poet-goddess Hopoe and to picking blossoms from the tropical trees. But out of dedication to her sister, Hiiaka set off, first making Pele promise to tend her gardens.

Passing through many trials, often relying on her magic to defeat threatening monsters, Hiiaka reached Lohiau's home just as he died, pining away for his lover Pele. But Hiiaka caught his soul and pushed it back into his body, reviving him. Then they set off for Kilauea.

Although touched by the man's beauty, Hiiaka fully intended to fulfill her task and bring Lohiau untouched to her sister. But Pele was a jealous spirit, and she soon began to burn, imagining Hiiaka in Lohiau's arms. The crater began to spit out lava fretfully. Pele was growing angry.

Hiiaka understood the messages from the distant crater and hastened along. Even though challenged for possession of the man by a sorceress (probably Pele in disguise) and even though Lohiau told Hiiaka he loved her more than Pele, the goddess would not betray her sister's trust. All the way to the crater she conveyed the prize, only to find that Pele had not kept her part of the promise, that the volcano goddess had in jealous fury killed the poet Hopoe and scorched Hiiaka's lovely gardens.

Right then and there, on the rim of the crater, Hiiaka made love to Lohiau. Pele, erupting in fury, burned the man to death but could not destroy her immortal sister. Hiiaka, not about to lose to her angry sister, descended to the underworld to free Lohiau's soul. When she arrived at the deepest circle of the underworld, the point at which the rivers of chaos were held back by a gate, it occurred to her that flooding the entire world would thoroughly extinguish Pele and her wrath.

Her conscience kept her from such folly, however. Hiiaka, after freeing Lohiau's soul, determined to return to the surface and demand her lover from Pele. The lustful, angry goddess would not have been willing, except that Lohiau's comrade Paoa arrived in timely fashion to satisfy the goddess's heat. Hiiaka was reunited with Lohiau, and they retired to his country. Pele, meanwhile, found herself a lover of sturdier stuff in the combative hog-god Kamapua'a, inventor of agriculture, whose idea of courting a goddess included all but dousing her flames with heavy rain and stampeding pigs across her craters. To this day, their turbulent affair continues on the islands called Hawaii.

Penelope Behind the familiar figure of the faithful wife Penelope, weaving by day and unwinding her work each night, looms a much more powerful queen: the spring-goddess who, as owner of the land, chose its king; a goddess whose activity of weaving and unwinding showed her power over life itself. Even dwarfed into the queen of Ithaca, Penelope's original character was hinted at in the *Odyssey*'s ending. After the happy reunion of Penelope and Odysseus, where our memories seem to end the tale, came the king's second banishment, which again left Penelope to rule alone. Then, the epic said, Odysseus returned again, to be killed, unrecognized, by his son by *Circe*; Penelope then married Circe's son while her own married Circe. Still other stories claimed that during Odysseus's absence his wife was far from faithful: it was Penelope who brought forth the wild woodland god, Pan, fathered on her by the ram-shaped Hermes—or by all her suitors in one long orgy.

Penthesilea   One of the greatest of the fighting *Amazons*, she led a troop to Troy to fight the Greeks; they nearly turned the tide of battle. Penthesilea herself engaged in single combat with the Greek hero Achilles. Some accounts of the war say that she killed him; the more common account is that the contest was close but Penthesilea was finally killed by the Greek warrior. Achilles, tearing off her helmet to see what worthy opponent he had bested, was overcome with her fierce beauty and regretted destroying her. But his destructiveness was untamable, for he then raped her corpse and killed a comrade who suggested that this lust was unnatural.

Perasia   The name of a goddess like *Artemis* in Cappadocia, where priestesses used to walk unharmed through sacred fires.

Perchta, Berchta, Percht   An ancient mother-goddess has survived throughout modern Germany, Switzerland, and Austria under the name of this "elf woman." Perchta is said to make the fields fertile and the cattle bear strong calves. Sometimes, it is said, you can see her float across the fields to nurture them, her white cape looking exactly like a soft mist.

Of course, she has her difficult side as well. She cannot tolerate laziness; she carefully inspects distaffs and spinning wheels, looking for wasted bits of wool. If she finds them, she scratches the guilty spinner or, worse yet, tears open her stomach and stuffs the remnants into the cavity.

She herself, however, is rather sloppy in appearance, with long, white matted hair and tattered clothes. Her face is wrinkled like an apple doll, but her eyes are lively. Her favorite time of year is the "twelve days of Christmas," which culminate in Perchta's Day, when everyone eats pancakes of meal and milk in her honor. Leftover bits of the cakes are left for Perchta herself; she will come secretly to enjoy them, but if anyone tries to spy on her, he will be blinded for the year. See also **Frau Holle.**

Perkuna Tete   The oldest goddess known in the Baltic was this "mother of thunder," who survives in only a single myth fragment as welcoming the sun-goddess *Saule*, after her day's work, with a hot bath. She was later hidden under the Christian name *Maria*.

Pero, Perone   She was the granddaughter of *Niobe* and daughter of Chloris. A great beauty of legend, she bore a title of the pre-Hellenic moon-goddess, of whom Pero may be a vestigial form.

Perse, Persea, Perseis "Light-bearer" or "destroyer," she was the early Greek moon-goddess, wife of the sun and daughter of the ocean. Her own daughters were the Cretan goddess *Pasiphae* and the famous witch *Circe*; possibly she later developed into *Persephone*.

Persephone The Greek world was divided into three parts, in honor of the threefold goddess. *Hecate,* the moon, wandered through the sky; *Demeter* ruled the surface of the earth; and underneath the world, in the afterlife, the pale queen Persephone lived. Sometimes Hecate would join her there; sometimes Persephone would visit her mother, Demeter, on earth. But they were never completely separate, for these three goddesses were really a trinity, like the Christian god, three persons perceived as facets of the same divinity.

According to the Greeks, Persephone originally lived aboveground. One day, surrounded by companions, the maiden goddess was picking flowers. Suddenly the chariot of Hades appeared; the god of death snatched her up and carried her through a crack in the earth, which instantly closed after them. Hearing her daughter's cries, Demeter immediately sought her, but no trace remained.

Demeter went into mourning, broken only when the Olympian gods demanded the return of the raped maiden—on condition that she was not to have eaten anything in the afterworld. Hades, hearing the heavenly verdict, pressed a single pomegranate seed into Persephone's mouth. So the goddess was condemned to spend one-third of the year belowground, while the rest of the time she enjoyed the company of her mother on earth.

While Persephone was with her, Demeter caused the earth to spring forth with blossom and fruit. While Persephone was absent, however, the earth wilted and died, and the earth-goddess mourned her annual separation from the daughter who was also Demeter's incarnate younger self. This annual cycle of joy and sorrow was celebrated at the town of Eleusis in solemn mysteries that the Greeks said made humans ready to face death, revealing the beautiful Persephone who waited to welcome them.

But what of those who died while Persephone was away from her domain? Did they wait for months to be initiated into the spirit realm? Persephone was known to be a gracious and gentle queen of the dead—indeed, she was called the reason for life itself, the goddess who lived with Eros, the goddess who had no children but allowed others to give birth. Some scholars, pointing out this confusion in the Greek conception of the afterlife, suggest that Persephone was originally the queen of death and that Demeter's daughter was *Kore* ("maiden"). As Greek theology grew, assimilating various figures into fewer but more complex ones, these maiden goddesses were joined.

That would explain variants of the Persephone story, like the one that tells how the goddess was sitting in a cave, guarded by snakes and weaving the entire world on a loom. Zeus came to her in the form of a snake and had intercourse with her; she gave birth to the wine-god Dionysus, who was instantly ripped apart by Titans and died. This tale—which fits in poorly with the more familiar tale of the virgin goddess—shows Persephone more clearly associated with symbols of regeneration: the snake and the loom; she was perhaps a remnant of the earliest Persephone, the queen of death and rebirth. See also **Anieros, Freya, Libera.**

Phaedra   After the Athenian hero Theseus had abandoned the helpful Cretan heroine *Ariadne,* he returned to his city, ascended the throne, and married his deserted mistress's sister, Phaedra. She soon became infatuated with Theseus's son by another abandoned mistress, Hippolytus, son of *Hippolyta.* She offered her bed to her stepson, but he refused; she cursed him so that he was dragged to death by magical sea-dwelling horses. This Greek Phaedra seems to be a literary creation based on an original Cretan goddess of whom only the name, "bright one," survives intact.

Pheraia   In Thessaly in the north of Greece, this Great Goddess was worshiped by her descendants, the Perai. All that is known of her now is that she carried a torch and rode a bull; this suggests she was a moon-goddess.

Pherenice   This Greek woman bore a son who became a famous wrestler. She coached him to victory after victory, until he was ready to enter the Olympics. All women except *Hera*'s priestesses were barred from the games, but Pherenice nonetheless put on male clothing to coach her son in the ring. He won, and her disguise was discovered; but in recognition of her coaching excellence, she was dismissed without punishment.

Philemon   Once, Greek legend says, there was an old man and woman who lived together so long and tenderly that they became inseparable, almost indistinguishable. Although age bent their backs, their eyes still shone with care and concern for each other; often they told themselves how empty life would be without such love.

Once, looking for adventure, the gods Zeus and Hermes went wandering the earth. Stopping at the poor hut where Baucis and Philemon lived, they begged a meal. The impoverished couple generously served what food they had, though they knew it meant a week of gruel for them. The gods revealed themselves; in recognition of the old couple's kindness, they granted a single wish. The pair wished quickly: to live together forever, never to be separated. Their hut instantly changed into a temple, where they served the gods for years. Then one day, as they stood outdoors, their feet took root and their arms stretched up to the sky, and they lived on forever as a pair of intertwined linden trees.

Philomena, Philomela   In Thracian legend, this sister of Procne (or Progne) was raped by her brother-in-law, King Tereus, who, to keep her from reporting the crime, cut out her tongue. But Philomena still had hands to bear witness, and she wove a tapestry picturing the brutal act. When she sent this to her sister, the two women began to plot revenge. They cut up the five-year-old son of Procne and her husband and served the child to his father for dinner. During the meal, Philomena brought in the boy's head and flung it upon the table. At that point they were all transformed: Philomena into the first nightingale; Procne, into a swallow; King Tereus, into a hawk; and the boy Itylus, into a sandpiper.

Phoebad, Phoebas   The name of a priestess of Delphi in Greece; this word was used later for any inspired woman prophet.

Phyllis   There were two Greek heroines by this name. The first was a Thracian queen, courted by an Athenian king who sought to control her country. She agreed to wed him, thereby giving him title to Thrace. But he heartlessly left her to return to the pleasures of Athens. So Phyllis ended his rights to Thrace, and her life, by throwing herself into the sea.

Another famous Phyllis was a free-living woman who took as a lover the young Macedonian king, Alexander, who was wildly infatuated with her. His teacher, the philosopher Aristotle, warned him against giving such power to a woman. Phyllis found this attitude insulting; she avenged herself by so bewitching Aristotle that he served her as a mount, walking on his hands and knees while she rode astride, controlling his head with a bridle.

Phyrne   "Toad," a name for *Hekate.*

Pidari, Kala-Pidari, Pitali   This South Indian snake-goddess was depicted with flaming hair and three eyes; she held a noose and a drum, apparently to frighten away evil spirits from the villages she guarded. Her worship has been traced to the first millenium of the Christian Era.

Pietas   Roman goddess of duty and filial respect.

Pi-Hsia Yuan-Chin   The Princess of the Blue and Purple Clouds was, to Chinese Taoists, a major divinity and one of the most beloved. With her train of six divine helpers—one for each stage of labor—she attended every birth, bringing health and good fortune to the newborn, as well as protecting its mother. She was sometimes thought to be identical with the Buddhist *Kuan-Yin* and was called by the names Sheng-Mu ("holy mother"), Yu Nu ("jade maiden"), and T'ien Hsien ("heavenly immortal").

Pitho, Suada, Suadela   This minor Greek "goddess" was really only a literary allegory. Said to rule seduction and persuasion, she was the daughter (appropriately enough) of the lustful goddess *Aphrodite* and tricky Hermes.

Plataia   *Hera* as a woman seeking a mate.

Pleiades   The seven daughters of the nymph Pleione, they were born in wild Arcadia and followed the wild goddess *Artemis* until they were turned into the stars that bear their name, the "seven sisters." Individually, their names were Alcyone, Calaeno, *Electra, Maia, Merope,* (A)Sterope and Taygete—almost all names also borne by early Greek goddesses, which suggests that the legend linking them has been lost.

Po Ino Nogar   Among the Chams of Cambodia, the world's goddess-ruler, creator of rice, was called Po Ino Nogar ("Great One, mother of the kingdom"). Born either from sea-foam or from clouds, she had 97 husbands and 38 daughters. One of her offspring was Po Bya Tikuh ("mouse queen"), a maleficent virgin goddess; another was the goddess of disease, Po Yan Dari, who lived in caves and grottoes to which worshipers would bring stones, asking for miraculous cures. Another Cham healing-goddess was the divine priestess Pajau Tan, said to be a 30-ish woman who lived on earth as a healer but who was finally sent to live in the moon because she kept raising all the dead; there she still lives, providing flowers to the newly dead to ease their transition.

Pohjan-Akka   In the European subarctic, among the Scandinavian Saami, this goddess was said to be mistress of the northern hell called Pohjan, where anyone who died a violent death would live forever, wearing blood-drenched garments. The "man-eating village" of Pohjan was sometimes thought to be the aurora borealis, floating with red fringes through the wintry sky. Witches were said to be able to visit Pohjan in their living bodies, but no other breathing humans could even find the place, located somewhere in the Arctic Ocean.

Poine An avenging ghost promoted to a goddess, she was to the Greeks an attendant of *Nemesis* and to the Romans the embodiment of righteous punishment.

Pok Klai An agricultural goddess of upper Burma.

Poldunica In eastern Europe, the goddess of midday was a white lady who floated about the fields on gusts of wind, killing people with a touch of her hand. That was her most familiar form, but there were variants. In Moravia, she was a white-gowned old woman with horse hoofs, staring eyes, and wild hair. In Poland, Poldunica was very tall and carried a sickle; she asked difficult riddles of those she caught wandering the fields at midday, and if they could not answer she would reap them. In Russia, she was very beautiful—something her victims noticed just before she twisted their heads around, bringing death, or at least intense pain. In Serbia, she guarded the corn from thieves and careless children; in Finland, she kidnapped children caught abroad at noon. Finally, in Siberia, Poldunica appeared as a scantily clad woman of great age, who hid in nettle patches and pulled naughty children into her den.

Polycaste The sister of the great Greek architect Daedalus, she bore a son who, as he grew up, was found to be even more brilliantly inventive than his uncle. Seeing the boy as a threat to his reputation, Daedalus murdered him; the grieving mother flew away, transformed by sorrow into a bird. When Daedalus's son died by his own carelessness and pride, Polycaste was there, chattering in derision as Daedalus dug the grave.

Polydamna, Polydama A famous queen of Egypt whom *Helen* of Troy visited as she traveled back to Greece, Polydamna was an herbalist who gave Helen a drug to banish melancholy and heartbreak.

Pomona In the spring, the Romans honored *Flora*, the flower-goddess; fall was the season of fruit, of Pomona. Although she had no actual festival, Pomona was nonetheless significant enough to be endowed with one of the 12 flamines, or high priests, of the city and with a shrine 12 miles from Rome called the Pomonal. Ovid tells us that she was courted by several of the male fertility-gods, including Pan, Priapus, and Silenus.

But she was won when Vertumnus came courting—disguised as an old woman, with whom Pomona fell in love.

Port-Kuva Many cultures believe that a home has its own spirit, and the Cheremis of eastern Russia were no exception. They called her Port-Kuva ("house woman") and said she was invisible to human eyes unless a disaster or illness was about to befall the residents of her abode. She was a *Norn* or Fate, however, and controlled such events; people could, therefore, if they saw Port-Kuva, suspect that they had hurt her feelings and could repair the breach before ill befell them. Sacrifices of black animals, buried in the earth, were helpful in such events. Bread and pancakes, however, also sufficed; they were absolutely necessary to make Port-Kuva feel at home in a new house.

Poshjo-Akka "She permits shooting" is the name of the Saami hunting-goddess; to her, offerings were poured out on winter solstice in the hunting camps. The goddess's image stood within the storage hut of the hunters so that she could observe the condition of all slaughtered animals. Once butchered, their skulls were buried at the statue's feet in thanksgiving and in sorrow that we must kill to live. Without such care, the animals would be unable to reincarnate, and all life would cease.

Postvorta The Romans, like many other peoples, considered prophecy logically related to childbirth; perhaps this represented a natural curiosity about the fate of newborns or a recognition of the wisdom of midwives. In any case, they provided two goddesses to assist the laboring mother and to provide oracles of the future: Postvorta and her companion, called *Antevorta*, Prorsa, or Porrina.

Potina This Roman goddess was honored as the spirit of weaving and of drinking.

Poza-Mama Among Siberian peoples, this most sacred goddess lived in the hearth fire; she was also mistress of the mountains. Like the Ainu *Kamui Fuchi* or the Roman *Vesta*, she was the bond that kept the family intact, as well as the heat which kept them alive. The Ulchi spit the first mouthful of every meal into the fire as a kind of grace and a prayer for food in the future; the Khakass had the same ritual to honor the braided-haired goddess.

The Negidals kept pictures of the fire-goddess Kutug-a next to the hearth and revered the spot as sacred to the goddess. Among the Shors, fire was called Otuz Pastu Ot Ana, "thirty-headed Mother Fire," and Altyn Tondu Ot Ana, "Mother Fire in her golden coat." The Altai called her Ot Ana, "Mother Fire," and Kyz Ana, "Virgin Mother," for it was believed that she perpetuated herself without need of a male principle; she was responsible for all family members, living and dead, for she lit the way to the afterlife with her bright flame.

Among the fire taboos of the Altai were the following restrictions: no garbage is to be thrown into the fire; the fire must never be unnecessarily put out; no iron may touch it; no one should jeer or mock the fire. Because Mother Fire was the mediator between humanity and the world beyond, no shaman functioned without first asking her help.

Prakriti, Prakrti Two points of collision between patriarchal Indo-European culture and indigenous mother-goddess religions saw the rise of splendidly complex mythologies: classical Greece and ancient India. In India, the melding of two disparate philosophies created Hinduism and its offspring, Buddhism, which both employ vocabularies compounded of insights from the two streams that converged to form them.

From the ancient religions of *Devi* ("The Goddess"), there remained a strong tendency toward the worship of female divinity. In Hindu philosophy, three concepts are given feminine form: *Maya*, the dancing goddess who keeps creation alive; *Shakti*, the force of life itself, and Prakriti, or nature. These three theological concepts are closely connected and—because no myths illustrate them—sometimes difficult to separate. In fact, each is identified with one or another of the triad, for the force of life cannot be segmented into neat categories.

As Prakriti, this energy is the creative principle, the unitary pattern behind all movement. Self-knowing, endless, and perfectly alone, Prakriti exists everywhere but is nowhere actually manifest, for although she herself, the material of the universe, is singular, that form takes immeasurably various individual forms. She is therefore paradoxical, divinely alone in her uncountable forms, which humans can perceive only because we, too, are parts of Prakriti.

Praxidike A three-faced head symbolized this Greek goddess of vengeance and enterprise, who punished evil actions and rewarded the good.

Prithivi, Prthivi, Pritha Hinduism embodies the earth in female shape, calling her Prithivi ("broad one") and saying that she appears like a cosmic cow, full of milk for her children. She figures in few myths but appears in many prayers.

See Le-Hev-Hev, p. 205. Field Museum of Natural History (Neg# A109628), Chicago.

Procris   Princess of Athens, she married Cephalus. But the man soon drew the eye of the lustful dawn-goddess *Eos*; she spirited him away, but Cephalus refused to sleep with her. Eos, disgusted, returned the man to earth, first changing his appearance completely.

When Cephalus entered his home, he seemed a handsome stranger, and Procris, infatuated, welcomed him into her bed. When Cephalus resumed his own shape, Procris, horrified to be caught in infidelity, fled the palace.

In the forest, she joined a band of wild-roaming women, servants of *Artemis*. Later reconciled to her mate, Procris grew jealous and possessive; she began to spy on Cephalus. Eos, to avenge Cephalus's rejection, had the man mistake Procris for an animal and kill her. Some interpreters see this as a nature allegory, in which the dew (Procris) is slain by the rays of the sun (Cephalus) while the dawn looks on.

Proserpine, Proserpina   Roman name for *Persephone*.

Protagenia   The "firstborn" daughter of *Pyrrha* after the great flood, she was the legendary ancestor of many Greek tribes.

Providentia   "Forethought," a Roman goddess.

Psyche   The heroine of a Greek allegory, Psyche represented the human soul, married to the loving heart personified as the god Eros. Psyche, the story goes, spent her days alone, making love each night in darkness with a husband she never saw; only under these conditions would he remain faithful to her. For a while she lived happily enough. But finally a fearful curiosity about his identity and a deep spiritual loneliness drove Psyche to bring a lamp into the bedroom. Hardly had the woman seen the beautiful winged body of her lover than a bit of oil fell from her lamp, awakening him. Instantly Eros flew away. Thus the soul, the Greeks knew, could remain happy in romantic union, until unmet needs demanded conscious knowledge of the lover's real identity.

Next, the tale goes, Psyche was charged with many near-impossible tasks to gain back her beloved: sorting overnight a roomful of seeds; catching the sun-sheep's fleece; traveling to the underworld to ask for magical beauty ointment. Intent on regaining Eros, she overcame these obstacles one by one.

But as Psyche returned from Hades with *Persephone*'s ointment box, vanity overcame her. She opened the jar to rub beauty cream on her weary face. Psyche fell into a swoon and might have died, but Eros persuaded the Olympian divinities that she had struggled enough. She ascended to heaven and was reunited with her lover, bearing two children named Love and Delight. In this allegory, the Greeks produced a magnificent tale of the relations of heart and mind, the journey through romance to real marriage, and the human joy born of the victorious struggle.

Ptesan-Wi   Brule name for *White Buffalo Woman.*

Ptrotka   In late Jewish folklore, a name for *Lilith* as a "winged creature."

Pukimna   The protector of land animals among the Ighuliks

Puta   Roman goddess of tree-pruning.

Pyrrha   Many peoples have legends of a great flood sent in punishment for humankind's iniquity. The Greeks placed this flood far back in the mythic era, when Bronze Age people occupied the earth. Brazen indeed, they provoked the Olympian divinities to decide the whole race should be drowned.

There was, however, one honorable couple: Deucalion, son of Prometheus, and Pyrrha, daughter of the earth-goddess *Pandora*. Only the perfect righteousness of their lives stayed the anger of the Olympians, who allowed the pair to escape death by floating nine days and nine nights in a wooden box. When the great flood receded, the couple found themselves on the sacred mountain of Parnassus. There they offered sacrifice for their salvation and, granted one boon, they asked that the earth be repopulated

They received an answer: as they descended to the flood-wet valley, they should cast the bones of their mother behind them. Quickly Pyrrha penetrated the enigma. Picking up stones, the bones of the earth mother, she began to walk downhill. Deucalion joined her, throwing stones over his shoulder. Behind them sprang up the "stone age" people, men from stones cast by Deucalion, women from Pyrrha's.

Pythia   A woman had to have seen 50 years through mortal eyes before she could be called by this name, borne by the Oracle of Delphi; only women distinguished by age could endure the power that rose from the earth at that spot. Pythia also had to be married, in deference to the original owner of the shrine, the earth mother *Gaea* or *Hera*; in later Greek history, it was dedicated to the newly arrived god Apollo.

Pythia's duties were as follows: on the seventh of each moon, she underwent ritual purification. Then, seated on the three-legged stool, or tripod, she chewed bay leaves and breathed in fumes that rose from a chasm, inducing a state of ecstasy in the prophet. Eventually she spoke complicated, often enigmatic, prophecies, which were then interpreted to questioners by her male attendants. These seekers, who could ask questions of the oracle only once each year, had to be ritually purified beforehand.

Python   This is one of the names—another being Delphyne ("womb")—given to the great snake of sacred Delphi, born of the mud left after the great deluge and a parthenogenetic daughter of earth. She nested near the flower-filled spring of the Greek shrine. Some legends said that she was killed by the invading god Apollo, when he took over the famous oracular spring; others, giving the name Python to her dead mate, said the she-snake lived forever at Delphi, where only women were allowed to prophesy even after the earth mother, the original owner of the oracle, was ousted by the Greek sun-god.

See Qocha Mana, p. 292. Field Museum of Natural History (Neg# A95952), Chicago.

Qadesh "Holy one," originally a title of *Ishtar* the wanton, later applied to an Egyptian goddess who rode a lion, holding out snakes and lotus buds. Sometimes Qadesh wore the headdress of the local pleasure-goddess *Hathor*, evidence that the holiness she embodied was a sacramental reverence toward sexuality as an expression of divine force.

Qamaits Among the Indians of the Pacific Coast, "Afraid-of-Nothing" was the highest heavenly goddess, a great warrior woman who lived in the east of the world. Although she created the earth, she brought death, famine, and disease to humanity when she visited; better for all the people, the Bellacoola and others said, when she stayed in her sea home with its salty bathing pool.

Her name means "sorrow-maker." She has another name, Dji Sisnaxitl ("slave-owner"), for to her all humans were merely slaves. Researchers in the early part of this century found evidence that she had once been the most important of the Bellacoola divinities, but in recent times, information about her has become scantier, and prayers were addressed to her less and less often. Thus, it seems this great death-goddess, within very recent times, lost her grip on her worshipers, just as earlier underworld queens from *Hel* to *Persephone* became mere metaphors rather than divine aspects of femininity.

Qebhsnuf With *Selkhet*, an Egyptian guardian of the embalmed dead.

Qocha Mana Hopi "white corn maiden."

Quetzapetlatl The incestuous twin sister of Mexican hero Quetzacoatl.

Rabie Among the Indonesian islanders of Ceram, the moon was not originally in the sky but lived on earth with her parents. There her loveliness drew the eye of Tuwale the Sun-Man, who demanded her in marriage. Her parents, however, loath to give up their daughter, waited till nightfall and put a dead pig into Tuwale's bed. Humiliated by the swap, he decided to get revenge. A few days later Rabie simply sank out of sight. After a three-day funeral feast, the people saw Rabie return, when the first full moon rose in the sky.

Rachel One of the four great matriarchs of Israel, she was the most loved of the husband they shared. Like her sister *Leah* and like their servant-doubles Zilpah and *Bilhah*, she gave birth to sons from whom the tribes of Israel descended. As befitted her status as favored spouse, she gave birth to the favored sons, Joseph and Benjamin.

A prophet, she foresaw the birth of her second son, but was said to have been cursed for her pride, for she said at Joseph's birth, "I will bear another son," rather than praying that it might occur. She did bear one son more, but died in labor. Not herself Hebrew but Aramaic, Rachel continued the worship of the *teraphim*, or household gods, even after joining the Hebrew household of Jacob.

Radha "Beloved one," said to be an incarnation of the Indian goddess of abundance, *Lakshmi*, was the adulterous lover of Krishna, the incarnation of Lakshmi's consort, Vishnu. The love of Radha and Krishna is the source of some of the most famous love poetry in existence, and Radha is still honored today in the rituals of *Shakti*, female energy. Although other goddesses sometimes appear as priestesses of these rites, most often it is the voluptuous Radha who stands before her worshipers, putting on a mortal woman's body for the occasion. Naked except for jewelry and flowers, the woman is given reverence due the essence of femininity by groups of male and female worshipers, bound to utter secrecy about their participation in the ceremonies.

Radien-Akka On Saami shamans' drums, this goddess is pictured as part of a holy trinity of father, mother and child.

Radien-Kiedde Among the Saami, the creator-goddess who handed over souls to mother-goddess *Madder-Akka* just before they were to be incarnated. See **Madder-Akka.**

Rafu-Sen The Japanese plum-blossom goddess, the hardy beauty of springtime, was said to be a lovely maiden, forever chaste, who wandered through moonlit groves of blossoming plums, drawing out their perfume, with her long veils floating in the springtime darkness.

Rakshasi A female demon in India.

Rambha Seductive female demigoddess of India.

Ran The great sea-goddess was, to the Scandinavians, also the queen of the drowned. Ran was a mighty woman who held a seafaring ship steady with one hand while with the other, sweeping her magical net into the water, she snared the sailors. These captives she took under the waves to her realm, where they lived as if on earth; because it was believed they were allowed to return to earth to attend their funerals, anyone seen at his own wake was assumed to be safely in Ran's keeping. Because she loved gold, Scandinavian sailors kept gold coins in their pockets as tokens of admittance to her domain, in case of death by drowning, called "faring to Ran" in eddic poetry.

    The sea, called "Ran's road," had a male form as well named Aegir. With Ran he had nine giant daughters, the waves, which poets also called "the claws of Ran." Like their mother, these wave women could appear to humans as mermaids. Ran was most likely to make herself visible during the cold, dark Scandinavian winter, when she splashed as close as she could to her worshipers' warm campfires.

Rana Neida Among the southern Saami, this springtime goddess had a specialized task: she turned south-facing hills green early in the season, giving winter-starved reindeer fresh growth on which to browse. To gain her favor—and an early spring—the Saami ritually rested a spinning wheel against her altar and covered it with blood, a sacrifice the goddess apparently liked.

Ranaghanti This Assamese goddess of war was worshiped in the shape of a huge red stone; she granted not only victory but protection on the field of battle.

Ranu Bai   Barren women prayed to this ancient goddess of India's Nimadi people. On a silver cord she bore a golden pitcher with which she filled in all the rivers of India.

Rati   The goddess of passionate night in Indian Hinduism, Rati was an embodiment of *Kali* ("Mother Time"). But while Kali was the perpetual night that ends creation, the fruitful cosmic destruction from which all would be reborn, Rati was the "giver," the earthly night in which all beings rest, the time of greatest procreative activity. In esoteric tradition, Rati was one of the great symbols of enlightenment, for if *Maya's* dance of creation so confuses the senses that we cannot understand the universal essence, Rati's darkness permits somewhat less confusion and therefore—paradoxical as it seems—greater consciousness and clarity.

Ratis   British Celtic fortress-goddess.

Rauni, Akko, Maan-Eno, Ravdna, Roonikka   The Finno-Ugric thunder-goddess bore many names, probably because she was one of the people's most powerful divinities. Wife of the oak-god of thunder, Rauni was incarnated in the rowan tree or mountain ash, whose red berries were sacred to her. Some myths say that she first brought plant life to the earth's face by having intercourse with the thunder-god.

Rebecca, Rebekah   The counterpart in later Hebrew legend of the great heroine *Sarah*, she was the mother of Jacob and Esau—symbolically, of the Hebrews and their non-Hebrew neighbors in the ancient Near East. Like Sarah, with whom she shared many attributes, Rebecca came close to having the stature of the great earth-goddesses of her territory: she was prescient, had an unearthly beauty, and lived under a magical cloud that never left her tent. Like Sarah, too, she lived with a man who, in times of danger, pretended she was his sister; divine sister-brother marriages were common to the mythology of the surrounding non-Hebrew tribes. A shrewd mother who, in classic matriarchal fashion, favored her younger son over her older one, Rebecca engineered the famous birthright-stealing episode whereby Jacob snatched Isaac's blessing from Esau.

Regina   A name for *Juno* as the "queen."

Renenet   When an Egyptian child was born, this goddess was on hand to pronounce its name, define its personality and bestow its fortune. Then she began to suckle the child, for Renenet was the personification of the force of nurturing and its effect on a child's destiny. In a larger sense, she was the earth itself, which offered milk and grain to her people, who hoped to flatter her as the "goddess of the double granary."

Renpet, Renph A newly sprouted palm was the emblem of this Egyptian goddess of youth and springtime, who also symbolized the extension of measurable time into immeasurable eternity. The goddess of "the year"—the meaning of her name—she was shown in ancient art wearing a calendar for a hat.

Rhea In late Greek legend she was a vague motherly figure—the Titan who gave birth to the Olympian gods. But earlier, Rhea was the primary goddess, the great mountain mother (called *Ida* as goddess of Mt. Ida), the earth who gave birth to the creatures of her wild and fruitful surface.

Rhea's name is Cretan. In the art of that island, Rhea was depicted as a huge stately woman surrounded by worshipful animals and small, subservient human males. Her religion was a fervent one, celebrated in great musical processions of pipes and cymbals, leading to mystical orgies among her reveling children. The blazing torch, the brass drum, and the double-ax were her symbols, and she was invoked with these words: "Earth sends up fruits, and so praise Earth the Mother."

When the wide stream of Aegean mother worship touched the later freshet of patriarchal religion, the confusion of divinities was such that multiple pantheons were defined, forming what we now call Greek mythology. Rhea was incorporated into Greek legend as a Titan, one of the second generation of deities. It was said that she was the wife of Cronos ("time") and the mother of the most powerful gods and goddesses, among them *Hera*. But reminders of her majestic past crop up: she was said to have been transformed into *Demeter*, to have been a snake-goddess raped by her own son Zeus, and to have borne as many fatherless children as she had fingers. Even in late legend, the earlier identity of Rhea as goddess of the living earth was subtly acknowledged.

Rhea Silvia, Ilia, Silvia The mother of Rome was originally the daughter of a king, Numitor, who was unseated by his younger brother, Amulius. The usurper kidnapped Silvia and made her a Vestal to keep her from reproducing her father's royal line. But she secretly slept with the war-god Mars and bore twin sons—the city-fathers Romulus and Remus. Discovered with her infants, she was commanded by Amulius to drown the children. Instead, she took up with Tiberinus, god of the Tiber River, who gently carried the children in a box downstream to safety. (Upon landing, they were nursed by a she-wolf whom some say was Rhea Silvia herself.) Some modern interpreters consider this legend to be an expression of Italy's change from matrilineal to patrilineal succession.

Rhiannon The beautiful Welsh underworld-goddess traveled through earth on an impossibly speedy horse, accompanied always by magical birds that made the dead waken and the living fall into a blissful seven-year sleep. Originally named Rigatona ("Great Queen"), she shrank in later legend into Rhiannon, a fairylike figure who appeared to Prince Pwyll of Dyfed near the gate of the underworld. He pursued her on his fastest horses, but hers—cantering steadily and without tiring—exhausted any mount of Pwyll's. Finally, the queen decided to stay with Pwyll; she bore him a son soon afterward.

What can one expect of a goddess of death? Her son disappeared, and the queen was found with blood on her mouth and cheeks. Accused of murder, she was sentenced to serve as Pwyll's gatekeeper, bearing visitors to the door on her back; thus she was symbolically transformed into a horse. All ended happily when her son was found; Rhiannon had been falsely accused by maids who, terrified at finding the babe absent, had smeared puppy blood on the queen's face.

Behind this legend is doubtless another, more primitive one in which the death queen actually was guilty of infanticide. This beautiful queen of the night would then, it seems, be identical to the Germanic *Mora*, the nightmare, the horse-shaped goddess of terror. But night brings good dreams as well as bad, so Rhiannon was said to be the beautiful goddess of joy and oblivion, a goddess of Elysium as well as the queen of hell.

Rhode, Rhodos A vague figure in late Greek mythology, she was the daughter of the sea queen *Amphitrite* and goddess of the island named for her, Rhodes—a place also sacred to her mate the sun-god Helios.

Rhpisunt The people of the Haida Wolf clan in southeastern Alaska possess a story of the Bear Mother, Rhpisunt, who long ago was a noblewoman, daughter of the Wolf clan's chief. Out walking one day, she stepped into the droppings of a bear and, a dainty and somewhat vain woman, became enraged that her feet should be soiled. Not only did she curse the bears then but she continued to exclaim against the animals for many days.

Later, while picking berries, Rhpisunt became separated from her party and, roaming farther and farther into the forest, finally filled her basket. But almost as soon as the basket was full, she felt the straps give way, and all her carefully harvested berries fell to the ground. It took some time to gather them together; by that time there was no sign of her friends' canoe.

Happily enough, she came upon a handsome young man who led her down a path until they came to his village. He introduced Rhpisunt to the chief, his father, a huge fat man who sat in a log house lined with bearskin cloaks. Suddenly, at Rhpisunt's side, a little fat lady named Tsects ("Mouse Woman") appeared; she whispered that Rhpisunt should give her some grease and wool and that she should never relieve herself without breaking off a piece of copper and placing it on the ground above the buried excrement.

Rhpisunt did as she was told and soon saw why she'd been so instructed: the Bear People, finding copper left behind after the woman's trip to the bushes, judged her complaints about the bear's leavings justifiable, as she herself passed shiny metal. Thereupon, Rhpisunt was allowed to marry the Bear Prince, and Mouse Woman provided a huge feast, miraculously created from the bits of fat Rhpisunt had given her.

But the woman's family was seeking her; they'd found her prints, with those of bears, leading away from where she'd been lost. The Haida raged through the forest killing bears, and in the village of the Bear People there was mourning for the loss of life. Eventually, led by Rhpisunt's little lapdog, Maesk, one of the woman's brothers found her, together with her Bear Prince and their twin sons, in a cave. The visionary Bear Prince knew he would die, so he shared magical formulas with his wife before he was speared by her brother. Rhpisunt was brought back to the Haida village, where she grew to a great and revered age. Her sons, taking off their bear jackets while in human company, returned at her death to their father's people, but afterward the people of the Wolf clan recognized bears as their blood relatives.

Ri, Re   The moon-goddess of ancient Phoenicia, of whom little is known but her name, which seems to mean "light."

Rind, Rinda   In Scandinavian legend, Rind was originally a Russian princess who, it was prophesied, was the only one who could bear a child to avenge the death of the god Balder. The god Odin traveled to her court disguised as a soldier to conceive the avenger, but Rind rebuffed him. Odin came the next year disguised as a skilled smith able to make beautiful ornaments, but Rind still did not find her heart moved. A third time Odin came wearing a third disguise, that of a young courtier. Rind again refused his advances.

Finally Odin disguised himself as a young leech maiden, a healer,

*See Rhpisunt, p. 297. Field Museum of Natural History
(Neg# 109380), Chicago.*

and became a servant of the princess. It was in this form that he finally drew Rind's eye and, when she fell sick of a strange malady (brought about, some legends say, by the curses of Odin himself), Odin cured her. At last Rind agreed to sleep with Odin, conceiving the hero Vali.

Worshiped throughout Scandinavia as a goddess, Rind was, some scholars believe, a symbol of the wintry earth, refusing the embraces of the fertilizing god. More convincing is the argument that Rind was a sun-goddess, for she was described as "white as the sun" and as leaving her couch each morning and returning each evening. As the Scandinavian sun was considered to be female, this interpretation has the force of tradition behind it.

Risem-Edne　"Twig Mother" of the Norwegian Saami.

Rohini　Once, Indian mythology tells us, Daksha had 27 daughters, all married to the moon. But though the moon promised to spend his favors equally, he fell in love with Rohini ("Red One") and began to spend more and more time with her. Daksha cursed the moon with consumption, but his daughters prevailed on him to lighten his curse, so he allowed the disease to be chronic rather than fatal.

A later Rohini appears in the myths of Krishna as the mother of his half-brother.

Rona　To the people of New Zealand, the moon was a man, and a tease at that. One night when Rona was walking to the stream to draw water, the moon-man covered himself with a cloud so that she could not see; Rona stubbed her toe on a big rock. Annoyed, she cursed the moon. She insulted him. She called him names. Aggravated, he came down to argue with her. When the moon-man reached earth, Rona was still so irritated that he grabbed her by the shoulder and took her and her basket with him back to the sky, where she still clings to the moon's face.

Rosmerta　Goddess of water or the sun of British Celts.

Rudrani　Indian goddess of storms who spreads disease and death.

Rugiu Boba　"The Old One of the Rye" was a Lithuanian harvest-goddess honored, like the *Carlin* in Scotland, when the last sheaf to be reaped was formed into her likeness. Brought into the village at the time of the harvest festival, her effigy was kept in a place of honor in the home until replaced the next year.

Rukko   In the cosmology of the Mandan people, Rukko was a goddess of materiality and darkness who created human bodies, while a male spirit provided animating souls.

Rumina   The Roman goddess of nursing mothers was worshiped at a fig tree. There the founders of Rome, the twins Romulus and Remus, were said to have been suckled by a wolf bitch. Fittingly, the offering made to Rumina was milk—to assure plentiful milk for healthy babies.

Rumor   The last-born daughter of the earth mother *Gaea*, Rumor was seen by the Greeks as feathered and fleet-footed. Rumor, they said, ran through the earth bearing messages that should be attended to, for some of them were disguised messages from the gods.

Rusalky   These Russian water spirits were originally human women who drowned or committed suicide. The company of naked, wild-haired Rusalky rose each spring from streams to beg bits of white linen from humans. The Rusalky hung them from trees after carefully laundering them. (One who accidentally stepped on the Rusalky's wash would be spastic thereafter.)

   Their spring cleaning done, the Rusalky began their nightly magical dances that help plants grow and mature; sometimes for these occasions they wore long white unbelted tunics or robes of green leaves. Humans could lose their souls by witnessing the beautiful dances of the Rusalky, which usually brought rain to the growing plants. When summer was over, the Rusalky retreated to feather nests at the bottom of their streams, where they hibernated until the next spring.

Saba, Saar, Sabia   Although married to a warrior, this Irish heroine retained such a horror of bloodshed that she died of horror because of her husband's cruelty in war. The most famous legend concerning her tells how, bewitched by a jealous Druid into a deer, she had to bear her young son in the woods. He was born in human form, but the princess could not resist licking his brow—where he sprouted fawn's hair and whence he was named Oisin ("little fawn"), the legendary poet.

Sabrina   Goddess of Severn River; see **Sequana**.

Sabulana   The savior-heroine of the African people of Machakeni rescued her people from starvation when—although previously they had lived on the earth's bounty—they neglected proper sacrifice to the goddess and found themselves unable to gather food from their gardens. Even wild food escaped them. Women trying to gather wild honey found that their hands broke off at the wrist when they reached into honey-bearing trees.

Only Sabulana apprehended the problem, and she instructed her people to seek divine help. Then she went alone—for no one was brave enough to accompany her—to the sacred ancestral grove. There she met ghosts and sang a melody for them so stirring that their hardened hearts melted. Telling Sabulana that her people had been sacrilegious and to make offerings to the earth for her gifts, the ancestral spirits sent the young woman back to the village, where she and her mother were honored as chiefs.

Sadarnuna   In Sumerian mythology, the goddess of the new moon.

Saga   The all-knowing goddess came second, after *Frigg*, in the Scandinavian pantheon; to some scholars she was an aspect of the mighty Frigg herself. The eddas said that Saga lived at Sinking Beach, a waterfall of cool waves where she offered her guests drinks in golden cups. Her name, which means "omniscience," was applied to the epic heroic tales of her people.

Saibya   This Hindu heroine was a devoted worshiper of Vishnu, the god who preserves life; she was married to a somewhat less devoted Vishnuite named Sata-Dhanu. He fell into error and was reincarnated as a dog; Saibya, however, was rewarded for her virtue by being reborn as a princess. Also as a reward, she retained knowledge of her former lives on earth.

One day the princess met the dog, whom she petted and reminded of his sinful ways. And so it went for generations, the woman being incarnated in human form while the man worked his way up through the shapes of jackal, wolf, crow, and peacock. Eventually, however, her diligence—for in every life she met him and reminded him of his crime—resulted in his being born again as a man. She married him again, and this time he remained true in faith; they ascended after death to eternal gratification.

Sakkala-Khatun   The drunken fire-goddess of Mongolia.

Sala   Babylonian or Kassite "light," a goddess of whom nothing but her name remains.

Salacia   The Roman name for *Aphrodite*, the "salacious" love-goddess.

Salmacis   In the Greek colony of Caria in Asia Minor, it was said, this fountain nymph lived, a force so female that anything that drank her waters became feminine. Even human males could not resist the power of Salmacis.

One day the son of Hermes and *Aphrodite*, who bore both parents names, chanced by her fountain. The nymph fell in love with him and reached to embrace him. Alas for her, he drowned in her waters. Salmacis pleaded with the Olympians to revive him and unite them forever; they approved her wish and the two became the first hermaphrodite, according to the Greeks. Earlier mythic hermaphrodites had been known, not coincidentally in the part of Asia Minor from which this fanciful Greek story derives.

Salus   Roman goddess of health.

Sambatu   To the Gallas, a Cushite tribe of Abyssinia, the "Sabbath" was personified as a goddess, a tradition that survives in the modern Jewish prayers that welcome the day of rest as "bride and queen."

303

Samjuna, Saranya "Knowledge" was the Indian wife of the sun, whose brilliance finally so tired her that Samjuna hid in the wilderness disguised as a mare. But he found her and, approaching her for intercourse, took the form of a stallion; from this union came the twin gods of agriculture, the horse-headed Aswins. Then Samjuna agreed to return to the sky with the sun-god, but first she had her father trim away some of the sun's rays to diminish his brightness. From the extra pieces of the sun were fashioned the weapons of other gods.

Samsin Halmoni These three goddesses of birth in Korea are celebrated at birthday parties throughout life. Women shamans, or *mudang*, specializing in childbirth and birthday rituals are called by the goddesses' name. These rituals include offerings of steamed rice, wine and soy sauce, laid out like a dinner for the divine women. When a child is born, the *mudang* uses a floating gourd like a drum to beat out prayers for a safe delivery.

Samundra Goddess of rivers in India.

Saning Sri Javanese rice-goddess.

Saosis, Jusas The Egyptian goddess, identified with *Hathor*, who was emblemized in the acacia tree in which it was said that "death and life are enclosed." See **Hathor**.

Sao-Ts'ing Niang In Chinese legend, the reason the sky cleared after rain was that "broom lady" swept the clouds away. She also had the power to gather them, and she was called on in time of drought to save her people.

Sarah, Sarai The greatest of the ancient Hebrew matriarchs, she also had the most in common with the ancestral goddesses of the non-Hebrew tribes of the ancient Near East. Her attributes and legend make it clear that she must be viewed as a vestigial goddess among the patriarchal Hebrews. Even as a mortal, Sarah was recognized as alien to the Hebrews. She was described as a Chaldean princess who bestowed wealth on Abraham by consenting to marry him.

Sarah was brilliantly beautiful and ageless; she was said to be so lovely that human women seemed like apes beside her. She did not bear a child until she had lived nearly a century; then, rather than exhausting her, the birth rejuvenated her. From her face an unearthly radiance shone; a miraculous cloud marked her tent as long as she was alive. Apparently her life had a particular health-giving power, for while Sarah was alive, her land was fertile and her husband did not age; when she died, the land ceased to bear and her husband, Abraham, suddenly aged and died.

She was so close to divine that she actually held conversations with Jehovah. She was prescient, called Iscah ("seer"), and acknowledged to be a more gifted prophet than her husband. Finally, she had a curious trait in common with the Great Goddesses of her region: she was called Abraham's sister as well as his spouse. Because the mythic intention was unclear to the Hebrews, they explained that Sarah was only *called* Abraham's sister when danger threatened, but in reality was only his wife. While so "disguised," Sarah married several kings, rather like goddesses who grant sovereignty to a man by "marrying" him, while remaining constantly in love with their "brothers," the fertile gods of growth and reproduction.

Sar-Akka, Sar-Edne, Sadsta-Akka   Among the Swedish Saami, this daughter of *Madder-Akka* was considered the supreme deity and creator of the world. In one myth, she was said to have invented physical life when, given a soul by her mother, she formed a body to house it. This recalls her duty as a birth-goddess; her specific charge was to create the fetal flesh within the womb. She is sometimes called Skile-Qvinde, or "dividing woman," because of her rulership of the division of child-flesh from mother-flesh at birth. She appears, together with her mother and sister, on Saami drum paintings, recognizable because of the forked stick in her hand, symbol of division.

Sarasvati, Vach   As every Hindu god must have a *Shakti*, or enlivening female force, to function, so Brahma the creator needed Sarasvati for the world to come into being. She is not only the water-goddess, one of a trinity that also includes *Ganga* and *Yamuna*, but she is also the goddess of eloquence, which pours forth like a flooding river.

Inventor of all the arts and sciences, patron of all intellectual endeavors, Sarasvati is the very prototype of the female artist. She invented writing so that the songs she inspired could be recorded; she created music so the elegance of her being could be praised. In her identity as Vach, goddess of speech, she caused all words to come into being, including all religious writings. Sometimes it is said that she is the rival of *Lakshmi*, goddess of material wealth; if anyone has the favor of one goddess, the other will turn away so that no one is ever blessed with both Sarasvati's genius and Lakshmi's riches.

Sarbanda   The king of the Babylonian city of Erech worshiped this "queen of the bow" and declared himself her son, while the wealthy among

Sarbanda's people enriched her temples with huge annual endowments. Like many other goddesses of the ancient Near East, however, Sarbanda was assimilated into the mighty figure of *Ishtar*.

Saris The most ancient goddess of Armenia, she may have been identical to the Babylonian *Ishtar* or derived from her. In any case, she later merged with the local goddess *Semiramis*.

Sarna Burhi Tree-goddess in Bengal.

Sarvari Indian water-goddess.

Sasti "Goddess of the sixth," a birth-goddess form of *Durga*.

Sasura A name for *Mami* as protector of the fetus.

Sati Anglicized, her name becomes *suttee*, for Sati was the first woman to follow her husband into death. An incarnation of *Devi*, she was married to that aspect of the destroyer Shiva called Rudra; when he was killed, Sati committed suicide.

Sati, "she who runs like an arrow," also known as Satis and Satet, was an Egyptian archer-goddess who personified the waterfalls of the river Nile. Her sanctuary was at Aswan, in ancient upper Egypt, on the island of Seheil.

Satine The underworld queen, to the Indonesian people of the island of Ceram, was the daughter of the banana tree. At first she lived on earth, but after the death of the goddess *Hainuwele*—who had been danced into the earth by human associates—Satine decided that she, too, would leave the earth and live on the death mountain. In that peaceful land, she ruled kindly, although to enter her domain humans had to pass through the black gate of death.

Saule The greatest goddess of the Baltic peoples—the Lithuanians and Latvians—was the shining sun, the sky weaver, the amber-goddess Saule. She ruled all parts of life, from birth into her light to death when she welcomed souls into her apple tree in the west. Even the name of the ocean on which the Balts lived was hers, named for Balta Saulite, "little white sun." She was worshiped in songs and rituals which celebrated her nurturance of earth's life, for she was Our Mother.

She was married in the springtime of creation to the moon-man Meness. Their first child was the earth; after that, countless children became the stars of heaven. Saule was a hard-working mother, leaving the house at dawn each day and driving her chariot across the sky until dusk. Meness, however, was fickle and carefree, staying home all day and only sometimes driving his moon-chariot.

The light of Saule's life was her daughter (variously named *Austrine*, Valkyrine, and Barbelina, but most generally called *Saules Meita*, the sun's daughter), the beloved lady of the morning star. Each evening, after she had bathed her weary horses in the Nemunas River, Saule looked for the child. But one evening she could not find her—for in her absence, Saule's beautiful long-haired daughter had been raped by Meness.

Furious beyond words, Saule took a sword and slashed the moon's face, leaving the marks we see today. Then she banished him forever from her presence; thus, they are no longer seen together in the sky— the end of the happy paradise before evil came into our world.

Saule was worshiped each day when her people would bow to the east to greet Mother Sun. But she was especially honored on summer solstice, *Ligo*, when she rose crowned with a braid of red fern blossoms to dance on the hilltops in her silver shoes. At that moment, people dived into east-flowing streams to bathe themselves in her light. All the women donned similar braided wreaths and walked through the fields, singing goddess songs, or *daina*. Finally, they gathered around bonfires and sang the night away.

Because Lithuanian is the oldest extant Indo-European language, it is thought that the Baltic mythologies hold clues to the original beliefs of that people. But scholarly convention has it that the Indo-Europeans worshiped a sky father embodied in the sun. Whence, then, this powerful Sun Mother? Marija Gimbutas, herself Lithuanian, believes Saule to be an Old European goddess of that woman-honoring culture that preceded the Indo-European invasions; Saule was too vital to her people, according to this theory, to give way to a male solar divinity. But sun-goddesses in other Indo-European areas (see **Sunnu, Sulis, Brigid, Wurusemu**) show there is room for study.

Saules Meita   The daughter of the sun in the Baltic, sometimes called *Austrine*, Valkyrine or Barbelina, was called a "little sun," possibly a star. In Lithuanian and Latvian legends, there are many sun daughters who climb rose trees in the sky to follow their mother. When they stayed at home, they were charged with keeping the house clean; sometimes they played hooky and ran off to Germany to play.

Saules Meita was said to be courted by a pair of twin stars; in some songs they are her brothers. When she was in danger of drowning—as when she dropped her golden ring into a fountain—it was their duty to save her. For the tale of her rape by the moon-man, see **Saule**.

Savitri The primary Hindu ancestor, Savitri was impregnated by Brahma early in creation. She gestated for a century, then began to give birth. From her womb poured music and poetry, the years, the months, and the days, the four ages of creation, and innumerable other offspring, including death. Called Sata-Rupa ("hundred-shaped"), she is also said to have been the first woman, daughter of Brahma and wife of the first man. See also **Ganga.**

Sayo-Hime A legendary woman of Japan, she married a man who often traveled by sea. And so often she would stand by the seashore watching for his boat that she turned into the famous "Wife Rock" of Futami in the province of Shima.

Scathach The "shadowy one," who lived on an island near Scotland, was the greatest female warrior of her time. Heroes from all the Celtic nations would travel to study with her, for she alone knew the magical battle skills that made them unconquerable: great leaps and fierce yells, which seem in ancient legend like puzzled accounts of Oriental martial arts.

One of her most famous students was the Irish warrior Cuchulain. When the princess *Emer* sized him up as a possible husband, she thought him too unskilled in his profession; therefore, she suggested that he study with Scathach, the foremost warrior of her day. While Cuchulain was away, he learned more than martial arts, for through an affair with Scathach's enemy, *Aife*, the warrior produced a son whom he later unwittingly killed. See also **Ess Euchen.**

Scota A vague figure in Irish legend, she was called a "daughter of Pharaoh" in the post-Christian historical annals that amalgamated ancient lore with biblical legend. She was probably an Irish ancestor-goddess, for the people of the island were called in ancient times "scoti" or "scots," a name that later came to rest in another Celtic homeland.

Scylla Once this legendary Greek monster, *Lamia*'s daughter, was a beautiful woman, so beautiful that she roused the jealousy of the sea queen *Amphitrite*, who poisoned her bath with magic herbs. When Scylla rose from the water, her 12-footed body ended in six dogs' heads with six mouths each, each mouth with three sets of teeth. This horrible barking creature was no longer a threat to the sea-goddess.

The embittered Scylla stationed herself on the seacoast, where she trapped sailors and ate them. But she hated her life so much that she flung herself into the sea between Italy and Sicily and was instantly transformed into rocks that continued to devour sailors. No one could safely pass the treacherous petrified woman, it was said, unless *Hecate* allowed it.

There was another figure in Greek legend with the same name, whom some scholars claim was actually the same woman. She was the princess Scylla, daughter of King Nisus who had a magical golden hair in the middle of his head that protected him from harm. But his daughter, infatuated with King Minos, during a Cretan siege of her city, betrayed her father by pulling out the golden hair and presenting it to Minos. The Cretan king spurned Scylla, however, and she committed suicide in shame; in death, she was transformed into a lark, and her father into a hawk. See also **Echidna**.

Sedna Beside the water, there once lived an old widower and his daughter, Sedna, a woman so beautiful that all the Eskimo men sought to live with her. But she found none to her liking and refused all offers. One day, a seabird came to her and promised her a soft life in a warm hut full of bearskins and fish. Sedna flew away with him.

The bird lied. Sedna found her home a stinking nest. She sat, sadly regretting her rejection of the handsome human men. And that was what she told her father, when she listed her complaints when he visited her a year later.

Anguta ("man with something to cut") put his daughter in his kayak to bring her back to the human world. Perhaps he killed the bird husband first, perhaps he just stole the bird's wife, but in either case the vengeance of the bird people followed him. The rising sea threatened the escaping humans with death. On they struggled, until Anguta realized that flight was hopeless.

He shoved Sedna overboard to drown. Desperate for life, she grabbed the kayak with a fierce grip. Her father cut off her fingers. She flung her mutilated arms over the skin boat's sides. Anguta cut them off, shoving his oar into Sedna's eye before she sank into the icy water.

At the bottom of the sea, she lived thereafter as queen of the deep, mistress of death and life, "old food dish," who provided for the people. Her amputated fingers and arms became the fish and marine mammals, and she alone decided how many would be slaughtered for food. She was willing to provide for the people if they accepted her rules: for three days after their death, the souls of her animals would remain with their bodies, watching for violation of Sedna's demands. Then they returned to the goddess, bearing information about the conduct of her people. Should her laws be broken, Sedna's hand would begin to ache, and she would punish humans with sickness, starvation, and storms. Only if a shaman traveled to her country, Adlivun, and assuaged her pains would the sea mammals return to the hunters, which, if the people acted righteously, they did willingly.

In Adlivun in a huge house of stone and whale ribs, Sedna dragged along the ground with one leg bent beneath her. A horrible dog guarded her, said by some to be her husband. Anguta himself lived there too; some versions of the myth say that, hoping the seabirds would think Sedna dead, he allowed her back into the kayak and returned home. But she hated him thereafter and cursed her dogs to eat his hands and feet; the earth opened and swallowed them. In any case, Anguta served Sedna by grabbing dead human souls with his maimed hand and bringing them home. These dead lived in a region near Sedna's home through which shamans had to pass to reach the goddess. There was also an abyss, in which an ice wheel turned slowly and perpetually; then a caldron full of boiling seals blocked the way; finally, the horrible dog stood before Sedna's door, guarding the knife-thin passageway to her home. Should the shaman pass all these dangers and ease Sedna's aching hands, the goddess permitted him to return, bearing the news that Old Woman had forgiven her people, that the seals would again seek the hunter, that the people would no longer starve.

Seia, Segetia, Tutilina   Three Roman goddesses who had power over seeds beneath, sprouting, and above the ground.

Seimia   "Star of Babylon," she was that ancient city's original patron goddess, ruling Babylon as *Athene* ruled Athens.

Sekhmet, Sehmet, Sekmet, in Greek, **Sakhmis**   Once, long ago, the lion-headed sun-goddess of Egypt became so disgusted with humanity that she commenced a wholesale slaughter of the race. Her fury terrified even the gods, who deputized Ra to calm down the goddess. She refused to be restrained. "When I slay men," she snarled, "my heart rejoices."

Ra, attempting to save the remnant of humanity from the blood-thirsty goddess, then mixed 7,000 vats of beer and pomegranate juice. He set the jugs in the path of the murdering lioness, hoping she would mistake them for the human blood she craved. Indeed she did, and she soon drank herself into a stupor. When she awoke, she had no rage left.

The intoxicating red drink was henceforth prepared and consumed on feast days of *Hathor*, so some say that Sekhmet was the negative side of that pleasure-ruling goddess. Others say that she was the opposite of the cat-goddess *Bast*, the cat embodying the sun's nurturing rays; the lion, her destructive drought-bringing potential.

Madagascar sculpture; see Sabulana, p. 302; Maruwa, p. 225. Field Museum of Natural History (Neg# 59082), Chicago.

Sela   In Kenya, the Luhya say the first woman bore this name and that she lived in a house on wooden stilts because the earth, in primordial times, was infested with crawling monsters. Her children—the human race— were bold enough to descend from her hut and live in houses built on the ground.

Selci Syt Emysyt   In Siberia, this goddess was named "mother of all snakes." Little is known of her ritual.

Selene, Mene, Selena   Also called Phoebe and perhaps *Helene* (see **Helen**), this early Greek full-moon goddess was the daughter of *Thea* (Titaness of Light) and spouse of the sun. Winged and crowned with a crescent, she drove the lunar chariot across the night sky, whose goddesses *Leto* and *Hecate* were her daughters; this radiant chariot was drawn by two white horses or oxen. When she was not visible, Selene was said to be in Asia Minor, visiting her human lover Endymion, for whom she had won the prize of eternal life and youth. Some legends say that he had to pay a price for this: he slept perpetually, even when his eyes were open, in his dark cave bed.

Selkhet, Selk, Selquet, Serk   In Egypt's pyramid tombs, mourners placed little golden figures of the guardian goddesses of the dead. One of these was Selkhet, a scorpion-goddess of great antiquity who, with *Qebhsnuf*, protected the vessels that held the corpse's intestines. Selkhet was also one of the deities who led the deceased into the afterlife and offered instructions in the customs of that world. She was shown as a woman with a scorpion headdress, or as a scorpion with a woman's head, and symbolized the rebirth that follows death.

Selu   "Old corn-mother" of the Cherokee.

Semele, Thyone   Daughter of *Harmonia*. Late in Greek legend she was called a mortal and the mother of the wine-god Dionysus. But her name came from Asia Minor, where it meant the "subterranean," and Dionysus's mother was in some legends called the queen of death (see **Persephone**). Semele had been worshiped as a goddess for ages before the introduction of Dionysus to Greece; she probably represented the earth in its darkly fruitful form, the earth that devours life so that, fertilized, she may reproduce it.

    The complex Greek story of Dionysus's birth has him first born of Persephone and killed in infancy. His father, Zeus, however, made a broth of the baby's heart and brought it to Semele, who became pregnant with the divinity to be reincarnated. But Semele mistakenly asked

Zeus to appear before her in Olympian glory. When he did so, she was consumed by his magnificence. Zeus picked up the fetus, sewed it into his thigh, and gave surgical birth to the child later.

But the young wine-god, it was said, never really freed himself from the influence of his mother, whom he adored so much that he descended to death's realm to reclaim her, bringing her back to Olympus and installing her as the foremost of his *Maenads* under the title Thyone ("ecstatic madwoman"). Thus Semele, who started as a goddess and was demoted to mortality, was restored to divinity.

Semiramis Some said the Syrian goddess *Alurgutis* bore this daughter and placed her in the desert to be raised by doves. Others disagree: Semiramis was not originally divine but was a canonized queen, Sammuramat. In either case, when Semiramis was a nubile maiden, she attracted the attentions of Prince Omnes. They married, and he remained so infatuated with her that, when Semiramis decided to become queen of Babylon with a second husband, Ninus, as king, Omnes committed suicide in despair.

He was not the only man destroyed by love of Semiramis. "She of the exalted name" was one of the most lustful of queens. Unwilling to share her life with a man, she took handsome soldiers to bed and had them killed afterward (compare the Breton princess *Dahut*). Across western Asia, there are mounds of Semiramis, said to be graves of the one-night lovers she buried alive.

Once, they said in Armenia, Semiramis fell in love with the sun. When he did not return her affection, Semiramis attacked him with a huge army. The queen took the day, and Er, the sun, was killed in the battle. But then Semiramis repented her fury and begged the other gods to restore the sun to life—a tale that may have been derived from that of *Ishtar*.

Sentia Roman goddess who heightened feelings.

Sequana Among the Celts, the earth-goddess was thought to be most easily visible in the rivers that drained each land. Thus their earth river-goddesses could best be defined as watershed deities. Sequana ruled the Seine and its valleys; her special shrine was at the river's source. During festivals, an image of Sequana was drawn along the river in a ship that looked like a duck holding a berry in its bill. At the shrine, worshipers tossed votive offerings, often tiny statuettes, into the water as they prayed for health; many of these trinkets came to light in 1964 during excavations of the Seine's source.

The names of a number of other Celtic river-goddesses are known:

Sabrina of the Severn; Clutoida of the Clyde; *Belisama* of the Mersey; Briant, whose river bears her name, and Devona of the Devon; Verbeia of the Wharfe; Matrona of the Marne. When depicted in art and statuary, these goddesses often reclined lazily, wearing long flowing dresses with folds as soft as river waves. Often they held cornucopias, fruit, or other symbols of the fertility their waters brought to the land.

In Ireland, where the goddesses' myths as well as their names were remembered, *Boann* and *Sinann* and Banna were all said to have been curious girls who, seeking immortal wisdom, traveled to the well at the mouths of their rivers—the Boyne, the Shannon, and the Bann. The wells, furious at being disturbed and unwilling to give forth secrets, rose from their holes and drowned the seekers. Thus, said Irish Celtic legend, were the great rivers of the earth formed. It is likely that similar stories of the river-goddesses were told in Britain and Gaul.

Seyadatarahime   In the *Kojiki*, the ancient compilation of Japanese folklore, this woman was struck in the vagina by a red arrow while defecating outside her village. Taking the arrow home, she took it to bed with her. There it turned into a young man, a form of the snake-god named Omononushi, to whom she bore a child. Carmen Blacker, scholar of women's shamanic traditions in Japan, finds in this tale a reflection of the tradition that shaman women took otherworldly or animal lovers. See **Tamayorihime.**

Shait   This infinitely divisible Egyptian goddess was human destiny, born at the instant of birth. Invisible Shait rode through life with each person, observing all virtues and vices, crimes and secret prides. Thus it was Shait who spoke the final judgment on a soul after death, and that sentence, based on such intimate knowledge, was not only perfectly just but inescapable.

Shakti   Just as divinity is symbolized in Hindu India as a phallus (*lingam*) surrounded by a vulva (*yoni*), so goddess energy is thought to surround and animate the energy of a god. Maleness, in divine terms, is thought of as passive and inert, a kind of passive being, while female divinity provides the activating energy that invigorates and empowers the god. Thus, in religious iconography, Hindu artists show the goddess having intercourse on top of the god, activating his previously languid body.

Worship of *Devi* ("The Goddess") appears to have been the rule in pre-Aryan India. Generations of invasions by Indo-Europeans, with their patriarchal mythology, led to the apparent religious conquest of the area. But the goddess's worshipers did not give up her image; as the

Aryans mingled with the indigenous races, the goddess began to reappear in Indian religious texts. Eventually, in the complexity of Hinduism that exists today, the goddess as the Shakti or energy of divinity was inseparable from the male god.

Each member of the Hindu trinity was provided with his Shakti: *Maya* enlivening creative Brahma; *Lakshmi* empowering nurturing Vishnu; and *Parvati* or *Kali* as the consort of destructive Shiva. But Shakti is sometimes used as a name for Shiva's energy alone, consistent with the philosophic understanding that all life, all energy, ultimately leads to destruction.

Shamshu, Shams   Ancient Arabian sun-goddess.

Shapash, Shamash   In the ancient Near East, the sun was more often female than male, and Shapash ("torch of the gods") was one of her names. In the Ugaritic *Epic of Baal*, this goddess retrieves the fertility-god's plaything from the underworld, an allegory of the return of moisture and growth to the earth's surface, of the annual defeat of drought.

Sharrat Shame   "Queen of heaven," a famous title of *Ishtar*.

Shatagat   Ugaritic healing-goddess who could conquer death.

Shauskha   An *Ishtar*-like Hurrian divinity, whose winged beauty seduced even monsters. The kings of Anatolia served her; she commanded them through dreams, oracles, and the augury of her female soothsayers. Probably a form of the Hittite sky queen *Hannahanna*.

Sheila na Gig   Smiling lewdly out from rock carvings, this goddess of ancient Ireland can still be seen in remaining petroglyphs: a grinning, often skeletal face, huge buttocks, full breasts, and bent knees. What most observers remember best, however, is the self-exposure of the goddess, for she holds her vagina open with both hands.

She is the greatest symbol of the life-and-death goddess left in Ireland, where her stones have in some cases been incorporated as "gargoyles" in Christian churches. Her name means "hag"; her grinning face and genital display are complicated by the apparent ancientness of her flesh. Laughter and passion, birth and death, sex and age do not seem to have been so incompatible to the ancient Irish as they are to the modern world.

315

Sheilah Daughter of the careless Jephthah, this Hebrew maiden was sacrificed because her ambitious father promised to kill the first thing he met upon returning home from a battle. Furious at his lack of foresight, Sheilah uttered a famous lament when she realized that he could not be convinced to let her live. In particular, she wept that she would die a virgin. "Ye beasts of the forest," she wailed, "come and trample on my virginity." Her death did not go unavenged: Jephthah was cursed by Jehovah and died by dismemberment.

Shekinah The Talmud tells us that human senses cannot perceive Jehovah, but that we can see, hear, and touch his Shekinah. This word (meaning an emanation Jehovah allows us to sense) is feminine in gender. Eventually (like Sabbath and *Hokkma*) the word took on a feminine personality as well, until Shekinah became a rather disputative but compassionate demigoddess who argued with the high god in support of his creatures. Like the Greek Dike, Shekinah was said to have abandoned the earth when humankind became too evil.

Sheol To the Hebrews, the underworld womb of rebirth was personified in this "clamorous woman."

Sherua Ancient goddess whose identity was merged with that of *Ishtar.*

Sheshat, Seshatu Like *Nisaba*, a similar goddess to the east, this Egyptian goddess was "mistress of the house of books," inventor of writing, and secretary of heaven. She was also "mistress of the house of architects," the goddess charged with studying the stars to determine the axes of new buildings. Finally, Sheshat invented mathematics, for which she was appointed goddess of fate, measuring the length of our lives with palm branches.

Shiju-Gara Bird-goddess of Manchuria.

Shina-To-Be Japanese wind-goddess.

Shita-Teru-Hime Japanese heroine of family loyalty.

Shiwanokia This primal divinity was, to the Zuni, a powerful being who, by spitting in her hand, caused the great earth mother, *Awitelin Tsita*, to be born. Her worshipers called their priestess Shiwanokia in honor of this creator.

Shulamite, Shala, Shulamatu The goddess after whom the Assyrian city of Shulman was named, she was the "heavenly female who designed heaven and earth." Her name survives, in part, in "Jerusalem," and in the mysterious Shulamite, the beloved sister of the biblical Solomon.

Sibilaneuman The goddess of songs to the Cágaba Indians of Colombia, she was hailed as the "mother of songs and dances, the mother of the grains and the mother of all things . . . She is the mother of dance paraphernalia and of all people, and the only mother we have."

Sibilja A cow who was worshiped as embodying divinity, she accompanied Eysteinn Beli, a legendary Swedish king, into battle. Her presence was a sure token of victory, for her roaring and bellowing so frightened Beli's enemies that they lost their nerve and ran from the battlefield. Great sacrifices were offered to Sibilja, who was buried next to her chief worshiper, the king, when she died.

Sibyl, Sibylla There were 10 famous female prophets of the ancient world, one each in Persia, Libya, Delphi, Samos, Cimmeria, Erythraea, Tibur, Marpessus, and Phrygia, and one—most renowned of all—in Cumae near Naples, where Sibyl's cave was discovered in 1932 to have a 60-foot-high ceiling and a 375-foot-long passageway entrance.

The Cumaean Sibyl wrote her prophecies on leaves, which she then placed at the mouth of her cave. If no one came to collect them, they were scattered by winds and never read. Written in complex, often enigmatic verses, these "Sibylline Leaves" were sometimes bound into books. It was said that the Sibyl herself brought nine volumes of these prophecies to Tarquin II of Rome, offering them to him at an outrageous price. He scoffed, and she immediately burned three volumes, offering the remaining six at the same high price. Again—rather less casually—he refused. Again she burned three volumes, again asking the original price. This time the king's curiosity was high, his resistance low, and he purchased the Sibylline prophecies.

The volumes were carefully kept in the Capitol and consulted only on momentous occasions by the Senate. Some were destroyed by fire in 83 B.C. while the rest survived until A.D. 405, when they perished in another fire. The people of Rome searched the world looking for prophecies to replace the Sibylline Leaves but were unable to find any. The Sibyl herself, it was discovered, had vanished. So the way was left clear for the production of pseudo-Sibylline prophecies, a profitable business until the end of the Roman Empire.

The Sibyl of Cumae gained her powers by attracting the attention of the sun-god, Apollo, who offered her anything if she would spend a single night with him. She asked for as many years of life as grains of sand she could squeeze into her hand. Granted, the sun-god said; and Sibyl, glad to win her boon, refused his advances. Thereafter she was cursed with the fulfillment of her wish—eternal life without eternal youth. She slowly shriveled into a frail undying body, so tiny that she fit into a jar. Her container was hung from a tree; Sibyl needed, of course, no food or drink, for she could neither starve nor die of thirst. And there she hung, croaking occasional oracles, while children would stand beneath her urn and tease, "Sibyl, Sibyl, what do you wish?" To which she would faintly reply, "I wish to die."

Sicasica   A mountain-goddess of the Aymara of Bolivia, she was said to reside in the peak named for her and to try to seduce young men by taking the shape of a woman and luring them into her fatally cold glaciers.

Siduri, Sabitu, Shiduri, Shidurri   When the hero of the Sumerian epic, Gilgamesh, sought treasure at the world's end, he found this bawdy innkeeper living on the border of the ocean abyss. The merry Siduri sang of the fleetness of time and the pleasures of life, telling Gilgamesh, "Dance and play, night and day . . . make each day a festival of joy." He refused, demanding instead directions to the ferryman of death. Siduri— who was the goddess *Ishtar* in her guise as a winemaker—told him, although the wise goddess knew Gilgamesh could not hold his prize once he found it.

Sien-Tsang   Chinese goddess of silk cultivation.

Sif   The beautiful Scandinavian grain-goddess was most renowned, legend says, for her long golden hair—the autumn grass. Sif lived with the thunder-wielding Thor; the lightning was seen to mate with the fields on summer nights.

   The wicked Loki, however, cut off Sif's hair one night, and Thor made him travel to the lands of the dwarfs to bring back master artisans. The dwarfs were set to work making hair of spun gold that, when attached to Sif's head, grew like the original.

Sige   "Silence," a Phoenician goddess worshiped in Egypt, of whom little is known.

Sigurdrifta   The wisest of the *Valkyries*, she once stole from battle a hero to whom Odin had promised victory; in punishment Odin stung her with sleep thorns. Sigurdrifta sank into a trance, saying she would never

*See Sala, p. 303. Field Museum of Natural History
(Neg# 97071), Chicago.*

awaken until a man utterly without fear came to claim her as his wife.

When the hero Sigurd was riding in search of adventure, he found a mountain lit by fire; in the center of the light was Sigurdrifta, fully armored. Cutting her armor from her, he awakened the warrior and asked her to teach him wisdom.

Sigurdrifta made reverent gestures toward night and day, toasting the deities of each, before answering. She spoke at length with the hero, telling him magic runes and the ways of sorcery. Finally, she sank back into sleep. Some legends, however, say she was the same woman whom Sigurd later encountered under the name of *Brynhild*.

Sila "Good behavior," an Indian goddess.

Silige Fraulein *Buschfrauen* that appear as vultures.

Silkie She took her name from the silk clothing she wore, this Scottish house-goddess who sneaked into homes to clean whatever was left in disorder; of course, too careful housekeeping was as bad as slovenliness, for if she found nothing to clean, Silkie messed up the rooms instead.

Sin This Irish "fairy woman" was probably a remnant of an early goddess, for she was said to have created wine from water and swine from leaves to feed the battalions of warriors she had created with her spells.

Sinann, Sinend The goddess of Ireland's famous Shannon River was—like most other Celtic river-goddesses—originally a curious and heedless woman. Seeking knowledge from the sacred well at the world's end, Sinann enraged the waters of wisdom with her audacity. Connla's Well, as it was called, rose up in fury and drowned her, but could not return to its cage and henceforth streamed through Ireland as a river. Virtually the same legend is told of the Boyne River goddess, *Boann*. See also **Coventina, Sequana.**

Sinjang Halmoni Korean military-goddess who also assists birthing mothers.

Sipna Etruscan goddess depicted carrying a mirror, probably a goddess of light and beauty.

Sipylene "The Mother," the goddess of the city of Smyrna.

Sirens   Today we picture these sweet singers in only female bodies, but in early Greece the Sirens were both male and female bird-bodied prophets of the future and omniscient readers of the past. Above their strange egg-shaped bodies rose beautiful human heads; the breasts and faces of women were borne only in later days on the Sirens' feathered bodies.

There were variously two or three Sirens, given different names by different ancient authors. Homer mentions two Sirens but names only one: Himeropa ("arousing face"). Three others are elsewhere named as Thelchtereia ("enchantress"), Aglaope ("glorious face"), and Peisinoe ("seductress"). Finally, in Italy, the Sirens were named Parthenope ("virgin"), Leucosia ("white goddess"), and Ligeia ("bright-voiced").

They were servants of *Persephone* the death queen, charged with bringing souls to her. This they did by singing sweetly to passing ships so that the enchanted sailors would be smashed on the rocks beneath the Sirens' coastal meadow. In form and function they are easy to confuse with *Harpies*, but the Sirens seem to represent death's sweet call, while their vulturelike sisters signify unsought, terrifying death.

Siris, Sirah   This Babylonian bird-goddess of banquets also ruled rainbearing clouds—for it is difficult to eat, drink, and be merry in the midst of drought.

Sirona   Continental Celtic sky-goddess.

Sita   The Hindu goddess *Lakshmi* incarnated herself as this girl so that she could marry her consort, Vishnu, in his incarnation as the hero Rama. Her name means "furrow," for Sita sprang forth from the earth when it was cut with a plow (appropriately, Lakshmi is the goddess of abundance and productiveness).

Sita came to earth to assure the destruction of the demonic King Ravena. While traveling with Rama, Sita was kidnapped by Ravena; Rama fought and destroyed Ravena. But even divine incarnations are imperfect, and Rama doubted Sita's chastity during her imprisonment. Though Sita successfully underwent a test of fire, Rama continued to doubt. Sita, pregnant, retreated to the wilderness to bear her twin sons who, recognized as adolescents by Rama, brought about the couple's reunion. But still Rama doubted and, wounded by his rejections, Sita called for a final test: earth, which gave her birth, should take her back if she were innocent. The earth opened and Sita disappeared, leaving Rama convinced of her purity and heartbroken at her loss.

Sitala, Shitla, Sitala-Devi   When one is stricken with smallpox in India, he is said to be possessed by the "cool goddess" Sitala, who owns all people and therefore can visit them in her feverish form. (The name "cool one" is clearly a flattering one, intended to keep the goddess at bay.) Sometimes said to be the death-goddess *Kali*, Sitala is still worshiped annually in India, particularly in Bengal. There it is said that Sitala, born after other goddesses, had difficulty getting humans to pay enough attention to her; she invented smallpox to force humanity to invent rituals for her. The tactic clearly worked, as Sitala is one of the most worshiped goddesses of India, called the Mata ("mother") of each village. A similar goddess is *Marahi Devi* or Marai Mata, the cholera-goddess.

Siva   Polish and Russian goddess of life.

Sjofn   One of the servants of the great Scandinavian goddess *Frigg*, this maiden had the special task of stirring infatuation in human hearts, a kindling that might lead to love.

Sjojungru   Scandinavian sea-goddess.

Sjora   Swedish sea-goddess.

Skadi   The goddess for whom Scandinavia was named dwelled high in the snow-covered mountains; her favorite occupations were skiing and snowshoeing through her domain. But when the gods caused the death of her father, Thjassi, Skadi armed herself and traveled to their home at Asgard, intent on vengeance. Even alone, she was more than a match for the gods, and they were forced to make peace with her.

Skadi demanded two things: that they make her laugh and that she be allowed to choose a mate from among them. The first condition was accomplished by the trickster Loki, who tied his testicles to the beard of a billy goat. It was a contest of screeching, until the rope snapped and Loki landed, screaming with pain, on Skadi's knee. She laughed.

Next, all the gods lined up, and Skadi's eyes were masked. She intended to select her mate simply by examining his legs from the knees down. When she'd found the strongest—thinking them the beautiful Balder's legs—she flung off her mask and found she'd picked the sea-god Njord. So she went off to live in the god's ocean home.

She was miserable there. "I couldn't sleep a wink," Skadi said in a famous eddic poem, "on the bed of the sea, for the calling of gulls and mews." The couple moved to Thrymheim, Skadi's mountain palace, but the water-god was as unhappy there as Skadi had been in the water.

Thereupon they agreed on an equitable dissolution, and Skadi took a new mate, more suitable to her lifestyle: Ullr, the god of skis.

Skogsnufvar   The wood-wives of Scandinavia were said to be sweet-voiced, fur-garbed creatures whose duty was to herd wild woodland animals. Before any animal was hunted, the Skogsnufvar had to be contacted for assurance that the prey was not their pet. If well courted by the hunter, the Skogsnufvar would direct him to animals they were willing to do without; coins and food left at fallen trees signified the intent to honor the wood-wives' will.

Skuld   In Scandinavia, the goddess or *Norn* of the future was also a powerful sorceress and the elf queen. Skuld was said always to be veiled and to carry the scrolls of fortune with her.
     There was also, in Norse legend, a half-elf mortal woman of this name, said to have the power to raise the dead, even if the bodies had been chopped in pieces; she was invincible because of this talent.

Smilax   This Greek shepherd loved a man named Crocus; both were changed into the flowers that bear their names.

Sneneik, Tsonoqua   Along the Pacific Coast, the Bellacoola and others acknowledged the power of this cannibal woman, who sneaked through the world stealing children and robbing graves, throwing bodies into the woven basket she carried. She owned a home far away from our world, where she offered visitors food that, should they eat it, paralyzed them; she had many children, but they all were wolves.

Snotra   Scandinavian goddess of wisdom.

Snutqutxals   Bellacolla death-goddess.

Spako   This name was given to the stepmother of King Cyrus, founder of the Persian Empire, but was probably originally that of a wolf-goddess who nursed the king, thereby guaranteeing his power.

Sparta   The famous Greek city-state bore the name of its founding mother, who was also said to be the mother of *Eurydice* and of *Danae*.

Spear-Finger, Stone-Dress   One of the most powerful mythic figures of the Cherokee was Spear-Finger, a giantess who ate human livers. Though she could change her shape at will, her natural form was an old rock-skinned woman with a bony forefinger which she used for stabbing the

323

unwary. She had special powers over stone: she could lift huge boulders, cement rocks together just by touching them, and build mountains of pebbles. Like the *Cailleach* and other winter hags, she had to die for life on earth to go on.

Always hungry, she often lured children from their play and stole their livers. She caused no pain, left no wound, but the afflicted eventually died. Thus, she was greatly feared. Anyone who ran into an old woman singing "Uwela natsiku. Su-sa-sai," which means, "Liver, I eat it. Su-sa-sai," quickly ran away.

When a council was held to rid the earth of Spear-Finger, it was decided that a trap would be the best way. So a pitfall was dug in a trail and a big bonfire lit to lure the old woman. It worked: very shortly she came down the path, looking for all the world like a member of the tribe. She was not shot immediately because the men felt kinship with her.

But when she fell into the hole they'd dug and immediately turned into a stone-skinned woman with a bone finger, they lost all sympathy for her. The hunters emptied their quivers to no avail. Nothing could penetrate her skin. She was immensely strong, and it seemed as though she would climb out and kill them.

Then a titmouse nearby sang "un, un, un," which the hunters thought meant "unahu," or heart. So they shot at Spear-Finger's heart, but the arrows glanced off her stony chest. So they caught the bird and cut out its tongue for lying.

Then they heard another sound. It was the chickadee, who bravely flew into the pit and landed on Spear-Finger's right hand. The hunters began to shoot there, and the old woman fell down dead, for her heart was hidden in her wrist. The earth was freed from Spear-Finger, who lived on only in myth.

Spes, in Greek, **Elpis**   An early Cretan goddess, she was ruler of the underworld and of death's cousin, sleep; her plant was the poppy, but otherwise nothing is known of her legends and meaning. In Greece and Rome, Spes became the personification of hope, worshiped in temples dedicated to her as early as the 4th century B.C.

Sphinx   The "strangler" started her life in Egypt, where the lion-bodied monster had a bearded male head and represented royalty. But in Greece—in a city with the Egyptian name Thebes—the Sphinx became female. She was said to have been a *Maenad* who grew so wild in her intoxicated worship that she became monstrous: snake, lion, and woman combined.

The guardian of Thebes, she prevented travelers from passing by strangling them if they could not answer a mysterious riddle. (Possibly she descended from the underworld guardian-goddess who, in many cultures, prevented the passage of the living into death's territory.) What, the Sphinx would ask, walked on four legs in the morning, two at noon, and three in the evening? Finally one traveler, who would become King Oedipus of Thebes, answered her: Human beings, who crawl as children, walk upright as adults, and rely upon canes in age. Her reason for existence having been destroyed, the Sphinx destroyed herself. See also **Echidna.**

Sreca In Serbia, this was the name of the fate-goddess when she appeared as a lovely maiden spinning golden thread; this vision meant good fortune. Bad luck, however, was brought by the same goddess, in the guise of Nesreca, a sleepy old woman with bloodshot eyes who could not be roused from bed when needed.

Srinmo Tibetan witch-goddess of the afterlife.

Sroya Slavic virgin war-goddess.

Strenua Roman goddess of strength.

Styx Under the earth, the Greeks said, lay the land of the dead, and between the two worlds wound the seven tributaries of the River Styx. The goddess of this sacred river was Styx herself, the "hated one" who prevented the living from crossing into the realm of *Persephone* without first undergoing death's torments.

   The eldest, strongest daughter of the ancient sea, Styx was the mother of three daughters, the most famous of whom was *Nike* ("Victory"); the others were Strength and Valor. The mother of this triad was as much revered as feared. Because she sided with the Olympian gods in their battle with the land's earlier divinities, the Greeks said, Styx was honored as the source of all oaths. Even among the Olympians, an oath taken on the name of Styx was held inviolable; if broken, it meant the sinner was deprived of *Hebe*'s ambrosia and nectar, the food and drink that kept the gods young and immortal.

Sudice The goddesses of fate in eastern Europe had names that varied from land to land: Rojenice in Croatia; Sudicky in Bohemia; Sudzenici or Narucnici in Bulgaria; Sojenice in Slovenia; Sudice in Poland. All were said to be beautiful old women with white skin and white clothes, wearing a white handkerchief on their heads and many necklaces of gold and silver. They glistened as they walked; sometimes they decked themselves with garlands of flowers or carried lit candles.

Generally these goddesses were invisible to human eyes, but they did appear at birth, when three of them arrived to cast the newborn's fate. Two spoke wishes for the child's fortune, but the words of the last could not be undone. To make sure she spoke good wishes, parents offered her gifts of wine, candles, and bread.

Suhijini-no-Kimi The goddess of settled sediments, a Japanese Shinto divinity who was among the first to emerge as the earth formed.

Suki In India, the cow-goddess, wife of the sun.

Sulis The ancient British goddess of healing waters had her special shrine at the spa we call Bath, where her power was strongest. Some scholars say that she was a solar divinity, deriving her name from the word that means "sun" and "eye." This interpretation may account for the perpetual fires at her shrines; the fact that her springs were hot, rather than cold, is additional evidence in favor of considering her a sun-goddess.

She was honored into historic times; the Roman occupiers called her *Minerva Medica* ("healing Minerva"). In statuary and bas-reliefs, she was shown as a matronly woman in heavy garments with a hat made of a bear's head and her foot resting on a fat little owl. See also **Coventina, Nemetona.**

Suliviae The multiple form of *Sulis*, a triple goddess who may have been a form of the great Celtic divinity *Brigid*. One inscription at Bath in England addresses the goddess this way, but the same name has been found at water shrines in France as well.

Sundi-Mumi The "Sun Mother" of the Finno-Ugric Wotjakians was invoked as follows: "We remember you with good broth and with bread. Give us warm days, and fair summer, and warm rain."

Sungmo, Chunwang In ancient Korea, this goddess lured a monk into her mountain sanctuary as he passed by causing a stream to suddenly become a torrent. She then appeared to him as a giant, bewitched him with a spell, and made him her lover. From their union she bore eight daughters whom she trained as healers.

Sunkalamma Goddess of south Indian pariahs.

Sunna, Sunnu, Sol "Mistress Sun," the ancient Scandinavians used to sing, "sits on a bare stone and spins on her golden distaff for the hour before the sun rises." To the people of the north, as to many others, the bright day-bringing star was feminine, the goddess Sunna—still honored whenever we point to the sun.

Her people said that Sunna lived at first on earth; she was such a beautiful child that her father, Mundilfare, named her after the most brilliant star. But such presumption annoyed the gods of Asgard. They took Sunna from earth to her namesake, where she forever after rode the chariot of day. Pulling her were divine horses, Arvak ("early-waker") and Alsvid ("all-strong"); under their harnesses were bags of wind that cooled them and the earth as they traveled with their mistress through the sky. Likewise Sunna carried the shield Svalin ("cool"), which protected the earth from too intense contact with her rays.

Sunna was not really immortal, for like other Scandinavian gods, she was doomed to die at the Ragnarok, the end of this universe. She was said to be constantly chased through the sky by the wolf Skoll, off-spring of a female giant; on the last day he would catch her and devour her. But, say the eddas, "one beaming daughter the bright Sunna bears before she is swallowed," and this new sun daughter would take her mother's place in the new sky following the destruction of Sunna's realm.

The "bright bride of heaven" had, in addition to the familiar powers we grant the sun, a special function in Norse mythology. She was the "elf beam" or "deceiver of dwarfs," for those creatures were petrified by her glance. Stone was important to her in another way, for her worshipers carved deep stone circles across the Scandinavian landscape as part of her sacred rites.

Suonetar Finnish life-giving goddess.

Sura Indian goddess of wine.

Surabhi One of the beings who emerged from the ocean as it was churned, says one of the most famous and evocative Hindu myths, was the cow Surabhi, goddess of plenty called the "fragrant one." She forthwith produced all luxury—and a daughter, *Nirriti* ("misery"), as well.

Surasa A demon queen of India.

Swan Maidens In Germanic and Scandinavian mythology, these women were *Valkyrie*-like figures who flew through the air in bird-disguises. They would, however, shed their feather cloaks to dance by the shores of quiet lakes. There, human men could capture the Swan Maidens as brides by stealing the victim's feather cloak and keeping it hidden from her. Should she find it, no matter how long and happily she had lived with the man or how many children she had borne, the Swan Maiden would don her cloak and fly instantly away. Sometimes, legend says, these women wore their souls on golden chains around their necks which, if removed, meant the girl's death.

Sweigsdunka   This Lithuanian star-goddess was bride of the sky and ruler of both the morning and evening stars. A weaver, she created the star cloth that covered the sky each night.

Syn   The goddess gatekeeper of heaven was, among the Scandinavians, named Syn ("denial") because she denied entry to anyone she judged unworthy. Because she was all-seeing and perfectly just, Syn was the goddess on whom oaths were sworn; she was also invoked in lawsuits so that justice would prevail.

Syrinx   This Greek nymph escaped from an attempted rape by changing herself into a reedy marsh. Her repentant assailant, the wilderness-god Pan, cut down the reeds and made himself a pipe, which afterward was called by the nymph's name.

Tabiti, Tabiti-Vesta   The Scythian Great Goddess ruled fire and animals. To her these early eastern Europeans swore oaths, suggesting a connection with the earth who witnesses all things. She was worshiped in southern Russia even before the Scythians arrived, little pottery statues of her were found there, showing an upright goddess bearing a child. The later Scythians showed her as half serpent, often seated between a raven and a dog. Strabo says Tabiti was the protective goddess of the Black Sea sailors, who sacrificed to her any who strayed into their territory.

Tacoma, Dah-Ko-Beed, Tacobud, Takkobad, Takobid, Tehoma   The great earth-goddess of the Cascade Mountains was embodied in the snowy peak of Mt. Rainier. Among the Salish, Nisqualli, Puyallup, Yakima, and other peoples of that area, Tacoma was the protector of the country's fresh waters, which brought nourishment upriver in the form of spawning salmon. Many legends were told of her, usually connecting her with the other mountains of the Cascades and Olympics.

One legend says that she was originally a hugely fat woman who shared a man with two other wives. The man, angered at their constant quarreling, set them far apart—two on one side of Puget Sound, and Tacoma on the opposite shore, where there was plenty of room for her bulk. This did not deter her, however, from shooting insults at her co-wives.

Another version has it that the woman was kept constantly on the move by her husband and co-wife until, exhausted, she just sat down and stayed put. But she continued to hate the other wife, at whose head she threw hot coals, so that Mt. Constance today is bald.

Yet another story says that Tacoma was always a mountain, but that, when she was a womanly young mountain, she married a mountain prince. But not yet full-grown, she soon outstripped her husband in size. So, to make room for her husband and his people, she moved across Puget Sound, taking berries and salmon with her,

Tacoma grew so huge that she became a mountain that ate anything that set foot on her slopes. Voraciously, she ate people as well as animals. Finally the great god Changer turned himself into a fox and dared Tacoma to swallow him, after he'd magically pinned himself to another mountain. When Tacoma tried to swallow the god, she engorged vast quantities of rock and water, but Changer could not be moved. One more try—and she burst open, hot blood flowing down her sides. Her corpse still sits there, covered with snow, a petrified woman's body.

Ta-Dehnet The "peak," a title of the death ruler *Mertseger.*

Tahc-I The sun-goddess of the Louisianan Tunica was originally courted by the kingfisher, who took a man's shape for the occasion. Successful in his pursuit, he took Tahc-I home in the dark, telling her he lived in an upstairs room. When the girl woke up, however, she was out on the limb of a hackberry tree in a nest. She was perplexed and ashamed. She was also hungry and was not delighted when the kingfisher—now in bird form again—brought her a tasty lapful of minnows for breakfast. She began to sing mournfully, and as she did she rose into the sky, radiating light. In her honor the Tunica annually danced the Sun Dance and placed her statue, together with that of a frog, on altars in their homes.

Tai Yuan The Chinese saint of this name lived on clouds high in the mountains and remained celibate until the age of 80, by which time she had become totally androgynous as well as ethereal. A beam of light, wandering by, saw the shining "Great Original" and penetrated her uterus; a year later Tai Yuan gave birth to a heroic child who became the ruler of the underworld.

Taillte The goddess of August in ancient Ireland was said to be foster mother of the light, embodied in the god Lug. One of the great earth-goddesses of the land, Taillte lived on the magical Hill of Tara, from which she directed the clearing of an immense forest, the wood of Cuan. It took a month to create the Plain of Oenach Taillten, where Taillte then built her palace; it remains on Irish maps today as Teltown, near Kells.

A festival was celebrated annually in her honor, lasting the whole of August. For generations it was celebrated, complete with mercantile fairs and sporting events; even into medieval times Taillte's festivities were held. Eventually they died out, but in the early part of this century the Tailltean Games—the Irish Olympics—were revived in an attempt to restore Irish culture.

*See Tara, p. 334. Field Museum of Natural History
(Neg # 37006), Chicago.*

Tamar   This Hebrew heroine—like goddesses of many cultures—outlived husband after husband; it was typical of earth-goddesses that they reigned with a series of mortal men, bedding and burying each "king" in the course of a year. Tamar's first husband, Er, was killed by a curse; then she married his brother Onan, who quickly died as well.

Tamar took matters into her own hands. As a prophet, Tamar could see that her children would have glorious descendants. So, disguised as a holy woman, offering herself sexually as an embodiment of the goddess, she caught the eye of the father of her husbands, Judah the Hebrew. He failed to recognize her because Hebrews kept their women veiled, while promiscuous pagan women left their faces self-confidently uncovered.

Tamar took Judah to bed and conceived by him, later reveiling herself and returning to his household, where she lived as a widow. Although there was a period of tension when her pregnancy was discovered, Tamar showed Judah love tokens he had given the holy woman and forced him to acknowledge the fatherhood of the twin sons she bore.

Tamayorihime   Like her sister Japanese heroines *Ikutamayorihime* and *Seyadatarahime*, she was a young woman who became Mother Ancestor to an important family after mating with an otherworldly creature. He used to come under cover of darkness, which apparently did not disturb the girl until she became pregnant. Then, to discover his identity, she sewed a long hemp thread to his hem, and, next morning, followed it to a dark cave. At its mouth she called out for her lover to show his face. "You would burst with fright," a deep voice answered from the earth's center. Unafraid, she continued to make her demand until he appeared, a scaly monster with a needle stuck in its throat. Tamayorihime fainted, but lived to bear the hero Daida, greatest warrior of Kyushu. The heroine's name, meaning a woman (*hime*) possessed (*yor*) by a god (*tama*), may have been a title borne by the Japanese shamans called *miko*. Similar stories are told of *Psyche* and *Semele*.

Tamfana, Tanfana   Tacitus mentions this Germanic goddess, so we are certain of her name but, alas, nothing else.

Tanaquil   Behind King Tarquin of Rome stood the wise queen Tanaquil, interpreter of omens, political genius, domestic manager. She came with Tarquin from Etruria to Rome and, when an eagle swooped down and stole his hat, she knew instantly that he was destined for success in the Italian town. When that success came, in the form of kingship, Tanaquil served as Tarquin's chief adviser. And she also provided the suc-

*See Tara, p. 334. Field Museum of Natural History
(Neg# A100399), Chicago.*

cessor to the throne—not by giving birth, but by noticing an omen that *Ocrisia* would bear the next king and by generously ensuring that conception took place. In the late 19th century, J. J. Bachofen analyzed the myths of Tanaquil and contended that she was a legendary disguise for a goddess who, like *Cybele* or *Ishtar* to the east, granted kingship to her favorite but retained the land's sovereignty for herself.

Tanetu *Hathor* as a goddess of light, allowing us to see the beautiful things of her creation.

Tanith When the conquering Romans saw the image of this goddess—just before they destroyed the Carthaginians who worshiped her—they named her *Dea Caelestis* or simply Caelestis ("heavenly goddess") for she seemed to rule the sky. Indeed, the winged goddess with a zodiac around her head and the sun and moon in either hand was the sky-goddess of the Punic people. (Some oversimplify her status, calling her a moon-goddess, but she ruled the sun and stars as well.) Her children called her "mother," seeing the sky as their source, just as other peoples have called themselves earth's children.

Tapa Another name for *Hina* as moon-goddess.

Tara In Indian Hinduism, the star-goddess Tara is a manifestation of the queen of time, *Kali*. Her symbol, the star, is seen as a beautiful but perpetually self-combusting thing; so Tara is the absolute, unquenchable hunger that propels all life.

Among Buddhists and Jains, and particularly in Tibetan Lamaism, Tara became a symbol of other hungers as well, in particular the spiritual hunger for release from the purely physical world. As such, Tara is the goddess of self-mastery and mysticism, invoked under her 108 names on a rosary of 108 beads. The compassionate goddess, she appears as a playful adolescent, for Tara sees life for the game it is; she also appears as a celestial boat woman, ferrying her people across from the world of delusion to that of knowledge. As the Green Tara she is terrifying, but the White Tara of meditation stares at us from her three eyes to remind us that if we look through the terror of death she waits to enlighten us.

Taranga, Hua-Henga The mother of the Polynesian hero Maui did not carry him to term; she gave birth prematurely and, as was right according to her people, wrapped him in her hair and tossed him into the sea. But she offered prayers and sighs for her son, which protected him from turning into a demon, the usual fate of such children.

In the sea's great womb, the child was carried to term and then raised by the gods until he was old enough to see Taranga's home. Happy to see her miscarried babe, Taranga welcomed Maui and made him her favorite son.

Taranga spent each day far from home, and her children did not know where she went. One day Maui decided to follow her; he saw her disappear beneath the earth. Continuing his pursuit, he found her tending the miraculous underworld gardens from which all food on this earth derives. Because of his obvious daring, Taranga allowed Maui to go through the manhood rituals.

Tari Pennu In Bengal, this earth-goddess was propositioned by the sun-god; she refused him. So he created human women, but they took up the worship of the earth-goddess, and so the struggle between Tari Pennu and the sun continues to this day.

Tarkhu Some scholars contend that the goddess *Atargatis* was derived from a Hittite goddess of this name.

Tasimmet Hittite weather-goddess.

Tatsuta-Hime Each autumn this Japanese goddess wove a beautiful multicolored tapestry. She then incarnated herself as wind and blew her own work to shreds.

Tauret, Apet, Opet, Taur, Toeris This was the animal form of the great Egyptian mother-goddess *Mut*. As a nurturing force, she was a pregnant hippopotamus with long tits, standing on her hind legs and carrying the scrolls of protection. But as the fierce animal force, as the mother who defends her brood, she was a lion-headed hippo with a dagger.

Tauthe Among the Babylonians, the female first principle who, with Apason the male principle, existed before our creation. See **Tiamat**.

Tava-Ajk Saami Mother Goddess.

Teczistecatl An ancient Mexican moon-goddess.

Tefnut Taking her name from the dew that appears each dawn, she was a goddess of daybreak like *Eos, A (Aja)*, and *Aurora*. Like them, Tefnut was associated with the mountains from which the sun rises. Sometimes, as the "heavenly cow of creation," she seemed to be a form of *Neith*; sometimes she was a lioness or a lion-headed woman, suggesting a similarity to *Bast* or *Sekhmet*.

Teleglen Edzen A Mongol name for the earth-goddess.

Teleia "Full-grown," the second phase of *Hera*.

Telesilla A poet of the Greek town of Argos, she was the heroine of a war with neighboring Sparta. When the Spartans besieged Argos, this poet fought her way out of the siege—at the head of an army of Argive women, worshipers of the ancient *Hera*.

Telete Roman spirit of mystery religions.

Tellus Mater The Roman "Mother Earth" was honored each April 15, when a pregnant cow was sacrificed and the unborn calf burned. The Romans tried to offer appropriate tribute to each divinity and they felt that the earth—pregnant in spring with sprouting plants—would appreciate this sacrifice.

　　Tellus's constant companion was *Ceres*, the grain-goddess, and the two of them interested themselves not only in vegetative reproduction but in humanity's increase as well. Therefore, they were invoked at every marriage that they might bless it with offspring. Tellus too was considered the most worthy goddess on whom to swear oaths, for the earth, witnessing all doings on her surface, would see that an oath taker kept his promise. Finally, Tellus, to whom the bodies of the dead were returned as to a womb, was the motherly death-goddess. See also **Damkina.**

Telphassa "Wide-shiner," she was an early Greek goddess of light who was probably imported from Phoenicia; she remains in legend only as the mother of the cow-goddess *Europa*.

Telphusa This water nymph had prophetic powers, said the Greeks, but the water of her fountain was so bitterly cold that it killed anyone who tried to gain prophetic speech by drinking there. Some legends say that the famous seer Tiresias died when he tried to increase his foreknowledge by sipping Telphusa's water. When Apollo, the invading god who took prophecy from the ancient earth-goddesses, was seeking a place for his oracle, he first selected Telphusa's renowned spring. But she persuaded him to look elsewhere, directing him to *Gaea*'s Delphi—where the nymph knew Apollo would have a fierce fight with the guardian serpent *Python* before he could control the oracular spring.

See Taranga, p. 334. Field Museum of Natural History (Neg# 99081), Chicago.

Tempestates   Roman goddesses of wind and storm.

Tethys   The most ancient pre-Hellenic sea-goddess, she was part of a trinity of world-creators with *Nyx*, the primeval darkness, and *Gaea*, the fertile earth; all were said to have mothered the world we inhabit. Gradually, the ages eroded Tethys's power, until classical Greek mythology contained little information about her. Homer tells us she has ceased giving birth, being content with 6,000 children: half of them sons, half the daughters called *Oceanids*, most famous of whom is her mother's double with a similar name, *Thetis*. By Hesiod's time, Tethys was even less important; that poet scrambled her history by calling her a Titan, a created goddess rather than a creator. But she still remained important enough to have been named as the nurse of the infant *Hera*, the great women's goddess of Greece. See **Thalassa.**

Thalassa, Thalath   In one Greek account of creation, she was the mother of all, possibly the same goddess as *Tethys*. Later she was said to be the fish mother, creator of all sea life. Her name, which means "sea," survives in the word for a mercantile sea kingdom, *thalassocracy*.

Thalestris   This *Amazon* queen practiced an early form of eugenics. Rather than mating with anonymous males in the yearly fertility ritual, she kept her eyes open for likely kings and princes to press into sexual duty. She had apparently borne several children this way when she first cast eyes on Alexander of Macedon. Recognizing a superior specimen of manhood, she invited him to fertilize her, an offer that, apparently, he took as a high compliment.

Thalna, Thana   Etruscan dawn-goddess.

Tharatha   Armenian name for *Atargatis*.

Thea, Theia, Thia   The pre-Hellenic goddess of light, mother of the dawn and the luminaries, bore a name that means simply "goddess." Although this hints at earlier eminence, nothing is left of Thea but her name and the list of her children; like many elder Greek goddesses, she was replaced by divinities of the invading Indo-Europeans. See also **Eos.**

Themis   The "steadfast one," the daughter of *Gaea*, was the earth-goddess personified as an unshakable power. By Homer's time, she had come to signify a second powerful steadfastness: the social contract among people living on the earth (similarly *Fides*). One of the most ancient and most hallowed of goddesses, Themis later became a vague and abstract personality. Yet evidence of her original precedence is suggested: no Olympian gathering could take place unless she called it, and neither could any divinity lift the cup of nectar before she had drunk.

In the language of her people, *themis* was a common as well as a proper noun, the former indicating the power of convention, of whatever is fixed in society as steadfastly as the earth beneath us. The personification of such social cohesion, Themis was shown bearing a pair of scales; as the fruitful earth, she was shown holding the cornucopia. She was mother of the seasons, or *Horae*, goddesses who determined the proper moment for the fruitful earth's budding and exhaustion, and the proper times as well for human events. One of Themis's daughters, the fierce Dike, was her own maiden self, a stern uncompromising virgin.

Themis ruled prophecy, for she knew human nature and the nature of human society and so could predict the outcome of any struggle; thus she shared with Mother Gaea the famous Delphic Oracle. For her worship, she demanded group dancing, the symbol of a group's bonding through graceful action. Eldest of Greek goddesses, she was the first to whom temples were built, for before her there was no human community to offer worship.

Thesmophoros   *Demeter* as "she who lays down the law."

Thetis   Reading late Greek mythology, you would believe this goddess merely the mother of the hero Achilles. But clues in her legend suggest that she was originally one of the Great Goddesses, daughter and double of the sea queen *Tethys*, much as *Hebe* was to *Hera*. She was apparently a goddess of womanhood, for she was raised by the threefold deity of femininity, Hera. Thetis also nursed the two gods associated with women's rites: the appealingly dissolute Dionysus and the crippled artisan Hephaestus.

Sometimes legend called Thetis not Tethys's daughter but an offspring of another sea-goddess, *Doris*. In either case, she was gifted with the oceanic power of shape-changing. Thus, when the Olympians— fearing the prophecy that she would bear a son greater than his father— condemned Thetis to marry a mortal, she resisted in the time-honored fashion of sea queens. She changed herself into monsters and microorganisms, but her husband-to-be, alerted to her powers, held fast until she resumed human form.

She agreed to marry Peleus. At the wedding the prankster-goddess Eris tossed her famous apple, marked "to the fairest," into the crowd, which resulted in the Trojan War and the death of Thetis's mortal son, Achilles. After Achilles's death, Thetis abandoned Peleus, who until that time had remained youthful by her immortal powers; he immediately aged and died.

Thordis   Scandinavian wise woman and healer.

Thorgerd   Her full name was Thorgerd Holgabrud. Originally a human woman, she was deified because of her unprecedented skill in divinity and sorcery. She and her sister Irpa were the special goddesses of Jarl Haakon, who built them a special temple in the south of Iceland.

Thorgerd was a mighty warrior-goddess, charged with protecting her people from enemies; if they were attacked, she sprang to life, arrows flying from each finger, each arrow killing a man. In addition, she had power over natural forces necessary for her people's happiness; thus she was invoked for luck in fishing and farming. Her worship was among the last vestiges of the ancient religion, remaining vital into Christian times. The Christians, denouncing her, called her Thorgerd Holga-Troll, although she had no troll blood in her.

Thyone   "The ecstatically raging," the deified *Semele.*

Tiamat, Tamtu   Before our world was created, said the Babylonians, there was only Tiamat, the dragon woman of bitter waters, and her mate Apsu, god of fresh water. In those timeless days in a frenzy of creativity, Tiamat began to bring forth offspring: monsters, storms, and quadrupeds, the like of which exist today only in our dreams.

Eventually, the gods came forth as well from the almighty womb of Tiamat. They set up housekeeping in another part of the universe. But they were a rowdy bunch, who disturbed Apsu with their noise. He approached Tiamat with the suggestion that, because she had created them, she could readily do away with the gods. Mummu Tiamat ("Tiamat the mother") was taken aback by the suggestion and refused.

But the gods got wind of the conversation and, in retaliation, killed Apsu, the goddess's lover. At that her fury exploded and, with Kingu, her firstborn son, she attacked the gods. They waged a battle that, some say, goes on annually to this day, with the hero Marduk each year swallowed by the enormous dragon. Tiamat, according to this version of the story, became a civilizing fish mother (like *Atargatis*) to the people of earth. But others contend that Marduk, hero of the new gods, killed his mother in the battle. Her body fell into the lower universe; one half became the dome of heaven, the other half the wall to contain the waters. See also **Cipactli, Lamamu, Leviathan.**

*See Tauret, p. 335. Field Museum of Natural History
(Neg# 94968), Chicago.*

Tien-Hou, Tien Fei   She was born Mei Chou, a natural psychic and the sister of four seafarers. One day she fell into a deep trance, which worried her parents deeply. They tried everything to break the spell and at last succeeded, much to Mei Chou's anger. Soon afterward, three brothers returned home with the news that the fourth had been lost at sea; they, too would have drowned, they said, had not their sister walked across the water in her astral body to save them. Mei Chou lived on earth only a few years longer before being elevated to the heavens as Tien-Hou.

The Chinese Empress of Heaven should not be confused with *Hsi Wang Mu*, the queen of the West and empress over all divinities. Tien-Hou was the ocean-goddess who rode across the sky on clouds, consulting her wind servants to find sailors in danger. She then hastened to their rescue, just as she had when she lived on earth.

Tien-Mu   To make lightning, this Chinese goddess had only to flash two mirrors at each other; from their intersecting rays, lightning bolts shot out.

Titania   Roman moon-goddess.

Tlazoltéotl   "Dirty lady" or "earth's heart" was the Aztec goddess of the fourfold moon, the witch-goddess of sexuality and license. Gambling, temptation, and black magic also fell to her rulership; however, she was also the purifier of her people, for only her priests could hear confessions of guilt. This confession was only effective once in a lifetime, so Aztecs put it off as long as they could, rather than die impure.

The four aspects of Tlazoltéotl had individual names: Tiacapan, Teicu, Tlaco, and Xocutxin. All were witches who rode broomsticks through the sky, clad only in the night and a tall peaked hat. Like other witch-goddesses of other lands, they were particularly fond of crossroads: the literal ones, which they were said to haunt, and the crossroads of life, the points at which decisions lead to good or evil.

Tlitcaplitana   The Bellacoola of the Pacific Northwest were always eager to meet this heavenly woman, who descended from her home in the sky to heal the sick; often she would grant them secret knowledge and chants as well as health. Sometimes, alas, her power was too much for the human vessel, and they died from the contact. But that was not because of any ill will on the goddess's part, for she was the most generous of heavenly spirits, though ugly in the extreme, with a snout and ropelike breasts. Her singing, however, which carried across the calm waters and through the dense rain forests, was as beautiful as she was not.

Toci, Teteoinnan "Our grandmother" was one of the great Aztec goddesses, the embodiment of nature's healing powers, and therefore invoked in sweat baths where the body was purified. She was said to wear a skirt of shells and carry the sun disk on her shield.

Toci's festival was particularly celebrated by doctors, midwives, surgeons, and fortune-tellers, who danced for eight days as though entranced, moving only their blossom-filled arms. Without speaking, they danced before a woman chosen to represent the goddess. Some researchers contend that in early times, the people of Mexico did not sacrifice humans to their divinities; Toci may have originally been worshiped without human slaughter, but by the time of the Spanish invasion her festival ended with the midnight sacrifice of the woman who had received the prayers of the Aztec healers.

Toh Sri Lam A crocodile-goddess of Indochina.

Tomyris Most history books mention that Cyrus the Great died on a military campaign. But it is seldom acknowledged that he was bested in battle and executed by an amazonian queen, ruler of the Massagetae, a Scythian people. When Cyrus's imperialism led him to invade Tomyris's country, she attempted to negotiate a truce. He refused; she sent her son against the invader, who took him prisoner; then the young prince killed himself in shame.

Just prior to the suicide, however, Tomyris gave Cyrus a last warning: "Restore my son to me . . . Refuse and I swear that, bloodthirsty as you are, I will give you your fill of blood." Cyrus was not disposed to listen to the queen's threats, and Tomyris forthwith destroyed his entire army and captured the king. Flaying his corpse and beheading it, she held his severed head above a skinful of blood and tossed it in, instructing him to drink his fill.

Tonan, Ilamatecuhtli, Tonantzin One of the Aztec mother-goddesses, she was honored in a winter-solstice festival at which a woman dressed entirely in white and covered with shells and eagle feathers danced, weeping and singing, through the crowds. A priest accompanied her and, taking the goddess's mask from the woman, killed the year's incarnate deity. The next day, Aztec men struck the women of the community with little bags full of green paper, apparently a magical act to renew the life force.

Torah The "Law" was a female force in Jewish legend, as stern and demanding as any goddess. She appeared as an adviser to Jehovah, and a skeptical one at that. Torah opposed the creation of humanity on the grounds that "The man thou art creating will be few of days and full of trouble and sin." Only after Jehovah had convinced Torah that repentance was possible did she cease her protest.

Tou-Mou   The Chinese goddess of the polestar was the judge of all peoples, keeping records of their lives and deaths. In addition, she was the scribe of heaven, keeping a tally of all the divinities, their duties, and their various estates in the nine heavens.

Toyota-Mahime   This sea-goddess, "Lady Abundance-of-Jewels," appears in the *Kojiki*, the Japanese scriptures. Like *Melusine* and other mermaids, she married a mortal but warned him not to look upon her while she was birthing their child. Then she hid in a hut thatched with cormorant feathers. Of course her mortal mate, unable to contain his curiosity, peered inside to see Toyota slithering around in her true serpent form. Discovering his perfidy, she retreated to the ocean and forever closed the door joining her realm to his.

Toyo-Uke   A food-goddess whose gold-filigreed shrine stands at Ise, she is sometimes considered an early sun-goddess whose worship was made secondary to that of the powerful *Amaterasu*, ancestor of the dominant Yamato clan and of Japan's 20th-century emperor Hirohito.

Triduana   A Scottish name for *Brigid* from the Edinburgh area. Of Triduana was told the famous Brigid tale that she tore out her eyes to destroy her beauty, rather than be preyed upon by a lecherous king—in this case Nechtan, king of the Picts. Triduana's sacred place was a well beneath a Druidic oak.

Trung-Trac, Trung-Nhi   These rain-goddesses of the Tonkin were originally warrior women who led a revolt of their people against a tyrannical Chinese governor. The uprising was successful, and Trung-Trac, the elder sister, became queen. Later, however, they were again invaded and conquered by the Chinese. The women were deified after death.

Tsan Nu   The Chinese silkworm-goddess also called Lady Horsehead.

Tsi-Ku, Tsi Ku Niang   When a Chinese woman wanted to know what the future held, she went to the toilet and asked Tsi-Ku ("purple lady"), the goddess of the outhouse.

Tsun Kyanske   Khymer goddess who rules the afterlife.

Etruscan bust; see Turan, p. 347. Field Museum of Natural History (Neg# 110969), Chicago.

Tsuru   When Japan was under the rule of shaman queens, this woman offered herself as a human sacrifice in the building of a dyke against a raging flood in Oita prefecture. Buried alive in the river, she successfully diverted the waters so that the village was safe. Probably she was a *miko*, or shaman, for there is a tradition—the *hito-bashira* or "human pillar" tales—that only such women could hold back ravaging floodwaters, provided they were willing to lay down their lives; in some interpretations, this "death" was metaphoric and meant retirement to an ascetic life in the shrine. Tsuru was worshiped at Aibara shrine near the site of her sacrifice.

Tuchulcha   The Etruscans pictured death as a woman with horrifying eyes staring over a beak, ass's ears, serpent hair, and a snake twisted around one arm.

Tuli   As the great father-god of Samoa watched the watery chaos of primeval time, the bird-goddess Tuli flew across it. As she tired, he threw stones from heaven, giving her temporary perches; these became the islands of Polynesia. As she rested on a rock, Tuli grew weary of the sun blazing on her head, so she flew back to heaven and brought herself a fresh vine as an umbrella. She left the vine behind her, and from it swarmed maggots who became the first human beings.

Tulsi   Indian goddess of the basil plant.

Tundr Ilona   The Ugrians, including the Hungarians, said that this goddess created the world. The sun was an egg which she, taking the shape of a swan, laid in the sky.

Tu-Njami, Tkuriz, Tuurm, Fadzja, Bokoj, Locia Amai, Togo Musun   The Siberian "Mother Fire" looked like a small naked girl, but she was strong enough to protect the whole family that worshiped her at their hearth—especially the women, since she was their ancestor. She was a goddess of purification and healing whose special concern was the removal of disease and filth. Tu-Njami also ruled birth, for she was an incredibly productive mother herself, birthing small versions of herself— daughters—on every twig in the fire.

Tuonetar   The queen of death, according to the *Kalevala*, lived in a jungle of darkness somewhere on the earth, divided from the land of the living by a black-watered river. It was thought to be possible to reach Tuonela, Tuonetar's country, by hiking seven days through underbrush, seven through woodlands, and a final seven days through dense forest.

Finally, the traveler reached the banks of the River Manala, where Tuonetar's swans floated and where her daughters laundered their dark robes. Only these daughters could—if they would—convey the traveler into the country of Tuonetar. But few would survive their assistance, for they were goddesses of disease. Once Loviatar, Kipu-Tytoo, or another of Tuonetar's daughters had brought the visitor to the death queen, Tuonetar herself would offer a magical brew of frogs and worms; if one drank that, return to the land of life was impossible.

Turan Before Rome conquered the Italian peninsula, the area now called Tuscany was the home of a rich and complex culture. The Etruscans who lived there evolved a theology and a philosophy of life quite different from the Romans—a culture that perished with the Roman victory, leaving only vestiges in the most biased source possible, the records of their conquerors.

The Etruscans left their own words as well, but their inscriptions are written in a language not yet deciphered and apparently unrelated to any language known today. The mysterious Etruscan culture was said by Herodotus to be a migrant from Lydia, a matriarchal culture where children bore their mothers' name and assumed their mothers' social status.

This Lydian heritage seems to have survived in Etruria, for Etruscan women enjoyed more social equality with men than did their peers in other Mediterranean countries of the ancient world. All the more unfortunate, then, that only the names of their goddesses survive. Although there is no proof that strong goddesses either lead to, or reflect, similar social prominence among their human counterparts, this connection seems probable; therefore, the Etruscan goddesses may have been the most feminist in the ancient world.

One Etruscan goddess about whom the modern world does know something is Turan—who survived as Turanna, the "good fairy" of peace and love in modern Italy. She took her name from the same word as the Greek *tyrannos*, or ruler. Thus Turan is assumed to be the queen of life, sometimes called *Aphrodite*. She was the "mistress," in both modern senses of the word, a divinity of sex and dominance. And apparently her worship included the former, for her temples were placed outside the city walls so as to be less obvious to young people and mothers of small children.

Turesh The Ainus of northern Japan remembered a golden age when humans did not have to work for a living, a happy time when the god Okikurumi caught fish in the celestial sea and sent down the catch in baskets with the goddess Turesh. But there was, as in many paradises, a single law in this land: no Ainu should ask their benefactress's name or seek to discover her appearance. One Ainu was villainously curious, however, and grabbed the ministering hand as it set food upon his table, pulling into the house a squirming sea monster. The wrath of heaven fell upon the Ainus that day, and since that time they have had to struggle for the meager food their harsh land provides them.

Turrean   The Irish wolfhound-goddess was, legend said, originally human, but was changed by the spiteful fairy queen Uchtdealbh into the most beautiful bitch that ever lived. Turrean was kept prisoner for many years on Galway Bay until her nephew Finn MacCool freed her and restored her to human form. In the meantime, she bore two sons, who retained their canine shape; they lived with their uncle and traveled with him as his half-human dogs, Bran and Sgeolan.

Tursa   Early Italian goddess of terror.

Tuulikki   Finnish goddess of forest animals.

·U·

Uadgit, Buto, Himbuto, Per Uadjit, Uazit, Uto   The sovereign cobra-goddess of Lower Egypt and the Nile delta, she joined with *Nekhebet* to form the "two mistresses" of the land, the *Neb-Ti*, a political symbol of the unification of Egypt.

Uairebhuidhe   Irish bird-goddess.

Uke-Mochi   Japan's food-goddess had her own way of providing for the world's needs: she vomited. If she faced the land, rice, boiled and ready to be devoured, poured from her mouth. Facing the sea, she regurgitated fish and seaweed. Looking to the mountains, she vomited game creatures ready for capture.

    Unfortunately, she set her table this way when one of the male gods was visiting her. It disgusted him, so he killed her. Her fertile body, falling to earth, dissolved into food: cattle stampeding from her head, silkworms crawling from her eyebrows, rice plants popping up from her belly. The god's behavior, however, so angered heaven's queen, *Amaterasu* the sun-goddess, that she withdrew her light, causing the world's first winter.

Ukepenopfu   Among the Angami Nagas of India, she was the great ancestor-goddess.

Uks-Akka   The "door woman" of the Saami, she was said to live under the doorway and to change girl children into boys in the womb, which is the correct biological development.

Ulsiga   *"Ishtar* of heaven and earth," a title of reverence.

Umaj   Russian Siberia was home to many different tribal traditions, but almost all worshiped a birth-goddess of this name. The Khakass believed she lived in the placenta; among the Shors, she protected newborns.

The nearby Altais believed the sacred mountains of their land were occupied by big-breasted women who appeared naked, even in winter; anyone who made love with one always had good luck in hunting.

Umm Attar "Mother Attar," an Arabian goddess similar to *Hathor* or *Asherah*, benevolent deities of sexuality and reproduction.

Unelanuhi Among the Cherokee, as among many peoples, the sun was seen as a lovely young woman and the moon as her brother-lover. Her name, Unelanuhi, means "divider" or "apportioner," for she was the one who marked off time into units.

She came into the world with the help of *Spider Woman* (see **Hatai Wugti**), for originally this planet had no sun, and earth's animals could not bring one from the underworld. The opossum tried and burned off his tail. The vulture tried to carry Unelanuhi on his head and scorched his feathers off. But Spider Woman wove a web that pulled Unelanuhi into the world.

Unelanuhi used to sleep with a young man who visited her once a month, a lover who refused to tell her his name. Determined to discover who was pleasuring her, she dipped her hands in ashes and rubbed his face in the dark. When daylight came, her brother met her at breakfast with ash on his face—the same one visible today in the moon, for the young man ran in shame from his sister and stayed as far away in the sky as he could. Once a month, however, he could not resist visiting her in the new moon's darkness.

Uni One of the few Etruscan goddesses the modern world knows, Uni—whose name may later have evolved into *Juno*—was benefactor of Etruscan cities and of the women who lived there. Queen of the sky, she hurled thunderbolts when angered and, when pleased, granted safe passage to the infant at birth. Her major sanctuary was at Pyrgi, a port of the city of Caere, where she was endowed with silver and gold by her worshipers.

Unxia Roman goddess of wedding anointment.

Urania *Muse* of astronomy; also a title of *Aphrodite* in Sparta.

Ursula, Horsel, Orsel The Slavic moon-goddess of this name was honored on her feast day, October 21. Later, Christians in the same area adopted her as a saint, calling the old moon feast St. Ursula's day.

*Uzume, p. 353. Field Museum of Natural History
(Neg# 49436), Chicago.*

Urvasi, Apsaras When the Hindu gods churned the ocean, among the beings that emerged were the Apsaras ("daughters of pleasure"), multiple spirits of all possibility, incarnations of parallel worlds that exist beyond our perception. The dancers and singers of the heavens, they are renowned for wantonness, taking as lovers whomever they please, never counting the number of men and gods who have shared their beds.

They are described as large-hipped and languid, with soft inviting eyes. Most famous was Urvasi (a name sometimes used of the dawn-goddess *Ushas*), born when a sage surrounded by tempting Apsaras slapped his thigh.

Urvasi once consented, as other nymphs did on occasion, to live with a human king, but she told him that human nakedness disgusted her. He promised she would never have to see him unclothed, but he forgot one day, and she fled. When he promised to leave his throne and become an erotic singer-dancer, she agreed to return.

Ushas The Hindu dawn-goddess—sometimes called *Urvasi*—was said to stay eternally young but to make men grow constantly older. She appeared each morning, throwing off her blouse to reveal shining breasts that filled the heavens with splendor. Like other dawn-goddesses (*Eos, Aurora, Hekt*), she was wanton, and said to be either the mother or the lover of the sun.

Uso-Dori Japanese goddess of singing who appears as a bullfinch.

Uti Hiata This is the Pawnee name for "Mother Corn," one of the most important divinities of the Plains Indian culture. Their neighbors, the Arikara, told the Corn Mother's story in detail. From the great blue lake of creation, diving ducks brought up bits of silt to build prairies and foothills. Sky father Nesaru, seeing giants populating the earth, sent a great flood to destroy them; he replanted the earth with maize seeds, which sprouted into human beings. Then he sent Mother Corn to assist at their birth.

Finding no one on earth, Mother Corn walked and walked. Suddenly the thunder kidnapped her and hid her beneath the earth. There, she gathered the underworld animals—the mole, the mouse, the badger—and with their help dug through the ground and burst out into the sun. As she emerged, so did the people of the plains, to whom she taught secrets of life and magic and the methods of agriculture and of religious ritual. Satisfied that humanity would live in abundance, she disappeared from the earth, leaving the cedar as an emblem of her existence. See also **H'Uraru**.

Utset and **Nowutset, Uretsiti** and **Naotsiti**   The first mothers of humanity were, to the Sia and Navaho of the southwestern American desert, two sisters who were the first humans in this world. They lived for a time in peace, until a rivalry began between them. Some stories said they started a riddle contest, and that Nowutset, being the duller sister, lost to Utset, who then killed her. Another version has it that the sisters argued and decided that the one whom the sun touched first in the morning would be judged the winner. Nowutset was taller, but Utset cheated and won. The contest was restaged; Nowutset pushed her sister suddenly and a fierce fight began. The sisters, unable to live with each other, separated. Utset became the mother of pueblo-dwelling people, and Nowutset, of all the others.

Uttu   This Sumerian goddess of plants lost her offspring to her great-grandfather and lover, Enki. See also **Ninhursag.**

Uzume   Ancient Japan's shaman-goddess was the one who lured the sun-goddess *Amaterasu* from the cave where she'd hidden. She did so by a merry mockery of shamanic ritual. Tying her sleeves above her elbows with moss cords and fastening bells around her wrists, she danced on an overturned tub before the heavenly Sky-Rock-Cave. Tapping out a rhythm with her feet, she exposed her breasts and then her genitals in the direction of the sun. So comic did she make this striptease that the myriad gods and goddesses began to clap and laugh—an uproar that finally brought the curious sun back to warm the earth.

    Shaman women who followed Uzume were called *miko* in ancient Japan. First queens like *Himiko*, later they were princesses and even later, common-born women. Some Japanese women today, especially those called *nuru* and *yuta* in Okinawa and the surrounding Islands, still practice shamanic divination.

Vacuna   This early agricultural goddess evolved into a Sabine divinity of license and fun; but the more serious Romans decided she was a war-goddess (perhaps their idea of a good time) and identified her with *Bellona*.

Vagitanus   Roman goddess who induced the first cry of babes.

Vajravaraki   The goddess "wanderer of the air" was said in Tibet to incarnate herself regularly as a Buddhist abbess who never slept; she had magical powers to protect the nuns under her care. Once, when a Mongol chieftain tried to take over the abbey, he could not find it. In its place, there was a herd of pigs with a very large wild sow at its head. After the danger passed, the glamour was unnecessary, and the nuns were restored to human form.

Vakyrine, Vakarine   Lady of the evening star, daughter of the sun in Lithuania and Latvia. See **Saule** and **Saules Meita**.

Valetudo   Early Italian goddess of health.

Valkyries, Valkyrjr   The helmeted battle maid, the chooser-of-the-slain who flew on her supernatural horse over war's carnage, is probably the only still-familiar female image from Scandinavian mythology. But there was another picture of the Valkyries—one more violent and powerful—that has been virtually forgotten. For before the battle started, the Valkyries wove the web of war, raising the warp of spears and weighting it with human heads, running a dripping red weft through the spears, using arrows as shuttles. When they had determined the battle's outcome, they flew from their blood-drenched house like carrion-seeking ravens to devour the bodies of the slain.

   These goddesses thus had much in common with the *Moirae*, the *Norns*, and other fate rulers who spun or wove human life in a supernatural home. The Anglo-Saxons identified the Valkyries with the Greek *Erinyes*, goddesses of vengeance who hunted down anyone spilling the blood of kin. Current interpretation sees these divine women simply as the servants of Odin, flying to earth to retrieve his select heroes; this ignores stories that show the Valkyries opposing Odin's will, selecting their own favorites, and teaching magic to the heroes they intended to save.

They did not always ride horses to battle; sometimes they appeared on wolves or disguised themselves as ravens. Some writers claimed there were two kinds of Valkyries: divine ones, of whom there were nine, or nine times nine; and the half-mortal Vaetter-maidens, visible as humans to the second-sighted, while the average eye saw only the aurora borealis leaping excitedly over the field of battle. See **Brynhild, Freya, Gondul,** and **Sigurdrifta.**

Vanths The most famous of the winged beauties called the Vanths was Culsa, the serpent-goddess of the underworld. The Etruscans thought death spirits were numberless and pictured Vanths as hunters in short skirts and high boots, carrying torches or snakes, waiting to accompany each of us past the grave.

Var Although this Scandinavian love-goddess had nothing to do with marriage, she did concern herself with promises lovers made to each other outside wedlock. She took fierce vengeance on anyone who broke such vows. An aspect of the all-knowing earth, Var saw and heard everything that happened: nothing could be hidden from her, so when a lover complained of wrongdoing by a love partner, Var knew instantly if the accusation were correct.

Varia This legendary Irish woman had such a temper that one day Donagha, her lazy husband, drove her into an extremity of anger. She leveled so furious a curse at him that it flung him to the farthest point distant from her in Ireland—to Donaghadee in Ulster, opposite her home in Kerry, Teach na Vauria.

Vashti A minor Elamite goddess, she appears in the Hebrew Book of *Esther* as a queen of the Persians who served also as the state's high priestess. A diplomat and daughter of a king, Vashti was unfortunately married to a fool, who drunkenly demanded that she appear before his friends naked. She refused. "Have you lost your reason from drinking? I am Vashti, daughter of Belshazzar, a son of Nebuchadnezzar who scoffed at kings. Shall you, a fool, be the master of so much beauty as mine?" But a Hebrew adviser, intent upon replacing Vashti with a woman of his tribe, urged the king to sentence her to death as a fearful example to other women who insisted on control of their own bodies. The king, proving himself more foolish by the moment, followed the Hebrew's advice. Queen Vashti's people rose against him, and the uprising was only put down when Esther ascended the throne.

Vatiaz   Among the Mongolian Buryat, this heroine was said to have traveled to heaven after her brother's murder in order to compete for the hands of three daughters of the chief god. There were many games of physical skill, all of which she won. Even though shamans warned the gods that she was a woman, they could not deny her strength and skill. So she was allowed to take the sisters back to earth, where she had them revive her brother.

Ved-Ava, Ved-Azer-Ava   One of the most important goddesses of the Finno-Ugric Mordvins was Ved-Ava, the water mother or water hostess. The spirit of the earth's fertility and of all who live on her face, she was also the one who sent fish into the nets of fisherfolk. See **Azer-Ava.**

Veden Emo   The Finnish "mother of the water" was responsible for guiding fish into the nets of the hungry. She is a very ancient goddess; her worship was recorded almost 2000 years ago by Agricola.

Vegoia, Begoe   When the Etruscans were first settling Tuscany, this goddess appeared to help them form a civilization pleasing to the gods of ancient Italy. Vegoia showed the Etruscans how to worship properly in rituals, how to divine the wishes of the deities through augury, and finally how to measure the land and set boundaries for human territory.

Veleda   One of the most famous of the legendary warrior queens of the ancient Continental Celts, Veleda ruled the Bructeri people. They once captured a Roman ship and towed it up the River Lippe as a present for their queen, outraging the Romans. But the legions, afraid of war with the fierce Bructeri, used diplomatic means to regain their vessel.

Vellamo   The Finnish sea-goddess lived underwater with her daughters, the waves, who tended cattle and raised mysterious crops on the ocean's floor.

Venus   We use her name, or words related to it, often: in *vain*, and *winsome*, *fain*, and *win*—and in that particular form of adoration, *veneration*. (She

*From Roman Pompeii, see Venus, p. 356. Field Museum of
Natural History (Neg# 58619), Chicago.*

was the goddess of *veneral* as well.) But when we speak of "Venus on the half-shell," we confuse her with the Greek *Aphrodite* rising from the sea.

The confusion is ancient, for the Romans themselves identified their kitchen-garden goddess with the Great Goddess of sexuality from the East. Although it is now impossible to distinguish Venus from Aphrodite, the Roman goddess was originally a spirit of charm and beauty, goddess of wild strawberries and herbs, of pine cones and cypress trees, served by virgin priests and priestesses. Wherever a large stone rested near a tall tree, there was Venus's sanctuary; there her altar could be erected for bloodless sacrifices. In this early Italian form, Venus was far less complex than the goddess with whom she was merged: a delicate, delightful, and, yes, "winsome" goddess of a youthful kind of love, the kind that took place on berry-picking excursions and in flirtations in Venus's own kitchen gardens.

Veritas   Roman goddess of truth, who hid at the bottom of wells.

Verplace, Virplace   Roman goddess of family harmony.

Veshtitze   In Slavic tradition, this was an old woman who left her body at night and flew through the air in a hen's body. She sought human children to kill, for she existed on the hearts of infants.

Vesna   Slavic goddess of spring, possibly identical to *Ostara* (see **Eostre**).

Vesta   Vergil said that Vesta is more easily felt than explained. Ovid, another great Roman poet, said Vesta and fire required no effigy—because Vesta was fire, and fire was Vesta. Like the Greek *Hestia*, Vesta was never originally shown in human form; when, in later days, she was pictured on coins, it was as a veiled figure.

Behind that veil was the central divinity of the Roman family, the goddess to whom a daily offering was made in each home at her sacred place, the hearth. In her public worship, Vesta was honored in the only round Roman temple, where a sacred fire burned, tended by the famous sisterhood of Vestal virgins. One day a year, on March 1, the Vestals doused and then relit the fire. Vesta's other sacred day was June 9, the Vestalia, when barefoot Roman matrons offered food baked on their own hearths and the Vestals sacrificed salt cakes baked on Vesta's fire; after eight days of such offerings, the Vestals closed the temple, cleaned it thoroughly, threw the refuse into the Tiber River, and reopened for the year.

Unlike her virgin priestesses, however, Vesta was honored as a mother, and there is evidence that a phallus-shaped effigy was reverenced in her temple down to imperial Roman times. That and the tradition of rekindling the Vestal fires by rubbing wood together—always a sexual symbol—indicate that Vesta was a goddess of generation, a symbol of the continual renewal of the family and of the Roman state. The light of the Vestal hearth, and of the hearth in each Roman home, showed the intention of the people to reproduce and continue their state; it was considered an ill omen for the public fire to go out, an omen of the end of the civilization. But if war threatened the city, the Vestal abbess was considered the appropriate person to mediate a peace.

Vesuna Erinia   An early Italian hearth-goddess like *Vesta*, but married.

Vila   One of the most powerful eastern European goddesses was called Samovila, Vila, or Judy according to the language of the people, who pictured this woodland force as a fair-skinned winged woman with glistening garments and golden hair falling to her feet. She lived deep in the woods, where she guarded animals and plants as well as cleaned streams of rubble and assured sufficient rainfall.

Hunters were wary of beautiful, well-dressed women speaking the languages of animals, for the Vila was fiercely possessive of her wild herds. Should one be injured or—worse yet—killed, the Vila mutilated the offender or lured him into a magic circle and danced him to death. Alternatively, the Vila might bury him in rocks by starting an avalanche, or simply cause him to keel over with a heart attack.

The Vila was able to masquerade as a snake, swan, falcon, horse, or whirlwind. Born on a day of soft misty rain, when the sun formed miniature rainbows on the trees, she knew all the secrets of healing and herb craft. Should a human wish to learn her skills, blood-sisterhood was forged with the Vila. The applicant appeared in the woods before sunrise on a Sunday of the full moon. Drawing a circle with a birch twig or a broom, she placed several horsehairs, a hoof, and some manure inside the circle, then stood with her right foot on the hoof calling to the Vila. Should the spirit appear and be greeted as a sister, the Vila would grant any wish.

Vinata   The Indian Mother of Eagles who argued with her sister; see **Kadru.**

Viran-Akka   Saami hunting-goddess.

Virginia   Roman goddess of politics.

Vitsa-Kuva "Cattleyard lady" lived among the Cheremis people of eastern Russia, appearing every night among the flocks in the folds, a white-dressed lady who caused animals to mate if she liked their owner, thus increasing the family wealth. Woe to the person, however, to whom Vitsa-Kuva took a dislike; she would drive the cattle through the fields all day until, unable to stop long enough to eat, they fell down dead.

Viviane, Chwimbian This Welsh sorceress was stronger even than the mighty magician Merlin, for when Viviane decided to keep Merlin forever as her lover, she bewitched him into believing himself trapped in a high tower, when in fact he sat in the middle of a meadow.

Vodni Panny These Slavic water-goddesses appeared to human eyes as beautiful sad women dressed in green translucent robes; they lived under the rivers in crystal castles surrounded by silver paths.

Volumna Roman goddess of will power.

Voluptas Roman goddess of sensual pleasure.

Voluspa This name, like Volva, was given to wise women in Scandinavia. The most famous seer in Norse legend was the one for whom the poem "Voluspa" is named. Born before this world began, Voluspa was asked to tell the history of the world. Once started, she did not stop, even though the gods did not wish to hear of their own death at Ragnarok, the doom of gods.

Vor Scandinavian goddess of prudence.

Vut-Imi From the Siberian village of Kazym comes this creator-goddess's myth. She first lived on the Arctic Ocean from whence she traveled around the world, occasionally leaving mittens which became rivers, sleds which became hills, and reindeer which became pine trees. After thus creating the Arctic world, she retreated to an island in Lake Num-to, her principal sacred site.

   The highest divinity of the Khanty tribespeople of Kasym and neighboring areas, Vut-Imi was honored with songs at bear festivals, sacrificial fires at other times. Her image was made of sheets of silver or gold; it was kept in a small building near which caldrons were hung on human-shaped hooks. See **Kasum-Naj-Ekva.**

Wahini-Hai The demonic mother figure of Polynesia looked like a seductive woman, except for her protruding eyes and her tongue, hanging to her toes. She sneaked through the world stealing and eating small children.

Wah-Kah-Nee The "drifting maiden" was born among the Chinook people of the Pacific Coast, a people once struck with a terrible endless winter. The ice never moved on the rivers, neither did the warming winds blow across the forests, and people begin to fear for their survival, for they would soon have no food.

   A council was called, and the elders recalled that endless winter always resulted from murdering birds. Each person was asked if he or she had been guilty of such a crime. Everyone denied it. But the children pointed to a little girl who, crying, confessed that she had struck a bird with a stone, and it had died.

   The Chinook dressed the girl in the finest garments and exposed her on a block of ice as an offering to the winter spirits. Almost immediately the ice crashed from the river, and summer came like a flood into the country. Nearly a year later, when the ice again was moving, they saw a block of ice containing the girl's body and fetched it to shore. Miraculously, the girl revived and afterward lived among them a sacred being, able to walk unprotected, even barefoot, through the winter and to communicate with its spirits.

Wakahirume Favorite weaving maiden of the Japanese sun-goddess *Amaterasu*, she died when the evil Susano-o threw a flayed piebald colt through the roof of the Heavenly Weaving Hall. Terrified, she fell onto her shuttle, which fatally punctured her vagina. This so enraged Amaterasu that she closed herself into the Sky-Rock-Cave, and only the creation of the world's first mirror could lure her hence. In some interpretations, Wakahirume is the sun-goddess's younger sister or a younger dawn form of the divinity. See **Amaterasu**.

Waldmichen "The Woodnymph" was a form of *Freya* found in Lower Saxony. Her servants were rabbits; two of them held the train of her cloak while two others lit her way with candles. She lived in a grotto, where a visitor could see the souls of unborn babies cavorting; she owned a mill where she ground old men and women young again.

Walo The Australian aboriginals of Arnhem Land called the sun-goddess by this name and said that she lived with her daughter *Bara* and her sister-in-law, the world-mother *Madalait*, far to the east. Each day Walo journeyed across the sky accompanied by Bara, until one day the sun-goddess realized that the reason the earth was so parched was their combined heat. She sent her daughter back to the east so that the earth could become fertile and bloom.

Walutahanga The eightfold snake-goddess of Melanesia was born to a human mother who was afraid of her husband and hid the serpent girl. But he discovered the deception and, shocked at his daughter's form, cut Walutahanga into eight pieces.

After eight days of rain, the girl's body rejoined into a whole. Walutahanga traveled through the islands, tormenting humans in retaliation for her murder. Captured, she was again chopped into eight pieces and her bones thrown into the sea; everyone except a woman and her daughter ate the goddess's body.

It rained for another eight days. Then the bones under the sea again formed themselves into the goddess. To punish humanity, Walutahanga covered the islands with eight huge flooding waves, which killed everyone but the woman and her child, the only one who had not eaten the goddess's flesh. The goddess gave them many gifts, including coconut and clear-water streams, before again retreating to the ocean.

Wanne Thekla In the Netherlands, this elf queen ruled witches' gatherings; she may have been a form of *Habondia*, ruler of abundance. She is believed to be of Celtic origin.

Waramurungundji, Imberombera The all-creating mother of Australia, she gave birth to the earth and then fashioned all its living creatures. She then taught her creations to talk and divided each language group from the next. She is an analogue of Mother *Kunapipi*.

Wari-Ma-Te-Takere In the Cook Islands of Polynesia, this goddess was "the beginning and the bottom," a coconut-shell divinity who parthenogenetically produced the other gods from her right and left sides.

The first part of her name means "mud," and Wari symbolizes the fertile slime of primordial times.

Wawalag Sisters, Wauwalak Sisters   The civilizers of Australia, these two women wandered the continent domesticating plants into edible foodstuff, evolving language for each territory, and naming all the land's creatures. At the end of their journey, they camped with their children next to the pond where the great mother serpent *Julunggul* lived, a taboo place where menstrual blood was prohibited. Unaware of the taboo, however, the older Wawalag bathed. Julunggul reared out of the water in fury, calling on the skies to drench the women with rain. The women danced and sang, hypnotizing the snake, but every time they stopped she moved toward them. Worn out at last, the Wawalag Sisters fell asleep, and Julunggul swallowed them whole.

But the snake-goddess, when visiting the other supernatural snakes of the universe, was made to feel ashamed for eating the women and their children. She vomited them up; the women were revived by ant bites, but Julunggul could not restrain herself and ate them again. Again she vomited them up. Again she ate them—as she probably does to this day.

Wazit   Original name of *Uadgit*.

Weisse Frauen   The "white women" of Germany and other northern European locations were said to be goddess-worshiping witches who disappeared ages ago into the woods. They lived deep in the forests where they helped lost travelers, foretold the future, and helped the earth produce its fruit by their ritual dances. Some say they were the ghosts of old goddesses, enchanted by Christianity, seeking magic to release them into fuller life again.

Whaitiri   One of the common figures of Polynesian mythology was "blind Grandmother," a powerful figure who owned the thunder and ate human flesh. Once she descended to earth to marry a warrior chief, misunderstanding his title, "man-killer." When Whaitiri had taken up residence with her husband, she found that he did not, after all, share her affection for eating humans. Not only that, but he complained about the smell of their children's excrement. She invented the latrine, showed humans how to use it, and returned to the sky, where she still lives.

White Buffalo Woman, Buffalo Calf Maiden   Ages ago, this sacred woman brought secret knowledge to the Oglala of the midwestern forests and plains. It was said that she first appeared to two young men, a white-clad lady whose clothing was lavishly embroidered with porcupine quills in exquisite patterns.

One of the young men was overtaken by lust, but the second recognized that she was no earthly woman. The first, although warned, could not contain himself; he rushed open-armed toward the woman. She smiled, and a soft white cloud descended to cover their embrace.

When it passed, the woman stood alone with the young man's skeleton at her feet. Smiling, she told the second man that the dead had been awarded just what he sought. She instructed the man to return to his village and set his people to building a huge sacred tent.

Then she entered the village, and the people were enraptured by her presence. Walking seven times around the central fire, she spoke to them, giving them a bag containing a sacred pipe and teaching them the ceremonies that went with these objects. Then, recalling that this was the third of seven revelations to the Oglala, she reminded them of the mysteries of their mother, the earth. Urging them always to honor her, she disappeared in the shape of a white buffalo. See **Ptesan-Wi.**

Wilden Wip   The forest women of Germany were usually seen alone, seeking a human as a playmate. But they disappeared after lovemaking, never staying long enough to share their vast knowledge of healing and magic.

Wlasca   After more than a generation of rule by princesses, the women of Bohemia refused to be led by the magician Przemislaw. Instead, under the leadership of the warrior Wlasca, they drank a magical potion to make them heartless, then killed all the men in their region—lovers and sons included. They ruled themselves for seven years (c. A.D. 690) before Przemislaw took over their fortress by magical means.

Wuriupranili   In northern Australia, this sun-goddess was said to make bark into a torch, carrying the flame through the sky from east to west. At the western sea, she dipped it in the water, then used the embers to guide her under the earth to reach her eastern starting point again. The brilliant skies of dawn and dusk, it was said, came from Wuriupranili's red ochre body paints misting up into the sky as she powdered and beautified her body.

Wurusemu   The Hittite sun-goddess, also called Arinna. Her consort was the weather-god; her rituals were performed by a high priestess, who also ruled the country as queen. See **Hebat.**

Xatel-Ekwa The Hungarian goddess of the sun, who rode through the sky mounted simultaneously on three horses.

Xochiquetzal The goddess of flowers, this Aztec divinity was, like the Roman *Flora*, a deity of sexual license as well. Marigolds were her favorite blooms, but she loved every plant and every creature to such excess that she was sometimes called "bitch mother." Her other names were "flower of the rich plume," "flower-feather," and "blue-skirted lady." Much loved by Aztec women, she was honored with little pottery figurines that showed her with feathers in her hair; these are still frequently unearthed in Mexico.

In some legends, this goddess was the only female survivor of the great flood that destroyed the world preceding this one. With a man, she escaped the torrent in a small boat. Faced with the prospect of repopulating the world, they set to work as soon as the flood receded. But all of their children were born without speech. Finally a pigeon magically endowed them with language, but every child received a different tongue so that each was unable to communicate with the others.

Xoli-Kaltes The Hungarian goddess of the dawn, a hot-blooded young woman who baked men who came to court her.

Yabme-Akka One of the death-goddesses of the Scandinavian Saami was named Yabme-Akka ("old woman of the dead"), a goddess who demanded black cats buried alive to appease her ill temper. Her servant was a blue-clad little man who tortured souls in the afterlife.

Yak Mother earth in Malaysia.

Yamato-Hime-no-Miko Early Japanese princess who, possessed by the goddess *Amaterasu*, founded the Great Shrine at Ise as her sanctuary. See **Amaterasu.**

Yama-Uba Mountain-goddess of the Japanese.

Yamuna One of India's great river-goddesses, ruler of the Jumna.

Yaparamma Business-goddess of eastern India.

Yasodha This Indian heroine was the stepmother of the semidivine Krishna.

Yaya-Zakura This Japanese cherry-tree goddess was a beautiful young woman each spring. She remained celibate while her beauty lasted, only taking lovers when her petals had fallen.

Yebaad Female chief deity to the Navaho.

Yemanja In Brazilian Macumba, this ocean-goddess is seen as the crescent moon; when Venus appears beside it, the love-goddess *Oshun* has come to visit Yemanja.

Yemaya Among the followers of Santeria, she was the beloved mother of 14 divinities or *orishas*. Some of her variants are Yemaya Ataramagwa, the wealthy queen of the sea; stern Yemaya Achabba; violent Yemaya

Oqqutte; and the overpowering Yemaya Olokun, who can be seen only in dreams.

Ymoja The river mother of spirits in the Yoruba area of West Africa, she was a goddess of women, who offered her yams and fowls in the hope of receiving children in return. She evolved, in the new world, into *Yemanja* and *Yemaya*.

Yohuatlicetl Ancient Mexican moon-goddess.

Yolkai Estsan, Yolaikaiason The sister of the turquoise sky-goddess *Estsanatlehi* was a Navaho moon-goddess. Called "white shell woman" because she was made from abalone, she was the ruler of the dawn and the ocean, the creator of fire and maize. Some legends said she was only an aspect of the great Estsanatlehi herself.

Yondung Halmoni An ancient wind-goddess of Korea, she is celebrated in shamanic rituals when she is fed rice cakes. Like many goddesses, she is sometimes transformed into a male god, though her female form takes historical precedence.

Yuki-Onne The "snow maiden" of Japan was the spirit of death by freezing, a calm, pale woman who appeared to the dying, making their passage quiet and painless. To those lost in blizzards, struggling futilely against the cold, she came, soothing them, singing to lull them to sleep, then breathing a deathly cold breath on them.

Once, it was said, a young man and an old one were lost on a snowy mountain. Yuki-Onne appeared, easing the older into death but merely touching the younger, telling him never to speak of their meeting. Terrified, he kept silent when searchers found him and the body of the old man.

Years later he met and married a thin, pale woman named Yuki, with whom he was very happy. One evening, as a storm roared by their home, he casually told her the story of his meeting with the snow maiden—told it as an amusing tale, as though she had been a fantasy. Instantly his wife stood up, her face draining of blood, her body growing thinner until she seemed to be just a bit of snowy mist. In cold fury, she reminded him of his promise that night on the mountain, said that only their children kept her from murdering him, and disappeared.

Zanaru "Lady of the lands," a title of *Ishtar*.

Zaramama, Mamazara The "grain mother" of ancient Peru was occasionally incarnated in her own fields in the form of strangely shaped ears of corn or ears that joined in multiple growths. Sometimes these goddess images were made even more like Zaramama by being dressed as human women in a robe and shawl with a silver clasp. Sometimes, Zaramama came to earth in cornstalks, which were hung by her worshipers on willow trees; festive dances were held around the willows, then the cornstalks were burned, assuring a plentiful supply of corn.

Zarpandit, Zerbanit, Zerbanitu, Zerpanitum, sometimes **Beltis** "Silver-shining," or "seed-creator," in early Assyro-Babylonian pregnant goddess who was worshiped each night as the moon rose.

Zemyna, Zemina, Zemes Mate, Semmes Mate, Zemynele, Sieroji Zemele Because all life came from her, the Lithuanian earth-goddess was honored at the birth of every child, when she was tenderly kissed in the morning and evening; food offerings were laid in front of stones, tied to tree boughs, or cast into flowing water to thank her for the new life.

Her name means simply "earth," and Baltic poems exalt her productiveness by calling her "blossomer," "bud raiser," and "flower-giver." Her special area of concern was plant life—not only foodstuffs but weeds, trees, the algae scum of ponds, the Arctic lichen. Trees with three leaves or nine branches were especially connected with Zemyna; the oak, the linden and the spruce were her favored trees. And of those trees, the most revered part was the top, where the secret of life was believed to hide.

Plant and human life were believed to flow together, with souls taking up residence after death in trees. Women lived on in lindens and spruce; men, in oaks, maples and birches. Virginal young girls survived as lilies; village ancestors resided in fruit trees. The passionate love of the Baltic people for the earth's plant life resounds through the *dainas*, the spiritual and mythological folksongs of the culture. "Green linden, my mother," a poem addresses a tree, or "green oak tree, my father." Even the most familiar tree in the yard easily became the cosmic tree leading to *Saule*'s heaven; the birds that rested or nested there became emblems of the force of life itself.

Zib   *Ishtar* as the evening star that inspires sexual desire.

Zima   Mother Winter to the Masures, a Slavonic group; the festival dedicated to her was similar to that of the Polish *Marzana*.

Zintuki   The granddaughter of *Wurusemu*, the Hittite sun-goddess, of whom little is known.

Zipporah   The magical wife of the Hebrew hero Moses, she could only wed a man who could touch a man-eating tree. Moses, by a miracle, was able to survive the tree's attack, but Zipporah's father then threw him into a deep pit. The girl, however, liked Moses's looks, secretly fed him for seven years, and then suggested to her father that if Moses had survived then he was indeed a man of miracles. Moses, emerging from the pit hale and well fed, became Zipporah's husband. Later in his life, she had to save him from death again—this time by outwitting the evil angel Satan.

Zirna   The Etruscan moon-goddess was the companion of *Turan* and was represented with a half-moon hanging from her neck.

Zisa, Cisa, Ciza   The Germans devoutly honored this goddess in a festival on September 28, suggesting that she was connected with the harvest.

Zlota-Baba   Ugrians and Voguls in Russia once worshiped this goddess in the form of a golden statue which spoke in clanging tones.

Zonget   The ancient goddess of hunting among the Mansi and Khanty of Siberia, she ruled all bird and animal life, as well as those who hunted them. According to her command, birds and animals would either come to the snare or leave it empty. To human eyes she looked like a greyhen, a kind of Arctic bird. See also **Vut-Imi** and **Kasum-Naj-Ekva**.

Zuleika   The most passionate woman of Jewish legend, she is often referred to merely as "Potiphar's wife," as though her own given name were unrecorded. She fervently desired the Hebrew prince Joseph, so much so that she tied him down while she fondled herself in front of him; he, however, utterly rejected her advances at first, though later she nearly had her desire satisfied.

Once, to show her friends how unnerving Joseph's beauty was, she threw a banquet. At each place, she set knives and put oranges on each plate. When Joseph entered, the guests lost awareness of anything but him, cutting their hands unconsciously as they tried to peel their oranges; the table ran with blood and orange juice while the guests felt no pain, entranced by Joseph's presence. Afterward they sympathized with the woman's passion for the man.

Like *Phaedra* and other mythic women, Zuleika got her revenge on Joseph by accusing him of the opposite of his crime. Sick with longing, she contended that he had assaulted her in bed. Joseph was thrown into prison and whipped.

Zytniamatka   Prussian Corn Mother.

Zywie   Polish Great Goddess, "The Living."

· Calendar of Goddess Feasts ·

January 1: Nanshe
January 5: Befana
January 11-15: Carmenta
February 2: Brigid
March 1: Juno, Vesta
March 15: Anna Perenna
March 17: Libera
March 19-23: Minerva
March 25: Mati Syra Zemlja
April 15: Tellus Mater
April 19: Ceres
April 21: Pales
April 28-May 3: Flora
May 1: Maia
May 6: Inghean Bhuidhe
June 9: Vesta
June 11: Matuta
June 21: Aine, Beiwe, Hu-Tu
July 7: Juno
July 25: Furrina
August 15: Diana
August 25: Ops
September 28: Zisa
October 1: Fides
October 13: Camenae
October 21: Ursula
October 31: Carlin
November 15: Feronia
December 1: Bona Dea
December 19: Ops
December 21: Angerona, Beiwe, Colleda, Tonan
December 23: Acca Larentia
December 25-January 6: Frau Holle, Perchta

· Index of Associations ·

SUN

Aega, Aghyu Gugu, Aine, Akewa, Akycha, Amaterasu, Ban Noamha, Bara, Bast, Beiwe, Bila, Bisal-Mariamna, Bomong, Brigid, Chup-Kamui, Dia Griene, Djanggawul Sisters, Etain, Gillagriene, Gnowee, Grian, Hae-Sun, Hathor, Hekoolas, Kanene Ski Amai Yehi, Keca Aba, Kou-Njami, Marici, Medusa, Olwen, Paivatar, Paive, Rind, Rosmerta, Saule, Sekhmet, Shamshu, Shapash, Sulis, Sundi-Mumi, Sunna, Tahc-I, Toyo-Uke, Unelanuhi, Walo, Wuriupranili, Wurusemu, Xatel-Ekwa.

MOON

A, Andromeda, Anunit, Arianrhod, Artemis, Artimpaasa, Auchimalgen, Bil, Britomartis, Candi, Chang-o, Coatlícue, Coyolxauhqui, Dae-Soon, Diana, Europa, Gnatoo, Gorgons, Hanwi, Hecate, Helen, Helle, Hina, Huitaca, Io, Ishtar, Isis, Ix Chel, Juno, Lalal, Leucothea, Luna, Mama Quilla, Mawu, Motali, Pandia, Pero, Perse, Pheraia, Rabie, Ri, Sadarnuna, Selene, Tapa, Teczistecatl, Titania, Tlazoltéotl, Ursula, Yemanja, Yohuatlicetl, Yolkai Estsan, Zarpandit, Zirna.

STARS

Al-Uzza, Andromeda, Astarte, Austrine, Belit-Ilani, Byul-Soon, Cassiopeia, Cynosura, Dilbah, Esther, Gendenwitha, Hesperides, Hulluk Miyumko, Ishtar, Istehar, Lemkechen, Maia, Matariki, Mayi-Mayi, Merope, Nish-Kan-Ru Mat, Omecíhuatl, Pleiades, Saules Meita, Sweigsdunka, Tara, Tou-Mou, Vakyrine, Zib.

SKY

Aditi, Agasaya, Amayicoyondi, Anatu, Aponibolinayen, Atargatis, Azer-Ava, Bau, Chih Nu, Dea Caelestis, Diana, Dione, Estsanatlehi, Ganga, Hannahanna, Hathor, Hebat, Hera, Ilma, Inanna, Irdlirvirisissong, Kuan-Yin, Lemkechen, Luonnotar, Maia, Mawu, Mayáhuel, Mylitta, Naila, Nambi, Nin-Si-Anna, Nu Kua, Nut, Qamaits, Saule, Shauskha, Sirona, Tanith, Tien-Hou, Tlitcaplitana, Uni.

WEATHER

Abhramu (clouds), Anahita, Ardat Lili (storms), Aryong-Jong (rain), Azer-Ava (rain), Bardaichila (storms), Cailleach, Cally Berry, Coatrischie, Dames Vertes (wind), Doda (rain), Feng Pho-Pho (wind), Frau Holle, Fulgora (lightning), Gentle Annie, Gna (wind), Guabancex (wind), Horae, Horephoros, Idothea, Ino (rain), Io (rain), Iphigenia, Irdlirvirisissong (aurora borealis), Iris (rainbow), Julunggul (rainbow), Junkgowa, Kadlu (thunder), Kunapipi (rainbow), Louhi (storm), Mardeq Avalon (wind), Menrva (thunder), Mokosh (rain), Muireartach (storm), Naru-Kami (thunder), Nephele (cloud), Ninlil (wind), Nut, Ochumare (rainbow), Oya (storm), Pa (drought), Panope (storm), Parewhenua-Mea (rain), Perkuna Tete (thunder, lightning), Rauni (thunder), Rudrani (storm), Sao-Ts'ing Niang, Shina-To-Be (wind), Siris (rain), Tasimmet, Tatsuta-Hime (wind), Tempestates (storm), Tien-Mu (lightning), Trung-Trac (rain), Uni (thunder), Whaitiri (thunder), Yondung Halmoni (wind), Yuki-Onne.

LIGHT, DAY

A, Akewa, Alectrona, Anunit, Bau, Bila, Bisal-Mariamna, Bomong, Brigid, Circe, Dag, Diana, Gerd, Helen, Inaras, Jocebed, Kanene Ski Amai Yehi, Lampetia, Lucina, Norwan, Poldunica, Ri, Sala, Sipna, Tanetu, Telphassa, Thea.

DARK, NIGHT

Breksta, Eriskegal, Eumenides, Evaki, Hecate, Khon-Ma, Korrigan, Laima, Leto, Maia, Marinette, Mayáhuel, Nott, Nyx, Rafu-Sen, Rati, Rhiannon, Rukko, Tuonetar, Zarpandit.

DAWN

Aja, Al-Uzza, Amba, Astarte, Atanea, Aurora, Austrine, Bau, Dilbah, Eos, Gendenwitha, Hanwi, Hekt, Hina, Ishtar, Matuta, Tefnut, Thalna, Thea, Ushas, Wakahirume, Xoli-Kaltes, Yolkai Estsan.

EVENING, SUNSET, TWILIGHT

Akusaa, Astarte, Bast, Belit-Ilani, Hanwi, Hesperides, Ishtar, Nephthys, Norwan.

EARTH

Aeracura, Ala, Al-Lat, Altan-Telgey, Ama, Amymone, Anieros, Apia-Fellus, Asase Yaa, The Augralids, Awitelin Tsita, Banba, Becuma, Bercyntia, Beruth, Campestres, Chaabou, Coatlícue, Da, Damkina, Demeter, Dharti Mata, Diti, Ebhlinne, Egime, Erce, Eriu, Etugen, Frigg, Fulla, Gaea, Gefjon, Hegemone, Hertha, Hippia, Hlin, H'Uraru, Hu-Tu, Hybla, Ila, Ja-Neba, Jord, Ki, Lilwani, Luminu-Ut, Madder-Akka, Ma-Emma, Maeve, Mami, Mastor-Ava, Mati, Mawu, Mayáhuel, Medusa, Meter, Mindhal, Mokosh, Mou-Njami, Muk Jauk, Nar, Nerthus, Ninlil, Nokomis, Nott, Nsomeka, Oanuava, Omamama, Omecíhuatl, Onatah, Ops, Oreads, Pandora, Papa, Prithivi, Rhea, Rind, Semele, Shiwanokia, Sita, Tacoma, Taillte, Tamar, Tari Pennu, Teleglen Edzen, Tellus Mater, Themis, Waramurungundji, Yak, Zemyna.

AIR

Gna, Guabancex, Iphigenia, Litae, Mardeq Avalon, Ninlil, Nin-Si-Anna, Norwan, Nut, Poldunica, Shina-To-Be, Tatsuta-Hime, Vairavaraki, Yondung Halmoni.

FIRE

Aetna, Aibheaog, Biliku, Brigid, Brynhild, Caca, Camilla, Chantico, Chuginadak, Darago, Davata, Durga, Dzalarhons, Eos, Feronia, Fuji, Goga, Gula, Hestia, Het, Holika, Izanami, Kupalo, Latiaran, Loo-Wit, Mahui-Iki, Maia, Masaya, Matergabiae, Mylitta, Ocrisia, Oya, Pele, Perasia, Pheraia, Poza-Mama, Radha, Sakkala-Khatun, Tabiti, Tu-Njami, Vesta, Yolkai Estsan.

WATER

Aige, Ailsie, 'Aisha Qandisha, Amberella, Amphitrite, Anadyomene, Anahita, Angeyja, Anuket, Aphrodite, Asherah, Atanea, Atargatis, Atla, Avfruvva, Bentakumari, Benvarry, Boann, Britomartis, Cacce-Jienne, Chalchiúhtlicue, Cipactli, Cleone, Dabaiba, Danae, Doris, Egeria, Fand, Fideal, Galatea,

Gamsu, Ganga, Guabancex, Hsian Fu-Jen, Hypermnestra, Imd, Ix Chel, Julunggul, Juras Mate, Jurate, Khala Kumari, Korobona, Korrigan, Lakshmi, Latis, Liban, Limnades, Louhi, Luonnotar, Ma Tsu-Po, Mem Loimis, Mere-Ama, Miriam, Mulhalmoni, Nahkeeta, Naiads, Nakineitsi, Nammu, Nanshe, Navky, Nemetona, Nereids, Niamh, Nimue, Ningyo, Niobe, Nixies, Nuliayoq, Oshun, Oto-Hime, Ran, Ranu Bai, Rosmerta, Rusalky, Sarasvati, Sarvari, Sayo-Hime, Sinann, Tiamat, Toyota-Mahime, Ved-Ava, Veden Emo, Vellamo, Vodni Panny, Yamuna, Yemanja, Ymoja.

NORTH

Branwen, Helle, Lemkechen, Louhi, Pohjan-Akka, Uadgit.

SOUTH

Hekoolas, Kou-Njami, Nekhebet, Nirriti, Omphale, Rana-Neida.

EAST

Aja, Al-Uzza, Atse Estsan, Aurora, Bau, Bila, Britomartis, Changing Woman, Eos, Hekt, Keca Aba, Matuta, Muireartach, Ninlil, Nish-Kan-Ru Mat, Qamaits, Ushas, Walo, Wuriupranili.

WEST

Akusaa, Ament, Bast, Bo Find, Echtghe, Estanatlehi, Hesperides, Hsi Wang Mu, Kadlu, Niamh, Pali Kongju, Saule.

SPRING

Anna Perenna, Antheia, Beiwe-Neida, Butterfly Maiden, Eostre, Flora, Freya, Frigg, Gauri, Hebe, Hlin, Hrede, Hu-Tu, Kono-Hana-Sakuya-Hime, Kore, Kostrubonko, Libera, Maia, Ma-Ku, Nana, Oniata, Pais, Penelope, Persephone, Proserpine, Rafu-Sen, Rana Neida, Renpet, Rusalky, Vesna, Yaya-Zakura.

SUMMER

Aine, Beiwe, Ceres, Diana, Ebhlinne, Freya, Frigg, Furrina, Inghean Bhuidhe, Kupalo, Luot-Hozjit, Ma-Emma, Olwen, Onatah, Taillte.

AUTUMN

Ahrenkonigin, Anieros, Anna Purna, Athana Lindia, Baba Yaga, Demeter, Feronia, Fides, Idem-Huva, Inari, Latiaran, Mama Allpa, Mamapacha, Morgay, Mother Friday, Pomona, Rugiu Boba, Sif, Tatsuta-Hime, Zisa.

WINTER

Acca Larentia, Angerona, Befana, Black Annis, Bona Dea, Bronach, Cailleach, Cally Berry, Carlin, Carravogue, Colleda, Frau Holle, Louhi, Marzana, Nicnevin, Poshjo-Akka, Rind, Tonan, Tonantzin, Wah-Kah-Nee, Zima.

TIME

At-Em, Juno, Kali, Laima, Menat, Mens, Nortia, Renpet, Savitri, Unelanuhi.

FATE, DESTINY, PROPHECY

Ananke, Antevorta, Auchimalgen, Ban Naomha, Bean Nighe, Bona Dea, Buan, Camenae, Carmenta, Cassandra, Cethlion, Cihuacóatl, Corra, Coventina, Deborah, Dekla, Dione, Dis, Dolya, Egeria, Eve, Feithline, Fortuna, Gestinanna, Gollveig, Hathor, Hecate, Istustaya, Laima, Lavercam, Mamitu, Manto, Masaya, Mati, Menalippe, Menat, Meskhoni, Minu Anni, Miriam, Moirae, Moneta, Morgan Le Fay, Nanshe, Necessitas, Nereids, Nessa, Nisaba, Nixies, Norns, Nortia, Nyx, Oddibjord, Ognyene Maria, Papaya, Parca, Phoebad, Port-Kuva, Postvorta, Pythia, Python, Rachel, Rebecca, Renenet, Sar-Akka, Sarah, Shait, Shauskha, Sheshat, Sibyl, Sirens, Skuld, Sreca, Sudice, Tamar, Tanaquil, Telphusa, Themis, Tien-Hou, Tlazoltéotl, Valkyries, Vegoia, Voluspa, Weisse Frauen.

MAGIC, SORCERY, SHAMANISM

Amaterasu, Angitia, Anuanaitu, Banba, Boann, Carman, Cerridwen, Chlaus-Haistic, Chuginadak, Circe, Devera, Devorgilla, Eriu, Freya, Groa, Hecate, Hekt, Hild, Himiko, Huitaca, Isis, Istehar, Jingo, Jocasta, Junkgowa, Kamrusepas, Kasum-Naj-Ekva, Kongsim, Kuma, Lara, Louhi, Marinette, Medea, Meroe, Moncha, Morrigan, Muses, Nimue, Ninlil, Pali Kongju, Pamphile, Sigurdrifta, Sin, Skuld, Sungmo, Thorgerd, Tlazoltéotl, Uti Hiata, Uzume, Vajravaraki, Vila, Viviane, White Buffalo Woman, Wilden Wip, Wlasca, Zipporah.

FORTUNE, LUCK

Acca Larentia, Benten, Dolya, Fama, Felicitas, Ghar-Jenti, Haltia, Nirriti, Norns, Pi-Hsia Yuan-Chin, Praxidike.

WISDOM

Ceibhfhionn, Danu, Egeria, Gatamdug, Genetaska, Hokkma, Kathirat, Metis, Providentia, Samjuna, Sigurdrifta, Snotra, Tanaquil, Tara, Thordis, Vashti, Vegoia, Veritas, Voluspa, Vor.

BEAUTY

Aega, Antiope, Aphrodite, Bebhionn, Becuma, Blodewedd, Bri, Clidna, Deirdre, Echo, Emer, Fand, Freya, Gerd, Guinevere, Helen, Leanan Sidhe, Lilith, Macha, Morgan Le Fay, Naamah, Niamh, Ningyo, Nixies, Omamama, Oniata, Oona, Oshun, Parvati, Pero, Poldunica, Radha, Rafu-Sen, Rebecca, Rhiannon, Sarah, Scylla, Sedna, Shauskha, Sipna, Sudice, Sunna, Venus.

WEALTH

Aida-Wedo, Amberella, Anu, Benten, Bona Dea, Copia, Fulla, Ganga, Gollveig, Habondia, Hada Bai, Jocebed, Kuan-Yin, Kuma, Lakshmi, Lan Ts'ai-Ho, Liberalitas, Louhi, Maruwa, Menrva, Mokosh, Mutyalamma, Nsomeka, Ops, Sarah, Surabhi, Wanne Thekla, Yaparamma.

SCHOLARSHIP, LEARNING

Aife, Alaghom Naom Tzentel, Brigid, Ceibhfhionn, Danu, Durga, Edda, Fu-Pao, Hiedo-no-Ame, Menrva, Minerva, Mnasa, Mnemosyne, Muses, Nisaba, Saga, Samjuna, Sarasvati, Sheshat, Tou-Mou, Urania.

LAW, JUSTICE, POLITICS

Acval, Ain, Ala, Arete, The Augralids, Basilea, Belit-Seri, Beruryah, Concordia, Daughters of Zelophehad, Deborah, Djigonasee, Egeria, Erinyes, Genetaska, Harmonia, Ishtar, Kadi, Maat, Marcia Proba, Megaera, Metis, Nanshe, Nemesis, Oya, Praxidike, Shait, Syn, Tanaquil, Themis, Thesmophoros, Torah, Tou-Mou, Virginia.

HANDICRAFTS

Arachne (weaving), Athene, Brigid (goldsmithing), Chih Nu (weaving), Dactyls (smithcraft), Eileithyia (spinning), Frau Holle (spinning), Giane (weaving), Gnatoo (tapa), Habetrot (spinning), Hsi-Ling Shih (weaving), India Rosa (pottery, weaving), Ishikore-Dome (smithcraft), Isis (weaving, spinning), Istustaya (spinning), Ix Chebel Yax (weaving, dyeing, spinning), Ix Chel (weaving), Junkgowa, Kanene Ski Amai Yehi (weaving, pottery), Kikinura, La Reine Pedauque (spinning), Lolmusu Deul (ironworking), Mami (pottery), Matergabiae (cooking), Menrva, Minerva, Moirae (spinning), Naru-Kami, Neith (weaving), Numma Moiyuk, Nyapilnu, Paivatar (spinning), Papaya (spinning), Penelope (weaving), Philomena (weaving), Potina (weaving), Rana Neida (spinning), Saule (weaving), Sreca (spinning), Sunna (spinning), Sweigsdunka (weaving), Tatsuta-Hime (weaving), Valkyries (weaving), Wakahirume (weaving).

MUSIC

Bast, Canola, Cred, Graces, Hathor, Hesperides, Huldra, Lan Ts'ai-Ho, Leanan Sidhe, Limnades, Menrva, Minerva, Moriath, Morrigan, Muses, Naamah, Oreads, Parooa, Sarasvati, Savitri, Sibilaneuman, Sirens, Syrinx, Tahc-I, Tlitcaplitana, Urvasi, Uso-Dori, Wawalag Sisters, Yuki-Onne.

ART

Castalia, Crocale, Graces, Hathor, Morgan Le Fay, Muses, Numma Moi-yuk, Sarasvati.

DANCE

Bast, Eurynome, Graces, Hathor, Hit, Huldra, Kali, Laka, Leanan Sidhe, Limoniades, Mahalat, Maya, Muses, Nereids, Nixies, Norwan, Rusalky, Saule, Sibilaneuman, Swan Maidens, Themis, Urvasi, Uzume, Vila, Wawalag Sisters, Weisse Frauen.

POETRY

Brigid, Chysothenius, Cred, Deborah, Eadon, Edda, Fachea, Gonlod, Ila, Karaikkal-Asmmaiyar, Koevasi, Lavercam, Leanan Sidhe, Miriam, Muses, Nausicaa, Saga, Sarasvati, Saule, Savitri, Telesilla.

HEALING, General

Airmed, Ajysyt, Angitia, Argante, Bebhionn, Brigid, Caolainn, Carna, Coventina, Eir, Ganga, Glispa, Groa, Gula, Habetrot, Iaso, Isis, Kamrusepas, Kongsim, Mama, Marahi Devi, Meditrina, Menrva, Minerva, Mokosh, Morgan Le Fay, Neith, Ninhursag, Ninkharak, Ninti, Nirriti, Pali Kongju, Panacea, Pi-Hsia Yuan-Chin, Salus, Sarah, Shatagat, Sitala, Sulis, Thordis, Tlicaplitana, Toci, Tu-Njami, Valetudo, Vila, Wilden Wip.

HEALING, Specialized

Aibheaog (toothache), Airmed (herbs), Angitia (herbs), Buschfrauen (herbs), Caolainn (eyes), Circe (herbs), Dziwozony (herbs), Kaya-Nu-Hima (herbs), Mulhalmoni (eyes), Polydamna (herbs).

TREES

Ailinn (apple), Asherah, Askefruer (ash), Aze (pine), Ba'Alat, Buan (hazel), Carya (walnut), Cuvto-Ava, Daphne (laurel), Druantia (fir), Dryads, Dryope (poplar), Embla (elder), Esther (myrtle), Eve (apple), Fangge, Helen, Heliades (poplar), Hsi Wang Mu (peach), Idunn (apple), Kono-Hana-Sakuya-Hime (cherry), Kualchink, Kupalo (birch), Lotis (lotus), Mayáhuel, Meliae (ash), Myrrha (myrrh), O-Ryu (willow), Philemon (linden), Puta, Rafu-Sen (plum), Rauni (rowan), Renpet (palm), Saosis (acacia), Sarna Burhi, Saule (apple), Uti Hiata (cedar), Venus (cypress), Yaya-Zakura (cherry), Zemyna (oak, linden, spruce).

FLOWERS

Acantha, Blathnat, Blodewedd, Clytie, Flora, Hebe, Lakshmi, Limoniades, Mary, Mehurt, Olwen, Oniata, Smilax, Spes (poppy), Xochiquetzel (marigold).

PLANTS, VEGETATION

Alakhani, Ariadne, Athana Lindia, Basho, Cocomama, Damia, Demeter, Gumshea, Haumea, Itzpapálotl, Limnades, Mentha, Ninsar, Nokomis, Norwan, Ohoyo Osh Chishba, Pandora, Rana Neida, Rauni, Tulsi, Uttu, Venus, Wawalag Sisters, Zemyna.

FOOD: Hunting

Ardwinna, Arganthone, Artemis, Artio, Banka-Mundi, Diana, Flidais, Hastseoltoi, Ja-Neba, Karpophoros, Kasum-Naj-Ekva, Luot-Hozjit, Mielikki, Poshjo-Akka, Pukimna, Sedna, Skogsnufar, Thorgerd, Tuulikki, Uke-Mochi, Umaj, Vanths, Vila, Viran-Akka, Zonget.

FOOD: Farming, Gardening

Abuk, Abundita, Ahrenkonigin, Ala, Anesidora, Anna Purna, Ashnan, Athana Lindia, Carna, Ceres, Charila, Chicomecóatl, Cihuacóatl, Cocomama, Damia, Demeter, Emboq Sri, Eshara, Eumenides, Hainuwele, Haumea, Hegemone, Idem-Huva, Inari, Ino, Junkgowa, Kait, Kornjunfer, Libera, Ma-Emma, Mama Allpa, Mamapacha, Marcia, Metanira, Morgay, Mother Friday, Onatah, Pandora, Pani, Perchta, Po Ino Nogar, Pok Klai, Pomona, Puta, Qocha Mana, Rugiu Boba, Saning Sri, Seia, Selu, Sibilaneuman, Sien-Tsang, Sif, Taranga, Thorgerd, Toyo-Uke, Uke-Mochi, Uti-Hiata, Vacuna, Venus, Zaramama, Zisa, Zytniamatka.

FOOD: Husbandry

Ajysyt, Amalthea, Amashilamma, Beiwe, Challalamma, Damona, Dil, Lahar, Lampetia, Luot-Hozjit, Mala Liath, Pales, Pandora, Pukimna, Vitsa-Kuva.

FOOD: Feasting and Drinking

Ashnan, Bast, Bona Dea, Dis, Dugnai, Flora, Ganymeda, Gauri, Hathor, Hebe, Hedrun, Huitaca, Inaras, Lyssa, Maenads, Maeve, Mami, Mayáhuel, Ninkasi, Potina, Sakkala-Khatun, Sekhmet, Siduri, Siris, Sura, Thyone.

MOUNTAINS

Agdos, Aine, Almha, Anu, Ararat, Banba, Becuma, Cailleach, Cally Berry, Clidna, Cybele, Ebhlinne, Echo, Echtghe, Gauri-Sankar, Hagar, Hsi Wang Mu, Huldra, Ida, Irnini, Jord, Kupapa, Kusumamodini, Magog, Mamapacha, Momu, Ninhursag, Ninkharak, Oreads, Pahto, Poza-Mama, Rhea, Saule, Sicasica, Skadi, Sungmo, Tacoma, Tefnut, Yama-Uba.

VOLCANOES

Aetna, Chimera, Chuginadak, Darago, Dzalarhons, Feronia, Fuji, Iztac-cihuatl, Loo-Wit, Masaya, Pare, Pele.

RUNNING WATER: Rivers, Streams, Fountains

Amymone, Anuket, Arnamentia, Avfruvva, Belisama, Biblys, Boann, Brigan-tia, Camenae, Castalia, Coventina, Danae, Dryope, Egeria, Epona, Fons, Ganga, Korobona, Korrigan, Limnades, Lo Shen, Logia, Mere-Ama, Miriam, Mnemosyne, Mylitta, Nekhebet, Nixies, Oba, Ranu Bai, Rusalky, Sabrina, Saga, Salmacis, Samundra, Sati, Sequana, Sinann, Styx, Sulis, Tacoma, Telphusa, Yamuna, Ymoja.

STILL WATER: Oceans, Seas, Lakes, Pools

Aige, Ailsie, Amberella, Amphitrite, Anuanaitu, Aphrodite, Asherah, Atanea, Atargatis, Bentakumari, Benvarry, Britomartis, Calypso, Ceasg, Cethlion, Ceto, Charybdis, Clidna, Creiddylad, Dea Syria, Dione, Diuturna, Domnu,

Doris, Dubh Lacha, Eurynome, Galatea, Gamsu, Huixtocíhuatl, Idothea, Isis, Julunggul, Junkgowa, Juras Mate, Jurate, Lakshmi, Liban, Lorop, Luaths Lurgann, Luonnotar, Mama Cocha, Mere-Ama, Meri, Morgan Le Fay, Moruadh, Muireartach, Mutyalamma, Naamah, Nahkeeta, Nereids, Niamh, Nuliayoq, Numma Moiyuk, Oceanids, Odras, Oto-Hime, Panope, Pohjan-Akka, Qamaits, Ran, Scylla, Sedna, Sjojungru, Sjora, Tethys, Thetis, Tien-Hou, Toyota-Mahime, Turesh, Vellamo, Walutahanga, Yemanja, Yolkai Estsan.

FORESTS

Ardwinna, Aricia, Artemis, Budhi Pallien, Buschfrauen, Callisto, Cuvto-Ava, Dames Vertes, Dea Dia, Dhat-Badan, Dziwozony, Fangge, Flidais, Giane, Gidne, Gwyllion, Gyhldeptis, Huldra, Irnini, Ivithja, Juno, Keca Aba, Kono-Hana-Sakuya-Hime, Kunapipi, Kupalo, Lignaco-Dex, Mardeq Avalon, Met-sannetsyt, Metsarhatija, Naru-Kami, Nemetona, Ovda, Parooa, Risem-Edne, Skogsnufvar, Vila, Waldmichen, Weisse Frauen, Wilden Wip.

DESERTS

Al-Lat, Al-Uzza, Dhat Badan, Hagar, Menat, Ningal, Pa, Semiramis.

WAR

Aeron, Agasaya, Alecto, Amazons, Anat, Andraste, Ankt, Artemis, Até, Badb, Baduhenna, Bellona, Dilbah, Eohara, Hariasa, Harimela, Menrva, Minerva, Morrigan, Nemain, Ranaghanti, Sinjang Halmoni, Sroya, Vacuna, Valkyries.

PEACE

Athana Lindia, Concordia, Djigonasee, Fengi, Genetaska, Horae, Irene, Kuan-Yin, Mengi, Saga, Turan.

ASCETIC GODDESSES

Kalisha, Karaikkal-Asmmaiyar, Parvati, Tai Yuan, Tara, Vajravaraki, Volumna, Yaya-Zakura.

ANDROGINES AND HERMAPHRODITES

Armaiti, Huligamma, Ia, Iphis, Julunggul, Lan Ts'ai-Ho, Mut, Omecíhuatl, Salmacis, Tai Yuan.

INCESTUOUS GODDESSES

Akycha, Anat, Biblys, Echidna, The Matronit, Nut, Quetzapetlatl, Rebecca, Sarah, Tamar, Unelanuhi.

SHAPESHIFTERS

Aife, Aige, Blodewedd, Carravogue, Cerberus, Cherubim, Dectere, Epona, Hippia, Inari, Iphis, Julunggul, Junkgowa, Kla, Lan Ts'ai-Ho, Lilith, Meta, Nemesis, Pamphile, Spear-Finger, Thetis, Vajravaraki, Valkyries, Vila.

LOVE GODDESSES, General

Artimpaasa, Branwen, Graces, Hnossa, Ingebord, Lofn, Oshun, Radha, Sjofn, Var, Venus.

LOVE GODDESSES, Sex

Absusu, Abtagigi, Achtland, Agrat Bat Mahalat, 'Aisha Qandisha, Anadyomene, Anat, Aphrodite, Astarte, Blathnat, Cotys, Eostre, Flora, Freya, Harmonia, Hathor, Ino, Ishara, Ishtar, Jezebel, Lilith, Mal, Mylitta, Myrrha, Naamah, Plataia, Qadesh, Sheila na Gig, Tlazoltéotl, Turan, Umm Attar, Vacuna, Voluptas, Zib.

LOVE GODDESSES, Fertility

Al-Lat, Anahita, Anna Perenna, Artemis, Asase Yaa, Bo Find, Boann, Deae Matres, Djanggawul Sisters, Epona, Eumenides, Fortuna, Freya, Helen, Hertha, Isong, Madder-Akka, Megaera, Niobe, Numma Moiyuk, Omamama, Po Ino Nogar, Ranu Bai, Ymoja, Zarpandit.

LOVE GODDESSES, Partnership and Affection

Ailinn, Cherubim, Deirdre, Edain, Eri of the Golden Hair, Eurydice, Galatea, Halcyone, Hero, Niamh, Oto-Hime, Penelope, Philemon, Psyche, Pyrrha, Rebecca, Saibya, Sayo-Hime, Zipporah.

AMAZONS, ATHLETES, WARRIORS

Aella, Aife, Aigiarm, Alfhild, Al-Uzza, Amazons, Anahita, Atalanta, Bia, Brynhild, Caenis, Callisto, Camilla, Candace, Cartimandua, Cetnenn, Cyrene, Dejanira, Ess Euchen, Estiu, Galiana, Gondul, Hera, Hervor, Hiera, Hina, Hippo, Hippolyta, Hyrrokin, Jingo, Judith, Luaths Lurgann, Lysippe, Macha, Maeve, Mami, Marpesia, Melanippe, Myrine, Nessa, Omphale, Otrere, Oya, Pantariste, Penthesilea, Pherenice, Qamaits, Sati, Scathach, Semiramis, Sigurdrifta, Strenua, Taillte, Telesilla, Thalestris, Thorgerd, Tiamat, Tomyris, Trung-Trac, Valkyries, Vatiaz, Veleda, Wlasca.

WILD WOMEN AND WANTONS

Achtland, Agave, 'Aisha Qandisha, Anat, Anna Perenna, Antianara, Arianrhod, Asherah, Astarte, Belit-Ilani, Bona Dea, Buschfrauen, Cocomama, Dakini, Dziwozony, Eos, Eostre, Ezili-Freda-Dahomey, Grainne, Ino, Ishtar, Jeh, Kilili, Kunti, Leucippe, Lyssa, Maenads, Maeve, Mylitta, Myrrha, Paphos, Pele, Phyllis, Qadesh, Semele, Semiramis, Sphinx, Thyono, Urvasi, Uohan, Uzume, Vacuna, Wlasca, Xochiquetzal, Zuleika.

BAWDY WOMEN AND LEWD JOKERS

Baubo, Hit, Iambe, Kakia, Sheila na Gig, Siduri, Tlazoltéotl, Uzume.

BOOGEY-WOMEN AND WITCHES

Agrat Bat Mahalat, Baba Yaga, Bila, Black Annis, Broxa, Cailleach, Carman, Ceiuci, Cer, Churalin, Cihuateteo, Dakini, Gollveig, Heith, Jezenky, Kalwadi, Khon-Ma, Kishimogin, Kunapipi, Kveldrida, Lamasthu, Lamia, Lilith, Mabb, Mahalat, Mara, Medea, Meroe, Mormo, Munanna, Myrkrida, Naamah, Nasa, Navky, Orthia, Ovda, Pahto, Parooa, Poldunica, Ptrotka, Rakshasi, Rusalky, Siren, Sneneik, Spear-Finger, Srinmo, Surasa, Tlazoltéotl, Veshtitze, Vila, Vitsa-Kuva, Wahini-Hai, Whaitiri.

SNAKES, DRAGONS, ALLIGATORS, ETC.

Abuk, Aida-Wedo, Angitia, Aspelenie, Bachue, Benten, Britomartis, Campe, Carravogue, Cipactli, Coatlícue, Corchen, Echidna, Eingana, Eurydice, Eurynome, Eve, Ezili-Freda-Dahomey, Gorgons, Hecate, Hekt, Het, Hit, Hydra, Ix Chel, Janguli, Julunggul, Kadi, Kadru, Kunapipi, Lamia, Leviathan, Mafdet, Mamapacha, Manasa, Medea, Medusa, Melusine, Mertseger, Morrigan, Nahab, Nasa, Ninhursag, Nisaba, Nu Kua, Olosa, Pidari, Python, Qadesh, Rhea, Selci Syt Emysyt, Sphinx, Tabiti, Tiamat, Toh Sri Lam, Toyota-Mahime, Turesh, Uadgit, Vanths, Walutahanga.

MAMMALS

Acca Larentia (wolf), Aige (deer), Aine (horse, cattle), Ajysyt (cattle), Amalthea (goat), Amashilamma (cow), Anat (cow), Anu (cat), Artemis (bear), Artio (bear), Audhumbla (cow), Bast (cat, lion), Bo Find (cow), Budhi Pallien (tiger), Callisto (bear), Cybele (lion), Durga (lion), Epona (horse), Eriskegal (lion), Etain (horse), Freya (cat, boar), Glas (cow), Hathor (lion, cow), Hecate (dog, horse), Hedrun (goat), Henwen (pig), Hera (cow), Hippia (horse), Hsi Wang Mu (tiger, cat), Inari (fox), Kuzu-no-Ha (fox), Le-Hev-Hev (rat), Lyssa (dog), Macha (horse), Mafdet (cat, mongoose), Mahakh (dog), Mala Liath (pig), Mehit (lion), Mehurt (cow), Menalippe (horse), Nehalennia (dog), Neith (cow), Ninkharak (dog), Norwan (porcupine), Nut (cow), Pales (cattle), Prithivi (cow), Rhea Silvia (she-wolf), Rhiannon (horse), Rhpisunt (bear), Samjuna (horse), Scylla (dog), Sekhmet (lion), Sibilja (cow), Spako (wolf), Suki (cow), Surabhi (cow), Tauret (hippopotamus), Tefnut (cow, lion), Turrean (dog), White Buffalo Woman.

BIRDS

Aedon, Aife, Aithuia, Asteria, Badb, Barbmo-Akka, Blodewedd, Branwen, Broxa, Caer, Clidna, Corra, Dechtere, Devorgilla, Estiu, Fand, Fionnuala, Frigg, Graeae, Halcyone, Holzweibel, Huitaca, Kasum-Naj-Ekva, Kilili, Liban, Loddis-Edne, Macha, Marinette, Mertseger, Minerva Medica, Morrigan, Munanna, Mut, Natosuelta, Nekhebet, Nemain, Nemesis, Pamphile, Panes, Philomena, Polycaste, Rhiannon, Scylla, Shiju-Gara, Silige Fraulein, Sirens, Siris, Swan Maidens, Tuli, Tundr Ilona, Uairebhuidhe, Uso-Dori, Valkyries, Veshtitze, Vinata, Zonget.

FISH, WHALES, AQUATIC ANIMALS

Amphitrite, Atargatis, Avfruvva, Ban Naomha, Bentakumari, Benvarry, Boann, Britomartis, Ceasg, Ceto, Chelone, Derceto, Hit, Liban, Lorop, Mama Cocha, Mere-Ama, Moruadh, Ningyo, Noogumee, Nuliayoq, Olosa, Sedna, Thalassa.

INSECTS

Arachne, Biliku, Hatai Wugti, Ituana, Itzpapálotl, Kanene Ski Amai Yehi, Le Hev-Hev, Lucina, Melissa, Mellonia, Nasa, Orore, Selkhet, Tsan Nu.

MAIDEN

Alfhild, Antheia, Artemis, Athene, Beiwe-Neida, Britomartis, Butterfly Maiden, Caer, Callisto, Cavillaca, Colleda, Despoina, Eir, Eos, Eostre, Fionnuala, Gefjon, Hathay, Hebe, Kore, Lalita, Ma-Ku, Ninlil, Odras, Oniata, Pais, Pallas, Pare, Persephone, Proserpine, Rafu-Sen, Renpet, Sar-Akka, Saules Meita, Scota, Sheilah, Sreca, Wah-Kah-Nee, Wakahirume, Yamato-Hime-no-Miko, Yaya-Zakura, Yuki-Onne.

MOTHER

Aka, Ama, Amba, Ba'Alat, Bau, Bontene, Ceres, Cybele, Cydippe, Damatres, Damkina, Deae Matres, Demeter, Epona, Eve, Frigg, Genea, Hera, Mami, Meter, Mut, Nowutset, Ocrioia, Oddudua, Ops, Pandora, Papa, Parvati, Renenet, Selci Syt Emysyt, Sundi-Mumi, Tava-Ajk, Tellus Mater, Uti Hiata, Utset, Vesta, Yemaya, Zaramama.

ANCESTRAL MOTHER

Abigail, Abuk, Acca Larentia, Adah, Amaterasu, Ammavaru, Angerboda, Anu, Apasinasee, Asase Yaa, Atabei, Atse Estsan, Awitelina Tsita, Bachue, Bestla, Bhavani, Bilhah, Brigantia, Bugan, Cessair, Claudia Quinta, Dido, Dinah, Dis, Don, Doris, Edda, Embla, Eve, Hagar, Hathor, Helle, Hina, Hybla, Itiba Tahuvava, Ja-Neba, Junkgowa, Kasum-Naj-Ekva, Kuma, Leah, Ligoapup, Luminu-Ut, Mama Ocllo, Mami, Mehurt, Meliae, Mokosh, Mu Olokukurtilisop, Muk Jauk, Mut, Nambi, Nammu, Nana Buluku, Natosuelta, Neith, Niobe, Nu Kua, Numma Moiyuk, Omamama, Otrere, Pali Kongju, Protagenia, Pyrrha, Rachel, Rebecca, Rhpisunt, Sarah, Savitri, Scota, Sela, Tama-yorihime, Toci, Ukepenopfu, Vegoia.

MOTHER CREATOR, GREAT GODDESSES

Aditi, Ararat, Asherah, Ataensic, Atse Estsan, Bhavani, Biliku, Bonto, Cally Berry, Cerridwen, Cipactli, Cleone, Coatlicue, Dabaiba, Danu, Deae Matres, Demeter, Devi, Diti, Eingana, Ekhe-Urani, Epona, Eriu, Eurynome, Eve, Frigg, Gaea, Ganga, Hera, Hina, Ila, Inanna, Indara, India Rosa, Ishtar, Isis, Isong, Ituana, Izanami, Kadru, Kali, Katau Kumei, Khon-Ma, Koevasi, Koro-bona, Kottavi, Kuma, Kunapipi, Kurukulla, Liomarar, Lla-Mo, Lorop, Luon-notar, Madalait, Madder-Akka, Mahakala, Mami, Mawu, Mayáhuel, Mehurt, Mokosh, Muk Jauk, Neith, Nemesis, Ninhursag, Nu Kua, Obatallah, Oma-mama, Omecíhuatl, Parvati, Pheraia, Po Ino Nogar, Qamaits, Radien-Kiedde, Rhea, Sarah, Sar-Akka, Sarasvati, Sedna, Sela, Shiwanokia, Tabiti, Tanith, Tethys, Thalassa, Thetis, Tiamat, Tundr Ilona, Uti Hiata, Vut-Imi, Wara-murungundji, Wari-Ma-Te-Takere, White Buffalo Woman, Yebaad, Zywie.

PARTHENOGENETIC MOTHER

Aditi, Arianrhod, Asase Yaa, Atabei, Ataensic, Bugan, Ceto, Dechtere, Diti, Djanggawul Sisters, Djigonasee, Eurynome, Finchoem, Fu-Pao, Gaea, Hen-wen, Hera, Kongsim, Ligoapup, Luminu-Ut, Mary, Mu Olokukurtilisop, Nana, Neith, Nessa, Nyx, Parvati, Poza-Mama, Shiwanokia, Tai Yuan, Tha-lassa, Tiamat, Wari-Ma-Te-Takere, Wawalag Sisters.

MOTHER PROTECTOR

Abeona, Adeona, Agave, Alemona, Anahita, Aphrodite, Auchimalgen, Caireen, Cerberus, Cuba, Cydippe, Dakini, Dea Nutrix, Djigonasee, Edusa, Ess Euchen, Europa, Fides, Fionnuala, Fylgja, Gnowee, Gula, Hlin, Hlodyn, Juks-Akka, Kasum-Naj-Ekva, Kishimogin, Korobona, Kuan-Yin, Lasa, Mac-ris, Matuta, Nut, Pi-Hsia Yuan-Chin, Rumina, Sarah, Sasura, Saule, Tabiti, Taranga, Tauret, Tien-Hou, Uks-Akka, Umaj.

CRONE

Baba Yaga, Befana, Bronach, Bugady Musun, Cailleach, Cally Berry, Chera, Edda, Eileithyia, Ess Euchen, Goga, Graeae, Hathay, Haumea, Hecate, Hel,

Hsi Wang Mu, Menat, Mnasa, Muireartach, Nirriti, Nokomis, Ohoyo Osh Chishba, Pele, Poldunica, Sarah, Sedna, Sheila na Gig, Sibyl, Spear-Finger, Sreca, Sudice, Ukepenopfu, Voluspa, Weisse Frauen, Whaitiri.

BIRTH, REBIRTH

Ajysyt, Artemis, Cihuateteo, Decima, Devayani, Eileithyia, Ermutu, Erua, Eve, Ituana, Ix Chel, Latona, Leto, Lucina, Madder-Akka, Mawu, Meng-Po Niang-Niang, Meskhoni, Nagar-Saga, Neith, Ninhursag, Nintur, Nona, Partula, Persephone, Saibya, Samsin Halmoni, Sar-Akka, Sasti, Saule, Savitri, Selkhet, Sheila na Gig, Sheol, Sinjang Halmoni, Skuld, Tu-Njami, Uks-Akka, Umaj, Ved-Ava, Vesta, Waldmichen, Wari-Ma-Te-Takere, Ymoja, Zarpandit, Zemyna.

MIDWIVES

Adamanthea, Artemis, Ban-Chuideachaidh Moire, Bhavani, Biddy Mannion, Candelifera, Carmenta, Cynosura, Dekla, Egeria, Eileithyia, Ermutu, Haumea, Hekt, Intercidona, Jocebed, Kapo, Luaths Lurgann, Mabb, Maia, Mami, Meskhoni, Miriam, Pi-Hsia Yuan-Chin, Postvorta, Sar-Akka, Uks-Akka, Umaj, Uni, Vagitanus.

WOMEN'S CYCLES, MENSTRUATION

Adamu, Jaki, Juno, Kali, Luperca, Mens.

HOUSEHOLD, HEARTH

Anna Purna, Aspelenie, Athene, Caca, Cardea, Chinnintamma, Chuang-Mu, Dugnai, Fornax, Ghar-Jenti, Gorgons, Groa, Haltia, Hestia, Hlin, Hlodyn, Kamui Fuchi, Kikimora, Laugo-Edne, Matergabiae, Port-Kuva, Poza-Mama, Silkie, Tu-Njami, Uks-Akka, Vesta, Vesuna Erinia.

OUTHOUSE, TOILET

No-Il Ja-Dae, Tsi-Ku, Whaitiri.

INDEX OF ASSOCIATIONS

DEATH: Grief

Achall, Aedon, Airmed, Althaea, Antigone, Banshee, Buan, Carman, Clytemnestra, Demeter, Etain, Isis, Korobona, Lysippe, Nana, Niobe, Polycaste.

DEATH: Suicide

Andraste, Arachne, Arria, Brynhild, Charila, Dido, Erigone, Hathay, Ia, Ixtab, Jocasta, Macaria, Metzli, Nuliayoq, Otiona, Pare, Phyllis, Rusalky, Sati, Scylla, Sphinx, Tsuru.

DEATH: Underworld

Ahemait, Ala, Alecto, Ambika, Angerona, Ariadne, Asase Yaa, Atalanta, Belit-Seri, Blathnat, Ceres, Clidna, Coatlícue, Erinyes, Eriskegal, Eve, Freya, Hathor, Hecate, Hel, Hikuleo, Hina, Husbishag, Ishtar, Izanami, Kali, Kalma, Kurukulla, Lara, Lyssa, Mahakala, Mahui-Iki, Malophoros, Mania, Mari-Ama, Meilichia, Mem Loimis, Mertseger, Mictecacíhuatl, Miru, Modgud, Natosuelta, Nephthys, Ninazu, Ninkigal, Persephone, Pohjan-Akka, Proserpine, Qamaits, Rhiannon, Saosis, Sati, Satine, Sedna, Semele, Sheila na Gig, Snutqutxals, Spes, Styx, Tellus Mater, Tsun Kyankse, Tuchulcha, Tuonetar, Vanths, Yabme-Akka, Yuki-Onne.

DEATH: Spirit Guides

Ament, Cihuateteo, Fylgja, Harpies, Hindi, Iro Duget, Le-Hev-Hev, Libitina, Maat, Maman Brigitte, Mania, Marzana, The Matronit, Miru, Modgud, Naenia, Neith, Poza-Mama, Qebhsnuf, Ran, Selkhet, Shait, Sirens, Sphinx, Srinmo, Styx, Vanths, Yabme-Akka, Yuki-Onne.

DEATH: Punishment

Aura, Cer, Clytemnestra, Cyone, Erinyes.

REVENGE

Althaea, Antigone, Anuanaitu, Caenis, Clytemnestra, Echenais, Electra, Erinyes, Furrina, Hecate, Itzpapálotl, Lemna, Medea, Melusine, Minachiamman, Munanna, Nemesis, No-Il Ja-Dae, Pele, Philomena, Poine, Praxidike, Sita, Skadi, Valkyries, Var, Zuleika.

RAPED GODDESSES

Akycha, Alcippe, Asteria, Austrine, Caenis, Cybele, Cyone, Danae, Daphne, Dryope, Hera, Hina, Leda, Lotis, Marpessa, Menalippe, Merope, Nemesis, Nessa, Ninlil, Oreithyia, Penthesilea, Persephone, Philomena, Proserpine, Rhea, Saules Meita, Syrinx.

VICTIM GODDESSES

Athaliah, Bebhionn, Iphigenia, Meta, Sedna, Sheilah, Vashti, Wakahirume, Walutahanga.

·Index of Alternative Names & Minor Goddesses·

Aberewa. See Asase Yaa.
Ablabaiae. Alternative name for Eumenides.
Abunciada. See Habondia.
Abyzu. See Lilith.
Acheloides. Patronymic of Sirens.
Acidalia. Aphrodite as fountain-goddess.
Adi Maya. Alternative name for Lakshmi.
Aeaea. Circe, named for her island.
Aebh. See Fionnuala.
Aedg. Mother of Fand and Etain.
Aegeria. See Egeria.
Aegilae. One of the Heliades.
Aegle. One of the Heliades.
Aello. See Harpies.
Aelo. See Harpies.
Aertha. See Hertha.
Aetheria. One of the Heliades.
Aethra. An Oceanid.
Afka. See Mylitta.
Agirope. Alternative name for Eurydice.
Aglaia. See Graces.
Aglaope. One of the Sirens.
Aglauros. See The Augralids.
Ahsonnutli. See Estsanatlehi.
Ailbe. Mother of Deirdre's lover.
Ailbhe. Same as Ailbe.
Aine An Cnuic. "Aine of the Hill," see Aine.
Ainippe. An Amazon warrior.
Aisyt. See Ajysyt.
Aja. See A.
Akko. See Rauni.
Akraia. A title of Hera.
Alagabiae. See Deae Matres.
Alcyone. See Halcyone and Pleiades.
Aletheia. Greek name for Veritas.

Alera. See Turan.

Alexandra. See Cassandra.

Alfhild Solglands. A name for Sunnu.

Alfsol. "Elf-sun," a name for Sunnu.

Alicibie. One of Penthesilea's troupe of Amazons.

Alilat. See Al-Lat.

Allita. See Al-Lat.

Alpanu. See Turan.

Alukah. See Allatu.

Amadubad. See Mami.

Amara. See Mamapacha.

Amatudda. See Mami.

Amaunet. See Ogdoad.

Amber. See Amba.

Ambrosia. One of the Hyades.

Ameretet. See Armaiti.

Amma. See Edda.

Amudubad. See Mami.

Anagita. See Angitia.

Anaitis. Greek for Anahita.

Anchiale. Mother of the Dactyls.

Andarta. See Artio.

Ane. See Ala.

Anelanuhi. See Unelanuhi.

Ani. See Mami.

Anit. See Anat.

Ankamma. See Ammavaru.

Anna. See Hannah.

Anta. See Anat.

Antandre. An Amazon who fought with Penthesilea.

Antibrote. An Amazon who fought with Penthesilea.

Antum. See Anatu.

Anukis. Greek for Anuket.

Aobh. See Fionnuala.

Aoide. See Muses.

Apet. See Tauret.

Aphek. See Mylitta.

Aphrodita. Italian for Aphrodite.

Apito. Alternative name for Atabei.

Apsaras. See Urvasi.

Aranrot. Early Welsh for Arianrhod.

Ardvi Sura Anahita. See Anahita.

Aridella. The deified Ariadne.

Arinna. See Wurusemu.
Ariope. Another name for Telphassa.
Ariu. Sister of Liban.
Arktos. Name for Callisto.
Arnakuagsak. "Old Sea-Woman," Sedna.
Arnarkuagssak. "Old Sea-Woman," Sedna.
Arrand. Alternative name for Aine.
Artini. Etruscan Artemis.
Artumes. Etruscan Artemis.
Asakhira. See Ishara.
Asase Efua. See Asase Yaa.
As-Ava. See Azer-Ava.
Ashdar. See Ishtar.
Asrapas. See Dakini.
Assa. The girl Nessa.
Astateia. Alternative name for Artemis.
Asterope. See Pleiades.
Athirat. Alternative name for Asherah.
Athtarath. See Astarte.
Atira. See H' Uraru.
Atlantides. The Pleiades.
Atropos. Oldest of the Moirae.
Attabeira. Alternative name for Atabei.
Aughty. See Echtghe.
Auiocersa. Daughter of Anicros.
Autonoe. "Wise unto herself," sister of Agave.
Auxo. See Graces.
Avilacoq. Name for Sedna as a human girl.
Axlocersa. Same as Auiocersa.

B

Baaltis. See Ba'Alat.
Bacchantes. See Maenads.
Ban-Ava. See Azer-Ava.
Banbh. See Banba.
Bandae. Alternative name for Banna.
Banna. Goddess of River Bann; see Sequana.
Banna Naomha. See Ban Naomha.
Barbelina. Alternative name for Saules Meita.
Base. Cappadocian alternative name for Athene.
Be Bind. See Behhionn.

Bechuille. Powerful Irish witch; see Carman.

Begoe. See Vegoia.

Belili. See Ba'Alat.

Belit-Matate. "Lady of Lands," Babylonian title of Ninlil.

Beltis. See Ba'Alat, Zarpandit.

Benzaiten. See Benten.

Bera. Alternative name for Scota.

Berchta. See Perchta.

Berlusianhena. Alternative name for Deae Matres.

Berooch. Irish mermaid.

Bertha. "Swan," alternative name for Freya.

Bhagvati. See Mindhal.

Bhdrakali. "Gracious" Kali.

Bildjiwuraroju. See Djanggawul Sisters.

Birrin. Daughter of Cessair.

Blaithine. See Blathnat.

Blama. Daughter-in-law of Cessair.

Blanaid. Maid to Ethne.

Bo Dhu. See Bo Find.

Bo Ruadh. See Bo Find.

Boabhan Sith. Highland Scots Banshee.

Boadicca. See Andraste.

Boba. Lithuanian Baba.

Bohu. See Bau.

Bokoj. See Tu-Njami.

Boudicca. See Andraste.

Boulaia. "Counselor," alternative name for Athene.

Bouvinda. Alternative name for Boann.

Brauronia. "Bear," alternative name for Artemis or Callisto.

Bremusa. An Amazon who fought with Penthesilea.

Briant. Welsh river-goddess; see Sequana.

Brigandu. Continental Celtic alternative name for Brigid.

Bubona. See Epona.

Buffalo Calf Maiden. See White Buffalo Woman.

Buschgrossmutter. See Buschfrauen.

Buto. See Uadgit.

C

Caelestis. See Tanith.

Caileach Cinn Boirne. See Bronach.

Cailleach Beara. See Cailleach.

Caitileen Og. See Clidna.
Calaeno. See Pleiades.
Calliope. See Muses.
Callipateira. See Pherenice.
Callirrhoë. Mother of Echidna.
Candika. "Fearful," alternative name for Kali, Durga.
Caprotina. Alternative name for Juno.
Carley. See Carlin.
Carline. See Carlin.
Carme. Mother of Britomartis; same as Charmel.
Carpo. See Horae.
Cat Ana. See Anu.
Celaeno. See Harpies.
Chalaiope. Sister of Medea.
Chamaine. Alternative name for Demeter.
Charis. See Graces.
Charites. See Graces.
Charmel. Mother of Britomartis; same as Carme.
Chia. See Huitaca.
Ch'll Kongju. "Seventh Princess," alternative name for Pali Kongju.
Chloris. See Flora, Niobe.
Chokmah. See Hokkma.
Chuan Hou. Alternative name for Tien-Hou.
Chunwang. See Sungmo.
Chwimbian. Welsh name for Viviane.
Cihuapipiltin. See Cihuateteo.
Cinxia. Alternative name for Juno.
Citlalinicue. See Omecîhuatl.
Ciza. See Zisa.
Cledoxa. One of Niobe's murdered daughters.
Cleodora. One of the Danaids.
Cleta. See Graces.
Clio. See Muses.
Cliodna. See Clidna.
Clonie. One of Penthesilea's troupe of Amazons.
Clotho. See Moirae.
Clothru. See Maeve.
Clutoida. Celtic goddess of Clyde River; see Sequana.
Cora. See Kore.
Cordelia. See Creiddylad.
Coronis. One of the Hyades.
Creidwy. See Cerridwen.
Crota. Mother of Pasiphae

Crete. Same as Creta.

Culsa. See Vanths.

Cupra. See Turan.

Cynthia. Alternative name for Artemis.

Cypris. Alternative name for Aphrodite.

Cytherea. Alternative name for Aphrodite.

D

Dah-Ko-Bed. See Tacoma.

Darine. See Fithir.

Dea Artio. See Artio.

Decca. See Fionnuala.

Decima. See Nona.

Deichtire. See Dechtere.

Deino. See Graeae.

Delia. Alternative name for Artemis.

Deliphobe. A Sibyl.

Delphyne. See Python.

Dendritus. See Helen.

Devo Dukryte. "God's Daughter," alternative name for Saule.

Devona. Goddess of Devon River; see Sequana.

Dhat-Hami. See Dhat-Badan.

Dia. See Dea Dia.

Dice. See Horae.

Dictynna. See Britomartis.

Digi No Duineach. See Digne.

Dii Involuti. Roman alternative name for Moirae.

Dike. See Horae.

Dindymene. Alternative name for Cybele.

Dirae. "Curses," alternative name for Erinyes.

Dirphya. Alternative name for Hera.

Discordia. Roman alternative name for Eris.

Dishimogin. See Churalin.

Dji Sisnaxitl. Alternative name for Qamaits.

Domiduca. See Juno.

Dwyn. Alternative name for Branwen.

Dwynacm. Alternative name for Branwen.

E

Edarlahm. Mother of Erinn.
Edji. See Eve.
Egee. An Amazon general of Libya; see Myrine.
Eidothea. See Idothea.
Eirene. See Irene.
Eithinoha. See Nokomis.
Eka Obasi. See Isong.
Ekki. See Aka.
Elissa. See Dido.
Elpis. See Spes.
Enyo. See Graeae.
Eodain. See Leanan Sidhe.
Ephesia. Alternative name for Artemis.
Epicaste. Alternative name for Jocasta.
Erato. See Muses.
Erda. See Hertha.
Ergane. "Worker," alternative name for Athena.
Erioboa. An Amazon.
Erytheis. See Hesperides.
Estine. See Estiu.
Ethlenn. See Ethne.
Eudora. One of the Hyades.
Eunomia. See Horae.
Euphrosyne. See Graces.
Euryale. See Gorgons.
Euterpe. See Muses.
Evadne. One of Penthesilea's troupe of Amazons.

F

Fadzja. See Tu-Njami.
Fainen. See Weisse Frauen.
Fakahoutu. Alternative name for Papa.
Fata Morgana. See Morgan Le Fay.
Fates. See Moirae.
Fatua. See Bona Dea.
Fauna. See Bona Dea.
Fea. "Hateful," alternative name for Morrigan.
Fenya. See Fengi.
Finda. See Fionnuala.

Fiorgyn. See Frigg, Hertha, Jord.
Firgunia. Alternative name for Hertha.
Fland. See Flidais.
Fluusa. Early Italian alternative name for Flora.
Folta. See Banba, Eriu.
Frau Harke. See Hertha.
Frau Herke. See Hertha.
Friis Avfruvva. See Avfruvva.
Fru Gode. Thuringian, Saxon alternative name for Frau Holle.
Furiae. See Erinyes.
Furies. See Erinyes.
Fyorgyn. See Frigg, Hertha, Jord.

G

Garbhog. See Carravogue.
Ge. See Gaea.
Gefn. Alternative name for Freya.
Geirronul. "Spear-Bearer," a Valkyrie.
Gello. See Lilith.
Gemmyo. See Hiedo-no-Ame.
Gentle Hannie. See Gentle Annie.
Gersimi. See Freya.
Gheareagain. See Carravogue.
Gilou. Alternative name for Lilith.
Girya. "Mistress of House," alternative name for Parvati.
Glauce. A Nereid.
Grandmother Toad. Ketq Skwayne; see Ataensic.
Grania. See Grainne.
Gratia. See Graces.
Grimhild. See Brynhild.
Guacarapita. Alternative name for Atabei.
Gudrun. See Brynhild.
Guimazoa. Alternative name for Atabei.
Gunabibi. See Kunapipi.
Gunlad. See Gonlod.
Guth. A Valkyrie.
Gwenhyfar. See Guinevere.
Gwragedd Annwn. Welsh lake maiden; see Nimue.

H

Hadassah. See Esther.

Hakahotu. Alternative name for Papa.

Hallat. See Al-Lat.

Hamadryads. See Dryads.

Haminga. Alternative name for Fylgja.

Harmonthoe. One of Penthesilea's troupe of Amazons.

Hauket. See Ogdoad.

Haurvatat. See Armaiti.

Heh. See Het.

Heian. Alternative name for Pele.

Heid. Alternative name for Gollveig.

Helde. "Brilliant," alternative name for Valkyries.

Hemera. See Eos, Nyx.

Heng-O. See Chang-O.

Hepatu. See Hebat.

Herentas. Early Italian form of Venus.

Herfjoter. "Panic-Terror," a Valkyrie.

Herophile. A Sibyl, daughter of Lamia.

Herse. "Dew," one of the Augralids.

Hespera. Sunset, last phase of Eos.

Hgoptchae Poridok. "Seventh Princess," alternative name for Pali Kongju.

Hiiaka. See Pele.

Himaji. "The Pearly," alternative name for Parvati.

Himbuto. See Uadgit.

Himeropa. One of the Sirens.

Hippothoe. "Impetuous Mare," Amazon who fought with Penthesilea.

Hiqult. See Hekt.

Hlok. "Shrieker," a Valkyrie.

Hluodana. Alternative name for Hertha.

Holle. See Frau Holle.

Holzfraulein. See Holzweibel.

Hora. Roman name for Graces.

Horn. Alternative name for Freya.

Horsel. See Ursula.

Horta. Alternative name for Angerona.

Hozbrauen. See Holzweibel.

Hrist. "Shaker," a Valkyrie.

Hua-Henga. See Taranga.

Hypsipyle. Queen of Lemnos; see Lemna.

I

Iaine. See Ain.
Ianthe. See Iphis.
Idaean Mother. See Ida.
Idya. An Oceanid, mother of Medea.
Iella. Alternative name for Atabei.
Iha-Naga. See Kono-Hana-Sakuya-Hime.
Ilamatecuhtli. See Tonan.
Ilia. See Rhea Silvia.
Ilithyia. See Eileithyia.
Imberombera. See Waramurungundji.
Ina. See Hira.
Innini. See Inanna.
Iord. See Hertha, Jord.
Irpa. See Thorgerd.
Iscah. Alternative name for Sarah.
Ishah. Alternative name for Eve.
Istaru. See Ishtar.

J

Jana. See Diana.
Judy. Alternative name for Vila.
Jurt-Azer-Ava. See Azer-Ava.
Juterna. See Diuturna.
Juventes. Roman version of Hebe.

K

Kadesh. See Qadesh.
Kala-Pidari. See Pidari.
Kalas-Ava. See Azer-Ava.
Kalika. See Kali.
Kamilla. See Camilla.
Kami-Naru. See Naru-Kami.
Kamui Katkimat. See Nish-Kan-Ru Mat.
Kandi. Alternative name for Durga.
Kandra. Alternative name for Durga.
Kara. One of the Valkyries.
Kardas-Jurt-Ava. See Azer-Ava.

Kauket. See Ogdoad.
Kaumaii. Alternative name for Shakti.
Kausiki. Alternative name for Durga.
Kerres. Early Italian Ceres.
Kesara. See Cessair.
Ketche Avalon. See Keca Aba.
Kethlenda. See Cethlion.
Kidaria. Alternative name for Demeter.
Kirisha. See Ki.
Kishar. See Ki.
Kleio. See Muses.
Klete. See Graces.
Klotho. See Moirae.
Korobonako. See Korobona.
Korythalia. Alternative name for Artemis.
Kotta-Kiriya. See Kottavi.
Kubaba. See Kupapa.
Kubabat. See Kupapa.
Kubele. See Cybele.
Kud-Azer-Ava. See Azer-Ava.
Kumari. Alternative name for Shakti.
Kururumany. See Korobona.
Kwannon. See Kuan-Yin.
Kweetoo. See Kadlu.
Kyn-Fylgja. See Fylgja

L

Lachesis. See Moirae.
Lair Derg. See Aine.
Lakhamu. See Lamamu.
Lamethusa. One of the Heliades.
Larentia. See Lara.
Lat. See Al-Lat.
Leucosia. One of the Sirens.
Leucothea. See Ino.
Lhianna Shee. See Leanan Sidhe.
Licho. Slavic Dolya.
Liganakdikei. See Lignaco-Dex.
Ligeia. One of the Sirens.
Ligoububfanu. See Ligoapup.
Likko. Slavic Dolya.

Liomarar. See Lorop.
Ljod. A Valkyrie.
Locha. See Maeve.
Locia Amai. See Tu-Njami.
Loddis-Edne. See Barbmo-Akka.
Lolita. See Lalita.
Losna. See Lalal.
Louisa. "Kindly," alternative name for Demeter.
Luatia. Alternative name for Juno.
Lucina. Alternative name for Juno.
Lucitia. Alternative name for Juno.
Lucna. See Lalal.
Lung Nu. See Kuan-Yin.
Luot Chozjik. See Luot-Hozjit.
Lusia. "Kindly," alternative name for Demeter.

M

Maan-Eno. See Rauni.
Maga. Mother of Dechtere.
Mahamaya. See Maya.
Mahuea. See Mahui-Iki.
Makhut. See The Matronit.
Malina. See Akycha.
Mamazara. See Zaramama.
Maniae. "Madnesses," alternative name for Erinyes.
Mara. See Mora.
Marai Mata. See Sitala.
Mardol. Alternative name for Freya.
Marena. Alternative name for Marzana.
Marga. Mother of Etain; same as Margo.
Margo. Mother of Etain; same as Marga.
Marpe. An Amazon warrior.
Martialis. Alternative name for Juno.
Marwe. See Maruwa.
Mastor-Ava. See Azer-Ava.
Mater Larum. See Lara.
Mater Turritia. Roman alternative name for Cybele.
Matronae. See Deae Matres.
Maut. See Mut.
Mebhdh. See Maeve.
Mechanites. Alternative name for Athene.

Megaera. See Metanira, Erinyes.

Megaira. One of the Erinyes.

Mei Chou. See Tien-Hou.

Melete. See Muses.

Melpomene. See Muses.

Mene. See Selene.

Mengi. See Fengi.

Menya. See Fengi.

Meskhent. See Meskhoni.

Mestra. See Meta.

Miao Shan. See Kuan-Yin.

Minithya. Alternative name for Thalestris.

Minthe. See Mentha.

Miralaidji. See Djanggawul Sisters.

Mist. "Mist," a Valkyrie.

Mitylena. See Myrine.

Mitylene. See Myrine.

Mneme. See Muses.

Modron. British alternative name for Matrona.

Momona. Alternative name for Atabei.

Morana. See Marzana.

Mor-Ava. See Azer-Ava.

Morrigu. See Morrigan.

Mortlock. See Lorop.

Moruach. See Moruadh.

Mothir. See Edda.

Mousae. See Muses.

Muilearthach. See Muireartach.

Muiriath. See Moriath.

Mujingga. See Kalwadi.

Mumuna. See Kunapipi.

Muta. Alternative name for Lara.

N

Nair. See Nar.

Naotsiti. See Utset.

Nar-Azer-Ava. See Azer-Ava.

Nata. See Nana.

Naunet. See Ogdoad.

Nea. See Niamh.

Nebthet. See Nephthys.

Nedolya. Alternative form of Dolya.
Neeve. See Niamh.
Neeve of the Golden Hair. See Niamh.
Neptunis. Alternative form of Artemis.
Nerrivik. See Sedna.
Nesreca. Alternative form of Sreca.
Net. See Neith.
Niang-Niang Sung-Tzu. Alternative name for Pi-Hsia Yuan-Chin.
Nicostrata. See Carmenta.
Nikkal. See Ningal.
Nina. See Nana.
Nin-Edin. See Belit-Seri.
Nini. See Inanna.
Ninmu. See Ninsar.
Nirdu. Alternative name for Hertha.
Niski-Ava. See Azer-Ava.
Nomoi. See Lorop.
Norov-Ava. See Azer-Ava.
Nowutset. See Utset.
Nox. See Nyx.

O

Obasi Nsi. See Isong.
Ocypete. See Harpies.
Ocyrrhoe. See Menalippe.
Oettar-Fylgja. See Fylgja.
Oiorpata. "Men-Killers," Scythian word for Amazons.
Onaugh. See Oona.
Opet. See Tauret.
Oreithyia. Queen of Amazons.
Orithya. Queen of Amazons.
Orsel. See Ursula.
Orthosia. Alternative name for Artemis.
Ostara. See Eostre.
Otsuved-Azer-Ava. See Azer-Ava.

P

Pachamama. See Mamapacha.
Padma. See Lakshmi.

Pajau Tan. See Po Ino Nogar.

Paks-Ava. See Azer-Ava.

Palagia. "Sea," alternative name for Aphrodite.

Pandrosos. See The Augralids.

Papaya. See Istustaya.

Parthenia. "Virgin," alternative form of Athene and Hera.

Parthenope. One of the Sirens.

Pasht. See Bast.

Pasikrateia. Alternative name for Persephone and Artemis.

Pasithea. A Nereid; alternative name for Aglaia of the Graces.

Pax. Alternative name for Concordia.

Peisinoe. One of the Sirens.

Pemphredo. See Graeae.

Per Uadjit. See Uadgit.

Perrephatta. Alternative name for Persephone.

Persipnei. Etruscan alternative name for Persephone.

Phaenna. See Graces.

Phatusa. One of the Heliades.

Pheme. See Fama.

Phillippis. An Amazon.

Phlea. "Fruitful," alternative name for Demeter.

Phoebe. Alternative name for Selene.

Phratria. "Lawgiver," alternative name for Athene.

Pinga. Alternative name for Sedna.

Pitali. See Pidari.

Plutos. "Richness," alternative name for Persephone.

Po Bya Tikuh. See Po Ino Nogar.

Po Yan Dari. See Po Ino Nogar.

Poldare. A Harpy.

Polyhymnia. See Muses.

Polymnia. See Muses.

Pontia. Alternative name for Aphrodite.

Populonia. Alternative name for Juno.

Porne. "Titillator," alternative name for Aphrodite.

Posidaeia. See Mnasa.

Potnia. See Mnasa.

Potniae. "Awful ones," alternative name for Erinyes.

Prajna. "Wisdom," alternative name for Sarasvati.

Prascovia. Alternative name for Mother Friday.

Praxidikae. "Vengeful ones," alternative name for Erinyes.

Primigenia. "Firstborn," alternative name for Fortuna.

Promoakkos. "Fore-fighter," alternative name for Athene.

Pronuba. Alternative name for Juno.

Prothoe. Famous Amazon warrior.
Prothyraea. Alternative name for Giane.
Pyatnitsa. Alternative name for Mother Friday.

R

Rangild. "Shield-Bearer," a Valkyrie.
Rata. See Laka.
Rathgild. "Plan-Destroyer," a Valkyrie.
Raura. "Fierce," alternative name for Durga.
Rav-Ava. See Azer-Ava.
Ravdna. See Rauni.
Raz-Akka. See Madder-Akka.
Re. See Ri.
Regina. "Queen," alternative name for Juno.
Reginleif. "Companion of Gods," a Valkyrie.
Rheda. See Hrede.
Roonikka. See Rauni.
Rota. A Valkyrie.

S

Saar. See Saba.
Sabbath. See Sambatu.
Sabitu. See Siduri.
Sadsta-Akka. See Sar-Akka.
Sakhmis. Greek for Sekhmet.
Sammuramat. See Semiramis.
Samovila. Alternative name for Vila.
Sangarius. Alternative name for Nata.
Saranya. See Samjuna.
Sar-Edne. See Sar-Akka.
Sata-Rupa. Alternative name for Savitri.
Saturnia. Alternative name for Juno.
Seena. See Sinann.
Seewa. See Mother Friday.
Segetia. See Seia.
Semmes Mate. See Zemyna.
Semnae. "Kindly ones," alternative name for Erinyes.
Sengen Sama. See Kono-Hana-Sakuya-Hime.
Sentu. See Nintur.

Senuna. See Sinann.
Seqinek. See Akycha.
Serk. See Selkhet.
Seshatu. See Sheshat.
Sessrymner. "Large-wombed," alternative name for Freya.
Shala. See Shulamite.
Shamash. See Shapash.
Sheng-Mu. "Holy Mother," alternative name for Pi-Hsia Yuan-Chin.
Shitla. See Sitala.
Shri. See Lakshmi.
Sibilla. See Weisse Frauen.
Sieroji Zemele. See Zemyna.
Silvia. See Rhea Silvia.
Sirdu. See A.
Sirrida. See A.
Skabas-Ava. See Azer-Ava.
Skegjold. A Valkyrie.
Skeyh. "Axe-time," a Valkyrie.
Skile-Qvinde. Alternative name for Sar-Akka.
Skogol. "Raging one," a Valkyrie.
Smrt. Bohemian alternative name for Marzana.
Smyrna. See Myrrha.
Sol. See Sunna.
Sospita. Alternative name for Juno.
Spakona. See Voluspa.
Spakonur. See Voluspa.
Spider Woman. See Hatai Wugti.
Sri Laksmi. See Lakshmi.
Sterope. See Pleiades.
Sthenno. See Gorgons.
Stone-Dress. See Spear-Finger.
Suada. See Pitho.
Suadela. See Pitho.
Subharda. Alternative name for Lakshmi.
Sulevia. Alternative name for Brigid.
Sumi-Zome-Zakura. Alternative name for Yaya-Zakura.
Syama. "Darkness," alternative name for Durga.
Syr. "Sow," alternative name for Freya.

T

Tacita. Alternative name for Lara.

Tacobud. See Tacoma.

Takkobad. See Tacoma.

Takobid. See Tacoma.

Talar-Disir. See Disir.

Talliju. Katmandu, alternative name for Tulsi.

Tamamo-no-Maye. See Inari.

Tamtu. See Tiamat.

Taurice. Alternative name for Artemis.

Taygeta. See Pleiades.

Taygete. See Pleiades.

Tea. See Taillte.

Tehoma. See Tacoma.

Tenso-Daijun. Alternative name for Amaterasu.

Terpsichore. See Muses.

Teteoinnan. See Toci.

Tetetka. See Kasum-Naj-Ekva.

Thaleia. See Graces.

Thalia. See Muses.

Thallo. See Horae.

Theira. Alternative form of Hera.

Thelchtereia. One of the Sirens.

Thermodosa. An Amazon in Penthesilea's troupe.

Thesmophoros. Alternative name for Demeter.

Thung. Alternative name for Freya.

Thurd. "Might," daughter of Sif.

Thurgai. See Minachiamman.

Thyiades. See Maenads.

T'ien Hsien. "Heavenly Immortal," alternative name for Pi-Hsia Yuan-Chin.

Tifantina. Alternative name for Diana.

Tisiphone. See Erinyes.

Tkuriz. See Tu-Njami.

Tlaltecuhtli. See Cipactli.

Toeris. See Tauret.

Togo Musun. See Tu-Njami.

Tol-Ava. See Azer-Ava.

Toyo-Uke-Bime. See Uke-Mochi.

Trivia. "Three," alternative name for Diana.

Trung-Nhi. See Trung-Trac.

Tsonoqua. See Sneneik.

Turachoque. Alternative name for Bachue.
Tutilina. See Seia.
Tuurm. See Tu-Njami.
Tyche. See Fortuna.
Tzitzimitl. See Mayáhuel.

U

Uathach. Daughter of Scathach.
Uazit. See Uadgit.
Uinigumissuintung. "Refuser of husbands," alternative name for Sedna.
Uma. See Amba, Ganga, Parvati.
Umm. See Ama.
Urd. See Norns.
Uretsiti. See Utset.
Ursa Major. See Callisto.
Uto. See Uadgit.
Uzza. See Al-Uzza.

V

Vach. See Sarasvati.
Valnad. Swedish alternative name for Fylgja.
Vama. "Left-handed," alternative name for Devi.
Vanabruder. See Freya.
Vanadis. See Freya.
Vardogr. Norwegian alternative name for Fylgja.
Vari-Ma-Te-Takere. See Wari-Ma-Te-Takere.
Varma-Ava. See Azer-Ava.
Varuni. See Gauri.
Verdandi. See Norns.
Vergilia. Roman alternative name for Pleiades.
Vete-Ema. Alternative name for Mere-Ama.
Vir-Ava. See Azer-Ava.
Vir-Azer-Ava. See Azer-Ava.
Volla. See Fulla.
Volon. See Voluspa.
Volva. See Voluspa, Gollveig.

W

Wang-Mu Niang-Niang. See Hsi Wang Mu.
Weiwobo. See Hsi Wang Mu.
Werzelya. Abyssinian alternative name for Lilith.
Wisin Wif. See Nixies.

Y

Yauni. See Ganga.
Yu Nu. "Jade Maiden," alternative name for Pi-Hsia Yuan-Chin.

Z

Zemes Mate. See Zemyna.
Zemynele. See Zemyna.
Zerbanit. See Zarpandit.
Ziva. See Siva.

·Bibliography·

ADAMS, CHARLES, ed. *Reader's Guide to the Great Religions.* 2nd ed. New York: The Macmillan Company, 1977.

AKURGAL, EKREM. *The Art of the Hittites.* New York: Harry N. Abrams, Inc., n.d.

ALBRIGHT, WILLIAM FOXWELL. *Yahweh and the Gods of Canaan.* New York: Doubleday & Co., 1968.

ANATI, E. *Palestine Before the Hebrews.* New York: Alfred A. Knopf, 1963.

ANDERSON, JORGEN. *The Witch on the Wall.* London: George Allen & Unwin, Ltd., 1977.

ANDRUPS, JANIS and KALVE, VITAUTS. *Latvian Literature: Essays.* Stockholm: M. Goppers, 1954.

ARRIAGA, PABLO JOSEPH DE. *The Extirpation of Idolatry in Peru.* Translated and edited by L. Clark Keating. Lexington, Ky.: University of Kentucky Press, 1968.

ASHE, GEOFFREY. *The Virgin.* London: Routledge and Kegan Paul, 1976.

BABB, LAWRENCE A. *The Divine Hierarchy: Popular Hinduism in Central India.* New York: Columbia University Press, 1975.

BACHOFEN, J.J. *Myth, Religion, and Mother Right.* Translated by Ralph Manheim. Bollingen Series. Princeton: Princeton University Press, 1967.

BAILY, CYRIL. *Religion of Ancient Rome.* London: Archibald Constable & Co., 1970.

BANKS, MRS. M. MACLEOD. *British Calendar Customs, Vol. 2: Scotland.* London: William Glaisher, Ltd., 1939.

BAROJA, JULIO GARO. *The World of the Witches.* Translated by O.N.V. Glendenning. Chicago: University of Chicago Press, 1964.

BATCHELOR, JOHN. *The Ainu of Japan.* London: The Religious Tract Society, 1892.

BENJAMINS, ESO. *Dearest Goddess.* Virginia: Current Nine Publications, 1985.

BENNETT, FLORENCE MARY. *Religious Cults Associated with the Amazons.* New York: AMS Press, 1967.

BHROLCHAIN, MURREAN NI. "Images of Woman in Early Irish Myths and Sagas." *The Crane Bag,* 4, No. 1: The Irish Woman. Dublin: Blackwater Press (1977-1981).

BIERHORST, JOHN. *The Mythology of North America.* New York: William Morrow & Co., Inc., 1985.

BLACKER, CARMEN. *The Catalpa Bow: A Study of Shamanistic Practices in Japan.* London: George Allen & Unwin, Ltd., 1982.

BLEEKER, C.J. *Hathor and Thoth: Two Key Figures in the Ancient Egyptian Religion.* Leiden: E. J. Brill, 1973.

BLOC, RAYMOND. *The Ancient Civilization of the Etruscans.* Translated by James Hogarth. New York: Cowles Books Co., 1969.

413

_____. *The Etruscans.* New York: Praeger Publishers, 1956.

BOAS, FRANZ. *The Central Eskimo.* 1888. Reprint. Lincoln, Neb.: University of Nebraska Press, 1964.

_____. *The Eskimo of Baffin Land and Hudson Bay. Bulletin* of the American Museum of Natural History, 15 (1901).

BORD, JANET and BORD, COLIN. *The Secret Country.* New York: Walker & Co., 1977.

BRANDON, S.G.F., ed. *Dictionary of Comparative Religion.* New York: Charles Scribner's, 1970.

BRANSON, BRIAN. *Gods of the North.* New York: Vanguard Press, 1955.

BRATTON, FRED GLADSTONE. *Myths and Legends of the Ancient Near East.* New York: Thomas Crowell, 1970.

BRAY, FRANK CHAPIN. *Bray's University Dictionary of Mythology.* New York: Thomas Crowell, 1935.

BRIGGS, KATHERINE. *An Encyclopedia of Fairies.* New York: Pantheon Books, 1967.

BROWN, CHEEVER MACKENZIE. *God as Mother.* Hartford, Vt.: Claude Stark & Co., 1974.

BROWN, VINSON. *Voices of Earth and Sky.* Harrisburg, Pa.: Stackpole Books, 1975.

BUDGE, E.A. WALLIS. *The Gods of the Egyptians: Studies in Egyptian Mythology.* vol. 1. New York: Dover Publications, Inc., 1969.

BUTTRICH, et al. *Interpreter's Dictionary of the Bible.* New York: Abingdon Press, 1962.

CAMPBELL, JOHN G. *Popular Tales of the West Highlands.* Edinburgh: Edmonston and Douglas, 1862.

_____. *Superstitions of the Scottish Highlands.* Glasgow: James MacLehose and Sons, 1900.

CAMPBELL, JOSEPH. *The Masks of God.* 4 vols.: *Oriental Mythology, Primitive Mythology, Occidental Mythology, Creative Mythology.* New York: The Viking Press, 1959-1965.

CAMPBELL, JOSEPH R. *The Fians.* London: David Nutt, 1891.

CHAMBERLAIN, BASIL HALL. *Ainu Folktales.* London: Folklore Society XXII, 1888.

CHAPMAN, JOHN W. *Ten'a Texts and Tales from Anuik, Alaska.* vol. 6. Publications of the American Ethnological Society. Leiden: E. J. Brill, 1914.

CLARK, ELLA. *Indian Legends of the Pacific Northwest.* Berkeley: University of California Press, 1953.

CONVERSE, HARRIET MAXWELL. *Myths and Legends of the New York Iroquois.* Port Washington, N.Y.: Ira J. Friedman, 1962.

COVELL, ALAN CARTER. *Ecstasy: Shamanism in Korea.* Elizabeth, N.J.: Hollym International Corp., 1983.

COXWELL, C. FILLINGHAM. *Siberian and Other Folk-Tales: Primitive Literature from the Empire of the Tzars.* London: The C.W. Daniel Company, 1925.

CRAWFORD, O.S.G. *The Eye Goddess.* London: Phoenix House, 1957.

CROSS, S.H. *Slavic Civilization through the Ages.* Edited by L.I. Strakhovsky. Cambridge: Harvard University Press, 1948.

CROSSLEY-HOLLAND, KEVIN. *The Norse Myths.* New York: Pantheon Books, 1980.

CURTIN, JEREMIAH. *Creation Myths of Primitive America.* 1898. Reprint. New York: Benjamin Blom, Inc., 1969.

————. *Myths and Folklore of Ireland.* Boston: Little, Brown, & Company, 1890.

DANAHER, KEVIN. *The Year in Ireland: A Calendar.* Cork: The Mercier Press, 1977.

DANIELOU, ALAIN. *Hindu Polytheism.* Bollingen Series. New York: Pantheon Books, 1964.

DAVIDSON, H.E. and GELLER, PETER. *The Chariot of the Sun and Other Rites and Symbols of the Northern Bronze Age.* New York: Praeger Publishers, 1969.

DAVIDSON, HILDA ELLIS. *Scandinavian Mythology.* London: Hamlyn Publishing, 1969.

DAVIS, ELIZABETH GOULD. *The First Sex.* New York: Penguin Books, 1971.

DE JUBAINVILLE, H. D'ARBOIS. *The Irish Mythological Cycle and Celtic Mythology.* Dublin: Hodges, Figgis & Co., 1903.

DEIGHTON, HILARY J. *The Weather-God in Hittite Anatolia: An Examination of the Archaeological and Textual Sources.* BAR International Series, 143 (1982).

DEUTSCH, HELENE. *A Psychoanalytic Study of the Myth of Dionysus and Apollo.* New York: International University Press, 1969.

DILLON, MYLES, ed. *Irish Sagas.* Cork: Mercier Press, 1968.

DIOSZEGI, V., ed. *Popular Beliefs and Folklore Traditions in Siberia.* Bloomington, Ind.: Indiana University Press, 1968.

DIOSZEGI, V. and HOPPAL, M. eds. *Shamanism in Siberia.* Budapest: Akademiai Kaido, 1978.

DOMITOR, TECKLA. *Hungarian Folk Beliefs.* Bloomington, Ind.: Indiana University Press, 1982.

DORSEY, GEORGE. *Traditions of the Arikara.* Washington, D.C.: Carnegie Institute, 1904.

DOWSON, JOHN. *A Classical Dictionary of Hindu Mythology.* London: Trubner & Co., 1874.

DRAGAMANOV, M.P. *Notes on the Slavic Religio-Ethical Legends.* Russian and Eastern European Series, vol. 23. Bloomington, Ind.: Indiana University Press, 1961.

DUMEZIL, GEORGES. *Archaic Roman Religions.* vols. 1 & 2. Translated by Philip Krapp. Chicago: University of Chicago Press, 1966.

————. *Gods of the Ancient Northmen.* Edited by Enar Haugen. Los Angeles: University of California Press, 1973.

DURDIN-ROBERTSON, LAWRENCE. *Goddesses of India, Tibet, China and Japan.* Ireland: Caesara Publications, 1976.

————. *The Goddesses of Chaldea, Syria, and Egypt.* Ireland: Caesera Publications, 1975.

EASTMAN, ELAINE GOODALE. *Indian Legends Retold.* Boston: Little, Brown & Company, 1929.

ELLIS, HILDA RODERICK. *The Road to Hel.* New York: Greenwood Press, 1968.

ELWIN, VERRIER. *Myths of the North-East Frontier of India.* Shillong: North-East Frontier Agency, 1958.

————. *Tribal Myths of Orissa.* Edited by Richard M. Dorson. Oxford: Geoffrey Cumberledge, 1954.

EMERSON, NATHANIEL B. *Pele and Hiiaka: A Myth from Hawaii.* Tokyo: Charles Tuttle Co., 1978.

ERDOES, RICHARD and ORTIZ, ALFONSO, eds. *American Indian Myths and Legends.* New York: Pantheon Books, 1984.

EVANS, ARTHUR. *The Earlier Religion of Greece in Light of Cretan Discoveries.* London: The Macmillan Company, 1937.

FERGUSON, JOHN. *Encyclopedia of Mysticism.* New York: Seabury Press, 1977.

————. *The Religions of the Roman Empire.* Ithaca, N.Y.: Cornell University Press, 1970.

FERM, VERGILIUS, ed. *Forgotten Religions.* New York: The Philosophical Library, Inc., 1950.

FLOOD, J.M. *Ireland: Its Myths and Legends.* London: Kennikat Press, 1916.

FOREMAN, CAROLYN THOMAS. *Indian Women Chiefs.* Washington, D.C.: Zenger Publishing Co., Inc., 1954.

FORLONG, J.G.R. *Encyclopedia of Religions.* New York: University Books, 1964.

FOWLER, W.W. *Roman Ideas of Deity.* Freeport, N.Y.: Books for Libraries Press, 1914.

FRAZER, SIR JAMES GEORGE. *The Golden Bough,* 3rd ed. New York: The Macmillan Company, 1935.

GARBER, CLARK. *Stories and Legends of the Bering Strait Eskimo.* Boston: Christopher Publishing House, 1940.

GASTER, THEODOR. *Thespis, Ritual, Myth and Drama in the Ancient Near East.* Garden City, N.Y.: Doubleday Anchor Books, 1961.

GIDDINGS, J.L. *Kobuk River People.* College, Alaska: University of Alaska, Department of Anthropology and Geography, Studies of Northern People, No. 1, 1961.

GIMBUTAS, MARIJA. *Gods and Goddesses of Old Europe.* Berkeley: University of California Press, 1974.

————. *The Slavs.* New York: Praeger Publishers, 1971.

————. *The Balts.* New York: Praeger Publishers, 1963.

GINZBERG, LOUIS. *Legends of the Jews.* Translated by Henrietta Szold. Philadelphia: Jewish Publishing Society of America, 1909.

GOLDENBERG, NAOMI. *Changing of the Gods.* Boston: Beacon Press, 1979.

GRAVES, ROBERT. *The Greek Myths.* 2 vols. Baltimore, Md.: Penguin Books, 1955.

GRAY, L.H., ed. *Myths of All Races.* 13 vols. New York: Cooper Square Publishers, 1946.

GREENWAY, JOHN, ed. *The Primitive Reader.* Hatboro, Pa.: Folklore Associates, 1965.

GRIMM, JACOB. *Teutonic Mythology.* Translated by James Steven Stallybrass. London: G. Bell & Sons, 1883.

GUERBER, H.A. *Myths of Northern Lands.* Detroit, Mich.: Singing Tree Press, 1970.

GURNEY, O.R. *Some Aspects of Hittite Religion.* Oxford: Oxford University Press, 1977.

GUYOT, CHARLES. *The Legend of the City of Ys.* Translated by Deirdre Cavanaugh. Amherst, Mass.: University of Massachusetts Press, 1979.

HACKIN, J., et al. *Asiatic Mythology.* New York: Thomas Crowell, 1963.

HARRISON, JANE ELLEN. *Prolegomena to the Study of Greek Religion.* 1903. Reprint. New York: Meridian Books, 1955.

HASTINGS, JAMES, ed. *Encyclopedia of Religion and Ethics.* New York: Charles Scribner's, 1924.

HAWKES, JACQUETTA. *Dawn of the Gods.* New York: Random House, 1968.

HENDERSON, JOSEPH, and OAKES, MAUD. *The Wisdom of the Serpent.* New York: George Braziller, 1963.

HERODOTUS. *The Histories of Herodotus of Helicarnassus.* Translated by Henry Carter. Baltimore, Md.: The Heritage Press, 1959.

HINNELLS, JOHN R. *Persian Mythology.* London: Hamlyn Publishing, 1973.

HOCH-SMITH, JUDITH and SPRING, ANITA. *Women in Ritual and Symbolic Roles.* New York: Plenum Press, 1978.

HODDINOTT, R.F. *The Thracians.* London: Thames & Hudson, 1981.

HOOKE, S.H. *Middle Eastern Mythology.* Baltimore, Md.: Penguin Books, 1963.

HOOKHAM, HILDA. *A Short History of China.* New York: New American Library, 1969.

HUBERT, HENRI. *The Greatness and Decline of the Celts.* London: Kegan Paul, Trench Brubner and Co., 1934.

HULL, ELEANOR. *The Cuchulain Saga in Irish Literature.* London: David Nutt, 1898.

HUTTER, CATHERINE. *The Norsemen.* Greenwich, Conn.: New York Graphic Society Publications, Ltd., 1965.

HYDE, DOUGLAS, tr. *Beside the Fire: A Collection of Irish Gaelic Folk Stories.* New York: Lemma Publishing, 1973.

————. *A Literary History of Ireland.* London: T. Fisher Unwin Ltd., 1899.

IDOWU, E. BOLAJI. *African Traditional Religion.* Maryknoll, N.Y.: Orbis Books, 1973.

JACKSON, KENNETH HURLSTONE, tr. *A Celtic Miscellany.* New York: Penguin Books, 1971.

JAMES, E.O. *Prehistoric Religion.* New York: Praeger Publishers, 1957.

JENNESS, DIAMOND. *The Corn Goddess and Other Tales from Indian Canada.* Bulletin no. 141, Anthropological Series no. 319. Ottawa: National Museums of Canada, n.d.

JOCHELSON, W. with SUVOROV and YACHMENEFF. *Aleut Traditions.* Fairbanks, Alaska: Native Language Center, 1977.

JOYCE, P.W. *Old Celtic Romances.* New York: Devin-Adair, 1962.

JUNG, C.G. and KERENYI, K. *Essays on a Science of Mythology.* Bollingen Series. Princeton: Princeton University Press, 1949.

KARSTEN, RAFAEL. *The Religion of the Sameks.* Leiden: E. J. Brill, 1955.

KATZENELEBOGEN, URIAH. *The Daina: An Anthology of Lithuanian and Latvian Folk-Songs.* Chicago: Lithuanian News Publishing Company, 1935.

KENNEDY, PATRICK. *Legendary Fictions of the Irish Celts.* London: The Macmillan Company, 1866.

KERENYI, KARL. *Athene: Virgin and Mother.* Translated by Murray Stein. Houston, Tex.: Spring Publications, 1978.

————. *Zeus and Hera.* Bollingen Series. Princeton: Princeton University Press, 1975.

KINSELLA, THOMAS, tr. *Tain bo Cuaillnge.* Dublin: Dolmen Press, 1969.

KINSLEY, DAVID. *Hindu Goddesses: Visions of the Divine Feminine in the Hindu Religious Tradition.* Berkeley: University of California Press, 1986.
_____. *The Sword and the Flute.* Berkeley: University of California Press, 1975.
KIRK, G.S. *The Nature of Greek Myths.* Woodstock, N.Y.: The Overlook Press, 1975.
KRAMER, S.N. *The Sacred Marriage Rite.* Bloomington, Ind.: Indiana University Press, 1969.
KUHN, A.B. *The Lost Light.* Elizabeth, N.J.: Academy Press, 1940.
KUPELRUD, ARVID. *The Violent Goddess: Anat in the Ras Shamra Texts.* Oslo: Universitets-forlaget, 1969.
LAING, GORDON J. *Survivals of Roman Religion.* New York: Cooper Square Publishers, 1963.
LAWRENCE, D.H. *Etruscan Places.* New York: The Viking Press, 1932.
LELAND, CHARLES. *Algonquin Legends of New England.* Boston: Houghton Mifflin Company, 1884. Reprint. Detroit: Singing Tree Press, 1968.
LICHTHEIM, M. *Ancient Egyptian Literature: A Book of Readings. Vol. 2: The New Kingdom.* Berkeley: University of California Press, 1976.
LOGAN, PATRICK. *The Holy Wells of Ireland.* Gerrards Cross: Colin Smythe, 1980.
_____. *The Old Gods: The Facts about Irish Fairies.* Berkeley, Calif.: Appletree Press, 1981.
LONNROT, ELIAS. *The Old Kalevala and Certain Antecedents.* Prose translations with foreword and appendices by Francis Peabody Magou, Jr. Cambridge: Harvard University Press, 1969.
MACALISTER, R.A.S. *The Archaeology of Ireland.* London: Methuen & Co., 1928.
MACGREGOR, A.A. *The Peat-Fire.* Scotland: The Moray Press, n.d.
MACKENZIE, DONALD. *Egyptian Myth and Legend.* London: The Gresham Publishing Co., 1907.
_____. *The Myths of China and Japan.* London: The Gresham Publishing Company, 1923.
MACNEILL, MAIRE. *The Festival of Lughnasa.* 2 vols. Dublin: Comhairle Bhealoideas Eireann, 1982.
MAILS, THOMAS E. *The People Called Apache.* Englewood Cliffs, N.J.: Prentice-Hall, 1974.
MARRIOTT, ALICE and RACHLIN, CAROL. *American Indian Mythology.* New York: Thomas Crowell, 1968.
MCILWRAITH, T.F. *The Bella Coola Indians.* Toronto: University of Toronto Press, 1948.
MCKAY, JOHN G. *More West Highland Tales.* vol. 2. Edinburgh: Oliver and Byrd, 1960.
MCNEILL, F. MARIAN. *The Silver Bough.* Glasgow: William Maclellan, 1959.
METRAUX, ALFRED. *Voodoo in Haiti.* Translated by Hugo Charteris. New York: Oxford University Press, 1959.
MILLS, CLARK and LANDSBIRGIS, ALBIRGIS. *The Green Linden: Selected Lithuanian Folksongs.* New York: Voyages Press, 1962.
MOOR, EDWARD. *The Hindu Pantheon.* Delhi: Indological Bookstore, 1968.

MUELLER, F. MAX and DORSON, RICHARD M., eds. *Peasant Customs and Savage Myths: Selections from the British Folklorists.* vol. 1. Chicago: University of Chicago Press, 1968.

MUNRO, NEIL G. *Ainu: Creed and Cult.* New York: Columbia University Press, 1965.

NEUMANN, ERICH. *The Great Mother.* Translated by Ralph Manheim. New York: Pantheon Books, 1963.

NICHOLSON, IRENE. *Mexican and Central American Mythology.* London: Hamlyn Publishing, 1967.

NILSSON, MARTIN. *Greek Folk Religion.* New York: Harper Torchbooks, 1965.

O'CONNOR, NORREY JEPHSON. *Battles and Enchantments.* Freeport, N.Y.: Books for Libraries Press, 1922.

O'FAOLAIN, SEAN. *The Silver Branch.* Freeport, N.Y.: Books for Libraries Press, 1968.

O'FLAHERTY, WENDY DONIGER. *Hindu Myths.* Baltimore, Md.: Penguin Books, 1975.

O'HEOCHAIDH, SEAN. *Fairy Legends of Donegal.* Translated by Maire MacNeill. Dublin: Comhairle Bhealoideas Eireann, 1977.

O'RAHILLY, T.F. *Early Irish History and Myth.* Dublin: Institute of Advanced Studies, 1957.

OCHS, CAROL. *The Myth Behind the Sex of God.* Boston: Beacon Press, 1977.

OINAS, FELIX J. and SOUDAKOFF, STEPHEN, trs. *The Study of Russian Folklore.* Hawthorne, N.Y.: Mouton Publishers, 1975.

OSBORNE, HAROLD. *South American Mythology.* London: Hamlyn Publishing, 1968.

PAKRASI, MIRA. *Folk Tales of Assam.* vol. 3. Mystic, Conn.: Lawrence Verry Inc., 1970.

PARK, YONG JUM. *Traditional Tales of Old Korea.* Seoul: Hanguk Munkwa Publishing Company, 1974.

PARKER, DEREK and PARKER, JULIA. *The Immortals.* New York: McGraw-Hill Book Co., 1976.

PARRINGER, GEOFFREY. *A Dictionary of Non-Christian Religion.* Philadelphia: Westminster Press, 1971.

_____. *West African Religion.* London: The Epworth Press, 1949.

PATAI, RAPHAEL. *The Hebrew Goddess.* New York: KTAV Publishers, 1967.

PATON, C.I. *Manx Calendar Customs.* London: London Folklore Society, William Glaisher, Ltd., 1934.

PAULSON, IVAR. *The Old Estonian Folk Religion.* Translated by J.K. Kitching and H. Kovamees. Bloomington, Ind.: Indiana University Press, 1971.

PERSSON, AXEL W. *The Religion of Greece in Prehistoric Times.* Berkeley: University of California Press, 1942.

POLLARD, JOHN. *Seers, Shrines and Sirens.* London: George Allen & Unwin, Ltd., 1965.

POWERS, WILLIAM K. *Oglala Religion.* Lincoln, Neb.: University of Nebraska Press, 1975.

RAFY, K.U. *Folktales of the Khasis.* New York: The Macmillan Company, 1920.

RANKE, KURT. *Folktales of Germany.* Translated by Lotte Baumann. Chicago: University of Chicago Press, 1966.

REICHARD, GLADYS. *Navaho Religion: A Study of Symbolism.* Bollingen Series. New York: Pantheon Books, 1950.

RHYS, JOHN. *Celtic Folklore.* Oxford: Clarendon Press, 1901.

RICE, PATTY. *Amber, The Golden Gem of the Ages.* New York: Van Nostrand Reinhold Co., Inc., 1974.

RINK, JOHANNES. *Tales and Traditions of the Eskimo.* London: W. Blackwood & Sons, 1875.

ROBERT, J.J.M. *The Earliest Semitic Pantheon: A Study of the Semitic Deities Attested in Mesopotamia Before Ur III.* Baltimore, Md.: The Johns Hopkins University Press, 1972.

ROHEIM, GEZA. *Hungarian and Vogul Mythology.* Seattle, Wash.: University of Washington Press, 1954.

RUSH, ANNE KENT. *Moon Moon.* New York: Random House/Moon Books, 1976.

RUSKIN, JOHN. *Queen of the Air.* New York: Hurst & Company, n.d.

RYDBERG, VICTOR. *Teutonic Mythology.* New York: Norroema Society, 1907.

SEBEOK, THOMAS A., and INGEMANN, FRANCES J. *Studies in Cheremis: The Supernatural.* New York: Viking Fund Publications in Anthropology, No. 22, 1956.

SEROS, KATHLEEN, adaptor. *Sun and Moon: Fairy Tales from Korea.* Elizabeth, N.J.: Hollym International Corporation, 1982.

SOBOL, DONALD. *The Amazons of Greek Myth.* New York: A.S. Barnes & Co., 1972.

SOUPAUL, RE. *Breton Folktales.* London: G. Bell & Sons, 1971.

SPENCE, LEWIS. *The Minor Traditions of British Mythology.* New York: Benjamin Blom, Inc., 1972.

STURLUSON, SNORRI. *The Prose Edda.* Translated by Arthur Gilchrist Brodeur. New York: The American-Scandinavian Foundation, 1929.

TACHEVA-HITOVA, MARGARITA. *Eastern Cults in Moesia Inferior and Thracia.* Leiden: E. J. Brill, 1983.

TERRY, PATRICIA, ed. *Poems of the Vikings: The Elder Edda.* New York: Bobbs-Merrill Co., Inc., 1969.

THOMPSON, STITH. *Tales of the North American Indians.* Bloomington, Ind.: Indiana University Press, 1972.

THORPE, BENJAMIN. *North German Traditions.* London: Edward Lemley, 1852.

TOULSON, SHIRLEY. *The Winter Solstice.* London: Jill Newman and Hobhouse, 1981.

TREVELYAN, MARIE. *Folklore and Folk Stories of Wales.* London: Eliot Stock, n.d.

TUVILLE-PETRE, O.G. *Myth and Religion of the North: Religion of Ancient Scandinavia.* New York: Holt, Rinehart & Winston, 1964.

UGUWIYUAK. *Journey to Sunrise: Myths and Legends of the Cherokee.* Claremore, Okla: Egi Press, 1977.

VERMASEREN, MAARTEN S. *Cybele and Attis.* London: Thames & Hudson, 1977.

VERNALEKAN, THEODOR. *In the Land of Marvels: Folk-Tales from Austria and Bohemia.* London: Swan Sonnenschein & Co., 1889.

VIEYRA, MAURICE. *Hittite Art.* London: Alex Tiranti, Ltd., 1955.

WARNER, MARINA. *Alone of All Her Sex.* New York: Alfred A. Knopf, 1976.

WEBER, MAX. *The Religion of China.* Translated by Hans Gerth. New York: The Macmillan Company, 1951.

WELLARD, JAMES. *The Search for the Etruscans.* New York: Saturday Review Press, 1973.

WERBLOWSKY, R.J., and WIGODEN, GEOFFREY, eds. *Encyclopedia of the Jewish Religion.* New York: Holt, Rinehart & Winston, 1966.

WHEELER, POST, tr. and ed. *The Sacred Scriptures of the Japanese.* New York: H. Schuman, 1952.

WHERRY, JOSEPH H. *Indian Masks and Myths of the West.* New York: Funk & Wagnalls, 1969.

WHITEHEAD, HENRY. *The Village Gods of South India.* Calcutta: The Association Press, 1916.

WHITLOCK, RALPH. *The Folklore of Wiltshire.* Totowa, N.J.: Rowman & Littlefield, Inc., 1976.

WILDE, LADY (JANE FRANCESCA ELGEE). *Ancient Legends, Mystic Charms and Superstitions.* London: Chatto & Windus, 1925.

WILDE, WILLIAM. *Irish Popular Superstitions.* New York: Rowland & Co., 1973.

WITT, R.E. *Isis in the Graeco-Roman World.* Ithaca, N.Y.: Cornell University Press, 1971.

YOONGSOOK, KIM HARVEY. *Six Korean Women: The Socialization of Shamans.* St. Paul: West Publishing Co., 1979.

ZIELINSKI, THADDEUS. *The Religion of Ancient Greece.* Translated by G.R. Noyes. Freeport, N.Y.: Books for Libraries Press, 1926.

ZIMMER, HEINRICH. *Myths and Symbols in Indian Art and Civilization.* Edited by Joseph Campbell. Bollingen Series. New York: Pantheon Books, 1946.

ZIMMERMAN, J.E. *Dictionary of Classical Mythology.* New York: Bantam, 1964.

ZOBARSKAS, STEPAS. *Lithuanian Folk Tales.* Brooklyn, N.Y.: Gerald Rickard, 1958.

ZONG, IN-SOB, ed. *Folk Tales from Korea.* New York: The Grove Press, 1953.

ZUNTZ, GUNTHER. *Persephone.* Oxford: Clarendon Press, 1971.